Praise for *The Tyranny of Experts*

"Easterly is one of the most consistently interesting and provocative thinkers on development." — *Bloomberg View*

"Easterly's stories unfailingly reinforce a select number of crucial themes, the boldest being that the people of the so-called underdeveloped world have been systematically betrayed by the technocrats in charge of the global development agenda." —*New York Times Book Review*

"William Easterly ...is one of the profession's most determined skeptics... In the real world, Professor Easterly says, development occurs as people identify problems and push for solutions through their political systems. Setting goals that nobody is truly responsible for achieving not only misrepresents what causes poverty but also substitutes goal setting for real action." —Eduardo Porter, *New York Times*

"Thought provoking." —*Economist*

"This powerful polemic against top-down aid projects convinces." —*Times of London* (UK)

"A passionate, if fitful, argument against the conventional approach to economic development." —*Washington Post*

"Easterly (New York University) has written a book that grabs a reader's attention from the first sentence…. Highly recommended" —*Choice*

"Fascinating." —*Lancet*

"Readable and fascinating…. I found a valuable if somewhat iconoclastic read and would recommend it to anyone in the social sector." —*Forbes.com*

"*The Tyranny of Experts* is intellectual comfort food for people … who are skeptical of the idea that the only things standing between us and a world free of poverty are insufficient funding and political will." —Cato Institute's *Regulation*

"Easterly makes essential points about human rights, the need to accommodate local factors in developing countries and the terrible mistakes that can result from deals with corrupt regimes or self-interested organizations. His argument is made with passion and ample illustration."
—*Shelf Awareness for Readers*

"*Tyranny of Experts* takes various tacks--historical, theoretical, technological, statistical—to explain, in theory and in practice, why international development economics should fundamentally rethink its premises and practices." —***Reason***

"Easterly delivers a scathing assault on the anti-poverty programs associated with both the United Nations and its political and private sector supporters....A sharply written polemic intended to stir up debate about the aims of global anti-poverty campaigns." —***Kirkus***

"Easterly's research may help start a dialog about identifying better methods for alleviating global poverty and should assist readers interested in humanitarian efforts who want to draw their own conclusions about how to aid the world's poor." —***Library Journal***

"This book is deeply radical and thought-provoking, and brilliantly entertaining. Easterly invokes Kahneman, Hayek, Hirschman; the free cities of 12th century Genoa and 18th century New York; the Erie Canal, Fujian and Benin; the "prison" of the nation state; the new generation of econometrics applied to human history, and more in making his argument: It is individual rights and political freedoms that safeguard spontaneous, shared and sustained development, and the prevailing technocratic approach subverts those rights at great cost to the global poor its adherents would help. Development insiders will, with some justification, complain about one-sidedness and exaggeration. But no one who starts this book will be able to put it down, or be able to undo its influence on her thinking about the deep determinants of development progress."
—**Nancy Birdsall, President, Center for Global Development**

"Knowledge and expertise are fountainheads of prosperity and freedom, yet experts, especially foreign experts, have frequently been instruments of the very oppression that they seek to alleviate. The Tyranny of Experts tells the extraordinary story of authoritarian development. Those not familiar

with Easterly's previous books are in for a revelation, and the many long time aficionados will be delighted to be back in the hands of the master."
—**Angus Deaton, Professor of Economics and International Affairs, Princeton University**

"Easterly's new book shows that the expert approach to development rests on an engrained but unexamined premise: that people in poor countries cannot be trusted to make their own decisions. As this wide-ranging and compelling account shows, this assumption is doubly flawed. It's morally offensive and a sure guide to bad policy."
—**Paul Romer, New York University**

"Bill Easterly is simply the most interesting and provocative economist writing on development topics today."
—**Francis Fukuyama, Olivier Nomellini Senior Fellow at the Freeman Spogli Institute for International Studies at Stanford University**

"In this impassioned book, William Easterly draws on a wealth of examples from history and from around the world to support his forceful call for a radical transformation in the way the world views development. Easterly shows that many of the contemporary debates about the nature of development have their roots in history and he argues that the rights of the individual and democratic values should not be trampled on by those seeking faster economic growth."
—**Joseph Stiglitz, Nobel Prize Winner, Professor of Economics at Columbia University**

"Bill Easterly is the development economist, and he has come up with yet another striking and original success. This is the book that puts together the role of government, the failures of experts, and the best way forward into one comprehensive package."
—**Tyler Cowen, Professor of Economics at George Mason University**

THE TYRANNY OF EXPERTS

ALSO BY WILLIAM EASTERLY

The White Man's Burden

The Elusive Quest for Growth

THE TYRANNY OF
EXPERTS

ECONOMISTS,
DICTATORS,
and the
FORGOTTEN RIGHTS
of the
POOR

WILLIAM EASTERLY

BASIC BOOKS

A Member of the Perseus Books Group
New York

Published by Basic Books,

A Member of the Perseus Books Group

Books published by Basic Books are available at special discounts for bulk purchases in the United States by corporations, institutions, and other organizations. For more information, please contact the Special Markets Department at the Perseus Books Group, 2300 Chestnut Street, Suite 200, Philadelphia, PA 19103, or call (800) 810–4145, ext. 5000, or e-mail special.markets@perseusbooks.com.

A CIP catalog record for this book is available from the Library of Congress.

ISBN (hardcover): 978-0-465-03125-2
ISBN (e-book): 978-0-465-08090-8
ISBN (paperback): 978-0-465-08973-4

10 9 8 7 6 5 4 3 2

To Lizzie

TABLE OF CONTENTS

PART FIVE:
CONSCIOUS DESIGN VERSUS SPONTANEOUS SOLUTIONS

PREFACE TO THE
PAPERBACK EDITION

The global battle of individual freedom versus autocracy has continued to generate headlines in the time since the hardback edition of this book went to press. Indeed, it generated multiple stories just in this morning's New York Times as I write these words. Protesters in Burkina Faso forced President Blaise Compaoré to resign after 27 years in power. Taiwan's democratic leader voices support for Hong Kong protesters demanding their democratic rights from the Beijing government. Myanmar's military rulers are backsliding on their promised transition to democracy. Yet another story about the Hong Kong protesters describes their plan to crash a meeting of world leaders in Beijing hosted by Chinese leader Xi Jinping. Defenders of liberal democracy in Turkey express alarm about how their leader Recep Tayyip Erdogan is acting more and more like Russia's Vladimir Putin. Defenders of liberal democracy in Hungary express alarm about how their leader Viktor Orban is acting more and more like Russia's Vladimir Putin. The battle for freedom versus autocracy has a high profile almost everywhere.

Yet the battle for freedom versus autocracy has a low profile in the community that works on economic development around the world, the community fighting against global poverty. This book describes how the development community too often winds up on the side of the autocrats—often unintentionally and often contrary to the private sympathies of development experts and officials for freedom.

Some recent news on the World Bank illustrates further development's blinders on individual rights. This book describes how the World Bank itself violated individual rights in Bank-financed projects in Uganda and Ethiopia, evicting poor people off their lands. It was alarming that the Bank was not accountable for this, despite some language in the Bank's own internal policies against involuntary resettlement. And yet, on July 30, 2014, the World Bank released a draft revision of its internal policies that makes it even less accountable for rights violations in its own projects.* A statement signed by 105 non-governmental organizations (NGOs) argued that the draft "acts to ... *weaken* land rights protections for poor and vulnerable groups," specifically protections against people being "evicted from their homes, land and livelihoods." The weakened internal safeguards, according to this statement, increase the risk that "Bank-financed projects" will "cause human rights violations." **

The NGOs who protested here give some hope that rights advocacy could have some impact. Yet these NGOs are mainly outside the development mainstream, which—as this book describes—usually takes a more technocratic approach, thinking of development action as mostly about implementing expert technical remedies to the problems of material poverty, such as fertilizers, antibiotics, or nutritional supplements. There is nothing wrong per se with these technical solutions or those who implement them, but it is an illusion that the technocratic approach makes irrelevant the global battle of ideas between individual rights and autocracy.

On July 26, 2014, the above-mentioned Hungarian leader Viktor Orban gave a speech to an audience of ethnic Hungarians in the town of Băile Tușnad, Romania (which Orban called by its Hungarian name Tusnádfürdő). Orban described the most important divide in the world today as around the "race going on to develop a state that is capable of making a nation successful." He described how "the most popular topic in thinking

---

* http://www-wds.worldbank.org/external/default/WDSContentServer/WDSP/IB/2014/07/30/000456286_20140730173436/Rendered/PDF/898130BR0CODE200Box385287B00PUBLIC0.pdf

** http://www.inclusivedevelopment.net/joint-statement-world-banks-draft-safeguards-fail-to-protect-land-rights-and-prevent-impoverishment-major-revisions-required/
accessed November 1, 2014

today is trying to understand how systems that are not Western, not liberal, not liberal democracies and perhaps not even democracies, can nevertheless make their nations successful." He cited expert "international analysts," who suggest the secrets to national development success are provided by autocratic "stars" such as Singapore, China, and Russia. Orban quoted another expert, an (unnamed) "internationally recognized analyst" on how "liberal values today embody corruption, sex and violence."

Apparently following this expert guidance, Viktor Orban declared that in Hungary, "we must break with liberal principles" such as individual rights, instead "serving the interests of the nation." Orban announced that what "we are constructing in Hungary is an illiberal state, a non-liberal state," serving "Hungarians living throughout the world" who "are part of the Hungarian nation." Orban's crackdown on non-governmental organizations in Hungary was justified because they were "attempting to enforce foreign interests here in Hungary."*

Orban was probably not fully aware of how much he was recapitulating a blend of authoritarianism, nationalism, and international experts as the key to development success, an idea that has been around for decades. This book describes the history and rise to influence of this idea of authoritarian development.

The Orban example is a small example of the famous quote by John Maynard Keynes: "the ideas of economists and political philosophers, both when they are right and when they are wrong, are more powerful than is commonly understood. Indeed the world is ruled by little else. Practical men, who believe themselves to be quite exempt from any intellectual influences, are usually the slaves of some defunct economist."**

This book discusses the defunct economists who produced influential ideas in the debate between freedom and autocracy in development over many decades. The usual focus in aid and development is on technical action plans, or perhaps on how to reform foreign aid policies, but this book

---

* Speech transcript at http://www.kormany.hu/en/the-prime-minister/the-prime-minister-s-speeches/prime-minister-viktor-orban-s-speech-at-the-25th-balvanyos-summer-free-university-and-student-camp Accessed November 1, 2014

** Keynes, John Maynard (2014-08-28). The General Theory of Employment, Interest, and Money (Kindle Locations 4800-4802). David Rehak. Kindle Edition.

argues all such action plans are premature before getting ideas and principles right (an approach that seems to have seriously disoriented some readers in aid agencies or philanthropic foundations). The focus on action plans has too often silenced the debate on getting ideas and principles right. If Keynes was right, having a debate to get ideas right is itself a powerful force to make the world a better place.

Notes on changes from hardback to paperback edition:

This edition makes a few corrections on minor errors and omissions, and provides a small update in the conclusion on the story that begins the book.

THE TYRANNY OF EXPERTS

PART ONE

The Debate That Never Happened

Chapter One

Introduction

The farmers in Wood County in rural northwest Ohio never saw it coming. The soldiers had arrived on the morning of Sunday, February 28, 2010, while the farmers were in church. Hearing gunshots, the farmers had rushed to their houses, which by then were already immersed in flames. While some soldiers kept the farmers at gunpoint from rescuing their homes, others poured gasoline over the recent grain harvest in the barns and burned that as well. One eight-year-old child was trapped and died in the fire. The dairy cows were dispatched more quickly and humanely with a burst of machine-gun fire. Then the soldiers marched the more than 20,000 farmers away at riflepoint. Never come back, they were told; the land is no longer yours.

The farmers, many of whose homesteads had been in their families for generations, were unhappy to learn that a British company was taking their land with the help of the soldiers. The company was going to grow forests and then sell the timber. The farmers were even more distressed to learn that the World Bank, an official international organization combating global poverty, had financed and promoted the project by the British company. The World Bank is not subject to Ohio or United States law or courts.

The farmers might have hoped that publicity would help them. And indeed, a year later a British human-rights organization, Oxfam, published a report on what had happened in Wood County in February 2010. The *New York Times* ran a story on the report on September 21, 2011. The World Bank the next day promised an investigation. That investigation has never happened.

As of this writing, now past the fourth anniversary of the tragedy, the whole event has been forgotten by almost everyone except the victims. The farmers could only wonder why nobody seemed to care.

THE RIGHTS OF THE RICH AND POOR

Is this story really true? It is true except for one geographic detail—the events did not occur in Wood County, Ohio; they occurred in Mubende District, Uganda. The World Bank had promoted the forestry project there to raise incomes, but those whose rights the Bank had overlooked would not be among the beneficiaries.[1] It is inconceivable that the story above could have occurred in Ohio. If it had, there would have been an outcry that produced justice for the victims and punishment for the perpetrators.

When Thomas Jefferson wrote the world's most famous statement of political ideals in 1776, he listed outrages of the king of England against his American subjects: "He has plundered our seas, ravaged our Coasts, burnt our towns, and destroyed the lives of our people." The following words were meant to prevent such outrages:

> We hold these truths to be self-evident, that all men are created equal, that they are endowed by their Creator with certain unalienable Rights, that among these are Life, Liberty and the pursuit of Happiness. That to secure these rights, Governments are instituted among Men, deriving their just powers from the consent of the governed.

Similar ideals would be repeated in other Western nations. For example, the Declaration of the Rights of Man, approved by the revolutionary French National Assembly on August 26, 1789, aimed

> to set forth in a solemn declaration the natural, unalienable, and sacred rights of man. . . . Men are born and remain free and equal in rights. . . . Liberty consists in the freedom to do everything which injures no one else.

These aspirations for freedom were those of poor people. The French in 1789 and Americans in 1776 were at an average income per person roughly similar to that of Africans today. The World Bank is based in the West and has many managers and staff who personally share in this dream. But the World Bank does not articulate such a dream for the world they cover, the world that at various times has been called "the Third World" or the "less-developed countries."

The World Bank can hardly avoid *some* discussion of the nature of government in development, and they have been preparing reports on this topic—what they have vaguely called *governance* for years now. One recent version is a 2007 World Bank report on governance that says:

> Implementing the strengthened approach to governance ... will require ... careful development of a ... detailed results framework, consideration of budget and staffing implications ... and further consultations with stakeholders. ... The specific initiatives needed to fully operationalize this strategy will be outlined in an Implementation Plan.[2]

The following concepts play little or no role in the "strengthened approach to governance": liberty, freedom, equality, rights, or democracy. These omissions are not accidents; they are part of a long pattern in World Bank reports. Questioned about the remarkably consistent omission of the word democracy from World Bank official reports and speeches, for example, the World Bank Press Office explained to this author that the World Bank is legally not allowed by its own charter to use the word democracy. We will retrace the revealing history behind this strange and important claim back to the 1940s.

The lack of commitment to such ideals is exemplified by the World Bank's successful evasion of any responsibility for burning down the homes of poor farmers. It is further exemplified by its linguistic evasion, such as a "strengthened approach to governance" complete with its "consideration of budget and staffing implications." The farmers in Mubende, Uganda, have reason to doubt whether they are included among the "men [who] are born and remain free and equal in rights."

THE TECHNOCRATIC ILLUSION

The conventional approach to economic development, to making poor countries rich, is based on a technocratic illusion: the belief that poverty is a purely technical problem amenable to such technical solutions as fertilizers, antibiotics, or nutritional supplements. We see this in the Bank's actions in Mubende; we will see the same belief prevalent amongst others who combat global poverty, such as the Gates Foundation, the United Nations, and US and UK aid agencies.

The technocratic approach ignores what this book will establish as the real cause of poverty—the unchecked power of the state against poor people without rights. In Mubende, Uganda, for example, the techniques of improved forestry offered a solution to poverty. But it was not a solution for the Mubende farmers. The illusion that the problem was technical only distracted attention from the soldiers' and World Bank's violations of the rights of the farmers.

By this technocratic illusion, the technical experts unintentionally confer new powers and legitimacy on the state as the entity that will implement the technical solutions. The economists who advocate the technocratic approach have a terrible naïveté about power—that as restraints on power are loosened or even removed, that same power will remain benevolent of its own accord.

What used to be the divine right of kings has in our time become the development right of dictators. The implicit vision in development today is that of well-intentioned autocrats advised by technical experts, what this book will call *authoritarian development*. The word *technocracy* (a synonym for authoritarian development) itself is an early twentieth-century coinage that means "rule by experts."

The sleight of hand that focuses attention on technical solutions while covering up violations of the rights of real people is the moral tragedy of development today. The rights of the poor—such as the right of Ugandan farmers not to have their homes burnt down—are moral ends in themselves. Morally neutral approaches to poverty do not exist. Any approach to development will either respect the rights of the poor or it will violate them. One cannot avoid this moral choice by appealing to "nonideological evidence-based policies" (a popular phrase in development today).

Authoritarian development is also a pragmatic tragedy. History and modern experience suggest that free individuals with political and economic rights—call it *free development*—make up a remarkably successful problem-solving system. Free development gives us the right to choose amongst a myriad of spontaneous problem-solvers, rewarding those that solve our problems. These public and private problem-solvers accomplish far more than dictators who implement solutions provided by experts. We will see how free development allows the squeaky wheel to get the grease, while authoritarian development silences the squeaky wheel— perhaps with a police raid and a prison term.

The technocratic illusion is that poverty results from a shortage of expertise, whereas poverty is really about a shortage of rights. The emphasis on the problem of expertise makes the problem of rights worse. The technical problems of the poor (and the absence of technical solutions for those problems) are a *symptom* of poverty, not a *cause* of poverty. This book argues that the cause of poverty is the absence of political and economic rights, the absence of a free political and economic system that would find the technical solutions to the poor's problems. The dictator whom the experts expect will accomplish the technical fixes to technical problems is not the solution; he is the problem.

AUTHORITARIANS ANONYMOUS

I have made clear the position this book argues. But this position could be completely wrong—that's why it will take a whole book to consider whether morality, theory, and evidence does or does not show a Tyranny of Experts.

Those who support autocrats in development do not see autocracy as an end in itself. They genuinely believe autocrats would deliver the escape from poverty faster than free systems will. They believe the experts advising the autocrats know better than poor individuals how to solve their problems. They could be right—after all, there are some development success stories that happen in the absence of individual rights, and many individual efforts do fail (among both rich and poor). The pragmatic case for free rather than autocratic development often goes against our intuitions.

A common concept among development observers over many decades is that of the "benevolent autocrat." According to this concept, the leader may have unconstrained power, but his intentions concerning what to do with that power are presumed to be good. He (and most autocrats are indeed male) just needs expert advice to accomplish good things. When good things do in fact happen to a country governed by an autocrat—such as high economic growth or rapid health improvements—the credit for these good things goes to the autocrat. The good outcomes are thereby taken as de facto evidence of the benevolence of the autocrat. These propositions could be correct—maybe it really does take autocrats to get things done, to avoid democratic stalemates—but they should at least be debated. This book will have that debate.

The support for an authoritarian approach to development is sometimes not overt but implied. It is often altruistic rather than self-serving. Support for autocrats is unintentional more often than it is intentional. There is no conspiracy against rights. I can sympathize with economists who, in their zeal to help the world's poor, unwittingly favor autocracy, because for a long time I was one of them myself.

The Story of the Authoritarian Idea

This book tells the story of authoritarian development. We will see that there *was* a debate between authoritarian and free development. But for the development experts who took over the field by the 1950s, the debate was already over—the authoritarian side had won. While eloquent advocates continued to make the case for free development, as we will see, the development community was no longer listening. It is still not listening today.

To see how this happened, we need to start before the official beginning of development in 1949, when Harry S. Truman first announced a US foreign-aid program, and look at a largely unknown history of development earlier in the twentieth century in places like prerevolutionary China and British colonial Africa. We will see debates between some of the first examples of what later would be called *development economists*.

When development was first conceived, open racism prevented

Western actors from seeing a free alternative—that is, an alternative based on individual rights and initiative—as possible in the rest of the world. Colonial and semicolonial actions by the West were directly violating the rights of the poor in the Rest. We will see how technocratic development gave these actions cover as technical measures to improve the well-being of colonial subjects.

Yet as overt racism and colonialism faded, the appeal of technocratic ideas remained. History also allows us to explore the political motivations that sometimes determine which side of each debate wins. Technocratic development turned out to be popular with a remarkable diversity of interest groups, including even racists and colonialists in the West, on one side, and the nationalist leaders in the Rest who were victims of racism and of colonialism, on the other. It had great appeal to philanthropists and humanitarians in rich countries who wanted to end global poverty, yet also to those who cared nothing about poverty and only about the foreign policy and national security needs of rich countries.

Technocratic development also held an understandable appeal for the group on which it conferred great importance: development experts. We will see how economists before and during the official start of development in the 1950s got seduced by missionary zeal to become anointed as development experts, while a brave and now-forgotten few economists resisted it.

Most observers agree that the political interests of the United States during the Cold War helped determine which countries got foreign aid—that is, donations from governments of rich countries to support development in less-developed nations—and how much. It is not a stretch to examine whether the ideas that justified that aid might also have been politically convenient for the Great Powers during the Cold War—and it turns out even long before the Cold War. These political interests continue to be on display today in the War on Terror.

This book will not automatically reject ideas that had political motivations. None of us are entirely free from political agendas, and political agendas do not automatically exclude altruistic agendas. I want to debate all ideas on their merits. But political motivations help explain why the debate on the merits of ideas has often failed to happen.

HOPE FROM NEW RESEARCH

The debate between authoritarian and free alternatives in development has been missing for six decades. But there is a new source of hope and inspiration, where this time some economists are the good guys. A new wave of research on economic history, politics, institutions, culture, and technology has provided plenty of material to finally have the debate. Alongside the story of how authoritarian development became the default consensus on global poverty reduction, the new research allows the reconstruction of the story of free development in reducing global poverty.

Three dimensions of the new research challenge the authoritarian consensus—three dimensions that already appeared in the protodebate that got squelched. One is an emphasis on history. Technocratic solutions view history as not really mattering, a view that we can call the *Blank Slate*. The new research revisits even old history, such as a battle in northern Italy in 1176, to show how a twelfth-century turning point for individual freedom still affects outcomes in Italy today. The opposite of the Blank Slate is recognizing that history matters, and learning from that history. This also opens the door to history itself being evidence for or against authoritarian development.

Another dimension of the new research is an emphasis on nonnational factors—for example, the technology, values, and network contacts that migrants take with them from one nation to another. We will visit with such surprising players as a Senegalese religious brotherhood that has migrated to major Western cities. This and many other stories and research findings shed light on the big development debate on the prerogatives of nations versus the rights of individuals.

Finally, the new research shows the importance of spontaneous solutions in politics, markets, and technology. It turns out that when the rights of local people are respected, new trades happen, new technologies happen, new public services happen. This challenges conventional wisdom about the "benevolent autocrats" behind many success stories. There is, for example, more evidence for attributing the rise of China as an economic superpower to the anonymous spread of the potato to China than to Chinese ruler Deng Xiaoping's economic policies. Appreciation of this phenomenon allows us, finally, to have the biggest development debate of all, on conscious design of development by experts versus spontaneous solutions by individuals.

Ironically, most of the economists involved in this recent research were not trying to solve the global poverty problem; they were just trying to better understand and explain the world. Nor were these researchers aware of the big debate that had failed to happen for six decades on authoritarian versus free development. So the development community of official agencies and philanthropic foundations has not changed its adherence to the authoritarian development consensus. But now we finally have the material to reopen the debate on the rights of the poor.

DANGEROUS DEBATES

The intellectual journey in this book toward a debate on autocracy versus freedom will be treacherous because the development consensus has a long history (as we will see) of disqualifying and dismissing its critics. There are many misunderstandings that tend to suppress dissenting views. Let's review them:

You are just repeating the tired argument about free markets versus state intervention. This is the main debate in development that seems related to the debate about authoritarian versus free development. But it is *not* the same debate, because the market-versus-state debate says nothing about the power of the state versus the individual. The market side of the debate wants the state to expand the scope of the market. For example, it could remove tariffs on trade that protect some industries, so that free trade determines which industries survive. The state could lift controls on prices and instead let markets determine prices. The state side wants the state to protect the poor with price controls on basic goods, and to use trade policy to pick the most promising sectors that will lead the economy into development. However, neither side of this debate is addressing restraints on state power. Regardless of which side wins the market-versus-state debate, the state is still able to violate the rights of private individuals with impunity. In the "market" side of the debate, it is still the leader of the state that gets to decide what is a "market" policy. The state leader is able to pick and choose whose rights and which types of rights individuals may temporarily enjoy, such as the economic freedom to trade with whom one wishes. These rights are never secure when restraints on state power are absent, or when the principle of equal rights for all individuals in all spheres of activity is not recognized.

The distinction between economic freedom and political freedom thrives on both sides of the market-versus-state debate, because some on each side insist on the primacy of the one kind of freedom over the other, while nonetheless disagreeing over which it is that is primary. However, while the distinction is helpful for analysis, only a unified vision of freedom is coherent as an ideal. Did the World Bank and Ugandan government violate the economic freedom of the farmers in the Mubende District of Uganda, or was it their political freedom? It is hard to separate the two: violating property rights violates economic freedom, while the soldiers' violent suppression of farmer protests violates political freedom. Whenever this book says *individual rights*, it includes both political and economic rights, the long list of those traditionally respected in today's mature capitalist democracies. It includes the political freedom from seizure of your person and the economic freedom from seizure of your property. It includes the political freedom to assemble with whom you wish and the economic freedom to trade with whom you wish. It includes the political freedom to replace bad public-service providers with good ones, and the economic freedom to replace bad private-service providers with good ones.

You are an ideologue. There is a slippery slope in perceptions of development writers. If you deviate from what the political Center deems to be centrist, you slide down a perceptional slippery slope toward "ideologue." Audiences sometimes look for code words that imply the writer is too extreme. Mention *markets* and you are presumed to favor a world with zero government. Mention *liberty* too often and you are presumed to be in favor of some extreme right-wing ideology. Mention Friedrich Hayek's book *The Road to Serfdom* and you are presumed to be to the right of ranting talk-show hosts.

Less commonly recognized is a perceptional slippery slope on the left. If you mention *colonialism, racism,* or *imperialism* too often, as concepts still relevant to understanding development past and present, you risk being seen as a leftist ideologue.

I hope to frustrate the search for code words, because I do not believe in them. Of course, there really are white supremacists, conspiracy theorists, and other extremists who should be disqualified from debate. If our exclusion of extremists is too broad, however, we will just wind up endlessly repeating a consensus whose origin is unclear. One of the most interesting features of the story you are about to read is that the rebels against the technocratic consensus come from both the left and the right, and they often hold incompatible views on almost everything else.

You are attacking a straw man. Another set of debate-sabotaging formulas are "the truth lies somewhere in between," or "there is no real difference between us," or "you are attacking a straw man."

Sometimes it is easier to see the debate in terms of the extreme each side is most desperate to avoid. Let's consider two opposing extremes: (1) conscious design of development by state leaders and First World experts, and (2) development emerging from the spontaneous solutions of individuals. Perhaps nobody is at the pure extreme of (1), yet most in development flee from (2) in a way they do not flee from (1), fearing (wrongly) that (2) leaves nothing for the development expert to do. The desperation with which the one extreme is avoided makes the other extreme seem closer to a reasonable, middle-ground position and therefore less of a straw man.

This book sometimes refers to a "consensus" of the self-described development community. The *development community* includes policy experts, public intellectuals, economists, and other social scientists. Its limits are defined as those who work for the aid agencies of rich-country governments, international aid agencies like the World Bank, think tanks like the Brookings Institution, and philanthropies like the Gates Foundation, or as consultants or advisers to any of the above. It does not include economics professors conducting purely academic research on development, unless those professors cross over into work for the kinds of agencies listed here.

The idea of a consensus that remains stable over time and across groups is an oversimplification, just as the extremes in the debate were an oversimplification. There are of course differing viewpoints within such a consensus as well as changes over time in the consensus. Yet simplification is necessary to clarify the issues that matter most.

The content of the consensus is likewise disputable. In describing the development-community consensus in this book, I am drawing on my own thirty years of experience in development, on reading decades of writings about development, and on direct quotations from official sources that I present in the remainder of the book.

This book just wants to have the debate. Let's not get obsessed with who and how many are located at each point between two opposing extremes, or who and how many belong to the consensus.

WHAT IS THE AGENDA?

Another device to suppress dissenting views is to attribute an agenda to the dissenter. It will help, therefore, to clarify what this book is *not* doing.

Not *about ideological debates in rich countries.*   There are lots of books about the debates between the Left and the Right in the United States or in other rich countries. They mainly tend to break down into arguments about state versus market (as described above). They also tend to focus on particular debates about particular rights such as gun control, abortion, or a right to privacy. This book is not about such debates in rich countries. Neither conservatives nor liberals in the rich societies would disavow the axiomatic existence of "unalienable rights" for rich people, although they might, of course, disagree about the definition and implementation of particular rights. Yet this book argues that development does not embrace unalienable rights for the poor, even as a starting point—and that is the missing debate that this book wants to have.

Not *implying guilt by association.*   Understanding the history of development requires grappling with racists and colonialists. Those who today hold some viewpoint that racists and colonialists used to hold—

for example, that poor people don't care about their own rights—are not thereby guilty of racism or colonialism. The history of ideas matters but does not automatically disqualify ideas that have some dubious progenitors. One of the surprises from the history of ideas is that the same ideas could appeal simultaneously to racists *and* antiracists, to colonialists *and* anticolonialists.

Not *about extending rights into new areas.* In addition to the traditional definition of individual rights given above, many have suggested additional rights such as a right to food or a right to health care. There is a debate about whether the word *rights* is appropriate for these cases. This book does not participate in that debate, which is well covered by many other books (such as the classic *Development as Freedom* by Nobel laureate Amartya Sen).

Not *a how-to manual for aid workers and philanthropists.* This book is not about "what we can do to end poverty." This book does share a common objective with aid workers and philanthropists: the end of poverty. But the exhortation that all development discussions must lead within five minutes to a recommended philanthropic action inhibits clear thinking. Actions follow from principles and understanding. This book addresses principles in development; it seeks to promote understanding of development; it does not recommend specific actions. There is a fear of inaction and indifference on the tragic problems of global poverty, which I share. But wrong actions are equally a danger, and they may create more indifference and disillusionment when they fail. It is critical to get the principles of action right before acting, and it is that task to which this book is devoted. I'll have more to say at the end about why it is unavoidable and absolutely necessary to focus on principles.

Not *an exposé of academics.* The experts and technocrats discussed in this book are not academic researchers; they are policy experts, public intellectuals, aid agency and philanthropic foundation staff, the odd billionaire, and think tankers—the already mentioned "development community." Academia is far from perfect, but here I have mainly good things to say about academic social-science research. In my experience, most academic researchers have exceptional integrity and rigor. Of course, some academics are also public intellectuals (including this author) and others become government officials. But it is only in the latter roles that they could fit the definition of technocrat. Only as public intellectuals or officials do they participate in the big debate about autocracy versus freedom.

Not *a critique of all expert knowledge.* When my toilet stops working, I am grateful for the expert plumber. When I get giardia, I am grateful for the expert doctor who prescribes Flagyl. Experts in sanitation, health, and education offer huge benefits for the world's poor. Medicines and antimalaria nets certainly save lives. This book is not about condemning all expertise, it is about distinguishing between good and bad ambitions for expertise in development.

Let us now spell out the debate in more detail with the help of two opposing Nobel laureates in economics who received their prizes on the same day. They were eloquent spokesmen for the opposite ends of the spectrum in development on individual rights, even though they never debated. After we review their views, we will see better how high the stakes were in this debate. We will also see how and why one wanted the debate to happen, and the other did not.

TWO NOBEL LAUREATES AND THE DEBATE THEY NEVER HAD

In December 1974, two men arrived in Stockholm, Sweden, to receive the Nobel Prize in Economics. Both were at the ends of long careers, having been born only six months apart in Western Europe three-quarters of a century earlier. They had known each other since 1931 and they both wrote on economic development.

The first of these two men, Friedrich Hayek, wrote about economic development before the field officially existed. He wrote amidst the epic confrontation in the twentieth century between Western liberal values on one side, and Fascism and Communism on the other side. This clash drove him to articulate a vision of how individual rights were both an end in themselves and a means by which free individuals in a free society solved many of their own problems. Hayek depicted the solutions, including both private goods and government services, as emerging from competitive economic and political entrepreneurs.

Hayek's fellow Nobel Laureate Gunnar Myrdal had very different views on how societies emerge from poverty into prosperity. The division between them was perhaps most fundamentally expressed by Myrdal's opposite views on individual rights in development.

Throughout his career, Myrdal did not feature an extensive role for individual rights in his writings about how development did or should happen. In his view, poor people were neither interested in rights nor capable of much individual initiative even if they had such rights. He said national governments needed to achieve development in spite of "a largely illiterate and apathetic citizenry."[1] Myrdal argued that even such rights

wow!

17

violations as that of the "autocratic element in Soviet Communism" often "satisfies a predisposition of the masses in these countries . . . [who] for centuries have been conditioned to respond positively to direction from authority."[2]

Myrdal thought that development efforts would "be largely ineffective" unless there were "regulations backed by compulsion," that is, "putting obligations on people and supporting them by force."[3] For example, growth of production requires more investment in machinery, but individuals might not save enough on their own to finance such investment. The government should force them to save by taking some of their income through taxes or mandatory savings schemes, and investing it for them. Likewise, the superior technical methods that experts brought might increase agricultural production, but peasants could not be trusted to adopt them voluntarily. In such an instance, the government should impose a technically superior mixture of crops and livestock to increase total production, "even if it required the killing of many half-starved cows."[4]

Hayek, in contrast, had been writing for years on how individual rights were both an end in themselves and the means by which societies escape poverty and move into prosperity. He celebrated changes from "a rigidly organized hierarchic system" into one in which people could "shape their own life," as the root of prosperity in the West.[5] Hayek declared himself appalled at the Fascist and Communist societies that he had observed in his lifetime in which "the individual is merely a means to serve the ends of the higher entity called society or the nation." From this followed the "disregard of the life and happiness of the individual," along with "intolerance and brutal suppression of dissent."[6]

Hayek denounced those with "a fondness for authority" along with those who displayed a "strident nationalism." He condemned those who do not protect the individual against "coercion or arbitrary power" as long as this power is used for what they regard as "the right purposes." Ironically for some who see Hayek as an icon of the Right, these criticisms were directed at *conservatives*.[7]

What were the "right purposes" for which Hayek feared conservatives used state power? Hayek went on to attack "anti-democratic" conservatives who defend privileges of some "small elite"[8] who use "the resort to privilege or monopoly or any other coercive power of the state in order to shelter such people against the forces of economic change."[9] Against that possibility, Hayek made a principled defense of individual rights that would continuously generate new opportunities for individuals and hence a continual turnover of the political and economic elite. For Hayek, "a policy of freedom for the individual is the only truly progressive policy."[10]

Hayek also could not agree with the conservative who uses the state to enforce morality or nationalist fervor, the conservative who "regards himself as entitled to force the value he holds on other people."[11] He realized, as we see below, the danger that such a use of state power posed to minority groups with different ethnic cultures or moral codes. Still attacking conservatives but noting that the critique applied to the Left as well, Hayek mocked the imperialist or colonialist thinker who considers "his own ways superior," who regarded it "as his mission to 'civilize' others," and who would do this "by bringing them the blessings of efficient government."[12]

Hayek and Myrdal had spent the previous decades espousing these opposite views. Hayek had made very clear why he rejected Myrdal's views, along with similar views, but Myrdal never addressed the argument that individual rights were crucial to development. He did not answer that argument by Hayek or by anyone else in his voluminous writings. He claimed that his approach to development was "unanimously endorsed by governments and experts in the advanced countries."[13]

Myrdal's claim of unanimity was correct in a strange way. By the 1950s, as we see in the next part of this book, a consensus on development of the Rest had emerged in the West among "governments and experts." Unanimous support for authoritarian development among development experts was achieved by declaring anyone opposed to this approach not to be a development expert. So there was never a debate between Hayek's and Myrdal's positions in development. The only debate that happened was that of state intervention versus markets, but we will see this was not the same as the debate on individual rights. The debate on individual rights as set out above never happened in development. It has still not happened today.

[handwritten marginal note: interesting distinction]

Hayek Dodges the Nazis

Hayek's life history may help us to understand his passion for individual rights. Friedrich August von Hayek was born on May 8, 1899, in Vienna, the capital of the Austro-Hungarian Empire. He came from minor nobility on both sides, which gave him the *von*. Noble titles would be abolished in 1919 and he would then drop the *von* (although his critics often continued using it for its derogatory associations).[14]

Hayek's first introduction to the Anglophone world came at the age of twenty-four, after he met New York University professor Jeremiah Jenks in Vienna. Jenks offered him a job in New York as a research assistant. Hayek would stay in New York from March 1923 to May 1924.[15] His New York stay had two important consequences for Hayek: he learned English, and he strengthened his knowledge of the English-language economics literature. The latter would allow him to be at the forefront of economics worldwide, the former would later allow him access to an international audience, especially in the United States and United Kingdom.

Back in Vienna, Hayek became part of a thriving intellectual community. Vienna had proportionally one of the largest Jewish communities in Europe, and Jews were well represented in academia. Hayek recalled later that "it is difficult to overestimate how much I owe to . . . [becoming] connected with . . . the Jewish intelligentsia of Vienna . . . who proved to be far ahead of me in literary education and general precociousness."[16]

An Austrian Nazi party grew in the 1930s in parallel with the German Nazis of Hitler (who was of course himself Austrian). Most of Hayek's Jewish Austrian friends would escape into exile. His close friend Fritz Machlup was one of the first. Hayek wrote Machlup on May 1, 1936, about Vienna: "The speed of the intellectual surrender and the corruption of politics . . . is shattering."[17] Hayek himself had already escaped to a position at the London School of Economics (LSE). Still a little-known thirty-four-year-old economist, Hayek had begun his appointment at LSE on March 1, 1933.

A month before, Hitler had assumed power in Germany. The day before Hayek started work at LSE, Hitler had used the Reichstag fire as a pretext to get the German President Hindenburg to issue the following decree: "On the basis of Article 48 paragraph 2 of the Constitution of the German Reich, the following is decreed as a defensive measure against Communist acts of violence that endanger the state . . . restrictions on personal liberty, on the right of free expression . . . including freedom of the press, on the right of assembly . . . and warrants for house searches, orders for confiscations as well as restrictions on property are permissible beyond the legal limits otherwise prescribed."[18]

Hayek was a precursor of a wave of Central and Eastern European refugees, some of them famous and others forgotten, who would write in the 1940s and 1950s about the origins and nature of totalitarianism: Hannah Arendt, Isaiah Berlin, Michael Polanyi, Karl Popper, and Jacob Talmon. They would demolish the conventional wisdom that Nazi and Communist totalitarianism occupied opposite ends of the right–left spectrum. Hayek thought, as did his fellow thinkers on totalitarianism, that the relevant spectrum was the individual versus the collective, with liberalism at one end and both Fascism and Communism at the other. Stalin and Hitler had in common the violent coercion of the individual to serve collective ends.

Hayek had appreciated this almost from the first moment that the Nazis took power. In a memo that he wrote the head of the LSE in the spring of 1933, he noted the common role in Germany and Russia of "universal compulsion" and of "intolerance and the suppression of intellectual freedom." He noted the "fundamental similarity of methods and ideas" in Germany and in Russia "is hidden by the difference in the phraseology and the privileged groups."[19] Hayek would later recall the effect of the rise of the Austrian Nazis on the intellectual life of Vienna, particularly at the University of Vienna: "at the beginning of the 1930s it dies, not only in economics, all of it."[20] In 1938, convinced the city held no future, he applied for and received British citizenship. He would avoid Vienna the rest of his life.

Anxiety about his friends and colleagues under the Nazis tormented Hayek. Hayek's mentor, Ludwig von Mises, was Jewish. Mises had escaped from Vienna to a position in Geneva in 1934, but the Swiss city would be no safer once the war began, with the Swiss turning Austrian Jews over to the Nazis. Hayek wrote to Machlup on June 21, 1940, less than a month after Dunkirk: "My main anxiety at the moment is whether Mises . . . got away from Geneva in time . . . The last letter I had from M. was from the end of May and he hoped then to leave almost any day. I have done my best through my French friend to secure him a French transit visa but I fear this will have come too late and the only hope is that he . . . got out by the Locarno-Barcelona air line before it was stopped." [21] It would be a while before Hayek got confirmation that Mises had indeed escaped.

THE ROAD TO SERFDOM

We will see throughout the present book that there are many excuses offered for avoiding debate of the ideas of anyone who advocates the free development alternative to authoritarian development. The most visible case of this is another book, which appeared seven decades ago. It is one of the best-known and most controversial books of the twentieth century. The author of the book had many notable development economists as his students or colleagues. The book is a direct attack on technocratic development and a defense of individual rights as the escape path out of poverty. But the book and its author never received a reply from development thinkers; they simply ignored the author and his book.

The author was Friedrich Hayek and the 1944 book was *The Road to Serfdom*. The excuse for ignoring Hayek is that he may or may not have implied a "slippery slope" in which any state intervention in the economy would start a downward spiral into totalitarianism. I do not agree with this idea. I also do not believe Hayek actually stated it (he himself said he didn't), but even if he did it is no reason to discard all of his other ideas. If we discarded all the good ideas of any thinker who had ever had a bad idea, we would have very few good ideas left.

The slippery-slope idea may have stuck to Hayek because *The Road to Serfdom* was alarmist about the threat to freedom in the United Kingdom that would emerge after World War II. We can cut Hayek a little slack on alarmism, considering that he had seen his own civilized Vienna succumb to the Nazis. And certainly, many advocates on both the left and the right make alarmist statements about what will happen if their ideas are not heeded. What seems to have happened with Hayek's reputation, though, is that his alarmism coincided with the alarmism of the right wing of the Republicans in the United States who were reacting against both the New Deal and the threat of Communism, and so he became identified with the extreme Right.

It is sadly ironic that the man who helped overturn the conventional left–right distinction in the debate on individual freedom would be lastingly seen by some as a right-wing extremist. In truth, as we have already seen above, there is ample evidence that Hayek was not the conservative ideologue his critics claimed. *The Road to Serfdom* advocated such nonconservative ideas as a minimum income guaranteed by the state: "there can be no doubt that some minimum of food, shelter, and clothing, sufficient to preserve health and the capacity to work, can be assured to everybody."[22]

In fact, Hayek condemned some of the very people he was identified with by his critics. In the pages of the 1956 version of *The Road to Serfdom*, he said British Conservatives were "paternalistic, nationalistic, and power-adoring . . . traditionalistic, anti-intellectual, and often mystical."[23] Hayek himself acknowledged after the fact that he had attracted some followers with whom he did not agree, at some cost to himself: "the manner in which [*The Road to Serfdom*] was used [in the United States] vividly brought home to me the truth of Lord Acton's observation that 'at all times sincere friends of freedom have been rare, and its triumphs have been due to minorities, that have prevailed by associating themselves with auxiliaries whose objects often differed from their own; and this association, which is always dangerous, has sometimes been disastrous.'"[24]

My argument here is not meant to address any debate on right versus left in US domestic policy. The argument of this chapter also does not depend on defending Hayek for his own sake. I am interested only in some of Hayek's ideas as valuable insights in and of themselves. The sole point of this section is that there was and is no basis for knee-jerk rejection of Hayek as an ideological extremist. Ignoring the slippery-slope controversy, this chapter covers some of the good ideas of *The Road to Serfdom*, many of which contradict the usual image of the book. The nonalarmist part of his book was a defense of individual rights, an explanation of how such rights explained a free society's development into prosperity.

The book's ideas were the opposite of those ideas emerging about technocratic development in the Rest. Hayek's former students and colleagues who were becoming development experts—including Gunnar Myrdal—were aware of Hayek's ideas, but they chose not to debate them. The debate that never happened between Hayek and Myrdal in development is one of the intellectual tragedies of the twentieth century. We will see in the next part of the book that an ideological misclassification of the advocates of free development was not the reason they were ignored in development debates of the last six decades. They were all ignored for other reasons, and we will discuss why. For now, let us see what the debate that never happened between Hayek and Myrdal would have been about. We will contrast the views of Hayek with those of Myrdal, drawing upon their writings throughout the career of each.

To address the richness of the debate about autocracy versus freedom, and to understand why autocracy won in development, it helps to break the big idea of autocracy down into three component ideas. We present them each here as a dichotomy in which few would be at either extreme (and the extremes will be less extreme today than in the 1950s):

1. The Blank Slate versus learning from history. Is the expert free to write upon a "Blank Slate"? Or does each country's past matter for its future—that is, does history constrain the expert's ability to draw up new solutions from scratch? Is completely fresh thinking needed, or is comparing the history of each country with those of other countries a valuable way to learn about how development happens?

2. The well-being of nations versus that of individuals. Is the object of development efforts to be the nation or the individual? Is development about meeting national goals, or letting individuals choose and meet their own goals? Can development only happen if it chooses the side of meeting national goals, or do individual goals find encouragement?

3. Conscious design versus spontaneous solutions. Was development the result of deliberate design by experts at the center, or did it emerge from unplanned solutions by individuals? Was development a set of technical problems to be consciously solved by technical

specialists? Or was it the emergence of solutions from competition between many different individual problem-solvers with many different pieces of knowledge?

The freedom side of the autocracy-freedom debate saw the first of each of these pairs as a threat to individual freedom and viewed the second element of each pair as both a value in itself and a means to achieve development. Let's examine each of these three component debates of the overall development debate.

DEBATE 1: THE BLANK SLATE VERSUS LEARNING FROM HISTORY

In 1955, the Swedish government appointed Gunnar Myrdal's wife Alva Myrdal as its ambassador to India. Gunnar followed and soon got a commission to do a major development study of South and East Asia. It would take him until 1968 to publish the 2,200-page *Asian Drama*, the result of a massive project to diagnose and cure underdevelopment in Asia.

American anthropologist Clifford Geertz objected to Myrdal's picture of India, which is a good example of the Blank Slate mind-set. Geertz said it was "completely stereotypic, . . . astonishingly abstract . . . . unnuanced and unparticularized. . . . It would seem impossible to write nearly a million words on a country with so rich a history, so profound a culture, and so complex a social system and fail to convey the force of its originality and the vitality of its spirit somewhere; but Professor Myrdal has accomplished it."[25]

The Blank Slate mind-set tends to ignore history and to see each poor society as infinitely malleable for the development expert to apply his technical solutions. The alternative would be to learn from history why each poor society is poor, to learn from history why other societies became rich, and to draw lessons accordingly for how to escape poverty. Since the Blank Slate ignores the particulars of history in each country, and technical experts start from scratch in every country, all poor countries seem equivalent. The best example of the pervasive Blank Slate mentality in development is the idea of "underdevelopment" itself. Categories like "underdeveloped countries" and "the Third World" homogenize otherwise diverse countries like China, Colombia, and Benin into one group.

The appeal of the Blank Slate is in part because it captures some truths—the per capita income levels of the Third World are much closer to each other than to those of the First World. And many other dimensions of society are associated with income: for example, low health, low education, and high corruption. On these dimensions, Third World members are very different from First World countries but similar to each other. This led Myrdal and others to think that the Third World had to attack first illiteracy, nutrition, and disease before they could expect that individuals would be able to look after themselves.

Blank Slate thinking thus opened the door for development experts to reject the utility of the West's history of individual rights and development as a precedent. If the Rest had nothing to learn from its own history, it also had nothing to learn from the West's history. Myrdal would later say that "all special advisers to underdeveloped countries" agree in that they "all assume a different approach to the social and economic problems of the underdeveloped countries today than that which historically was applied in the advanced countries."[26]

A malleable Blank Slate also fostered a great potential for technocrats to create one-size-fits-all fixes that could be applied widely instead of having to study the historical context in each instance. It is easy to see the appeal of solutions that promised to work everywhere in the Third World. Hayek addressed a Blank Slate mind-set in *The Road to Serfdom* when he criticized beliefs that one could simply erase the old and start over, the belief that "further advance could not be expected along the old lines."[27] He affirmed the traditional narrative that the triumph of individual rights had led to development, giving the example of science: "Perhaps the greatest result of the unchaining of individual energies was the marvelous growth of science which followed the march of individual liberty from Italy to England and beyond. . . . Only since industrial freedom opened the path to the free use of new knowledge, only since everything could be tried—if somebody could be found to back it at his own risk—. . . has science made the great strides which in the last hundred and fifty years have changed the face of the world."[28]

But now, in 1944's *Road to Serfdom*, Hayek feared there was a new disregard for learning from history about what "had made past progress possible." He also noticed the assumption of a completely malleable starting point, which made possible "a complete remodeling of society." He was alarmed at those who would not learn from history by "adding to or improving the existing machinery," whose approach was based instead on "completely scrapping and replacing" such machinery.[29]

Gunnar Myrdal early in his career had already provided an example of this Blank Slate mind-set that Hayek was criticizing in the rich countries. After Myrdal launched his successful academic career, which saw him get a prestigious chair at the University of Stockholm by 1933, he was eager for a new role as what today we would call a "public intellectual." Both Gunnar and his wife Alva had great ambitions to remake their own society at home. In the summer of 1934, they retreated to a cabin in the mountains of Norway to write a book, *The Population Problem in Crisis*. They were addressing what at the time seemed a crisis: the drastic slowdown in population growth in Sweden. The details of this problem and solution are less important than the Myrdals' willingness to embrace what Hayek would call "a complete remodeling of society."

The Myrdals' book recommended discarding what they called the "almost pathological" traditional family, with its excessive attention paid by parents to their children. Too much parental attention to each child meant parents were having too few children. So children should be raised largely by the state in state-run daycare centers as part of a "great national household." The Myrdals said they wanted all this "to shape a better human material."[30]

Myrdal embraced what he called "social engineering," a willingness to discard all previous institutions and traditions regardless of whether there was any historical evidence that they worked. Experts would design new institutions from scratch based on pure reason. Myrdal had explained in 1932 that the new social policy ideology is "rational, whereas the old . . . was quite sentimental." The expert reformer should be "liberated from the inhibitions" of any reverence for past experience. Myrdal captured well the new technocratic approach as "a purely technical analysis of a social policy question." Such an approach "has a certain tendency to go in an extremely radical direction." This was because the technical solution really did start from scratch and discard previous institutions, "quite simply because a purely technical analysis has no place in its schedule for institutional conventionalism."[31] This was the thinking that led Gunnar and Alva to propose supplanting the traditional family in Sweden.

Hayek was horrified at the technocrats' ambition to draw up a new society from scratch. He saw "the preoccupation with technological problems" as the root of Blank Slate thinking. It was a preview of the development mind-set still around today that seeks purely technical solutions from natural scientists and engineers trying to answer the question, "what must we do to end poverty?" To Hayek, technocracy represented "the uncritical transfer to the problems of society of . . . the habits of thought of the natural scientist and the engineer." The technocrats "tended to discredit the results of the past study of society which did not conform to their prejudices" as to what the right technical solution was. The decentralized solving of a problem by a free social system—with nobody in charge—was *not* analogous to an engineer solving one technical problem completely under his or her control.[32]

The Blank Slate had two important consequences for the role of individual freedom in development. First, it discarded positive evidence on how well individual freedom had worked in the past for development (as we will see in the rest of this book). This rejection of historical evidence made the rejection of freedom in development more likely.

Second, a Blank Slate approach itself required more autocratic coercion of individuals to get them to give up their previous institutions and accept the experts' new technical solutions. Technocracy mostly failed in the West because democratic institutions allowed people to keep the institutions they wanted to keep and to reject expert alternatives. The Swedes, for example, were not willing to give up what the Myrdals called their "pathological" traditional families and accept one "great national household" for their children. The option to evolve gradually, mostly sticking to tradition, was not the outcome of coercion, it was what came naturally.

Hayek defended those who wanted to keep their institutions, instead of expert blueprints, and did not require them to provide a complete, rational justification for every social practice. The technocrats did not understand that institutions (like the family) were complicated solutions to complex problems; they had evolved without expert guidance. They were "products of a social process which nobody has designed and the reasons for which nobody may understand."[33] The lesson was not to keep things always unchanged, it was that experts should have more humility in the face of traditions they could not completely understand. With their local knowledge, nonexperts may better appreciate than imported technocrats how traditions are working for them. Institutions could continue to evolve on their own as circumstances changed. The ultimate lesson was to let individuals choose.

Democratic institutions made the option of rejecting the Blank Slate approach possible in the West. In the Rest, autocrats and their expert advisors had more unchecked power to impose Blank Slate approaches. The debate on the Blank Slate versus learning from history had happened in the West, but it would not happen in the Rest. The side that lost the debate in the West would win without a debate in the Rest.

DEBATE 2: THE WELL-BEING OF NATIONS VERSUS THAT OF INDIVIDUALS

The objective of development as developing the nation-state—that is, development in, by, and for individual countries—is so taken for granted that it is rarely even noticed. In the various phrases in development discourse—*developing countries, underdeveloped countries, Third World countries*—the discussion is usually about which modifier to use while the word *countries* is never questioned.

The phrases above were ubiquitous in Myrdal's development writings. Whom did development advisers advise? They were "advisers to underdeveloped countries."[34] What problems did they study? It was the "problems of the underdeveloped countries." Who was going to act? The advisers "from advanced countries" were "urging the underdeveloped ones toward . . . their social and economic reforms."[35] He described the actions that "underdeveloped countries have to attempt." He regretted that "time does not allow them" any delay. His imperative was "they have to reform."[36] Myrdal's *they* is "countries," as it has remained in development up to the present. Of course, some action is inevitably at the national level, and much development analysis is also at that level; zero emphasis on nations is not tenable. However, exclusive emphasis on nations carries dangers of its own to individual rights, as Hayek pointed out.

One obvious danger is to the rights of ethnic minorities. Myrdal in *Asian Drama* described "religion, ethnic origin, culture, language" as "barriers" to be "broken down."[37] There are benign and less benign ways toward broken-down ethnic barriers, if indeed that is universally desirable. If it is simply a call for ethnic groups to show toleration toward each other, to abandon racist attitudes toward other groups, nobody would disagree with such benign ideals. A less-benign way is to deny minority ethnic groups the rights to assert their own, voluntarily chosen ethnic identity—for example, to ban minority languages or minority religious and cultural observances. The least-benign way of all is for one ethnic group to identify the nation with itself and actively promote hatred and discrimination toward all others.

Myrdal did not seem aware that his call for individuals to show a "firm allegiance" exclusively to the "national community" might promote nationalism and intolerance.[38] Hayek was far more aware of the potential threat of nationalism toward minority groups. He noted, for example, that nationalism is useful for autocrats, who are not above also manipulating hatreds toward nonnational groups to consolidate their own power: "The contrast between the 'we' and the 'they,' the common fight against those outside the group, seems to be an essential ingredient in any creed which will solidly knit together a group for common action . . . [for] the unreserved allegiance of huge masses. From [autocrats'] point of view it has the great advantage of leaving them greater freedom of action than almost any positive program."[39]

Hayek noted the particular vulnerability of ethnic minorities prominent in business or finance to nationalist hatreds. Envy of their success and ethnic prejudice make a toxic mix. National policies such as "expropriating the excess profits" of the capitalists could in fact be aimed more at minorities than at capitalists.[40] Hayek's warnings about minority businessmen would be tragically prescient as the examples of the East Indians expelled from Uganda by Idi Amin in 1972 and mass killings of the

Chinese in Indonesia in the 1960s would later show. The general minority problem would later become well known with examples like the Tutsis, Bosnian Muslims, Kurds, Tibetans, Darfuris, and many others.

But there was more to the risk that nationalism posed for freedom than just its threat to ethnic minorities. What exactly did the goal of "national development" mean? It could not make sense as just a unified aspiration of all individuals, when individuals have so many different goals of their own. Indeed, another Nobel laureate, Kenneth Arrow, was to demonstrate a famous "impossibility theorem" in 1950, showing that no method can exist to rank the choices of a collection of individuals in a way that satisfies the most elementary common-sense rules for consistency and coherence.

Hayek was blunt that a "national goal" just covered up the fact that some goals for some groups were attained at the expense of other goals for other groups. Economics and politics involve "the choice between conflicting or competing ends—different needs of different people." Making a particular set of choices and calling it "national development" really means making decisions on which goals "will have to be sacrificed if we want to achieve certain others." National development as advised by experts just means that the experts "are in a position to decide which of the different ends are to be given preference. It is inevitable that they should impose their scale of preferences on the community."[41] Since a democracy is unlikely to turn such vital judgments over to experts, the experts may even voice frustration at how democracies fail to get things done, how they fail to promote what the expert sees as development. The experts may actually welcome an autocrat, who in turn can use the expert promotion of development as part of his rationale for his autocratic rule.

If it is impossible to reconcile the national goal of development with individuals' own freely chosen goals, one must choose. It was clear that Myrdal and Hayek would make opposite choices. To Hayek, as we have seen in the introduction to this chapter, it was unacceptable that "the individual is merely a means to serve the ends of the higher entity called . . . the nation."[42]

Interestingly enough, Myrdal understood, like Hayek, that the combination of nationalism with a national goal like development was a path to power: "The political leaders of the new countries have to arouse ambitions among the masses" because "this is their means of acquiring power."

The leaders know that "the aspirations which they know they can arouse successfully are the cravings for . . . economic development." The leaders know that "the pliant, illiterate masses" can be "aroused by nationalist appeals."[43] Myrdal's difference with Hayek is that he thought such extensive power for the national state and its nationalist leader was a good thing. Myrdal thought development could only happen through such national development goals, enforced by leaders, using coercion of individuals if necessary.

Hayek and Myrdal occupied opposite sides of this debate on individual rights versus the prerogatives of nations in development, another debate that never happened. Let's now turn to the third debate between Hayek and Myrdal.

DEBATE 3: CONSCIOUS DESIGN VERSUS SPONTANEOUS SOLUTIONS

In February 2013, a well-known development veteran named Owen Barder gave a talk in which he defined development as an "emergent property of a complex adaptive system." By this he meant that development emerged from a whole system that was too complex to be run by any one leader. Yet the system was adaptive in the sense that problems generated decentralized feedback and responses that then allowed the system to correct the problems. The idea stimulated positive buzz on development blogs, and nobody called Barder a right-wing extremist.[44]

Hayek was unlucky to be ahead of his time. A large part of *The Road to Serfdom* was about what he called "spontaneous order." Among the examples he gave were markets, the evolution of the rule of law, and the evolution of social norms. Similar concepts abound today. Whether called *complexity, complex adaptive systems, self-organizing systems,* or *emergence,* and whether championed by natural scientists or Silicon Valley enthusiasts, all refer to systems that nobody designed, that display order that nobody ordered, and that deliver outcomes that nobody intended. Some examples are the Internet, evolution, language, cities, and anthills. The debate in development between conscious design and spontaneous solutions is similar to the evolution debate between religious believers in "intelligent design" as opposed to those who celebrate the "spontaneous order" of evolution.

Hayek's spontaneous order was related to an idea that was already a mainstream concept in economics—general equilibrium—which held that a system of uncontrolled markets in every possible consumer or producer product would be a self-regulating system that reconciled supply and demand in every market, with nobody in charge.[45] Kenneth Arrow summed it all up in a sentence that sounds a lot like Hayek: "The notion that through the workings of an entire system effects may be very different from, and even opposed to, intentions is surely the most important intellectual contribution that economic thought has made to the general understanding of social processes."[46]

Lawrence Summers, a Harvard economist who was treasury secretary under Bill Clinton (and coincidentally Kenneth Arrow's nephew), wrote about Hayek: "What's the single most important thing to learn from an economics course today? What I tried to leave my students with is the view that the invisible hand is more powerful than the [un]hidden hand. Things will happen in well-organized efforts without direction, controls, plans. That's the consensus among economists. That's the Hayek legacy."[47]

In *The Road to Serfdom*, Hayek had first of all stressed the insight that today excites us about undesigned order (as summarized above in the Barder talk): "the spontaneous and uncontrolled efforts of individuals were capable of producing a complex order of economic activities."[48] Hayek acknowledged how "impatience for quick results"[49] had led some to reject the "spontaneous forces found in a free society" and to propose instead "collective and 'conscious' direction of all social forces to deliberately chosen goals."[50] He noted the seduction of conscious direction because "the person who actually does things" is always going to be far more popular than "the economist [who is] the odious individual who sits back in his armchair and explains why the well-meaning efforts of the former are frustrated."[51]

But we have an alternative to the expert-solutions mind-set: spontaneous solutions through market competition. Competitive markets allow anyone with a possible solution to a particular need to offer it to consumers. Consumers choose the solutions that deliver the highest need-satisfaction at the lowest costs. In Hayek's words, "we trust the independent and competitive efforts of many" to produce what we want. Hayek's poetic touch was that even when we don't know what we want, spontaneous market competition produces "what we shall want when we see it."[52]

Those advocating conscious direction thought they knew better than individuals what was good for those individuals. They also thought they were smart enough to run the whole society, to identify and alleviate the constraints in the society that held back societies' progress out of poverty. The spontaneity and humility of individualism is the opposite: "Individualism is thus an attitude of humility before this social process and of tolerance to other opinions and is the exact opposite of that intellectual hubris which is at the root of the demand for comprehensive direction of the social process."[53]

Myrdal indeed said the opposite of Hayek, that the state should take "responsibility for economic development."[54] Myrdal envisaged a "government and its entourage as the active subject in planning, and the rest of the people as the relatively passive objects of the policies emerging from planning."[55] The word *planning* for Myrdal did not mean Soviet-style central planning. Myrdal clarifies that planning is just what we are calling here conscious design: "Development plans often explicitly define planning as a comprehensive attempt to reform all unsatisfactory conditions."[56] He noted "what these countries need is a programme that will induce changes simultaneously in a great number of conditions that hold down their growth."[57]

When he wrote *Asian Drama* in 1968, Myrdal could see no hope for spontaneous solutions to emerge from poor individuals: "The prevailing attitudes and patterns of individual performance in life and at work are from the development point of view deficient" and are marked by "low levels of work discipline" as well as "superstitious beliefs and irrational outlook; lack of alertness, adaptability, ambition, and general readiness for change and experiment."[58]

NOT STATE VERSUS MARKET

But in spite of misconceptions to the contrary, spontaneous solutions versus conscious design is not just an argument in favor of markets versus state intervention. This has been one of the biggest misunderstandings in the development debate for six decades. It has been the only debate on freedom that happened in development, but it was the wrong debate on freedom.

For example, the British-Hungarian economist P. T. Bauer published his book *Dissent on Development* in 1971, supporting many of Hayek's views and attacking Myrdal's authoritarian approach to development (I have quoted again here many of Bauer's quotes of Myrdal). But the development community saw Bauer's argument to be nothing more than the standard free market critique of government intervention. Bauer in 1971, like many before him and since, was unsuccessful in getting the development community to engage in a more fundamental debate about authoritarian versus free development.

There are three reasons why state-versus-market debate is the wrong debate. First, Hayek himself acknowledged the complementarity of state and market by identifying the need for government-supplied goods or interventions in areas the market doesn't cover. What Hayek called "a wide and unquestioned field for state activity" included roads, pollution, sanitation, a legal framework, the prevention of fraud, and social services.[59]

Second, government services work best when they, too, are the outcome of spontaneous order in a free society. Politicians supplying goods the voters want are rewarded with political support, and politicians neglecting or harming their constituents are punished with vociferous protesters. The system does not require a government services czar: a decentralized "squeaky wheel gets the grease" system will do the job. Autocracy denies individuals' rights to be squeaky wheels—such as the freedom of speech and assembly necessary to protest bad public services.

We underestimate how effective the political spontaneous order already is because of the things we take for granted in free societies. Teachers show up, the roads mostly remain in good condition, and the government doesn't burn down the houses of Ohio farmers—because there would be vociferous complaints otherwise. In autocracies that do not depend on popular support and that are able to suppress protesters, teacher absenteeism, disastrous roads, and stolen farms are a lot more likely.

Third, the real test case of the misunderstanding of the debate on conscious design versus spontaneous solutions as state versus market is the pro–free market autocrat. Where does he fit into the debate about state versus market? Such a dictator and his free-market advisors may consciously design development "as a comprehensive attempt to reform all unsatisfactory conditions," to use Myrdal's words again, where the unsatisfactory conditions include the absence of a flourishing private sector. We have already seen how Hayek criticized the probusiness conservative who would "not object to coercion or arbitrary power so long as it is used for what he regards as the right purposes. He believes that if government is in the hands of decent men, it ought not to be too much restricted by rigid rules. Since he is essentially opportunist and lacks principles, his main hope must be that the wise and the good will rule."[60]

Hayek objected to the idea of the benevolent autocrat on the principle of his opposition to unchecked power, which such an autocrat possesses. Hayek's principle is violated regardless of whether the objective of that power is to promote free markets or socialism. The autocrats and their expert advisers get to determine which policies do promote "free markets," with no safeguards against violating individual rights. The experts consciously designing market-driven development might replace those designing state-driven development, but the experts would still be in the service of unchecked power.

Hayek was so insistent that unchecked power could not be trusted to be held by "the wise and the good" that he devoted a whole chapter of *The Road to Serfdom* to "Why the Worst Get on Top." In an autocratic system, Hayek noted, "there will be special opportunities for the ruthless and unscrupulous."[61] In such a system, "the readiness to do bad things becomes a path to promotion and power."[62] Why do we think that the leader who winds up on top in such a system is likely to be benevolent? Why do we think he will stay benevolent when staying in power requires the same "readiness to do bad things" that brought him to power in the first place?

The promarket autocrat that is on the market side of the market-versus-state debate is on the state side of the individual rights–versus-state debate. Such an autocrat will sooner or later be a threat to economic freedom as well as political freedom.

THE KNOWLEDGE PROBLEM WITH CONSCIOUS DESIGN

Hayek had yet another insight into why conscious design could not work in development, the insight for which he is best known as a purely academic contributor. In 1945, Hayek published "The Use of Knowledge in Society" in the *American Economic Review,* the leading journal in economics. A big problem with conscious direction from the center, said Hayek, is the lack of sufficient knowledge at the center. In 2011 a panel of prominent economists selected Hayek's article as one of the top twenty articles of the last century in the *American Economic Review. (The Road to Serfdom* expounded the same ideas in accessible form; ironically, the ideas that harmed Hayek's reputation in the public marketplace of ideas enhanced his reputation in academic circles.)

When Hayek and Myrdal received their Nobel prizes three decades later, their talks in Oslo gave rather different views of the knowledge problem. Myrdal spoke first and concluded his Nobel lecture by saying that "I am hopeful about the development of our science. . . . Everything can be studied. We are free to expand and perfect our knowledge about the world, only restricted by the number of scientists working and, of course, the degree of their . . . brightness."[63]

Hayek had already generated puzzlement at the banquet the night before the ceremony, where he confessed that "if I had been consulted whether to establish a Nobel Prize in economics, I should have decidedly advised against it." He further unsettled his hosts with the suggestion that "the Nobel Prize confers on an individual an authority which in economics no man ought to possess."[64] Hayek was outrageously honest about the inability of experts to consciously design a society—he included even himself among those undeserving of such authority. In the Nobel lecture the next day, he contradicted Myrdal about the unlimited potential of science. Social scientists who claimed to be able to run a society did not really understand social science: "In the sciences of man, what looks superficially like the most scientific procedure is often the most unscientific, and, beyond this, . . . in these fields there are definite limits to what we can expect science to achieve."[65]

Hayek in his 1945 article had demolished the presumption that experts had sufficient knowledge to consciously design solutions to all social problems. He noted that the kind of knowledge to make investment, production, and consumption decisions was often very localized, context-specific, and personally idiosyncratic. Just as important as the science beloved by technocrats is the individual's knowledge of constantly changing details of other people, places, and opportunities. More important than how to build a machine is where and when and for what group of people a machine will really pay off, where the "right" answer keeps changing and is known only to those on the scene. The knowledge needed to generate prosperity is not contained in a single mind, it is dispersed among many minds. The free society creates the incentives for each individual to utilize his or her own particular bits of knowledge.

Even more inaccessible to conscious designers is *tacit knowledge*, which cannot be communicated as a list of instructions from one individual to another. Tacit knowledge is the kind of trained and mostly unconscious knowledge needed, for example, to ride a bicycle—it does not work to follow a recipe on how to balance and turn the pedals. Economics examples include on-the-job learning, which is the main reason workers' earnings rise with experience. Even purely technical solutions often require experience with that technology, in particular times and places, to fix the bugs. Tacit knowledge can only be gained through what Kenneth Arrow later called "learning by doing." Tacit knowledge can certainly not be accessed by centralized problem-solvers.

For Hayek, the advantages of a spontaneous order of free individuals is that it creates the incentives for individuals to utilize their own localized or tacit knowledge, without any need for anyone else to access it. For private goods, the prices and markets coordinate all the decisions of individuals based on their idiosyncratic knowledge in a way that top-down plans could never do. In any given area, the individual who has the knowledge to produce what customers want most is the one chosen through market competition to be the producer.

Hayek would later state this in a different way. We cannot rely on centralized expertise to run society "because every individual knows so little" relative to the vast knowledge needed to give us what we want. We don't even know enough to know who should be the expert, because "we rarely know which of us knows best."[66] A spontaneous order of competition among individuals with different kinds and degrees of knowledge to supply our needs will decide who knows best for each particular need.

The ideas of spontaneous solutions and the limits to knowledge were a severe challenge to aspiring experts in development. How would they respond?

WHY DID THE HAYEK–MYRDAL DEBATE NOT HAPPEN?

As we have seen Myrdal claimed unanimous support for what he called planning and what I am calling here the technocratic approach to development. It is striking how often he repeated this claim and how sweeping it was: planning "is unanimously endorsed by governments and experts in the advanced countries."[67] Myrdal affirmed yet again that "it is now commonly agreed that an underdeveloped country should have an overall integrated national plan." He notes that "positive and urgent advice to do so is given them by all scholars and statesmen from the advanced countries." Underdeveloped countries "under the encouraging and congratulating applause of the advanced countries" were "attempting to furnish themselves with . . . a plan."[68]

The group of "all special advisers to underdeveloped countries" in favor of plans included a broad range, no less than "all who have taken the time and trouble to acquaint themselves with the problems, no matter who they are— . . . experts from the [World Bank] or other international agencies . . . private foundations and consultant firms; independent social scientists, journalists or visiting politicians."[69] Myrdal seemed to think unanimity was something to brag about, something that showed how strong his case was for technocratic development.

Hayek, on the other hand, argued in *The Road to Serfdom* that dissent from the consensus was necessary for the "life of thought": "So long as dissent is not suppressed, there will always be some who will query the ideas ruling their contemporaries and put new ideas to the test of argument and propaganda. This interaction of individuals, possessing different knowledge and different views, is what constitutes the life of thought." Hayek argued that the absence of "different views"—that is, Myrdal's unanimity—in fact inhibits the progress of thought: "The growth of reason is a social process based on the existence of such differences."[70]

Hayek condemned those who wanted to suppress debate, what he called "the presumption of any group of people"—such as Myrdal's unanimous development experts—"to claim the right to determine what people ought to think or believe."[71] The absence of dissent would "produce a stagnation of thought and a decline of reason."[72] Hayek argued that it is not possible to know which innovation in thinking will succeed (otherwise it wouldn't be innovation!): "results [of thinking] cannot be predicted . . . we cannot know which views will assist this growth [of reason] and which will not—in short, . . . this growth cannot be governed by any views which we now possess *without at the same time limiting it*" (emphasis added).[73] For development to occur it is thus necessary to have the debate among many "different views."

There were many possible reasons for the reluctance in development then and now to consider the case for spontaneous solutions by individuals. Maybe people really are too illiterate, too malnourished, too sick, or too poor to act in their own long-term interests. Maybe national development efforts can mobilize more expertise than what is available to individuals. Maybe authoritarian methods really do enable more rapid catching up to the rich nations than do methods that respect individual freedom.

There was likely also a moral motivation. Many who cared then (or now) about global poverty may have feared that theories of spontaneous solutions may support an immoral indifference or inaction on poverty. The moral motivation is problematic, however. Even if we do judge theories by their moral consequences, these consequences are impossible to predict. It may be that a theory of development as spontaneous solutions by individuals will lead to insights that form a stronger moral case for action by outsiders and not a weaker case that justifies indifference.

All that *can* be predicted is that inhibiting debate is bad for the progress of reason. The absence of debate on the technocratic approach to development stifles progress in development, which in itself is immoral.

POLITICAL MOTIVES FOR NOT DEBATING

Myrdal's writings reveal another reason why he did not debate Hayek's ideas. It is surprising to learn, for all Myrdal's fierce advocacy of planning in development, that he feared it would fail. He noted in 1956 that the state in underdeveloped countries was "often a weak state, served by a comparatively ineffective and sometimes corrupt administration." Myrdal recognized that he and other experts were now asking for "what amounts to a sort of super planning" that "has to be staged by under-developed countries with weak political and administrative apparatuses and a largely illiterate and apathetic citizenry." Myrdal said these were "all reasons to expect numerous mistakes and in many cases total failure."[74] So why did he and other experts unanimously endorse planning?

Myrdal explained: "*the alternative to making the heroic attempt is continued acquiescence in economic stagnation which is politically impossible in the world of today*" (original emphasis). And, he continued, "this is, of course, the explanation why grand scale national planning is at present the goal in under-developed countries all over the globe and why this policy line is unanimously endorsed by governments and experts in the advanced countries."[75]

So Myrdal suggested that the appeal of technocratic development was in part political, and politics may help explain why experts from rich countries who held democratic and individualistic values at home chose the authoritarian side in poor countries. Here appears a momentous double standard on rights for the West and not for the Rest. The double standard arrives in Myrdal's writings in deceptively bland language: "[None of the American and European experts] sees any other way out of the mounting difficulties in under-developed countries, however different their attitude may be towards economic problems at home."[76] For Myrdal, Hayek's concerns about the consequences of a powerful state for individual rights did not apply to poor countries. Myrdal believed poor people did not care that much about their rights, and could not use those rights to do much for themselves.

There were going to be two different kinds of economics, based on two different kinds of values: one for underdeveloped countries and the other for advanced countries. By this time, development economists had asked the rest of the economics profession for a divorce, which had been granted. Hence, by a circular argument, Myrdal could claim unanimous support for the technocratic approach to development—amongst a group known as "development economists"—who were in turn defined as those who supported the technocratic approach to development.

We will explore the politics of development ideas in the next part of the book. We will see that these development ideas may have been helpful to the United States in the Cold War. In fact, similar development ideas were helpful to the Great Powers long before the Cold War, while at the same time they appealed in common to nationalist leaders in the Rest and humanitarians in the West.

PART TWO

Why the Debate Never Happened—
the Real History of the Development Idea

Most histories of the subject date the birth of economic development to a sunny, cold, and windy day in Washington DC at 1:29 pm on January 20, 1949. On that day, at that time, President Harry S. Truman announced an initiative to give foreign aid to poor countries in his inaugural address:

> We must embark on a bold new program for making the benefits of our scientific advances and industrial progress available for the improvement and growth of underdeveloped areas.
>
> More than half the people of the world are living in conditions approaching misery. Their food is inadequate. They are victims of disease. Their economic life is primitive and stagnant. Their poverty is a handicap and a threat both to them and to more prosperous areas.
>
> For the first time in history, humanity possesses the knowledge and the skill to relieve the suffering of these people.

In fact, it was not the first time in history that it was the first time in history.

Woodrow Wilson had noted about the League of Nations on January 8, 1919, that "For the first time in history the counsels of mankind are to be drawn together and concerted for the purpose of . . . improving the conditions of working people—men, women, and children—all over the world."[1] The 1949 birth date is part of the conventional view that ties development to the end of colonialism, addressing the needs of peoples in new independent states. Wilson's 1919 statement gives us an advance hint that this history gets it wrong.

The true history is that development ideas took shape while racism and colonialism still reigned supreme. And locating the formative years of development between 1919 and 1949 highlights a critical point: development ideas took shape before there was even the most minimal respect in the West for the rights of individuals in the Rest. We know this because many different actors in the West at the time told us so. Western commentators, from Presidents Wilson to Hoover to FDR, and from intellectuals like British scientist Julian Huxley to the Harvard lecturer and China expert Stanley Hornbeck made no effort to disguise their low view of people in the Rest. It was a time when the word *racism* had not even been invented, and when attitudes that were at best ethnocentric and at worst downright racist were still acceptable. This environment would allow an authoritarian approach to development to defeat any or all liberal alternatives based on equal rights for individuals in the Rest.

There were some who cared about freedom in the Rest despite this hostile environment. First, there were intellectuals in the Rest, who considered the free alternative to authoritarian ideas for their own societies.

Second, a more surprising source of support for freedom came from mainstream Western economists. Mainstream economics emerged out of free societies in the United States and the United Kingdom; it took freedom for granted in that it studied the behavior of individuals making voluntary choices. Confronted with the unfree situations of colonialism and indigenous autocracy in the Rest, some economists would create a special economics that discarded free choice and individualism. It would be called development economics. But those who remained in the economics mainstream adhered to the traditional respect for individuals and their choices. They applied a unitary economics across all societies that stressed freedom as the basis for development in the Rest as it had been in the West.

Those in charge of racist, colonialist, or imperialist policies in the United States and the United Kingdom could (and did) use the ideas of authoritarian development to justify or excuse racist, colonialist, or imperialist policies. For example, the colonial power could present itself as a benevolent autocrat, using its superior technology to better the welfare of colonial subjects. We will see other more subtle applications in the semicolonial situation of prerevolutionary China and the semi-imperialist relationship between the United States and Colombia after World War II.

Development without rights also made sense to humanitarians in the United States and United Kingdom who genuinely wanted to improve the lives of the world's poor. Western humanitarians focused on the technocratic solutions of the colonial power rather than on the rights violations by those colonial powers. The humanitarians also suffered from a patronizing view of colonial subjects (such as Africans) in which the rules that applied in the West did not hold in the Rest. Hence, they had little conception of rights for poor people. The same technocratic ideas amongst humanitarians gave cover for rights violations perpetrated by the West in China and Latin America.

The point is not to discredit particular ideas solely for their colonialist or imperialist origins. The point is the historical continuity of attitudes toward technocrats and rights. The colonial examples show a focus on technocratic solutions and a concomitant blindness to rights violations by the colonial autocrats who perpetrated them. These examples foreshadow today's development focus on technocratic solutions and blindness to rights violations by the indigenous autocrats who perpetrate them.

We will see how notions of benevolent autocrats in development were originally inspired by colonialism and racism in which the Western powers would be the benevolent autocrats. But, ironically and surprisingly, the same concept appealed even to anticolonialist and antiracist leaders in the Rest, because those leaders aspired to be the benevolent autocrats themselves.

What was the idea of ideal power?

The period between 1919 and 1949 would bring sharp debates on authoritarian versus free development. We will see debates on the issues that appeared clearly in the positions of Hayek and Myrdal on authoritarian versus free development, with the authoritarian side taking the first of each of these opposite pairs: the Blank Slate versus the learning from history, the prerogatives of nations versus the rights of individuals,

and conscious design versus spontaneous solutions. Mainstream economists in the West, as described above, adhered to their traditional preference for the second of each of these pairs. But the authoritarian side
(such as Chiang Kai-shek in China, as we will see), choosing the first of
each of these pairs, claimed to be formulating a "new economics" that
was better for rapid development.

Logic and evidence gave little support to the new economics of authoritarian development. But it would defeat free development anyway
because it offered power and a rationalization of that power to the key
groups: the Great Powers, the humanitarians in rich countries, and political leaders in poor countries.

This section of the book (Chapters Three through Five) seeks to understand why and how the illiberal version of development had already
defeated the liberal version by January 20, 1949. Our journey will take
us from the early years in China to crucial years during and immediately
after World War II in West Africa to the final triumph of official development in Colombia in 1948 through 1951.

CHAPTER THREE

ONCE UPON A TIME IN CHINA

In 1927 an economist from New Zealand named John Bell Condliffe arrived in China for a four-month visit. He was there to commission research by local Chinese economists on China's economic development. He brought with him American financing (primarily from the gigantic American philanthropy, the Rockefeller Foundation) for such research. Condliffe (1891–1981) was a typical economist of his generation, affirming core values of individual liberty and democracy, and holding to classical economists' ideas of markets and gains from international trade. For the next twenty-two years, until the victory of Mao Tse-tung's Communists in 1949, he would observe China as it sought to realize the hopes of its 1912 republican revolution that had ended thousands of years of imperial dynasties. Development experts would play a major role in this effort.

Condliffe would eventually question the role of the development experts in China. His early visit, ironically, would launch the career of such a development expert. This expert was H. D. Fong (1902–1985), an American-educated Chinese economist who would occupy the authoritarian side on the debates to come. Condliffe and Fong would become some of the first participants in the debate on authoritarian economic development, both in China and worldwide, although both are now completely forgotten.

The debate on Chinese development took place against a backdrop of some ugly Western attitudes and policies toward the Chinese. Most important was the toxic combination of two policies. First, the United States banned Chinese immigration to America for overtly racist reasons. Second, the United States asserted special privileges for American residents in China. Americans in China who lived in semicolonial "concessions" occupied by the United Kingdom or other Great Powers were not subject to Chinese law.

This backdrop would eventually explain why both sides—Westerners making development efforts in China, and Chinese leaders and their advisers (including Fong)—would embrace authoritarian development ideas and reject ideas based on individual rights. It would explain why an advocate for rights—like Condliffe—would wind up isolated, ignored, and then forgotten.

To understand the backdrop, we need to go back to three momentous decisions made in Versailles in the aftermath of World War I. These decisions reflected the West's struggle to come to terms with the Rest in the early twentieth century, so their story involves much more than discussions in smoke-filled rooms in 1919.

THREE BAD MOMENTS AT VERSAILLES

The negotiations in Versailles for a treaty to end World War I occupied the first half of 1919, until the participating nations signed the treaty of Versailles on June 28, 1919. Although twenty-seven nations participated in the Versailles talks, the dominant powers were the United States, the United Kingdom, and France. Three decisions came to have lasting significance for the history of development ideas in China and elsewhere: the decision to create League of Nations mandates, the decision not to endorse racial equality, and the decision to transfer Shantung Province in China from German to Japanese control.

League of Nations Mandates

The first decision was to transform former German colonies into "mandates." The mandates were places, not commands. They were regions whose trustees answered to the League of Nations (the precursor international organization to the United Nations) that was also created at the Versailles conference. This was the context for Woodrow Wilson's inaugural address quoted above about how "the first time in history the counsels of mankind are . . . concerted" to improve "the conditions of working people . . . all over the world." Wilson spelled out the idea of the mandates further "with regard to the helpless parts of the world": "All of those regions are put under the trust of the league of nations, to be administered for the benefit of their inhabitants—the greatest humane arrangement that has ever been attempted—and the rules are laid down in the covenant itself which forbid any form of selfish exploitation of these helpless people by the agents of the league who will exercise authority over them during the period of their development."[2]

The mandates were not directly relevant to China, which was not a colony. However, the idea of development as a neutral enterprise in some territories "for the benefit of their inhabitants" would indeed be relevant in China. It was one of the first statements of technocratic development, in which the focus is on the development of the "helpless" and not on who is doing the developing. It displays either naïveté or indifference to who actually holds the power.

In practice, the mandates were hard to distinguish from colonies. The League of Nations awarded the former German colonies to other colonial powers, notably Britain (e.g., Tanzania) and France (e.g., Togo). The League had no enforcement power to prevent "exploitation" by those colonial powers who "will exercise authority over them during the period of their development." So the mandates just became British or French colonies in all but name. Cynics could dismiss the whole exercise as a power grab by the British and French.

But the technocratic idea of focusing on development instead of on the rights of those to be developed was going to appear over and over again in the next three decades of development's formative period. It would be developed further in China, as we will see in this chapter. It would also influence British colonial policy in Africa and America's softer imperialism toward Latin America, to be discussed in the next two chapters.

Racism and Development

The second decision at Versailles—not to endorse racial equality—also had lasting consequences for China and for the formation of development ideas. The Japanese, as the first nonwhite Great Power, wanted respect and proposed a declaration of racial equality at Versailles in 1919. The British and the Americans shot down the equality proposal. The British did not want international attention on racial discrimination within the British Empire. Woodrow Wilson was a segregationist at home who also did not want international interference in white Americans' treatment of blacks.

What is important about this decision is that the idea of development solidified while the West was still unapologetically racist during the inter-war period of 1919 to 1939, as we will see with the example of China in this chapter. Racism would be even more at the center in colonial Africa in World War II, as we will discuss in the next chapter. While the Americans and British at Versailles had their own political self-interests at stake in rejecting the Japanese racial equality proposal, they also did so just because they were so racist. Let's sketch briefly the state of racial attitudes in the West during this crucial period.

The British and Americans directed their most severe racism at Africans. Lord Lugard, the longtime Governor General of Nigeria, whose 1922 book *The Dual Mandate* was the bible for British colonial officials in Africa, offered a tidy if disturbing view into colonial attitudes: "In character and temperament the typical African of this race-type is a happy, thrift-less, excitable person, lacking in self-control, discipline, and foresight. . . . 'His mind', says Sir C. Eliot, 'is far nearer to the animal world than that of the European or Asiatic.'" Lugard continued: "the virtues and the defects of this race-type are those of attractive children, whose confidence when once it has been won is given ungrudgingly as to an older and wiser superior . . . Sir Chas. Eliot, from personal experience extends his description to the West Indies and the Southern States of America." In short, concluded Lugard, "we are dealing with the child races of the world."[3]

The British believed in their racial superiority so much that they thought blacks themselves accepted it. Even a liberal such as the British biologist (and later first director of UNESCO) Julian Huxley claimed the African "native" had a "childlike belief in the white as an inherently superior being."[4]

Stanley Hornbeck, an American expert on the Far East who will play a role in this chapter, affirmed these attitudes toward blacks: "the average negro does enough work to get enough to live on and no more. . . . He is not interested in property or culture and you have to impair his freedom to make his economic standards higher."[5]

Of course, the rejection of racial equality at Versailles in 1919 was not limited to blacks. This became even more clear five years later in the United States with the passage of the Oriental Exclusion Act of 1924, which established a complete ban on Asian immigration, without even the nationality quotas that had occurred under previous immigration-restriction acts for many other nations. To the Chinese, this was another in a long string of racist insults by Americans that dated back to the Chinese Exclusion Act of 1882 (at a time of unrestricted and huge immigration flows from Europe). The Secretary of Commerce in 1924, Herbert Hoover, expressed support for the Act because there were "biological and cultural grounds why there should be no mixture of Oriental and Caucasian blood."[6] In light of these views, it's not surprising that American efforts at development in China would have little regard for the rights of the Chinese.

It Was All About May 4

The third decision at Versailles had the most immediate consequences in China. On May 4, 1919, word arrived in China that the Allies had decided not to give the German-controlled province of Shantung in China back to China. It would cede the rich and populous coastal province to the Japanese.

To make matters worse, the Allies had already given away Shantung twice during the war. In a secret treaty during the war, Britain and France had promised it to Japan as a reward for entering the war on the Allied side. Then Wilson, unaware of the promise, offered it back to China in return for entering the war on the Allied side. But by the end of the war, Wilson's focus had shifted to creating the League of Nations. He felt the organization would work only if it included all of the major powers, including Japan. Thus Shantung went to Japan. The Chinese delegation refused to sign the Versailles treaty that ended World War I, but nobody in the West cared.

Shantung had been not a German colony but a territorial "concession," one of many held by the Western powers in China as the result
of treaties imposed on the weak Chinese Empire over the previous eight
decades. Under the concession system, the Germans in Shantung had
their own military and police forces. German residents in Shantung were
under German rather than Chinese law, and they were tried in German
courts—a set of protections called *extraterritoriality*. Chinese citizens
could (and did) live in the concessions, but they were subject to the same
rule of German law, which effectively made them second-class citizens in
their own country. The other European powers had their own concessions
(also known as "spheres of influence") with the same rules in China.

It was bad enough to lose Shantung, but to lose it to Japan was intol-
erable. Japan had been everything that Chinese nationalists wanted China
to become—a country that had successfully modernized and defended itself against Western imperialists. However, Chinese admiration for Japan
had ended after Japan used that success for its own imperial aims, with
China as a prime target. Japan defeated China in an 1894 war and started
to put together its own concession in China (as well as making possible
new concessions for the Germans and Russians). It shocked the world
by defeating Russia in 1905 and then used that victory to take over yet
more Chinese land for its sphere of influence in Manchuria. By the end of
World War I, Japan looked to the Chinese to be the most threatening of
imperialist powers, as indeed would be borne out by later events.

The May 4 decision was particularly ironic in light of Woodrow Wilson's ideas about national self-determination, which broke up the prewar
empires and gave each ethnic nationality within those former empires its
own country. So, for example, new nations like Czechoslovakia achieved
independence from foreign rule by the old Austro-Hungarian Empire.
Clearly such ideas about independence from foreign control applied only
to Europe. Japan was able to exploit this double standard, pointing out
that none of the victorious powers in World War I had to give up their
own concessions in China, only the defeated power, Germany. The argument would help tilt the Allies at Versailles into giving Japan Shantung.

The Americans did not have concessions but did enjoy the same protections of extraterritoriality as other whites in the concessions of other

Great Powers. This created a toxic double standard, with lasting consequences, on Americans living in China versus Chinese living in America. Americans enjoyed special privileges living in China under extraterritoriality while the Americans banned the Chinese from living in America.

When the news on the Shantung decision at Versailles reached China on May 4, 1919, it provoked a nationalist outcry. Student riots broke out in Beijing, Tianjin, Shanghai, Nanjing, Wuhan, Fuzhou, Guangzhou, and elsewhere. A strike spread nationwide in June 1919, which developed into calls for a boycott of Japanese goods. Most important, a new movement— the May 4 movement—would help ensure the victory of a Chinese nationalist named Sun Yat-sen and his nationalist party, the Guomindang. In the process, it would give impetus to the autocratic side on the debate on authoritarian versus free development.

THE WORLD'S FIRST DEVELOPMENT PLAN

Sun Yat-sen's response to such national humiliation was a development plan in the form of a short book called *The International Development of China,* first published in November 1918.[7] Sun was one of the first to present the idea of technocratic development in its modern form. "I began my strategy for national construction by explicitly drafting a section on plans for developing industry. If we are to employ others and avoid being used by them, we must have a plan."[8] When the final version of his development plan was published in 1922, he made clear up front that "It is my hope that as a result of this, the present spheres of influence can be abolished."[9] In a 1924 speech, Sun Yat-sen said "the European powers are crushing China with their imperialism and economic strength."[10]

This is the first key moment in the history of the development idea as appealing to diverse—even opposite—groups. Sun Yat-sen suggested the idea of technocratic development to resist European imperialism in China, while at the same time in Versailles the Allies suggested technocratic development to expand European imperialism in Africa. The paradox is resolved if we remember what technocratic development takes for granted behind the scenes: a benevolent autocrat. The British Empire offered itself as a benevolent autocrat for the sake of development in Africa. Sun Yat-sen offered himself as a benevolent autocrat for the sake of development of China. The British were imperialist and Sun was anti-imperialist. The common theme is what the technocratic emphasis on development as the goal obscures: both Sun and the British simply wanted power.

Sun's idea of development did give a lot of power to the state he aspired to head: "I suggest that the vast resources of China be developed internationally under a socialistic scheme. . . . It was once thought by the economists of the Adam Smith school that competition was a beneficent factor and a sound economic system, but modern economists discovered that it is a very wasteful and ruinous system. . . . Therefore China should make all the national industries of China into a great Trust owned by the Chinese people."[11]

The passive voice and use of vague collective words like *Chinese people* or *China* obscure who is going to have that power. Behind the scenes, Sun's organization of his nationalist party, the Guomindang, did not seem to leave a lot of room for democracy or individual rights. In a speech to party insiders at the Whampoa military academy, which trained officers for the new Chinese army, Sun said on June 16, 1924: "you must first sacrifice your own personal liberty [and] everyone must obey the internal orders of the party. . . . Only the party as a whole has liberty. Individuals cannot have liberty."[12] One person listening closely to this speech was the head of the Whampoa military academy, Chiang Kai-shek.

Sun Yat-sen's idea of development immediately evoked one dimension of the authoritarian development debate: the prerogative of the collective (nation or party) to trump the rights of the individual. His remarks quoted above called upon conscious design ("China [is to] be developed internationally under a socialistic scheme") rather than spontaneous evolution as the basis of development. Lying in the background in that statement is the Blank Slate, in which modern economists disregard the lessons of history ("once thought by the economists of the Adam Smith school") and do something new ("make all the national industries of China into a great Trust").

Sun Yat-sen would die of cancer less than a year later after the Whampoa speech, on March 12, 1925. It would be Chiang Kai-shek who would carry on his ideas. The year 1925 also found a twenty-three-year-old Chinese student named H. D. Fong studying for his PhD in economics at Yale. That same year a group of American experts met in New York to discuss what to do about China. Chiang, Fong, and the American experts would wind up coming together on the ideas of authoritarian development in China.

AMERICAN EXPERTS

On a rainy February 22, 1925, in New York, a group of fifty-one men gathered at the Yale Club near Grand Central Station for the purpose of organizing a conference.[13] Brought together by the Rockefeller Foundation—the equivalent then of what the Gates Foundation is to development today—the group comprised ten journalists, fifteen academics, nine officials (including one from the League of Nations), seven businesspeople, and seven religious representatives. The group included the editor of the *New York Times* and the president of Stanford University. Academics included Stanley Hornbeck ("lecturer, Harvard University and Expert on China"), and the historian James Shotwell. One participant enthused about the "amazing response of the greatest American experts in the different fields that we are proposing to discuss" at the conference and noted that "with the leadership and participation of such able men, we will be able to carry out to a successful finish a plan of large proportions."[14]

What brought together this impressive assemblage to plan a conference? The United States had security interests in the Pacific, among them their recently conquered territories in Hawaii and the Philippines, but the region seemed menacing to those interests. A new Great Power, Japan, seemed to be growing stronger by the minute, presenting a specific threat to US interests (including those in China). Meanwhile, the new Republic of China remained mysterious to American observers. And while American policy makers and international relations thinkers wanted to maintain good relations with Japan and China, the racism toward Asians on display in the previous year's Oriental Exclusion Act had provoked hostile reactions in both countries. What to do?

One of the participants, Ray Wilbur, the president of Stanford University from 1916 to 1943, provided a clue. He had chaired a 1923 "Survey of Race Relations" to address racial tensions between whites and Asians on the West Coast. Wilbur enthused that this "scientific" research solved racial problems by establishing the material interests of each race. Wilbur's study found, for example, that Japanese agricultural laborers were "useful" to the local economy, so both the locals and the Japanese workers materially benefited from their presence in local agriculture. Wilbur thought racial problems could be solved by a "neutral" approach that just established the "facts"[15]—each group's material interests. Perhaps a similar "scientific" approach—an appeal to material interests of each nationality—could resolve international racial tensions as well.

The idea of experts improving international relations dated back at least as far as Woodrow Wilson, who had established a brain trust to advise him on the World War I peace negotiations. The historian James Shotwell at the Yale Club meeting had been part of that brain trust. The men at the Yale Club meeting thought relations across the Pacific could be improved by a dialogue that had the American experts talk to the Japanese and the Chinese experts to clear up misunderstandings. A Yale geography professor put it this way: "We have to get the Orientals to tell us what they think about us. The Orientals understand us a great deal better than we understand them. . . . We have to go to the conference primarily to learn from the Orientals."[16] This group of men was groping its way toward technical solutions in international relations, a path that would lead them eventually to embrace the technocratic development concept already conceived by the League of Nations and Sun Yat-sen.

The Yale Club group intersected with another group that was concerned more with humanitarian principles than US foreign-policy needs: the international Young Men's Christian Association. YMCA organizations on the West Coast and Hawaii had been seeking to use Christian principles to persuade whites to take a more benevolent view of their fellow men who happened to be Asians.

The YMCA could draw on its international network of YMCA clubs around the Pacific to further the cause of reducing racism toward Asians. By 1925, they hoped to repeal or mitigate the Oriental Exclusion Act in the

United States. The YMCA had independently begun planning an international conference in Honolulu on race relations as part of this effort. The international committee planning the conference comprised representatives from the major Pacific nations: Australia, Canada, China, Japan, New Zealand, and the United States. It sent out invitations to national committees of the YMCA in each of these countries on December 7, 1923, to "consider how [Christian ideas and principles] might be made a common basis of understanding and motivation for the Pacific peoples."[17]

The two groups that wanted an international conference on Pacific relations decided to join forces. The Yale Club men needed the YMCA's international network of contacts to get access to the experts outside the United States, especially in Japan and China. The YMCA needed the access the Yale Club men could provide to New York funding, especially that from the Rockefeller Foundation. The two groups reached agreement on a shared organization, the Institute of Pacific Relations, with its first conference to be held in Honolulu in 1925. The IPR was thus born as a mixture of those with humanitarian objectives and those concerned mainly with American foreign-policy needs. It was to be a lasting mixture in development, still existing today.

But the YMCA paid a price for the merger: those that paid the bills called the shots. The New York men needed good relations with the US administration for their business and professional interests, not to mention that some hoped to serve in government. This led them to heed the American government on its own concerns. The upcoming Honolulu conference was getting a high profile, and the last thing the State Department wanted was further embarrassment for the United States about the Oriental Exclusion Act. Assistant Secretary of State John MacMurray warned the organizers in January 1925 against providing publicity for Chinese and Japanese complaints about immigration exclusion from the United States: "you should not forget that the Government has a very great stake in how these matters are handled."[18] He asked the organizers to restrain the publicity for the conference.

So the American YMCA conference organizers agreed to abandon openly discussing the Oriental Exclusion Act, much less calling for its amendment or repeal. They could not stop the Chinese or the Japanese participants from bringing it up (as indeed they would), but the conference organizers could redefine the issue under discussion. The combined conference had initially been framed by the YMCA as about fighting white racism against Asians. Now, it would be a neutral forum for Asian and white experts to exchange factual information aimed at improving things for all the nations of the Pacific. Experts would "bring together accurate information" that would enable a consensus of experts on solutions to the as yet ill-defined "Problems of the Pacific" (which would be the title of the conference proceedings).

The Institute of Pacific Relations would advance Ray Wilbur's idea of the material interests of each nationality as a way to sidestep racial tensions. The material interests of the Chinese could distract China's attention away from white racism, American immigration restrictions, and extraterritoriality in the Western concessions in China. What was in the material interests of the Chinese, the IPR would elaborate, was the economic development of China.

In Search of Development

It would take a while for the IPR to get to development. The first IPR conference opened in Honolulu on June 30, 1925. In the end, 140 people would attend, among them 39 from the United States, 20 from Japan, and 14 from China.[19]

The most important aspect of the 1925 conference for our story was how one YMCA delegate from New Zealand made a strong impression on other participants. He was a thirty-two-year-old economics professor named John Bell Condliffe. Condliffe was a well-credentialed economist, with an amicable manner and an easygoing respect for Asian scholars. The IPR organizers realized that they needed research on their agenda item of "Industrialization in the Far East"[20] in order to offer credible technical solutions, and they needed someone to organize that research. The IPR quickly identified Condliffe as the best candidate to be the first research secretary of the IPR, beginning in February 1927.

This set the stage for Condliffe's four-month trip as research secretary to China in 1927.

He was under pressure to produce research projects by Chinese scholars for funding, yet China was still torn apart by conflict among rival warlords. Dodging various armies, he tried to identify leading Chinese researchers who had the technical qualifications but who would also do the projects that the IPR wanted. Condliffe began to realize the latter would dominate the former. He found toward the end of his trip that the IPR staff back in New York had already prepared an agenda of projects from China without consulting him. Reacting to this episode, Condliffe would later describe the IPR approach as too centered around what they wanted to hear: "There was too little attempt to study China and the Chinese, to discover what were their problems, how they were being faced, what the Chinese thought of and expected from us."[21]

On his 1927 trip, Condliffe would meet Chiang Kai-shek, who had succeeded Sun Yat-sen as head of the Nationalist party, the Guomindang, after the latter's death. By now, the IPR and the Rockefeller Foundation were enough of a local player that Chiang took their representative seriously. Chiang invited Condliffe to his upcoming wedding with May-ling Soong, a Wellesley-educated Christian. Chiang had purportedly converted to Christianity, and this, and his marriage to the Christian Soong, burnished Chiang's image among the YMCA men in the IPR, as well as among the network of missionaries in China upon whom they relied for information. This favorable image would result in Chiang becoming perceived as a benevolent autocrat, one of the first examples in the development of this enduring concept.

The reality in the meantime was not quite so benevolent. Chiang in 1927 was still consolidating power. It could have been a case study for Hayek on how "the worst get on top" in autocracy. Chiang up to this moment had been allied with the Communist Party, which had been founded in 1921, because he was so desperate for financing his own army that he had accepted Soviet military aid. The local Communist-led labor unions in Shanghai had followed Soviet orders to back Chiang. But Chiang now betrayed the Communist labor unions and ordered their massacre, carried out in part by the Chinese underworld in Shanghai, known as the Green Gang. At the same time, Chiang intimidated merchants into making large contributions to his Guomindang army, using the Green Gang to threaten and even kill those merchants who did not contribute enough *pour encourager les autres.*[22]

Other Guomindang party members followed Chiang's example of coercing payoffs from merchants. Guomindang corruption, following the old Chinese saying of "become an official, get rich," would tarnish the rest of the party's rule until its defeat in 1949. Officials could solicit payoffs from merchants to process paperwork, or even arrange partial ownership of profitable firms by well-connected officials. A later study of the Nationalist Government found that the organization meant to control corruption, the Control Yuan, had received allegations of corruption from 1931 to 1937 on 69,500 officials. Of these, the Control Yuan fired thirteen.

Condliffe faced a problem that would recur again and again throughout the history of development. The horrible political situation in China seemed itself to be a huge barrier to development. Anyone mixed up in this politics would seem to be part of the problem, not part of the solution. But if he didn't deal with the Guomindang, Condliffe risked returning home empty-handed. In this environment, the technocratic approach, which ignored politics, came to the rescue. The technocratic mind-set would allow Chinese economists to present themselves as neutral experts, no politics implied. In particular, Chinese economists who had been educated in the United States would have expert qualifications, some apparent distance from internal Chinese politics, and the ability to communicate with their funders.

It was around this time that Condliffe met H. D. Fong, who was such an economist. Fong was a coauthor of the "Tianjin Industrialization Project," a proposal with his mentor Franklin Ho (another convert to Christianity) at Nankai University in Tianjin. The proposal seemed purely descriptive and thus politically neutral. They would conduct case studies of four industries in Tianjin: carpets, hosiery, rayon, and cotton. They would identify factors that had helped and hindered these four industries. This would be a first step to diagnose the causes of China's lack of development, and thereby to recommend policies to make development happen. They offered the proposal to Condliffe, still desperate to find projects, and he readily accepted it.

THE WORLD'S FIRST LOCAL DEVELOPMENT ECONOMIST

There were few Chinese economists in a better position than Fong to use American connections necessary to get funding from the IPR. His life circumstances had provided him with an early opportunity to travel to the United States and he quickly took to life there.

Hsien Ding Fong was born in Ningpo (also the birthplace of Chiang Kai-shek) on September 6, 1903, the son of a jeweler who died when Fong was seven. His mother concentrated her limited resources on her only son, as was common in Chinese culture. She sent him to a Methodist primary school at age ten to begin learning English, which seemed like a good move just as China's empire collapsed and the future seemed to be with the Western-occupied (and English-speaking) districts of China. She apprenticed him at age fourteen to a Shanghai cotton magnate, H. Y. Moh, who would finance Fong's travel to the United States in 1921 and pay for his undergraduate education at New York University. Fong supplemented his income by giving mah-jongg lessons in Gimbel's Department Store to New York society matrons.

The year 1924 proved key for Fong's career. Fong joined a fraternity of Chinese students studying in America, called the Chen Chih-hui (CCH), or Society for the Fulfillment of Life's Ambitions. He developed a strong network of Americanized Chinese students through the CCH, and this would prove useful in furthering his career with the IPR. The most important person Fong met through the CCH was his mentor Franklin Ho, who was then studying for a PhD at Yale. Ho encouraged Fong to do the same.

Although Fong was in the United States at the time the Oriental Exclusion Act was passed, there is no evidence that it affected him at the time; nor does he mention it or any racial discrimination in the memoirs he published decades later. He makes only an oblique reference to the difficulty Chinese students had at that time in dating American girls, because of "racial differences."[23] There is no record in the rest of his career that Fong ever commented on Chinese exclusion in the United States. Yet another Chinese scholar visiting the United States made clear even much later in an article how much Chinese visitors noticed the racism: "A very large number of China's leaders have received their education and training in America. . . . the Chinese exclusion laws' . . . moral effect is very great, as the Chinese consider these laws a standing symbol of the much decried doctrine of racial inequality which should have no place in a brave new world."[24] Fong seems to have developed early on the technocrat's ability to ignore unpleasant realities.

After getting his PhD, Fong returned to China and joined Ho at Nankai University in Tientsin (today spelled Tianjin), where Condliffe discovered them on his 1927 trip. Soon Nankai University developed a stable of IPR grant writers and recipients, many of whom had been part of the CCH fraternity in the United States and hence were already friends. They maintained many Western customs. The young professors lived in Western-style housing, drank coffee imported from San Francisco, and played pool. In short, they were ideal intermediaries between the IPR's Western representatives and Chinese academia.

However, Fong and other Americanized Chinese economists did not emulate liberal ideas from the West. Based on Fong's initial IPR funded project, which looked at the growth of the Tientsin Carpet Industry, published in 1929, the 1929 IPR Conference report concluded: "technical knowledge of the processes of production and distribution has advanced so far that it ought to be possible for newly developing countries to take a good many short cuts and avoid much of the cost of readjustment and experiment through which the older industrial countries have had to pass." The report added that "the knowledge of the economies and improvements which can be effected by . . . rationalisation is at the disposal of the world. It is not inevitable therefore that industrial development in the future should be so marred by waste, unnecessary duplication and destructive competition as it has been hitherto."[25]

The implication was that someone was doing the rationalizing, but who that someone was is never mentioned. The passive voice would become a hallmark of the technocratic approach, an indication that this approach does not seem to care who is performing the recommended actions. On the spectrum of conscious direction versus spontaneous solutions, Fong inclined toward the former by suggesting "rationalization." For good measure, Fong leaned toward the Blank Slate, discounting the history of how industrial development had so far happened. We will see how this made Fong open to authoritarian approaches to development.

Perhaps part of the reason that Fong was not enamored of spontaneous entrepreneurship was that the spontaneous entrepreneurs were foreign. In a 1936 study of industrial capital, Fong noted that most industrial capital was in the foreign concessions and came from foreign sources, something he knew well from his apprenticeship in Shanghai cotton, which was dominated by the Japanese. The profits of this spontaneous entrepreneurship flowed out of China and back to Japan. Fong's answer to unwanted Japanese domination was to move away from such spontaneous investments and have conscious direction of development.

The Key Moment

We are reaching now the crucial moment—the convergence between Sun Yat-sen's early advocacy of a development plan and the approach to China's development by the Westerners in the IPR. The IPR-funded H. D. Fong was the link between the two. In a 1936 article, Fong called on everyone working on development in China to acknowledge "the far-sighted and comprehensive grasp of the need for economic control by Dr. Sun Yat-Sen."[26]

Fong's development plan would appeal to the authoritarian Chiang Kai-shek. "Rationalization" of an industry sounds apolitical. Choosing conscious direction over spontaneous solutions does not say who is doing the conscious directing. Yet in practice, there was only one possibility—the national state—which would need a lot of power to achieve comprehensive economic control. This sounded like a great approach to an aspiring autocrat like Chiang.

The convergence of ideas and political needs resulted in government appointments for the economists. In 1936, Fong's mentor Franklin Ho became head of the political department of the government administration, where he would be Chiang's chief economic advisor for the next decade. Fong would follow him as a top executive of the government's Central Planning Board. In that position, Fong gave advice to Chiang on a three-year development plan from 1936–37 to 1938–39 to develop heavy industries such as iron and steel, copper, zinc, tungsten, antimony, synthetic oil and alcohol, electrical equipment, and chemicals, with advice and financing from Germany.

Fong in his new position again highlighted the "need for centralized, coordinated economic planning and control." His models for development in the late 1930s were "Germany and Soviet Russia," which "have attempted industrialization in a new manner which China . . . may simulate with profit."[27] At the time, Fong could not have fully anticipated the awful realities we now know characterized his two models. The point is simply that he favored a model of conscious development by an authoritarian government.

To sum up, H. D. Fong was a crucial figure in the first practical appearance of technocratic development in any nation's economic policy anywhere. The long-forgotten Fong was perhaps the most important early contributor to the official development consensus that had already solidified by the time of development's "birth" in 1949.

THE ROCKEFELLER'S BLANK SLATE

The final missing link is to explain why technocratic development appealed to the IPR. It is easiest to explain if we look at the attitudes of their funders, the Rockefeller Foundation. The Rockefeller Foundation in the 1920s and 1930s was the world's premier international philanthropic organization. As its website today explains simply "John D. Rockefeller, Sr., established The Rockefeller Foundation in 1913 to promote the well-being of humanity around the world."[28]

The Rockefeller Foundation's own ambition in China in the 1930s kept escalating as it was increasing its funding to the IPR. An internal strategic review asked rhetorically "Is there no other sector of the world where we can hope to obtain as large a return in human happiness and welfare as we can in China?"[29] As one Foundation official saw it, China was a test site for ideas that might have a hard time getting a hearing in the United States: "demonstration of principle can take place in China long before it will occur in this country due to the absence of vested traditional interests in the former." China was "a vast laboratory in the social sciences, with implications that would be international in scope." It gave an opportunity to "bridge the gap between a rural medieval society and twentieth century knowledge."[30] In short, China offered a Blank Slate. It was "bound by few hampering traditions, and the plastic condition of her life and institutions at the present moment is an inviting challenge to a positive kind of service."[31]

Rockefeller also embraced conscious direction of development as opposed to spontaneous evolution. Rockefeller officials wrote that advances in one area such as health were "so dependent upon the progress in other fields of community activity, such as industry, agriculture, education, and transportation, that it should be closely coordinated with a program of national planning."[32] As one scholar puts it, Rockefeller sought to bring "together social scientists, public health experts, engineers, and agronomists for a concerted attack on China's rural problems."[33]

Conspicuously missing in Rockefeller's discussion of China is any respect for the initiative and rights of the Chinese people themselves. This is not surprising by 1930s standards, when Western racial attitudes made it difficult to allow that people in the Rest might deserve the same rights as those in West. But Rockefeller's blindness to the Chinese as individuals would prove a useful mind-set to US government officials, who could emphasize the material development of China in order to change the subject away from US policies on Chinese immigration and on extraterritoriality in China.

A Historian Ignores History

The Rockefeller Foundation's Blank Slate approach to China shows up also in one of the IPR's most credentialed Western grant recipients. One of Condliffe's first grants went to British historian R. H. Tawney, best known for his analysis of the rise of capitalism in Europe. Condliffe commissioned Tawney to draw upon this expertise by visiting China and then writing an analysis of how China could develop. Condliffe introduced Tawney to Fong and his colleagues at Nankai University, who, as we have noticed, served as cultural intermediaries between Western visitors and the locals. Fong impressed Tawney favorably, and Tawney would thank Fong in the acknowledgements to the study that resulted, *Land and Labor in China*, published in 1932. Tawney also visited another of Condliffe's Western grantees, agricultural expert J. Lossing Buck and his wife Pearl S. Buck. The latter had just published *The Good Earth*, the best-selling depiction of the Chinese peasantry that would win her the Nobel Prize in Literature, be made into a Hollywood movie (with white actors playing the Chinese peasants), and encourage a paternalist sympathy for China among the American public.

Tawney's report on China was notable for how little Chinese history it acknowledged. Like Rockefeller, Tawney perceived China as a Blank Slate: "China moved till yesterday in an orbit of her own, little influencing the West and little influenced by it." The "static civilisation of China" together with the "traditionalism which has sometimes been described as a special mark of Chinese economic life," said Tawney "is the characteristic . . . of one phase of civilisation. The greater part of the West lives on one plane, the greater part of China on another."[34]

THE ISSUE OF CHINESE MIGRATION
DISAPPEARS AT THE IPR

The usefulness of the technocratic development approach to the IPR and its Western backers made itself clear as it changed the subject from Chinese exclusion and extraterritoriality to Chinese development.

The IPR's third conference took place in Kyoto from October 23 to November 9, 1929. (The participants could not have known that the Wall Street crash during the conference was the beginning of what would become the Great Depression.) The IPR conference in 1929 was a milestone for the tension between political realities and technocratic development. It would demonstrate the potential of this approach to development in China to distract attention away from Western injustices toward the Chinese.

Technocratic development ideas would dominate the 1929 conference. Meanwhile, one politically sensitive issue had disappeared from the IPR conference agenda—Chinese immigration to the United States. It would never appear again on the agenda of IPR conferences over succeeding decades.

In spite of the US State Department's pressure to avoid discussion of the Oriental Exclusion Act and American racism at its first conference in 1925, the IPR had not at first succeeded in fully suppressing the toxic issue of US Chinese-exclusion policies. One attendee in particular had caused trouble in the first conference. Ta Chen was a thirty-three-year-old professor of sociology at Tsinghua University in Beijing, one of China's top universities. Chen was no stranger to the United States; he had lived there for seven years while earning his BA from Reed College in Oregon and his PhD from Columbia. He published his dissertation in 1923 as *Chinese Migrations*,[35] which quickly established him as an authority in the field. He had a great deal to lose by speaking out at the IPR conference, as IPR represented huge potential funding for his research. However, this did not stop him from making a strong statement at the 1925 conference, saying that all human beings had a right to live wherever they wanted.[36]

But the opportunity for such principled statements on Chinese migration to the United States had disappeared by the time of the 1929 IPR conference. The IPR had succeeded in changing the subject to development back in China. Anyone concerned about the lost opportunity of the Chinese to better their lot through migration could only take comfort that the new technocratic ideas promised a rapid escape from poverty back at home in China itself. Discouraging the idea of migration as an escape from poverty and promoting development at home instead would remain a standby of the official development consensus up to the present. Ironically, Ta Chen would turn out to be prescient on the economic potential of Chinese migration. Chen had anticipated the role of overseas Chinese migration in the development of East Asia, including the impact on China itself.

TECHNOCRATS AND RIGHTS: THE CONTROVERSY ON EXTRATERRITORIALITY

The IPR was initially less successful in making the sensitive issue of Americans' and other Westerners' extraterritorial privileges in China disappear. Nonetheless, technocrats displayed their skill at changing the subject from rights to development.

Extraterritoriality—the exemption of foreigners from Chinese law in the foreign concessions—had grown too large for the IPR to ignore by the time the 1929 Kyoto conference occurred. Condliffe would note in the conference proceedings that "extra-territoriality which, as far as immediate abolition was concerned, received only passing and rather academic discussion in 1927, appeared to have reached the stage where serious and detailed consideration was urgent." Factors pressuring such consideration included "the presence of foreign soldiers in force upon Chinese soil, the existence of powerfully organized foreign settlements with their own organs of government and police power, the penetration of foreign shipping enjoying extraterritorial privileges into the very heart of China, [and] occasional intervention, whether deliberate or unavoidable, in China's civil war." "All these," said Condliffe, "loom very large in Chinese eyes."[37]

James Shotwell, the historian who had been an advisor to Woodrow Wilson at Versailles and then one of the founders of the IPR, gave the semiofficial Western response in Kyoto: "the only concern at present on the part of any foreign government is juristic, not political." The Washington Conference of 1921, which was mainly about the naval arms race in the Pacific, "called into existence an international commission to study the question of Chinese extra-territoriality and recommend specific proposals for a juristic reform in China upon the completion of which the Powers would relinquish their extraterritorial claims."[38]

It was the classic technocratic move: transforming a political and moral problem—the occupation of parts of China by Western countries without the consent of the Chinese—into a technical issue. An international commission would decide the issue based on what the commission called "findings of fact." In language that sounds a lot like a modern-day World Bank or International Monetary Fund mission report, the commission would make "recommendations . . . to improve the existing conditions of the administration of justice in China, and to assist and further the efforts of the Chinese Government to effect such legislation and judicial reforms." Once that happened, extraterritoriality would end. Improving its own institutions was an aspect of China's development. Extraterritoriality—the West's violation of Chinese rights—was a problem that was up to the Chinese to solve, by achieving development. The technocrats had changed the subject from Western violations of the rights of the Chinese to a technical discussion of how best to accomplish China's development as rapidly as possible.

Moreover, technocratic development promised an escape from poverty as well as an exit from extraterritoriality. Fong presented his work in Kyoto on the Tientsin carpet industry, noting how learning from Western experts could speed up China's development.

Another Chinese presenter at the IPR conference was Wu Ding-chang, yet one more Nankai University economist linked to Chiang Kai-shek, and a former governor of the Bank of China. It was Wu who would express best the technocratic solution to extraterritoriality. Wu gave a talk at the IPR conference in Kyoto entitled "International Economic Cooperation in China." After noting how extraterritoriality had poisoned the atmosphere for international cooperation in China, Wu suggested the technocrats take over:

the writer begs to lay before the public the following proposition . . . The Government of China will request the League of Nations to appoint an international group of outstanding economists and financiers to form an International Commission on the Economic Development of China. This Commission will make its own investigation of conditions within a definite period of time and draw up a plan acceptable to the people of China and will have charge of the raising of funds from Chinese and foreign investors for the carrying out of the plan at an early date.

With such a Commission working on a comprehensive, scientifically formulated, progressive and practical plan of economic development, public support and ultimate success are assured.

The Chinese people should understand that the League of Nations, of which China herself is a member, is an organization for the promotion of international peace and goodwill and not a combination of governments for selfish aggression. International co-operation through the agency of the League, therefore, is not the same as international control of national economics or finances. Precedents have already been established in the case of Austria and Greece.[39]

Wu, too, had captured perfectly the reformulation of extraterritoriality as a technical problem. To work on China's development, Western powers with imperialist policies (what Wu called "selfish aggression") would be replaced by a neutral body: the League of Nations. The League would oversee the technical progress on the institutional development that Shotwell had said was necessary for extraterritoriality to end. The big payoff for China was that the marshaling of technical experts with a development plan would actually make China's development happen.

It was a remarkable precedent for how development would later and still today promise technical solutions, and stress the role of "neutral" actors like the United Nations or World Bank. It would do this later while overlooking the Western Powers' violations of individual rights in the Rest during the Cold War or the War on Terror.

On this occasion in 1929, however, things would not go well for Wu's international development plan. The feel-good play in Kyoto had an unhappy finale less than two years later. On September 18, 1931, the Japanese invaded Manchuria. The League's "promotion of international peace and goodwill" instead of "selfish aggression" did not work out as intended.

FREE CHINA

Despite the Japanese invasion of Manchuria in 1931, the IPR's development efforts hung on for a surprisingly long time in China. Only after Japan's general invasion of China in 1937 did the IPR have to withdraw. But the IPR was ready to reenter in 1942 after the United States became a meaningful ally of China, because the United States was now itself at war with Japan. America needed an economically successful China to defeat Japan. The United States also needed a beneficent image for its autocratic ally against Japan, Chiang Kai-shek. The old authoritarian approach to development that the IPR had embraced in its early work in China was perfect for presenting Chiang as a benevolent leader. The IPR now became a leading generator of wartime propaganda on China.

The result was a nation-builder's fantasy of "Free China," built with American aid and technical assistance. Like later nation-building fantasies during wartime in Vietnam, Iraq, and Afghanistan, the reality was that the United States was stuck with—and then promoted—a corrupt,

FIGURE 3.1   Cover of an Institute of Public Relations
pamphlet during World War II promoting the image of
"Free China."[40] (Source: American Institute of Public Relations)

autocratic, and weak leadership incapable of building a nation, much less
a free one. Nationalist army commanders siphoned off American aid into
their own pockets, leaving their conscripted soldiers half-starved and
short of guns and ammunition.

The IPR was so successful in creating the image of a "Free China"
that Senator Joseph McCarthy and his allies would later blame the IPR
for "losing China" to the Communists. If Free China was as great as IPR
propaganda made it out to be, so the charges went, then only betrayal
of Free China by Communist sympathizers in the West (and in the IPR)
could explain its defeat. However, the reality was not that the IPR lost
Free China, but that they had never found it.

NATION TRUMPS INDIVIDUAL

Meanwhile, as one of the original formulators of China's development plan, Fong had been advising Chiang Kai-shek on economic management during the war. Fong visited the United States again from 1941 to 1943 as a Rockefeller Foundation fellow, seeking to catch up on the latest trends in economics to bring back to Free China.

In Rockefeller's treatment of Fong and his colleagues, we can glean more reminders of Rockefeller's attitudes toward the Chinese. First, the Rockefeller stipend for Chinese fellows in the United States was less than that for Europeans. Second, Fong, though the most senior Chinese economist, received the same stipend as the most junior new Chinese graduates—apparently, Chinese were Chinese. Third, the Rockefeller Foundation policed the Oriental Exclusion Act, making sure their Chinese fellows left when their fellowship was up; there was no such enforcement for European fellows whose visas expired. [41] These matters highlight the disrespect of Western humanitarians, including the Rockefeller Foundation, for the Chinese as individuals, which made it possible for them to overlook the neglect of individual rights in China's authoritarian development model.

Fong remained silent on how he felt about all this, as he had on such issues throughout his career. But Fong was well rewarded in other ways for the prominence he occupied in the international discussion of Chinese development and in the government of Chiang Kai-shek. Technocratic development offered the local experts power and prestige—rewards that could offset the occasional eruption of disrespect by their Western sponsors.

Indeed, Fong articulated his economic development ideas for China further for a large wartime audience while in the United States. In May 1942, Fong published a short book called *The Post-War Industrialization of China*. He developed further his previous themes: "a thorough-going survey of Chinese resources must precede scientific planning of large-scale developmental projects for a postwar China. . . . In heavy industries, as well as in large-scale public works and public utilities, state ownership and operation seems to offer the best solution."[42]

Fong presented the findings of his report to Chiang Kai-shek in person after his return to China in early 1944. Chiang had published a book in 1943 under his own authorship, taking the side of the nation on the nation versus individual debate in development: "The scope of Chinese economics is much broader than that of Western economics," he noted, for the former "is the study of how to make the nation rich and strong—to build a nation into a wealthy, powerful, healthy and contented state." Unlike Western economics, "Chinese economic theory does not base itself on the individual or single unit" but calls on economists to "abandon their selfish individualism and materialism."[43]

An American writer, Creighton Lacy, pointed out at the time that the United States had to be content with suppression of individual rights in China because the United States also wanted to deny rights to the ordinary Chinese citizens in America. Any criticism of Chiang's antidemocratic ways would only create embarrassment for the Americans: "The United States cannot justly seek for democracy in China as long as 'yellow races' are looked upon as too inferior for American citizenship. . . . They cannot fairly look for democracy around the Pacific as long as an Oriental Exclusion Act refuses even the quota system given to all other immigrants."[44]

THE OTHER PATH

We have to back up again to the early days of the IPR in China. We have until now left out part of the story. The convergence of ideas and political interests on technocratic development and suppression of individual rights in China did not satisfy everyone. Not all of the participants in the IPR experience in China had been happy with the triumph of these ideas. There had been a critique of an authoritarian path to development in China all along, expressed by the IPR's original commissioner of research, John Bell Condliffe.

Perhaps because of this critique, Condliffe was never going to last long at the IPR. The IPR at the behest of American state department officials had tried to censor the report of the 1929 conference to eliminate embarrassing quotes about how unhappy the Chinese were about extraterritoriality. When Condliffe refused, the American power brokers succeeded in abolishing the position of research secretary, thereby getting rid of the excessively honest Condliffe.

Condliffe would go on to become research secretary of the League of Nations, a position in which he was finally free to say what he really thought. Although he remained friendly with Fong, he became a critic of the authoritarian development approach embraced by Fong and the IPR. If Fong exemplifies the technocratic approach to development, Condliffe illustrates that other views were possible. In the 1932 World Economic Survey he wrote for the League of Nations, Condliffe made clear his view on "conscious direction" versus "spontaneous evolution" in development. He disparaged the "possibility of adding to a country's economic stature" by merely having some experts reveal their expert thoughts on how to increase that stature.[45]

Condliffe would sharply disagree with Chiang and Fong on the nation-versus-individual debate. The powerful forces for development, he argued, are not at the national level, they are "scientific and technical progress" such as "the opening of the Panama Canal in 1913, the development of electrical communication." In other words, he was arguing that development happened through efforts of creative individuals who exchanged ideas, goods, and finance across national borders for mutual benefit. He noted poignantly, "The world as a whole hesitates between the contradictory principles" of the free flow of goods, technologies, and ideas and of an "economic nationalism" that would shut this down.[46]

He stated these ideas more forcefully in a 1938 article in the prestigious academic journal *Economica*: "The human race has made progress towards the good life as long as thought and economic activity were left free to cross national boundaries and creeds." "But now," he observed, "we face a new and more formidable superstition than the world has ever known, the myth of the nation-state, whose priests are as intolerant as those of the Inquisition. The struggle for the rights of the individual against the all-powerful and intolerant nation-state is the most difficult and crucial issue of our generation."[47]

Condliffe continued to write about China long after he left IPR, although it is unclear if anyone was listening. After 1940, Condliffe was professor of economics at Berkeley until his retirement in 1958. In a speech titled "The Industrial Development of China" given at the Chinese National Reconstruction Forum at Berkeley on Jan 24, 1943, he criticized the technocratic approach: "China cannot be turned overnight into a mechanically minded, industrial community. . . . It is too easy a solution to believe that economic development can be achieved simply by transplanting some of the mechanical tricks and tools of the West."[48]

Condliffe emphatically rejected the authoritarian development model that Fong and Chiang were promoting for China. He admitted that sometimes "autocratic and authoritarian controls have proved efficient for limited purposes." But Condliffe recognized the value of individual rights as an end in themselves. Even a temporary benefit of "efficiency" of "authoritarian controls" required an unacceptable "ruthlessness in their administration."[49] Condliffe's words remind us that Chiang was no more offering a "Free China" than were his Communist opponents. As a participant in the formulation of development in the 1920s through 1940s, Condliffe reminds us that another development alternative had been possible for China. The alternative would have recognized the political and economic rights of the Chinese.

In 1944 Condliffe received a book to review that would crystallize further what he had observed in China. Reviewing Hayek's *Road to Serfdom*, he observed that "the essential condition of effective planning is that the planners must be prepared to dragoon those who do not fit into their plans." Planners could not allow individual rights, because the plan could only work if individuals followed the plan. Condliffe joined Hayek against the idea "that in some mysterious fashion the concentration of all power, political and economic, in the hands of those who control the State machinery will endow them with wisdom to direct the affairs of men better than they can direct them for themselves." Condliffe understood that unchecked state power was one of the root causes of poverty, not one of the solutions. He closed his review by mocking the new bureaucratic machinery of the World Bank and other postwar international organizations, which offer "the apocalyptic vision of a new heaven and a new earth by reason of the apotheosis of the bureaucrat, as a result of which all the troubles which now vex us will pass away."[50]

Yet Condliffe's China experience had made him aware of how much the West had weakened the appeal of free trade and investment in developing countries through its privileges of extraterritoriality for European and American residents in China. Condliffe understood all too well from his IPR experience China's growing "mistrust of any foreign organization formed ostensibly for China's benefit."[51]

Condliffe was quick to respond to Truman's announced development program in 1949. He put it succinctly: "These United Nations activities and the projected programs of technical assistance do not constitute economic development." Instead, Condliffe argued, "Economic development is correlated with political liberty. . . . More is involved than mere technical efficiency. . . . If the peoples whose economic development has been retarded are to handle the equipment of modern machine industry and agriculture, their minds must be free. . . . [Individuals] must participate of their own volition."[52]

Condliffe thought Truman had missed one of the main obstacles to global development, which had happened in the interwar years and during World War II: the shutting down of international trade and finance:

> The basic difficulties we face arise from the progressive disintegration of the monetary and marketing mechanisms necessary for the smooth working of the international division of labor. Unless markets are opened up again, the programs projected for economic development may turn out to be just another unworkable expedient. Finally, the broad principles of a trading code . . . might be embodied in a multilateral convention. The International Trade Charter negotiated at Havana, but not yet ratified, constitutes such a code.[53]

The worst circle of hell is reserved for those who are right ahead of their time. The Havana trade charter mentioned by Condliffe would evolve into the General Agreement on Tariffs and Trade, which would help fuel the greatest international trade boom in world history, much to the benefit of post–Mao China.

The Debate Within China

Although H. D. Fong's technocratic approach had triumphed, there had always been other views among Chinese economists. Unfortunately, the most articulate Chinese critic of authoritarian development arrived too late to have much effect.

Yuan-li Wu had been a student of Hayek's at the London School of Economics in the late 1930s. His critique of Chinese planning, including a biting criticism of "the ten-year programme of economic development outlined [by] Generalissimo Chiang Kai-shek" was not published until 1946. It received little attention from American supporters of "Free China."[54]

Wu diagnosed why plans were attractive both to Chiang and his American supporters, all of whose interests were served by plans that had "a fundamental confusion of ends" between "economic welfare and national defense." Wu noted Chiang's "desire to emulate the example of the Soviet experiment and . . . that of [Nazi] Germany," and how Chiang was able to exploit "the state of national emergency consequent upon the long drawn-out civil war" and "Japanese aggression" to win domestic and foreign support for his "collectivist approach."[55]

Wu explained the politics left out of the planning narrative: "in all poor countries, the struggle for wealth and power . . . tends to be conducted unscrupulously. Hence any economic system conducive to an over-concentration of economic power in a few hands is dangerous from the point of view of economic welfare [and] the creation of an elite group of planners might be the outcome. To this objection China cannot claim exception."[56]

To Yuan-li Wu, Chinese democracy had little chance under "a system of economic regimentation involving forced savings and the central direction of investments," which "tends in all circumstances to undermine political democracy." Wu commented on why Hayek's warning about planning and democracy was more applicable to poor countries than to rich ones: "This tendency becomes even more ominous if political democracy is not yet mature and fully developed."[57]

After the Communist takeover, Yuan-li Wu looked back more in sorrow than in anger: "Because the [Chinese] government had played an increasingly important role in the actual allocation and use of resources both before and after the war, and because inadequate attention had been given to the development of the economy through individual initiative" the transition to Communism "was made all the easier both physically and ideologically."[58]

Wu spent the rest of his life in obscurity at the University of San Francisco.

THE ESCAPE OF H. D. FONG

Meanwhile, H. D. Fong was back in China in 1945 as the war against Japan ended and the civil war against the Communists began. With hyper-inflation destroying savings and lowering real incomes, with a family of four kids and a new wife, step-daughter, and mother-in-law to support, Fong later reported that he was working nine jobs concurrently to make ends meet. The job that would rescue him from the 1949 Communist takeover was in the new official development bureaucracy being created by United Nations agencies. His new employer was going to be the UN Economic Commission for Asia and the Far East (ECAFE), created by the UN in March 1947 and headquartered in Shanghai.

Fong joined ECAFE in October 1947, becoming chief of the research division, responsible for producing the annual economic survey of Asia and the Far East. ECAFE evacuated its staff, including Fong, from Shanghai just ahead of the advance of Communist armies in November 1948. The new headquarters wound up in Bangkok, where Fong would enjoy a secure refuge and career for the next twenty-five years.

It is hard to tell in the reports how Fong felt from exile about what had happened to his country and to his life's work. In the ECAFE report published in June 1950, Fong still insisted that "inadequacy of sound planning remains an important obstacle to economic development."[59] As far as "total economic planning," examining "parts of China under the control of the People's [Communist] Government," Fong noted blandly that "a trend in that direction has been recently visible."[60]

Gunnar Myrdal in 1955 cited a 1953 ECAFE Survey written by Fong in support of Myrdal's position that "the state will almost inevitably have to take the initiative."[61] Fong had won the argument for authoritarian development on China. He never commented on how Mao's even more extreme authoritarianism had exiled Fong from his home country.

THE END

Contrary to the legend of development's sudden birth with Harry Truman's address in 1949, China in the preceding two decades had been one of the formative places for the technocratic model of development. The technocratic mind-set had worked well for changing the subject away from the dignity and rights of Chinese individuals, both for US policymakers on immigration and extraterritoriality and for Chiang Kai-shek's aspirations to have unchecked power as China's leader. It did not work out for Chinese individuals whose rights were trampled, nor did it work to develop China.

As Harry S. Truman announced a "bold" and "new" American development program for poor countries on January 20, 1949, Mao Tse-tung's tanks encircled Beijing, ending America's bold new development program of more than two decades in China. Chiang Kai-shek and the Nationalists fled the mainland, crossing the strait to Taiwan from a port city called Quanzhou in a mountainous and infertile coastal province called Fujian. Development of the Chinese at home and abroad would not actually happen in the way set out by the IPR, Rockefeller Foundation, and H. D. Fong, but by 1949 they had helped win the argument for authoritarian development anyway.

Meanwhile, the two other momentous decisions taken at the Versailles peace talks after World War I—the failure to endorse racial equality, and awarding League of Nations mandates to develop former German colonies, as discussed above—were to affect the policy of Britain in its moment of great danger at the outbreak of World War II. We discuss next how this affected the debate on authoritarian versus free development.

CHAPTER FOUR

RACE, WAR,
AND THE FATE OF AFRICA

On October 6, 1939, Malcolm MacDonald, Britain's Secretary of State for the Colonies, called a special meeting on "Future Policy in Africa." The meeting included a veteran colonial official named Lord Hailey and many other notable British Africanists.

Why would Africa be high on the list of priorities only a month after Britain declared war on Germany? Many of the official class feared that Britain's survival, not to mention the survival of its empire, depended on the allegiance of non-European peoples. The British were going to need troops and raw materials from the empire to fight the war. And it was hard to keep the allegiance of colonial subjects when the empire was built around a racial hierarchy that reflected still-prevalent feelings of racial superiority by the British, feelings not lost on the victims of such racism. As one colonial official put it, "Colonial subjects might be tempted to say that they have not much freedom to defend."[1] Other officials and observers feared a worldwide revolt by nonwhites against white rule, perhaps led by the rising power, Japan, and destroying the empire. The British realized during the new war that racism was becoming a serious political liability. The failure to endorse Japan's racial equality proposal at the Versailles peace talks after the previous war was now a huge embarrassment.

Lord Hailey would attempt to remove this liability during World War II by reinventing yet again the idea of technocratic development as a justification for colonial rule. The empire's legitimacy was going to be based on its technical ability to achieve rapid development, not on the racial superiority of the British. The empire could present itself as a benevolent

autocrat for the colonial peoples. The British even banned racist statements by colonial officials to conform to the new narrative, although the
victims of racism knew that such a ban did not immediately change racist
attitudes.[2]

Ironically, Lord Hailey's justification for colonialism and his cover-up
of racism would later appeal to the anticolonial victims of racism, the
new African political leaders who would emerge after the sooner-than-
expected collapse of the British African empire in the 1950s and early
1960s. The new African leaders found state-led technocratic development
to be a justification for their own aspirations to unchecked power. The
new African leaders would inherit the role of benevolent autocrat from
the defunct empire.

This is another critical juncture in the history of authoritarian development, when it is in the process of becoming the new consensus on how to
escape poverty. Building upon the previous chapter on China, this chapter shows that Africa is yet another region where development ideas took
shape in the West at a time when Western attitudes toward the Rest were
still racist. With such racism, there was little likelihood that development
ideas would recognize the dignity and rights of the Africans who were
seen as the passive objects of development efforts. When the new African
leaders and their expert advisers endorsed the same authoritarian ideas,
without the racism, the debate between authoritarian and free development was over. At the time, a few dissident economists protested the suppression of the rights of the poor, but they would be ignored and then
forgotten.

We saw in the previous chapter the state of racism in the 1920s toward
both Africans and Asians. We now need to bring the story of racial attitudes forward to World War II as they continued to evolve.

RACISM AND FEARS OF RACE WARS

The many Western observers of Africa still expressing racist attitudes included Lord Hailey himself. In spite of Hailey's need to combat racism, he
was prone to heroic feats of racist extrapolation. After concluding a massive
survey of Africa in 1938 (discussed below), he noted that "in estimating the

future of Africans . . . I think we can only say that the situation of the negro in the United States, Hayti and Liberia must always cause us some hesitation and uneasiness."[3]

Frederick Pedler, secretary to Lord Hailey in his travels around Africa during the war, feared the Colonial Office's new antiracist effort was going to raise "embarrassing situations"; it was expecting too much to get British officials to accept Africans "as equals." The problem was that "most Africans are still savages and this sometimes renders it difficult to make an exception for the African who has acquired 'culture.'"[4]

Perhaps most revealing of the many Western observers of Africa is a report *attacking* racism. In 1942, Anson Phelps Stokes, a white American philanthropist, organized a Committee on Africa, the War, and Peace Aims, seeking to apply the language of FDR's and Churchill's 1941 Atlantic Charter on self-government and freedom to Africa. It included prominent black Americans such as W.E.B. DuBois, Ralph Bunche, and Walter White, and even took testimony from a young African studying in the United States identified as "Mr. Francis Nkrumah, of the Gold Coast," who later would become better known as Kwame Nkrumah, the first leader of independent Ghana.

This committee produced a cringe-inducing defense against the charge of African inferiority in an appendix to its report. It quoted an author who had spent fifteen years in the British Colonial Service that "the African is capable of equal education and responsibility with Europeans" although "it is obvious that such a development will take a very long time." A randomly quoted commander of French African troops chimed in that "the Negro is probably as competent as the white man to handle the scientific instruments of civilization." The committee noted other black success stories, for example: "the clerical tasks of government, industry, and commerce are largely and increasingly entrusted to young Africans." The report said of the committee that "almost all of [their] names are signed to this report." Perhaps a few of the black luminaries wanted to opt out.[5]

Yet, while racist attitudes continued among the British and Americans, they feared that World War I had caused a loss of white prestige. Julian Huxley articulated this: "in 1914 we Europeans could have pointed with some pride to the fact that we had for all practical purposes suppressed the constant violence of intertribal war in Africa. But by 1919 that boast seemed a little empty."[6] Such loss of prestige fed the paranoid fears of a global race war.

In 1920 the American historian Lothrop Stoddard caught the mood with a best-seller, *The Rising Tide of Color against White World-Supremacy*. World War I had been a tragic civil war "between the white peoples," which left them overstretched around the world. Now, "the colored races" threatened whites through sheer force of numbers, already outnumbering whites two to one and outbreeding them. Unfortunately, for Stoddard, the whites had contributed to this losing population race by sharing their scientific knowledge to bring down nonwhite infant mortality.[7] Another writer in 1931 suggested an even broader sympathy between the Negro in the United States, the African natives, blacks in the Caribbean, and Indian and Chinese nationalists, so that "the oppressed races have a common foe, the white peoples of Western Europe and their cousins of the United States."[8]

According to a white mentality that approached hysteria, white commentators thought nonwhites saw every military conflict everywhere as part of the color war. The Turkish victory over the Greeks in 1923 was "discussed in every bazaar in India . . . and in student debates from Cairo to Delhi, Peking and Tokyo."[9]

The famous anthropologist Bronislaw Malinowski wrote in the introduction to a book by one of his African students in 1938 that current events tended to unify the "world of coloured peoples against Western influence and above all against Great Britain and the United States." Malinowski's student was the Kenyan Jomo Kenyatta, whom the British would later accuse (falsely) of leading the Mau Mau revolt against British rule in Kenya.[10]

Not to mention that Japan's militarists could offer themselves as leaders of a nonwhite counterattack on white imperialism. The Japanese Army had come close to armed confrontations with British extraterritorial settlements in Shanghai and Tientsin during their war in China after 1931. Japanese broadcasts to British India (in Hindi) in September 1940 told listeners "Japan has no intention to subjugate China but to free China from white domination."[11] Although the British were not yet at war with Japan, they already feared in 1939 that the war in Europe left them stretched so thin as to leave the empire almost defenseless.

This was the background to the British officials' meeting on Africa on October 6, 1939, which would eventually result in Lord Hailey's new justification for empire. But first the British had to clamp down on their own racism, at least in public.

BANNING RACISM IN PUBLIC

When a BBC broadcast in December 1940 used the word *nigger*, George Ernest London, the colonial secretary in the Gold Coast (known today as Ghana) sent a telegram to O.G.R. Williams, the head of the Colonial Office for West Africa, on January 14, 1941, noting that his colonial subjects had complained about the BBC broadcast. The Colonial Office forced the BBC to apologize to Ghanaians and discouraged the use of the word, previously common. The BBC sent the apology on March 6, 1941.[12]

In late 1941, the British Minister of Labor Ernest Bevin took the US Ambassador John Winant to visit a training center for "coloured workers." Bevin announced to Winant that "in future Indians were not to be referred to as 'coolies' and Africans as 'niggers,' but as the great peoples they are."[13] Another British official advised other officials that "the cards to conceal" or "play down" are "our racial arrogance."[14] The Colonial Office also begged the BBC to minimize use of the word *natives*, on top of the new ban on the other N-word.

THE COLONIAL OFFICE CONFRONTS ITS OWN RACISM

The Colonial Office was already dealing with its own embarrassing race problem—nonwhite colonial subjects were eligible for neither the Colonial Service nor officers' commissions in the British Army. The League of Coloured Peoples, an organization made up primarily of Caribbean blacks fighting racism, met with the Colonial Secretary in October 1939 to protest these racist policies. The league brought up four test cases of colonial subjects applying for Army officer commissions. The meeting had some impact as all four quickly got commissions.

The meeting was also notable because one of the League's representatives was a twenty-four-year old black economist from St. Lucia named W. Arthur Lewis. The Colonial Secretary had no idea that he was discussing his racist Colonial Service with someone who would later become the first black winner of the Nobel Prize in Economics as one of the founding fathers of development economics.

The League's demand to make nonwhites officials in the Colonial Service was difficult for the Colonial Secretary to approve. It was an embarrassment that advertisements for Colonial Service openings specified that the applicant had to be of European parentage, at a time when such overt racism was becoming a liability. At the same time, the Colonial Office could point out that nonwhites in one British colony might resent being ruled by nonwhites from a different colony (the Colonial Office didn't say if they preferred being ruled by whites from a different country).

The Colonial Office settled for some face-saving gestures. First, it dropped mentions of race in advertisements for openings and considered nonwhite hires on a case-by-case basis. Second, it found an opportunity to hire a black economic adviser for the Colonial Office, the previously mentioned W. Arthur Lewis. Lord Hailey himself hired Lewis on September 4, 1941. Although Lewis was too young and too black to have any influence on colonial policy for the rest of the war, it was a notable milestone. [15]

The next step in saving the empire was Lord Hailey's formulation of technocratic development as a justification for colonial rule. The way Lord Hailey became the key colonial official on development ideas itself reflected a technocratic mind-set.

LORD HAILEY'S *AFRICAN SURVEY*

William Malcolm Hailey had been an unlikely member of the Colonial Service to become Britain's leading official Africanist. He had spent his career not in Africa but in India. He had arrived in India in 1894 at the age of twenty-two, an admirer of Kipling. He would spend the next four decades of his career in colonial India. Yet he wound up in charge of an African survey published in 1938. In an attitude inspired by a Blank Slate idea that persists today in development, experience in one part of what would later be called the Third World made you an expert on every other part. It was this African survey that was going to put Hailey in an ideal position to propose technocratic development as the basis for the continuation of colonial rule after World War II.

As Hailey's retirement from the Colonial Service in India at the age of sixty-one approached in the summer of 1933, one of Hailey's high-placed friends approached him about directing a massive research project on the development of Africa—it would be called *An African Survey*. Hailey accepted, explaining in October 1934 that "I would not have taken it had I seen any future in England for the retired service Governor. You know his fate."[16]

The idea for an African survey went back to 1925. A flare-up of racial tensions between white settlers and the locals in Kenya raised fears that British neglect of indigenous development would fuel a native revolt. In response, the British missionary J. H. Oldham proposed to the Rockefeller Foundation a survey that would lead "to the assembly and dispassionate study of the facts." It was another early example of the classic technocratic move: first, avoid the question of who has the power to do what to whom; that is, avoid the issue of rights of Africans against land grabs and exploitation by white settlers. Instead, study material development of Africans as a technical question with technical solutions. Oldham quoted American journalist Walter Lippman on the "the discipline of objective information."[17]

The Rockefeller Foundation declined, but Oldham did not give up. Veteran South African politician General Jan Smuts also proposed a survey of Africa, and Smuts and Oldham merged their efforts, managing to convince the Carnegie Corporation to finance it.

British Africanists were a close-knit bunch. The first discussions on the proposed *African Survey* took place over dinner at Blickling Hall, the country home of Lord Lothian, a long-time colonial expert. Dame Margery Perham, another notable Africanist, could ride her horse from her own country house over to the country estate of Lord Lugard, who had retired from being the long-time governor of British Nigeria. Other gatherings of Africanists happened in clubs like Chatham House or the Royal Empire Society or the Royal African Society.[18] British Africanists quickly settled on Lord Hailey to be the chief author of the *African Survey*, based on his high profile in colonial circles.[19]

Hailey was not able to start work until 1935 because of his India duties, and his health broke down during the work on the *Survey*. Yet the hard-working Hailey and his team produced an 1,837-page report by October 1938. It was a technocratic masterpiece.

The *African Survey* announced "a more scientific approach to the problems of health and material well-being" in Africa. Similar phrases like "a scientific approach to the questions of African development" recur throughout the report.[20] The preface by Lord Lothian contrasted the Survey's "clear and objective study of significant facts" with undesirable "political passion, and a scramble for control" in Africa.[21]

The scale of the *African Survey*'s technocratic achievement, and the lasting appeal of such an approach, is evident in how modern some of its recommendations sound. As one of many examples, the *African Survey* in 1938 recommended "Green manuring, the digging in of green-stuff as soon as the land goes out of cultivation."[22] It suggested in particular some green-stuff called mucuna, a nitrogen-fixing legume in the soil. More than seven decades later, on March 29, 2012, an article in the science journal *Nature* about the Gates Foundation's Africa program suggested "the key to tackling hunger in Africa is enriching its soil." One solution mentioned is nitrogen-fixing legumes.[23] The Food and Agriculture Organization of the United Nations in a 2010 article mentioned a specific nitrogen-fixing legume called mucuna.[24]

Given the emphasis on technical solutions, it is not surprising that the report closed with a call for yet more "intensive study" in science in Africa.[25] The lack of economics research on Africa led Lord Hailey to ask for a chair in colonial economics at Oxford. This chair did eventually happen in 1946, although we will see it would not have the result that Lord Hailey wanted.

When the *African Survey* came out in October 1938, the moment did not seem propitious for attention to Africa, for it was right after the Munich Agreement in which British Prime Minister Neville Chamberlain appeased Hitler to achieve "peace in our time." It is another sign of Africa's surprising importance in the war that the report still got plenty of notice.

It got reviews in many of the prominent places, and almost all the reviews were favorable.

JUSTIFYING COLONIALISM: THE ROLE OF THE STATE

Hailey's Africa report displayed the usual technocratic genius for recommending actions while avoiding the question of who should be given the power to take those actions. After the outbreak of war required a new justification for colonial rule to save the empire, Hailey was then ready to answer the question of who should have the power for action.

Hailey took the first major step in articulating his new justification for colonial rule on October 29, 1941, at a lunch-time lecture to the members of the Royal Empire Society. Entitled "A New Philosophy of Colonial Rule," its breakthrough insight concerned the role of the state in the colonies: "It is the primary function of the State to concentrate its attention on the improvement of the standards of living and the extension of the social services in the Dependencies. . . . We should within reason give some measure of assistance to territories which cannot afford the initial steps necessary to raise the local standard of life."[26] This was his "new philosophy of colonial rule." His view of the state included "systematic planning," which in turn implies "a far greater measure both of initiative and control on the part of the central government."[27]

Hailey in 1941 was siding with conscious direction instead of spontaneous solutions. Hailey took a low view of "the initiative of the native cultivator," so a market system that rewarded such initiative had little to offer.[28] The natives might even require coercion. The state could use "legal compulsion" to "improve the methods of cultivation of cash or export crops or to correct faulty methods of cultivation leading to soil exhaustion and erosion." Such coercion became "justified if it is shown that it is the only possible way to secure a reasonable increase in the standards of life."[29]

THE TECHNOCRATIC EVASION OF RIGHTS

The technocratic approach also offered an excuse to postpone indefinitely any native demands for political rights. This is another critical moment in the story of how useful technocracy was to evade discussions about rights. After all, the approach delivered material benefits, which Hailey thought trumped any concern for political rights for people who were starving. In May 1941, Lord Hailey said, "We should not give our native population cause to complain that when they had asked for bread, we had offered them a vote."[30] Hailey would in 1943 make a heroic extrapolation from such thinking to a sweeping generalization that "political liberties are meaningless unless they can be built up on a better foundation of social and economic progress."[31]

The shock of the Japanese conquests of the British territories of Hong Kong and Singapore would give Lord Hailey even more motivation to re-define colonialism. In a newspaper article on March 27, 1942, he noted how "the late unhappy events in the Far East" had created "a demand for a radical change in a colonial policy which seemed to have failed to rouse in the peoples concerned the necessary desire to defend themselves against Japanese aggression." Later that year he announced "a new conception of our relationship" with the colonies, in which the British Empire would join the "movement for the betterment of the backward peoples of the world."[32]

Combining his earlier experience with technocracy with state-led ini-tiative, Lord Hailey had once again independently invented authoritarian development. The idea of the state promoting development could seem progressive, while obscuring who ran the state. Even the British socialists, who might have been expected to question colonial oppression, embraced Lord Hailey's formulation. As the modern political scientist Suke Wolton, whose pioneering account I have followed closely here, described Hailey's achievement of a new consensus during the war: colonial rulers' new "le-gitimacy was based less on racial difference and more on their new role as protector and developmental economist."[33]

Lord Hailey had conceived of the state as about efficient administration—not about power and conflict. There was a contradiction here that persists to the present: development thinkers wanted the state's power to increase so as to jump-start development, while they expected the conflict over who wielded that power to decrease.

In February 1943, O.G.R. Williams, the head of the West Africa De-partment in the Colonial Office, and the same official who got BBC to apologize for the word "nigger" in early 1941, wrote a memo indicating that he was a convert to Lord Hailey's formulation. Williams' 1943 memo suggested that the Colonial Office prepare a development plan for West Africa, which would "serve as a framework to which a good deal of the detailed development plans of the West African Colonies could be related and it would enable His Majesty's Government to resist far more effectively and convincingly any tendency to rush them into making undesirable concessions to impatient hotheads."[34]

Sir George Gater, the Undersecretary of State for the Colonies, referring to Hailey's ideas, suggested in a cover letter to Williams' memo "a forward policy in material development and social welfare. We should not concentrate on the pursuit of political ideals to the detriment of the pre-eminent need for improving the physical and social conditions."[35] The Secretary of State for the Colonies, O.F.G. Stanley, read the memo and wrote a cover note:[36] This is excellent!

The effort to save the empire seems easy to dismiss, because we now know that virtually all British colonies became independent within a couple of decades after the war. But this was not the expectation of British officials at the time. The Secretary of State for the Colonies, Viscount Cranborne, said in October 1942 that "most of the colonies, especially in Africa, will probably not be fit for complete independence for centuries."[37] The British saw any Africans agitating for independence as weak and isolated. Reflecting this attitude, the head of the West Africa department, the same O.G.R. Williams, produced in July 1943 a gradualist five-stage plan that still stopped short of independence. Williams commented that even completing the first three stages would take "a good many years (perhaps a good many generations, though it would be impolitic to say so openly)."[38]

THIS LOOKS LIKE A REAL RACE WAR

The day after Pearl Harbor, December 8, 1941, the Japanese Army attacked Hong Kong, which fell on Christmas Day, 1941. The Japanese simultaneously invaded Malaya, defeating the British by January 31, 1942. The Japanese then attacked Singapore, which fell on February 14, 1942, after an anemic British campaign to protect it. The British feared further loss of racial prestige amongst their colonial subjects after these embarrassing defeats.

The old British fear of a race war suddenly looked like the real thing. A high official in the British Foreign Office noted, "We are nothing but failure and inefficiency everywhere and Japs are murdering our men and raping our women."[39] Japanese atrocities against British civilian prisoners in Hong Kong and Singapore seemed part of a deliberate strategy of humiliation. More concerned about PR than about Britain's own civilians, a British official sent a secret memorandum to his own government saying "the point is to emphasise by every means Japanese barbarity towards other Asiatics, but not to bolster up [the] Japanese self-proclaimed role as defender of Asiatics by putting out stories of their barbarous treatment of Europeans."[40]

The British could not help looking even worse despite their PR efforts. British evacuations in Hong Kong and Singapore prior to defeat were color-coded: whites got out first, even the most loyal Asians often not at all. Lee Kuan Yew, later leader of Singapore, at the time only eighteen years old, later recalled how the whites' alleged "superiority" did not survive the debacle, as "stories of their scramble to save their skins led the Asiatics to see them as selfish and cowardly."[41]

Both during the initial Japanese invasion and during the subsequent occupation, local Asian populations collaborated with the invaders, confirming the whites' worst fears of a united nonwhite front. A former Africa hand in the Colonial Office said that "the events of the last few months have shown the immense difficulty of successfully defending areas in which the native population is secretly hostile or sullenly indifferent. Our failure to win the sympathy and co-operation of the native inhabitants has largely contributed to the Japanese victories in the Far East."[42]

The Americans were also in shock. The first response was to blame the British. The old China hand and novelist Pearl S. Buck wrote secretly to her friend Eleanor Roosevelt on March 7, 1942, that US troops in India ""must be prepared for a revenge which may fall upon them, too, only because they are helping white men whom the Indians hate."[43] FDR told Eleanor that she could tell Pearl that he had read her letter with real interest. The US State Department worried that Japan could now gain a "secure place as the leader of . . . colored races of the world."[44]

The consequences of these events were that Lord Hailey's efforts to justify the Empire on nonracial, developmental grounds got even more widespread support among other British officials. But the Americans wondered whether a lot more was needed to win the battle for hearts and minds among the "colored races." The Americans saw an alternative to rationalizing the British Empire: end it. Now Lord Hailey would have to convince the Americans about his justification for colonial rule.

The American Attack on Empire

When the United States had joined the war after Pearl Harbor, they, too, had worried about a race war led by the Japanese under their slogan "Asia for the Asiatics." American government officials and soldiers wanted Asians to view them as liberators, not as bounty hunters intent on transferring them back to British captivity. American soldiers expressed their discontent in a jingle: "the Limeys make policy, Yanks fight the Japs, / And one gets its Empire, and one takes the rap.'"[45]

The influential American journalist Walter Lippman expressed the same discontent after the fall of Singapore: the Allies "have found themselves in a position where they could be accused . . . of fighting to preserve the rule of the white man over the peoples of Asia . . . for the restoration of empire." Sumner Welles, Roosevelt's chief foreign-policy adviser, gave such views official sanction in a Memorial Day Address at Arlington National Cemetery on May 30, 1942: "Our victory must bring in its train the liberation of all peoples. . . . The age of imperialism is ended."[46]

Lord Hailey responded with a major propaganda effort in America to defend the continuation of empire. He would be able to play upon white Americans' own racial problems at home. He also found an unexpected ally in an economist we have already met: Gunnar Myrdal. Myrdal was completing a landmark 1944 book on American racism toward blacks, called *An American Dilemma: The Negro Problem and Modern Democracy*. Myrdal said that there was a "disturbing racial angle to the Second World War" and also to "the planning for a world order after the War."[47] Myrdal said the "racial angle" inflamed racial tensions at home in the United States: "In this war there was a 'colored' nation on the other side—

Japan. And that nation had started out by beating the white Anglo-Saxons on their own ground. The smoldering revolt in India against British rule had significance for the American Negroes, and so had . . . the ambiguity of the plans for the colonial chessboard of Africa. Even unsophisticated Negroes began to see vaguely a color scheme in world events."[48]

Racial tension in America was indeed high during the war. A race riot broke out in Detroit in June 1943. Blacks complained about discrimination in the armed forces and in employment in arms factories. Isaiah Berlin, later to become a major political philosopher, was stationed in the British Embassy in Washington and was part of Hailey's propaganda effort. Berlin noted with satisfaction on April 17, 1942, that "Americans who are fond of criticizing the treatment of subject races by other people found similar troubles nearer to home this week. The Navy authorized for the first time the enlistment of negroes for general service, though not for commissioned rank, and this concession was criticized as both belated and inadequate by the negro organizations."[49]

Lord Hailey reviewed Myrdal's book on "America's Negro Problem" in the London *Times* on July 25, 1944. His concluding sentences showed Hailey's ability to use Myrdal as leverage against American critics of empire: "Nor can we overlook the effect of the growing recognition by the American public that . . . their country occupies a somewhat exposed position as a defender of the democratic faith. 'When we talk of freedom and opportunity for all nations', it has been said, 'some of the mocking paradoxes in our own society become so clear that they can no longer be ignored.'"[50]

Hailey knew in July 1944 that Roosevelt was in a trap. While Roosevelt tried to avoid the worst flare-ups of black discontent, he could not enforce desegregation or black voting rights in the South. Southern whites were solid supporters of the Democrats at that time, and losing them would threaten FDR's reelection in November 1944.

ANOTHER KEY MOMENT IN THIS BOOK

Lord Hailey's propaganda offensive in the United States during World War II was a combination of threat and opportunity. The threat was "if you keep harping on how we oppress our nonwhites, we will harp on how you oppress your nonwhites." The opportunity was to reformulate both American and British policies in a more positive light.

Lord Hailey suggested the British and Americans come together on the positive image of the state leading the development of backward areas (code for "backward races"). He suggested a parallel between British development of colonial Africa and America's New Deal promotion of development among its impoverished blacks: "Both in Great Britain and in the United States we now realize it is necessary to revise our system so far as will enable the State to give more help to the development of the underprivileged areas or communities."[51]

Hailey was well briefed on how the Roosevelt Administration had already tried to finesse the Negro Problem so as not to offend white southerners. Back in 1940, Eleanor Roosevelt lunched with black leader Ralph Bunche and suggested to him that racism was most "effectively attacked on the economic front." White New Dealers tried to convince blacks that they should "concentrate on the attainable goal of economic progress and to postpone the challenge to segregation."[52]

Through Lord Hailey, the United Kingdom offered the United States a choice between mutual accusations of a denial of rights to nonwhites, or a unified progressive agenda of raising standards of living for nonwhite peoples through state action. The United States chose the latter course, preserving the empire for the time being. Lord Hailey had won the day for the authoritarian idea of development, at the expense of political rights for nonwhites.

We have reached another key moment in this book. Today's emphasis on material development—focusing on "what must we do to end global poverty?" while neglecting the unequal rights for blacks and whites and the unequal rights in the West and the Rest—goes back to this moment and other similar moments in the history of the development idea. Development at moments like this accepted the bargain of the autocrat. The autocrats and their expert advisers asked us to give up our concerns about rights in return for a promise by autocrats to alleviate poverty faster than free societies would.

The Founding of the United Nations

The triumph of the technocratic idea of development was written into the charter of the new United Nations. On June 26, 1945, in San Francisco at the United Nations Conference on International Organization, representatives of the world's countries signed the United Nations Charter, which reads in part: "We the peoples of the United Nations," in order "to reaffirm faith in fundamental human rights, in the dignity and worth of the human person, in the equal rights of men and women and of nations large and small, and . . . to promote social progress and better standards of life in larger freedom," have determined "to employ international machinery for the promotion of the economic and social advancement of all peoples."[53] This sounds admirable, of course, but there is a fundamental omission. The UN Charter paid at least lip-service to rights and freedom, but it made no mention of independence for colonial peoples. Perhaps it helps to understand this contradiction to learn that the main author of the soaring language of the charter was Jan Smuts, the long-time South African leader and long-time advocate of white rule in Africa. At the conference in San Francisco, Smuts praised the United Kingdom as the "greatest colonial power" in the world. Smuts saw the United Nations as serving "men and women everywhere, including dependent peoples, still unable to look after themselves."[54] The "international machinery" to promote "advancement" of "dependent peoples" included the British Empire. At the time of the UN's founding, the United Nations and the British Empire were mutually supportive international organizations.

W.E.B. DuBois accused Smuts and the other UN founders of "lying about democracy when we mean imperial control of 750 millions of human beings in colonies."[55]

Friedrich Hayek had questioned the moral value of any real power given to an international organization in *The Road to Serfdom* in 1944. Hayek, with his realism about the Allies wielding such power and his suspicion of unchecked power at any level, reacted a lot like the left-wing anti-imperialist DuBois. He asked, "can there be much doubt that this would mean a more or less conscious endeavor to secure the dominance of the white man, and would rightly be so regarded by all other races?"[56]

Article 73 of the UN Charter said that some unspecified UN members have "responsibilities for the administration of territories whose peoples have not yet attained a full measure of self-government." As Lord Hailey pointed out in the 1956 revision of the *Africa Survey*, this provision did not give "the organization of the United Nations any authority to intervene in the control of these territories." The article requires such members to ensure for these peoples "protection against abuses." This article thereby firmly required colonial powers to protect their colonial subjects against—themselves.[57]

When the United Nations published its first report on development in 1947, *Economic Development in Selected Countries: Plans, Programmes and Agencies*, it included plans for "British African Non-Self-Governing and Non-Metropolitan Territories" and "French African Overseas Territories." The introduction to the report lumps together all "governments of the less developed countries," including the European colonial rulers of these territories next to local rulers like those in Argentina, Brazil, Chile, Poland, and Yugoslavia. The report declared that all members of this diverse group of autocrats, democrats, Stalinists, and colonizers shared the "ultimate aim in economic development" which "is to raise the national welfare of the entire population."[58]

POSTWAR EMPIRE

Was the new development justification for empire taken seriously after the war was over? There was a postwar surge in the British Colonial Service, adding about 15,000 new officers. Historians refer to this period as the Second Colonial Occupation. The new officers were the administrators and technicians necessary for colonial development. The Second Occupation makes it clearer than ever that colonial officials did not expect the collapse of the empire that happened only a few years later.

The language of racial superiority had disappeared, yet the problems confronting the empire did not go away. The fears of a global revolt of "colored peoples" led by Japan disappeared after the war, only to be replaced by the fears of an anticolonial revolt led by the Soviet Union. Moreover, the Soviet model of development was actually closer to the new synthesis of technocracy and state initiative than the Western countries' own development experiences. The Soviets seemed to offer the whole package to the non-Western world: anticolonialism with authoritarian development. The Americans would eventually realize this Soviet potential to win over anticolonial leaders as the Cold War erupted. The United States would soon reverse its support for the empire. We will see the Americans' own formulation of technocratic development to win the new "Third World" during the Cold War in the next chapter.

THE OXFORD CHAIR IN COLONIAL ECONOMICS

In 1946 Lord Hailey finally got the creation of a chair in colonial economics at Oxford that he had first requested in the *African Survey* eight years earlier, but not quite with the result he expected. The first (and as it turned out, the last) occupant of the chair was a white South African economist named S. Herbert Frankel (1903–1996), a critic of apartheid in South Africa. If Lord Hailey had wanted the occupant of the chair to apply and elaborate Hailey's authoritarian development model, Frankel had other ideas; he would favor free development and denounce authoritarian development.

Frankel's biggest moment in the chair came in 1951, when the United Nations published a *Primer for Development* that distilled the new consensus on technocratic state-led development. The *Primer* could not have put it any more plainly:

> Economic progress depends to a large extent upon the adoption by governments of appropriate administrative and legislative action. . . . We wish to emphasize that the masses of the people take their cue from those who are in authority over them. If the leaders are reactionary, selfish and corrupt, the masses in turn are dispirited, and seem to lack initiative. But if the leaders win the confidence of the country, and prove themselves to be vigorous in eradicating privilege and gross inequalities, they can inspire the masses with an enthusiasm for progress which carries all before it . . . all problems of economic development are soluble.

Frankel published a review of the UN *Primer for Development* in the prestigious *Quarterly Journal of Economics* in 1952 and quoted this section of the *Primer*. The "authoritarian ring" of these "admonitions" troubled Frankel. The report displayed the usual technocratic blind spot as to the nature of power. Exactly where, Frankel asked, would you find leaders dedicated to "eradicating privilege"? In the absence of democratic accountability to the majority, leaders tended to come from the privileged elite and to reinforce those privileges, not eradicate them. And yet the report wanted to give such leaders more power so as to overcome any reluctance "to pay the price of economic progress." Frankel commented, "It would have been useful to have been told more exactly what the authors meant by 'willingness to pay the price of economic progress.' Is it to be paid by the masses or by the leaders, by the young or the old, by the weak or the strong?"

Frankel was disturbed about how the values of individual freedom and dignity were so remarkably absent from the UN report. An approach that made everything depend on the "public will," said Frankel, is "not likely to find much room for the uniqueness of the potential contribution of the mere individual." Frankel noted that, according to the United Nations, the individual is just one of the masses who "take their cue" from the leaders.[59]

Frankel was aghast at the encompassing emphasis on simply mobilizing enough money for African investment, which did not recognize the lack of rights of Africans as the real problem: "as one who has spent the greater part of his life as an economist in dealing with the investment problems of Africa, and indeed in trying to contribute to the greater economic and political liberty of its inhabitants, I can say that a statement of this kind is so unrelated to the basic problems of the continent and its peoples as to be quite irrelevant."[60]

Frankel had a view of development that definitely did not fit the emerging development consensus and did not help justify continuing authoritarian colonial rule. Development did not depend "on the abstract national goals of, and the more or less enforced decisions by, a cadre of planners."

Instead, Frankel strongly took the side of spontaneous solutions to poverty, rather than that of conscious direction. Solutions happened from "the piecemeal adaptation of individuals to new circumstances." Frankel trusted individuals' knowledge over planners' knowledge. It was individuals who knew best as they "themselves become aware" of solutions to their own particular problems. Individuals running their own lives were the best judge of "what can and ought to be done next." Frankel here disagreed not only with the UN *Primer* but with Lord Hailey's 1941 speech that expressed Hailey's low view of "the initiative of the native cultivator."[61]

Frankel's high-profile review of the UN *Primer for Development* unfortunately turned out to be the high-water mark of his career in development. It was as close as he ever came to getting heard, which was not very close. His autobiography in 1992 gave the substance of many lectures that he continued to give throughout the 1950s, many of which now read as prescient and insightful. But he joined the long list of now-forgotten liberal economists that the new development economists of the 1950s did not deem worthy to debate.

The new rulers of independent Africa may not have liked Hailey's colonialism or racist paternalism, but they did see a lot to like in Hailey's ideas of conscious development instead of spontaneous solutions. They also admired much in Hailey's idea of the authoritarian state being in charge of development (i.e., everything), because now *they* were the authoritarian state. What was good justification for colonial authoritarian rule was just as good justification for anticolonial authoritarian rule. We can see this legacy of Hailey's ideas, and Frankel's fears of authoritarianism, play out with one development economist and one new African ruler in the 1950s.

SIR ARTHUR LEWIS AND KWAME NKRUMAH[62]

The principal author of the 1951 UN *Primer for Development* that Frankel criticized was W. Arthur Lewis, the thirty-six-year-old economist from St. Lucia who had been the token black hired by the Colonial Office in 1941. By 1951, Lewis had a PhD and a faculty appointment from the London School of Economics. Hayek had been one of his teachers and then one of his colleagues at LSE, but Lewis's views on development were closer to those of Hayek's would-be debate opponent, Gunnar Myrdal. Like Myrdal, Lewis claimed unanimity among development experts for a planning approach to development. In a 1949 book, he had written "the truth is that we are all planners now."[63]

Lewis would provide yet another example of technocratic development's ability to appeal to opposing groups. Lewis's state-centered approach was also close to the approach that Lord Hailey used as a cover-up for British racism and a justification of colonialism. As an advocate *against* colonialism, Lewis wanted developmental legitimacy for the independent African states that would succeed colonial rule.

It was Lewis who had seen investment in plant and equipment as the key variable driving economic development in the UN report, which Frankel had criticized as "so unrelated to the basic problems" of Africans when they lacked "economic and political liberty." Lewis would develop these ideas further. Unlike the forgotten Frankel, Lewis would achieve widespread recognition as one of the founding fathers of the new development economics. In 1979 Lewis received the Nobel Prize in Economics, five years after Hayek and Myrdal.

Lewis also had the opportunity to put his ideas into practice. On March 6, 1957, the Gold Coast became the first British African colony to become independent, changing its name to Ghana. Elected as the first president of Ghana was Kwame Nkrumah, a longstanding independence activist. We met him above as "Francis Nkrumah" while a student in America and as an observer of the 1942 Phelps Stokes Commission that gave a cringe-inducing defense of Africans against racism. Nkrumah almost immediately after independence invited Arthur Lewis to be his economic adviser. Lewis accepted the offer, arranging a two-year contract under United Nations auspices.

Lewis arrived in a politically polarized environment with an ethnic dimension. Nkrumah was from the coastal Akan people; his main opposition was centered in the interior homeland of the Ashanti people. Some of the roots of this ethnic conflict dated to the days of the slave trade run by the British and other Europeans. The Ashanti were among the African kingdoms that sold slaves to Europeans; the coastal Akan people were among their victims.

Nkrumah's development policies followed the prescription of Lewis and other development economists to raise investment to launch development.

Nkrumah did this by taxing Ghana's most valuable industry, cocoa production, and using the proceeds to increase public investment. Although following a technocratic recommendation, the cocoa-tax policy also exposed the illusion that technocratic development was politically neutral. Cocoa production was in the Ashanti region. So the tax could just as easily be seen as redistributing income from Nkrumah's opposition to his supporters. The tax only increased the intensity of opposition to Nkrumah among the Ashanti.

Lewis approved of the concept behind the policy to raise investment, but the political conflict and Nkrumah's response to it dismayed him. Already in the first year of independence, in 1957, Nkrumah's government was enacting measures to repress the opposition. After Lewis was already in the country, the government passed an emergency-powers bill at the end of 1957, allowing Nkrumah to declare an emergency in any local region—such as the Ashanti region—which would give him emergency powers. A preventive-detention bill in 1958 allowed the government to imprison anyone declared to be a threat to national security. Nkrumah's party used it to put opponents in jail. Just the threat of jail was sufficient to coerce many opposition members of parliament into joining the ruling party. Other opponents fled into exile.

Lewis kept quiet for the time being, but his own democratic principles did not allow him to tolerate such repression for very long. His final break with Nkrumah happened over a much smaller issue in late 1958—eradicating an insect parasite, the capsid beetle, that threatened the cocoa crop. Lewis advised Nkrumah to spend the modest sum necessary and use the well-qualified sprayers and equipment from the Ministry of Agriculture. Nkrumah agreed eradication was needed but wanted to give the job to a farmers' cooperative controlled by his party. Lewis understood correctly that this was pure political patronage. It would fuel corruption but would fail to kill capsid beetles, in yet another blow to the Ashanti cocoa growers. It was a small issue that reflected Lewis's pent-up anguish about Nkrumah's autocratic ways. Lewis wrote privately at this time to a correspondent: "the fascist state is in full process of creation, and I find it hard to live in a country where I cannot protest against imprisonment without trial."[64]

The end result of this conflict was that Lewis gave Nkrumah an ulti-
matum on December 18, 1958. The demand was for Lewis to have more
power over decisions. Ironically, Nkrumah had backed down on the capsid wars in the meantime. But Nkrumah could not agree to such an ulti-
matum and accepted Lewis's resignation, ten months before the end of
Lewis's two-year appointment as adviser.

Lewis did not speak out publicly against Nkrumah's abuses of power in
1958. As the world's most famous black economist, Lewis felt a duty to the
cause of African independence from colonial rule, which still had yet to
happen in most places. Lewis did not want public recriminations that (as
he explained privately to a correspondent) "would only comfort enemies
of Africans everywhere."[65]

Nkrumah would grow yet more dictatorial after this, and his policies
slowly strangled both the cocoa industry and Ghana's entire economy. He
would have little public support left when a military coup deposed him
in 1966. His successors continued the same repressive policies on cocoa,
however, and Ghana's economy (and cocoa) continued a long decline until economic reforms began in 1983.

In 1965 Lewis would finally take public his dismay at African dictatorships (including Nkrumah's) in a book called *Politics in West Africa*. He
criticized the whole apparatus of repression, the one-party state, the cult
of the leader, and the opportunities for corruption, which Lewis pleaded
we should remember "when we read in the political science books about
the 'charisma' of the great men now engaged in modernizing backward
societies."[66] Alas, this book had far less influence than Lewis's earlier writings on how to achieve technocratic development by raising investment
rates (see, for example, the paltry citation counts for the book relative to
the vast counts for his early articles). The technocratic indifference to political power and rights would continue.

CONCLUSION

As Lord Hailey turned ninety in 1962, the fall of the British Empire in
Africa was well underway with one country after another becoming independent. Lord Hailey's attempt to save the empire with the idea of

authoritarian development failed. His picture of British rule as benevolent autocracy proved unconvincing in the long run, but mostly because
the new nationalist leaders in the colonies wanted the role of benevolent
autocrat for themselves. The Americans sided with the new nationalist
autocrats as the competition with the Soviets for Cold War allies began.

Lord Hailey's advocacy for virtually unchecked state power at the center of development efforts proved far more lasting. Few worried about the
threat of so much state power to the individual rights of poor people. The
British and Americans at the time of Lord Hailey's work still had such
racist attitudes toward Africans that it was hard for them to conceive of
Africans' rights. Today, when racism is thankfully unacceptable, we don't
have the same excuse.

The authoritarian development ideas left behind by Lord Hailey would
achieve the final leap to acceptance when they also proved useful to the
United States during the Cold War. To see how, we move next to Colombia on a fateful day in 1948.

CHAPTER FIVE

ONE DAY IN BOGOTÁ

Three things happened on April 9, 1948, in Bogotá, Colombia, that changed the history of development, the history of Colombia, and the history of the Cold War.

By analyzing what led up to and what followed the events of this day in Bogotá, we will see the transition from the forgotten formative years of development to its modern practice. The previous two chapters saw technocratic development as justification for or distraction from Western policies that no longer exist: colonialism in Africa and the semicolonial occupation of parts of China. This chapter tells the story of how technocratic development became politically useful for Western policies that still do exist: support for allies in whatever war the West was or is fighting (originally the Cold War, today the War on Terror).

We will relate this story to the moment of original sin—the founding of the World Bank—in which the Bank disavowed the ideals of freedom, embraced the technocratic approach, and made itself available for supporting dictatorial Western allies. After the events of this chapter, the final piece was in place for the Tyranny of Experts, the embrace of benevolent autocrats, and the triumph of authoritarian development over free development.

THE OFFICIAL DEVELOPMENT HISTORY
OF APRIL 9, 1948

In the spring of 1948, World Bank President John J. McCloy made his first trip to Latin America. He had become president of the Bank a year earlier, and soon after realized that the Bank (whose official name was the International Bank for Reconstruction and Development) would soon have to shift from supporting European reconstruction to supporting development in the rest of the world.[1] The Americans were going to take the lead role in European reconstruction with the Marshall Plan, announced in 1947, leaving a diminished role for the Bank. April 9, 1948, found the World Bank President McCloy in Bogotá, meeting with Colombian President Mariano Ospina Perez.

McCloy suggested to Ospina on April 9 that the World Bank send a comprehensive survey mission to Colombia. The nation would serve as a test case for the World Bank's shift from European recovery to Third World development. Ospina accepted eagerly; he had his own reasons to welcome the Bank, as we will see below.

And so the next year McCloy dispatched a fourteen-man World Bank mission. The World Bank's 1949 use of the word *mission*, with its overtones of religious salvation, was to become standard. The mission included experts on such diverse fields as highways, industry, agriculture, health, banking, and railroads. The leader of that 1949 World Bank mission to Colombia was Dr. Lauchlin Currie, a veteran New Deal economist and adviser to FDR. The mission's assignment, as Currie would explain in his report, was "to formulate a development program designed to raise the standard of living of the Colombian people."[2]

Currie's flight touched down in Bogotá on July 11, 1949. For the next four months, he would travel through remote and often lawless regions of Colombia, saying he was struck by the contrast between the richness of the land and what he called the miserable and superstitious people.[3] Currie and his team departed on November 5, 1949, and, less than a year later, on August 13, 1950, the report was ready. On that date, the three-volume study of 950 pages was delivered to the Colombians.

The report's conclusion was that Colombians indeed had a development problem: "The great majority are inadequately fed, clothed and housed. Their health is poor and life expectancy short. A large proportion is illiterate, and few have had more than two or three years of primary schooling."[4] Yet the problem had a clear solution—which the report presented as a comprehensive attack: "Our approach is comprehensive, for the causes and characteristics of economic underdevelopment—poverty, ill health, ignorance, low productivity, and the like—are all interrelated and mutually reinforcing. The chances for success will be greatly enhanced if the attack proceeds simultaneously on several fronts."[5]

Already in 1950 we can see in the World Bank report on Colombia a number of statements that capture the solidifying consensus in development. First, on the debate between understanding development as conscious design or as spontaneous solutions:

> One cannot escape the conclusion that reliance on natural forces has not produced the most happy results. Equally inescapable is the conclusion that with knowledge of the underlying facts and economic processes, good planning in setting objectives and allocating resources, and determination in carrying out a program of improvements and reforms, a great deal can be done to improve the economic environment by shaping economic policies to meet scientifically ascertained social requirements.[6]

Second, on the Blank Slate versus learning from history: "Colombia is presented with an opportunity unique in its long history. Its rich natural resources can be made tremendously productive through the application of modern techniques and efficient practices."[7]

The "unique" opportunity suggests Colombia's previous history is not terribly relevant, while experts can now write new "tremendously productive . . . modern techniques" upon a Blank Slate.

Finally, on the emphasis on the prerogatives of the nation versus the rights of individuals:

> International and foreign national organizations have been established to aid underdeveloped areas technically and financially. All that is needed to usher in a period of rapid and widespread development is a determined effort by the Colombian people themselves. In making such an effort, Colombia would not only accomplish its own salvation but would at the same time furnish an inspiring example to all other underdeveloped areas of the world.[8]

All the emphasis is on action by the collective nation ("the Colombian people" or "Colombia"), while there is no discussion of whether such collective actions will violate any individual rights.

It is striking that nothing in these conclusions was based on anything specific to Colombia. In fact, the report's language echoed verbal formulations that had emerged from the New Deal and worked their way into international discourse on global poverty. The World Bank Report said about Colombia: "The great majority are inadequately fed, clothed and housed." FDR in his January 11, 1944, State of the Union address had said about conditions at home: "We cannot be content . . . if some fraction of our people—whether it be one-third or one-fifth or one-tenth—is ill-fed, ill-clothed, ill-housed, and insecure."[9] And Truman had prefaced his January 20, 1949, speech announcing a US development program with a similar reference to the world's poorest: "More than half the people of the world are living in conditions approaching misery. Their food is inadequate. They are victims of disease." The 1950 Colombia report said "Their health is poor and life expectancy short."

Likewise, where the 1950 Colombia report envisioned an "attack" that "proceeds simultaneously on several fronts," we see echoes even of the IPR and the Rockefeller Foundation in 1930s China. The latter had commissioned "social scientists, public health experts, engineers, and agronomists for a concerted attack on China's rural problems."

The government reception was very positive. The government began almost immediately to implement the World Bank recommendations. On September 28, 1950, it formed a Committee for Economic Development made up of Colombian officials, with Currie as expert adviser.[10] This gave way to a more powerful body, the National Planning Council, on April 25, 1952. The latter now included, in addition to Currie, an economist who would later become famous for his contributions to development thinking: Albert Hirschman.

Both Hirschman and Currie were to remain in Colombia through 1956. Hirschman then moved on to other countries; Currie actually settled in Colombia and spent the rest of his life as development expert for the Colombian government. The Colombian government gained a lasting reputation as a technocratic state drawing heavily on expert guidance. Unfortunately, the receptivity of the government to the expert recommendations was not quite what it seemed. There is a different narrative around April 9, 1948, that reveals a different perspective.

THE COLOMBIAN HISTORY OF APRIL 9, 1948

Colombians remember April 9, 1948, for reasons other than the commissioning of a World Bank report. On that day, a lone gunman in Bogotá assassinated Jorge Gaitán, a charismatic champion of Colombia's poor majority. Gaitán had been expected to win the next presidential election for the Liberal party and enact programs in favor of the poor. President Ospina, who had accepted the World Bank proposal of a development report on the same April 9, 1948, was a Conservative party member who had taken office in August 1946, ending a period of Liberal party rule from 1930 to 1946. There had already been some violence throughout the country as Conservative appointees replaced Liberals in countless local government posts. Ospina tried to reduce the conflict by including Liberal representatives in his government, but this attempt was short-lived. As Liberal party leader, Gaitán ended the coalition when Ospina failed to address Liberal grievances, and Conservative violence against Liberals in the countryside increased in 1947 and early 1948.[11]

It would never be known what had motivated Gaitán's killer, but the popular reaction was "they killed him," where "they" meant the oligarchs whom the Conservatives served.[12] In response to the assassination, enraged mobs began looting, raping, and killing in Bogotá, with atrocities from both Liberal and Conservative supporters. The riot, known as the Bogotazo, raged for days before the army finally stopped it.

Colombians also remember the following period, from 1948 to 1956, for things other than the implementation of World Bank reports by development experts. Instead they call it simply "La Violencia," a deadly political conflict that killed as many as 400,000 Colombians. The violence between Liberal and Conservative supporters spawned a whole new taxonomy of atrocities. For example, *picar para tamal* described a technique for cutting up the body of a political opponent while the victim was still alive, bit by bit. As one historian of La Violencia describes the conflict: "Crucifixions and hangings were commonplace, political 'prisoners' were thrown from airplanes in flight, infants were bayoneted, schoolchildren, some as young as eight years old, were raped en masse, unborn infants were removed by crude Caesarian section and replaced by roosters."[13]

The conflict was fueled by the actions of the same leaders discussing development plans with Currie and Hirschman. On October 12, 1949, as the Currie mission was still in Bogotá, the Conservatives nominated for president a candidate who destroyed any hope of compromise with the Liberals, ensuring that La Violencia would continue. The Conservative candidate was Laureano Gómez, who had an unfortunate history of favorable statements about Hitler and Franco. The Liberals withdrew from the elections, saying they could not campaign while their supporters were leading candidates for *picar para tamal*. As the Currie mission left in November 1949, the Conservatives declared a state of siege and closed Congress, while the terrified voters elected Gómez president, unopposed. The closing of Congress was to last until December 1951, the longest suspension of Congress in Colombia's history. La Violencia got even worse after the election.

On August 7, 1950, six days before receiving the World Bank report, Gómez began his presidency, announcing a "Revolution of Order" modeled on his hero Francisco Franco. By 1952, as Currie and Hirschman began advising the National Planning Council, Conservative mobs sacked the headquarters of the two prominent Liberal newspapers and attacked the homes of two Liberal ex-presidents. Finally, on June 13, 1953, General Rojas Pinilla staged a coup and began a military dictatorship that would last until 1957.

The World Bank report did not mention politics or violence as an item on its long list of obstacles to Colombian development. In private, behind the technocratic veneer, the World Bank mission in 1949 could hardly be unaware of the violence when their hosts at the Central Bank were stocking up on canned goods in the basement in preparation for a siege. Currie wrote in private correspondence that a Canadian electoral mission had told him that an honest presidential election was impossible, while also alluding to a "shooting incident" inside the Congress.[14]

We can now see why the Gómez government was enthusiastic about a World Bank report that lent legitimacy to his rule as the benevolent developer of the country. The World Bank even realized this at the time. After

Gómez won the election, a World Bank staffer in a confidential internal memo on January 19, 1950, worried that Bank actions "might be construed as an endorsement of the Colombian regime; it seems certain that the Government would try to make it appear so."[15]

The idea that the government was just following expert recommendations was, of course, doubtful. However, it was easy to justify government actions by citing some technological recommendation or another when there were multiple foreign experts, all with differing views and all eager to please their Colombian government counterparts. Hirschman in his private correspondence on September 20, 1952, admitted as much: the Conservative regime officials "just love to play one foreign expert out against the other." This way they could always cite "foreign expert opinion" as an "alibi" for "doing exactly what they want."[16]

Hirschman would write a poignant article many years later expressing remorse for the legitimacy given to autocrats by development economists, although not mentioning his Colombia experience. He had eventually dissented from the technocratic view, worrying in 1979 that development economics "brings with it calamitous side effects in the political realm, from the loss of democratic liberties at the hand of authoritarian, repressive regimes to the wholesale violation of elementary human rights."[17] Hirschman was dismayed at the brutal military regimes holding power in Latin America at the time he wrote, such as those in Argentina, Brazil, Chile, Paraguay, and Uruguay. Colombia no longer had military rule at the time Hirschman wrote. Colombia instead had a less-than-democratic formal alternation of the presidency between the two elite parties. The closed political process had spawned violent guerilla resistance that continues to this day.

But why did the World Bank and development experts go along with all this ugly politics at the time when they realized they were being used? We need yet another perspective.

THE INTERNATIONAL VIEW OF APRIL 9, 1948

A third time line, on international politics, helps us understand why the World Bank would have such a blind spot on the politics of member countries. That same crowded day in Bogotá, April 9, 1948, had one other significant event in addition to the World Bank mission and the Gaitán assassination. US Secretary of State George "Marshall Plan" Marshall was in Bogotá on that same day for the founding meeting of the Organization of American States (OAS). For Marshall, the significance of that day had nothing to do with Colombian politics or development. He was there to cement alliances with Latin American states against communism.

The Cold War had begun about a year earlier with the March 12, 1947, announcement of the Truman Doctrine, a commitment to defend Greece and Turkey against Soviet attempts at communist revolutions. Both the United States and the Soviets were scrambling to line up allies on their respective sides of the Cold War. The United States feared Soviet-supported communist takeovers would happen in its traditional sphere of influence in the Americas, the area that the Monroe Doctrine had long forbidden to European interference.

On November 1, 1947, a CIA agent wrote a secret memo describing "Soviet objectives in Latin America," mentioning Colombia among a number of Latin American countries thought to be vulnerable to communist penetration. Shortly after the OAS founding summit in Bogotá in April 1948, the Cold War would heat up with the June 25, 1948, Soviet blockade of Berlin. The Soviet Union would conduct its first successful nuclear test on August 29, 1949. As Laureano Gómez was about to take over as president of Colombia in 1950, the Korean War began. The US government was only too happy to have such a reliable anticommunist as Gómez during such a frightening early period of the Cold War.

The official history of the World Bank makes clear that the US government controlled the allocation of World Bank support to its favored countries.[18] For America, the idea of politically neutral, technocratic development was a great way to combine two goals that had two separate domestic political constituencies: to distribute World Bank loans to promote development, and to assign World Bank loans to authoritarian regimes to secure alliances with the United States against the Soviets. So the Colombia report and subsequent World Bank loan was yet another key moment of transition to the modern status quo in development—technocratic ideas that appeal to humanitarians who care about world poverty and that also appeal to foreign-policy realists who care only about US national security. We have seen some of the background to this transition already in other parts of the world, in the chapters on China and British colonial Africa. It is time to pick up the same thread in Latin America.

US AND LATIN AMERICAN DEVELOPMENT IN THE INTERWAR PERIOD

The idea that development began from scratch in 1949 was contradicted for China and Africa in the previous two chapters, and is equally mythical in Colombia. A theme across all three of these chapters is a different kind of expert use of the Blank Slate idea. Development experts favored not only a Blank Slate disregard for the history of each region but also a Blank Slate disregard for the history of development experts.

As Roosevelt's economic adviser, Lauchlin Currie had actually visited China in 1941 and 1942 to evaluate America's nation-building program there, and so Currie is a personal link between the two cases of China and Colombia. Currie gave a positive evaluation in 1941–1942 to the China development effort. Just as Currie was to say Colombia had a development "opportunity unique in its long history," he also reported in a 1942 memo to Roosevelt that there was "a unique opportunity to exert a profound influence on the development of China."[19]

The World Bank Mission of 1949 was also not the first "unique" time Colombia could draw upon experts for a development "opportunity." The Colombian government had started the Banco de la República (the Colombian central bank that hosted the Currie mission in 1949) during a previous mission of US experts. On March 10, 1923, a five-man mission led by American economist Edwin Kemmerer arrived in Bogotá, staying until August 20, 1923, to lay the groundwork for the central bank. The new central bank and its sound fiscal policy helped attract American capital during the rest of the 1920s to finance Colombian railroads, roads, and ports. American experts kept coming to Colombia during the 1920s and 1930s.

A UN report coming out about the same time as the 1950 World Bank report noted that "the Government of Colombia, by Decree 1157 of 18

June 1940, adopted a general plan for the development of the country's economic activities." There had already been a National Economic Council implementing the 1940 development plan, before the formation of the National Planning Council in 1952 after the World Bank mission.[20]

The Americans' political use of the technocratic idea in Latin America also had happened before the 1948–1950 World Bank mission and report. After FDR took over from Hoover in 1933, US foreign policy would have a new strategic reason to promote the development idea in Latin America: the fear of German and Japanese inroads into Latin America as war clouds gathered. If the United States hoped to win the propaganda campaign against the fascists, it needed to present a different face to Latin America than a long history of semi-imperialist bullying and military interventions to protect American interests. The outcome was FDR's Good Neighbor Policy. He later summarized it as a "new approach" to "these South American things." FDR unintentionally revealed that racism was a factor in American attitudes toward Latin Americans, saying that "They think they are just as good as we are and many of them are."[21]

The concrete implication of the Good Neighbor Policy was for the US Export-Import Bank to support and stimulate Latin American industrialization. A public works loan by the ExIm Bank to Haiti in 1938 set the precedent, followed by a steady stream of Latin American loans "to assist in the development" of the countries "of the Western Hemisphere."[22]

As war broke out, the United States lost no time. On September 23, 1939, the Inter-American Conference of Ministers convened in Panama City and pledged to cooperate against the Nazis. The Panama City Conference led to the founding of the Inter-American Development Commission in January 1940.[23] Just as the meeting on Africa in Britain a month after the war began showed the importance of Africa, the speedy US response revealed the importance of Latin America. Nelson Rockefeller, the chairman of the Development Commission, cited "technicians and specialists from the United States" and "American capital" as key parts of promoting Latin American Development.[24] American capital and experts helped develop Colombia's oil holdings in 1942.

An American government economist named Harry Dexter White had proposed an Inter-American Bank to cement economic and political alliances in Latin America at a conference in Havana in February 1940. Though the conference approved the plan, a backlash against regional blocs would later kill it off. But it would be replaced by an even larger proposal by the same Harry Dexter White to create a new organization: the World Bank.

THE ORIGINAL SIN AT BRETTON WOODS

The World Bank was founded in 1944 at the Bretton Woods conference, which had been set up by the soon-to-be victorious Allies to plan postwar economic cooperation. The Bank would provide long-term financing and expert advice to what would become known as "developing countries." It would be the most powerful institution at the heart of the development community, which would include rich-country government aid agencies, international philanthropies, the United Nations and other international agencies, and the development experts advising all of the above. The same Bretton Woods conference also founded the International Monetary Fund (IMF), which would bail countries out of short-term financial crises. Both the Bank and the Fund still have these powerful roles today.

A key moment in the hardening consensus for technocratic development was the approval at Bretton Woods of one particular clause in the Bank's 1944 Articles of Agreement. Article IV, Section 10, was a "nonpolitical clause," as it became known, which would make it easier to overlook unlovely autocrats among America's anti-Soviet allies during the Cold War: "The Bank and its officers shall not interfere in the political affairs of any member; nor shall they be influenced in its decisions by the political character of the government of the member or members concerned. Only economic considerations shall be relevant to their decisions."[25]

The nonpolitical clause had a political motivation in 1944. Ironically, this motivation for Article IV, Section 10, was originally to allow *support* for the Soviet Union—then a wartime ally. At the same time, the article perfectly reflected a technocratic viewpoint—what mattered were the technical solutions to be implemented by the state, not the "political character" of whether a state was authoritarian (or even totalitarian as in the Soviet case). The article made possible an alliance between those who wanted to

fight global poverty with technocratic means and those with political mo-
tives (in this case, cementing the wartime alliance with the Soviets).

The principal author of Article IV, Section 10, was Harry Dexter White.
An economist with a Harvard PhD, White (1892–1948) had worked in
the FDR administration since 1934 as the top adviser to FDR's Treasury
Secretary, Henry Morgenthau, who had a close personal relationship with
Roosevelt. White had been on the left wing of the New Deal: he advo-
cated national economic planning in response to the Great Depression.
He would lose that argument domestically but would be on the winning
side for planning in development. White had a particularly strong influ-
ence, through Morgenthau, on the international economic policy of the
United States.

Treasury Secretary Morgenthau on December 14, 1941 had directed
White to write a draft for an "inter-Allied stabilization fund" with a view
to "postwar international monetary arrangements."[26] White wrote a first
draft proposing both an international bank (which would become the
World Bank) and a stabilization fund (which would become the IMF)
in late 1941 and circulated it within the US government in early 1942.
In his first draft he had already included a clause that would eventually
morph into the World Bank's nonpolitical clause: "No restrictions as to
membership [of the fund] should be imposed on grounds of the particular economic structure adopted by any country."[27] One sentence later,
White makes clear why he wanted "no restrictions"—because "to exclude
a country such as Russia would be an egregious error." White believed
strongly in a US–Soviet alliance both during and after the war.

It seems surprising that the treasury secretary and his top adviser
would show interest in postwar organizations only a week after Pearl
Harbor, but the occasion is yet another example of development's prominence during World War II. White explained the urgency in his draft:
"serious discussion of specific proposals . . . will be a factor toward winning the war." Allies "must have assurance that methods and resources
are being prepared to provide them with capital to help them rebuild their
devastated areas."[28] Behind this "assurance" that the Allies "must have"
was an unspoken "or else"—that Allies might sign a separate peace with
the Axis powers.

White wrote his draft at a bad moment for the Allied cause. In Europe, the Nazi empire was at its greatest extent, which included control over most of the European part of the Soviet Union. The United States had a two-front war in Europe and the Pacific. The Americans needed their new Soviet ally to keep fighting hard on the Eastern Front in Europe while the United States for the moment could do little on the Western Front in Europe. But what could the United States offer the Soviets at the time? FDR would be receptive to White's ideas of offering whatever he could promise to the Soviets for assistance after the war.

For White, the technocratic rationalization for Article IV, Section 10, and the political motive to support the Soviets were linked. White's parents were Jewish immigrants who had fled the pogroms in the prerevolutionary Russian empire. White himself was a long-time admirer of Soviet planning. His 1941 proposal draft stated that Free Trade policy "grossly underestimates the extent to which a country can virtually lift itself by its bootstraps in one generation from a lower to a higher standard of living, from a backward agricultural to an advanced industrial country, provided that it is willing to pay the price."[29] In an unpublished note written around the end of the war, White said "Russia is the first instance of a socialist economy in action. . . . And it works!"[30] This was a common view at the time.

White's draft embodies the technocratic approval of state power and disregard for individual rights. He proposes "measures of control" over the economy, chosen solely on technocratic criteria that "will be the most effective in obtaining the objectives" of "sustained prosperity." He anticipated possible criticism that such controls may "have been abused" to violate individual rights. But to "cast aside" such "effective" controls for this reason would be just as "foolish as it would be to rely solely on the self-interest motive of individuals as a means of solving our economic problems."[31]

White's draft on the Bank was full of experts: "The task calls for the joint efforts of experts of many countries." Bank loans would be made by a "competent committee," which would have to certify that the loan will "permanently raise the standard of living of the borrowing country." Such loans subject to such an expert committee "will be based on more careful studies of their utility than has ever been true with most private investments made to foreign countries." This made clear "the necessity for selecting the most able men to manage the Bank." The Bank "should also have the authority to send the experts into the field."[32] When White as Morgenthau's deputy became the key American decision-maker at Bretton Woods, White's original 1941 draft became the basis for the Article IV, Section 10, nonpolitical clause for the World Bank.

Harry Dexter White died in 1948, just as the World Bank began operations. But White had a former Harvard graduate school classmate and lifelong friend—Lauchlin Currie—to carry on his technocratic legacy at the World Bank. Lauchlin Currie had enthusiastically supported all of the Latin American and World Bank initiatives as Roosevelt's chief White House economist since 1939.[33]

The irony, of course, is that the article *against* politics made it easier to use the Bank to *pursue* politics. First, cite the article to justify using the Bank in 1944 to support the Soviet autocrats. Then by 1950, cite the article to justify using the Bank to oppose the Soviet Union with Colombian autocrats.

Six decades later, the spokesman for the World Bank would quote Article IV, Section 10, to me to justify the World Bank's overlooking authoritarian violations of individual rights in countries receiving World Bank loans. The autocrats the Bank was supporting six decades later happened to be US allies in the War on Terror.

THE THIRD WORLD BLANK SLATE

Another clue about the political motivations of the new development consensus was the very definition of what part of the world was "Third World" or "underdeveloped." How did Colombia wind up lumped in the same category with other much poorer places (Togo, Cambodia, Papua New Guinea) as an "underdeveloped country"?

One can find no clear-cut economic criteria for what came to be known as the Third World. Only a few years earlier, in 1940, economic historian Colin Clark had published a much-discussed book, *The Conditions of Economic Progress*, in which he ranked countries by rough estimates of per capita income from 1925 to 1934. Countries such as Albania, Bulgaria, Romania, Portugal, and South Africa were below Colombia.

Colombia and most of the rest of South America was at roughly the same level as Greece, Finland, Italy, and Japan. Other Latin American countries like Argentina and Uruguay (later to be classified as Third World, like Colombia) were estimated to be as rich as Great Britain and France.[34] A classification of the amount of "machinery in use per capita" all the way back in 1925 had also classified Colombia with Greece and Portugal, and well above the Dutch Indies, Turkey, India, and Siam, who in turn were well above China.[35]

One of the first academic articles that would retrospectively form the canon of official development thinking appeared in 1943, authored by Paul Rosenstein-Rodan, a forty-one-year-old Polish émigré economist in London. The World Bank would later anoint Rosenstein-Rodan, along with Gunnar Myrdal, Arthur Lewis, Albert Hirschman, and P. T. Bauer, as one of the "Pioneers in Development."[36] Rosenstein-Rodan actually applied his development ideas to Eastern and Southeastern Europe (although he mentioned the same analysis could also cover the Far East).[37] In another article in 1944, Rosenstein-Rodan spoke of five "economically backward" areas: (1) the Far East, (2) colonial Africa, (3) the Caribbean, (4) the Middle East, and (5) Eastern and Southeastern Europe.[38] In this first sketch of the object of development efforts—what would later be called the Third World—Rosenstein-Rodan excluded Latin America.

As development began after 1949, the final cut for the Third World would drop Eastern Europe and include Latin America. Since we have seen there was no justification for this based on per capita income, the most plausible explanation is political. The First World was the United States and its rich, democratic allies. The Second World was the Soviet Union and its eastern European satellites. The Third World was simply defined as what was left over, the areas of the world where the United States desperately wanted to deny the Soviets additional allies. The World Bank would be helpful for this purpose, as it was demonstrating in Colombia.

THE COLOMBIAN DEBATE THAT NEVER HAPPENED

Colombia and the rest of Latin America had traditionally been thought to be part of the West; its strongest cultural and intellectual ties were to

North America and Europe. As we have seen, Latin American countries overlapped with European countries in their levels of income per person. It was not obvious whether Latin America would wind up with the free development that would prevail in the West, or the authoritarian development that would prevail in the Rest.

When suddenly Latin America became "underdeveloped" in 1949, the object of "development planning," some Latin American thinkers objected. Albert Hirschman faithfully recorded these objections in a 1961 essay "Ideologies of Economic Development in Latin America." He noted that the Latin American Adam Smith was the Argentine thinker Juan Bautista Alberdi (1810–1884), who advocated imitation of the North American success story: "in economics even more than in politics, the best example for Americans to follow is America herself . . . North America is the great model for South America."[39] Alberdi seemed to anticipate the coming debate on conscious direction versus spontaneous solutions and made clear which side he favored: "There is no better or safer way to impoverish a country than to entrust its government with the task to enrich it."[40] Noting that doubting the competence of the state to mastermind growth remained an intellectual tradition in twentieth-century Latin America, Hirschman quoted the Brazilian proverb "our country grows by night when the politicians sleep."[41]

In Colombia, many who were heirs to these intellectual traditions were not happy about the World Bank Report approach to Colombian development. Hernán Echavarría Olózaga, a Colombian businessman and writer on economic policy, wrote in a 1958 book (*Common Sense on the Colombian Economy*, quoted by Hirschman in 1961): "In the Latin American countries there exists an important school which maintains that economic progress must necessarily be directed by the State. . . . What foundation is there for such a statement? None. The public should not accept blindly development plans. It must recall that bureaucracy is always interested in elaborating such plans, since they give it economic power and advantages."[42]

Hirschman also expressed the reaction by American development economists to such statements in Latin America. He said this "aversion" to "development planning" seems "a bit hysterical and old-fashioned to us!"[43] Aside from Hirschman's idiosyncratic interests in intellectual history, liberal Latin thinkers like Hernán Echavarría Olózaga were ignored and forgotten.

The liberal ideas of free development could conceivably have won in Colombia, but they lost to the authoritarian ideas of Currie's report to the World Bank. As elsewhere, the debate never really happened. The outcome seems to have been predetermined by the political usefulness of technocratic development to America's Cold War foreign policy and the self-interest of Colombian rulers. The World Bank management and economists could not or did not resist such political interests.

CONCLUSION

We have documented a similar process at work so far in China, British colonial Africa, and Colombia in forming a technocratic consensus on development. In chronological order: First, Western semicolonial interests in China agreed with the interests of an autocrat in China on the suppression of Chinese individual rights. Second, British colonial interests in Africa agreed with postcolonial African rulers on the suppression of African individual rights. Third and finally, US Cold War interests in Colombia agreed with a Colombian autocrat on the suppression of Colombian individual rights.

The process was complete before the end of the decade of the 1950s. This was the time when development thinking was supposed to have started, but really it had already ended. We don't have to be content with that lack of debate after the 1950s. The rest of this book carries out the debates on the Blank Slate versus learning from history, nations versus individuals, and conscious direction versus spontaneous solutions, and, above all, authoritarian versus free development.

PART THREE

The Blank Slate Versus Learning from History

The technocratic approach, and the Blank Slate in particular, both still dominate development today, as the following story illustrates.

On January 25, 2013, the *Wall Street Journal* published an article by one of America's most famous philanthropists with the tag line "My Plan to Fix the World's Biggest Problems."[1] Bill Gates, the funder of nearly everything and everybody in development, tends to get large-type headlines. He emphasizes technical solutions: "You can achieve amazing progress if you set a clear goal and find a measure that will drive progress toward that goal. Given a goal, you decide on what key variable you need to change to achieve it and develop a plan for change."

As an example, Gates noted recent progress on the tragic problem of child mortality in Ethiopia, "thanks in large part to a government goal to bring primary health care to all Ethiopian citizens." In 2000, the United Nations had announced a series of goals called the Millennium Development Goals to be reached by 2015. The Ethiopian government had signed on to these United Nations goals, Gates explained, one of which was the "goal of reducing child mortality by two-thirds" relative to a 1990 benchmark. This goal of two-thirds reduction "created a clear target for success or failure."

For Gates, a key turning point for the success of the Ethiopian goal-based approach had come when the government of Ethiopia, inspired by a community-health program in India, "launched its own program in 2004." The key was government response to "data from the field," which helped "government officials see where things are working and to take action in places where they aren't." Child mortality fell rapidly after that.

The data now indicate that the government has come close to meeting the goal of a two-thirds reduction in the child mortality rate (measured by deaths of children under the age of five for every 1,000 births). Back in 1990, Ethiopia's child mortality rate was 198. That is, in 1990, for every 1,000 Ethiopian children born, a tragically high number—198 children—would fail to reach their fifth birthday. By 2010, boosted by the rapid reduction after 2004, the child mortality rate was down to 81. The decrease in the child mortality rate from 1990 to 2010 is 59 percent; if mortality reduction continues at the rate attained from 2005 to 2010, the Ethiopian government will surpass its goal of a two-thirds reduction from 1990 by 2015. For Gates, the lesson to be learned from Ethiopia is that "setting clear goals, choosing an approach, measuring results, and then using those measurements to continually refine our approach—helps us to deliver tools and services to everybody who will benefit."

Ethiopia's recent mortality success is so striking that Gates is not the only one to celebrate it. Former British Prime Minister Tony Blair had placed a lot of emphasis on helping Africa develop during his time in office, helping orchestrate a large increase in aid to Africa at a G8 summit he hosted in 2005. After leaving office in 2007, Blair set up an organization called the Tony Blair Africa Governance Initiative (AGI), dedicated to helping African governments achieve development results.

In May 2013, the AGI produced a report called *The New Prosperity: Strategies for Improving Well-Being in Sub-Saharan Africa*.[2] One of the success stories of a goal-based approach was exactly the same as Gates': Ethiopia's recent improvements in child mortality. AGI shared Gates' admiration for how the Ethiopian government had begun "a concerted effort" to improve health in Ethiopia and had shown "strong, accountable leadership in implementing the plan." The report repeats such praises: "most striking" was how the Ethiopian government leadership had an "intense focus on executing the plan well." The report then cites the same improvements in mortality that impressed Gates: from 2005 to 2010, mortality rates for children under five fell 23 percent, which put Ethiopia on track to meet the Millennium Development Goal by 2015.

The story is inspiring: a dramatic reduction in the great human tragedy of child mortality. Maybe the technocratic emphasis on forceful action from above is correct after all. Neither Gates nor Blair noted that the Ethiopian government was an autocracy, which, among other things, denied food aid to its political opponents. But maybe Gates believes (and is possibly correct) that solutions in health are technical and politics is indeed irrelevant. Or maybe Gates and Blair were correct to just look away from individual rights until the most tragic problems of mortality and hunger were solved. Maybe it even does take autocrats to effect these reductions in tragedy, to get things done, to avoid democratic paralysis.

Yet Gates and Blair unintentionally reveal the key weaknesses of the Blank Slate approach in development. They base a big conclusion about the success of the technocratic approach on remarkably little data—five years of mortality improvements under a single government program in a single country. This is very little to go on relative to the decades, not to mention centuries, of efforts in every part of the world to combat the tragedy of child mortality.

The attachment to the Blank Slate is so strong that Gates and Blair disregard some well-known realities. A single short episode is even shakier evidence because of a boring but severe problem. Gates uses Ethiopia's five-year improvement in child-mortality rates as a precise measure of success—which is significant because child-mortality rates are notorious for their imprecise measurement. Measurement error in child mortality is so large that it swamps changes over a short period like five years.

The problem is that government-statistics offices in poor countries do not comprehensively record every birth and death in the country—the statisticians either cannot afford it or simply do not try hard enough. Even Gates acknowledges that "the government previously didn't have any official record of a child's birth or death in rural Ethiopia." Lacking vital records, child mortality is based on imprecise fragments of information, like surveys of mothers asking them to recall recent deaths of children and at what ages they died. Even if Gates's hopeful claim that the government "now tracks those metrics closely" were true, it would not solve the problem, because

1990 would still have been a hugely imprecise starting point for the precise goal of two-thirds reduction from 1990 to 2015.

In fact, the World Health Organization (WHO) that reported the child-mortality rate of 198 in 1990 also reported margins of error that place the actual rate somewhere between 179 and 209. In 2010, WHO similarly reported margins of error around the base estimate of 82, in which the child-mortality rate was somewhere between 65 and 93.

Another independent source doing its best to get a good number is the official UN site that monitors the Millennium Development Goals. The UN reported a 2010 Ethiopian child-mortality rate even above the WHO range of estimates: 106 deaths before age 5 for every 1,000 live births. The UN source estimated that the child-mortality reduction between 2005 and 2010 was only 13 percent, not the 24 percent celebrated by both Gates and Blair. If the UN numbers are correct, Ethiopia will fail to meet the Millennium Development Goal for child-mortality reduction by a large margin.

Although measurement error seems like a boring topic, it is actually quite revealing. The claim that the Ethiopian government is following a rigorously measured goal-driven approach on child mortality falls apart if the measurement is so far from rigorous. Gates's argument holds in reverse also—if you measure carefully what you care about, you are also careless about measuring what you don't care about. Gates could have been forgiven for not getting right all the boring details about margins of error, different methodologies for measuring the same thing, and lack of vital records—if only he were not espousing an approach that requires getting it exactly right.

Given that Gates is forcing us to think about tedious details like measurement error, it is nice to know there is a partial solution to measurement error—the longer the period, the more data you have and the more confident you can be of a trend. Measurement error can be either positive or negative, so it tends to average out over longer periods. The emphasis here is on "longer"—the more data you have, the more likely it is that measurement error averages out, and the greater the signal is relative to the noise of measurement error.

We have just seen that even twenty years of child-mortality data from 1990 to 2010 may not be long enough to get precise estimates of how much it decreased for purposes of measuring Ethiopian government performance relative to other governments or relative to an exact Millennium Development Goal. Twenty years could only support a vague conclusion like "child mortality in Ethiopia from 1990 to 2010 decreased a lot, as it did in many other diverse settings around the world as well." To compare performances of different types of government, like authoritarian technocrats versus free democrats, an ever longer assessment period is required. I have tortured you with these boring statistical details because it meets Gates on his own technocratic measurement ground. Gates's own desire for precise measurement should have caused him to look at the longer run for evidence of what works on child mortality.

The Gates Foundation and Ethiopia could be the modern-day equivalent of the Rockefeller Foundation and China in the 1920s and 1930s, and the ideas are very similar. Ethiopia is a Blank Slate upon which the experts are writing new technical solutions to solve poverty and its health consequences. We will return to the Ethiopia story shortly.

Fortunately, academic economists have been breaking free of the Blank Slate in their research over the past decade or so, tracing the history of individual freedom and its consequences for the world today. The next chapter discusses the formation of cultural values that underlay the rise of freedom and democracy; the following two chapters consider the accompanying institutions of oppression versus freedom. We will see that all three chapters bring long-run evidence to bear on the connections between autocracy and development, and autocracy and health improvements. There is no reason to be stuck with only five years of child-mortality data from one African country to discuss the momentous issue of authoritarian versus free development.

In Chapter Six in this section, we look behind the Blank Slate in the Old World history of autocracy versus freedom, collectivist versus individualist values, and their consequences for development. In Chapter Seven the story moves to the New World and Africa, and we explore the consequences of the slave trade and associated oppression on both sides of the Atlantic. Chapter Eight covers the happier history in the northernmost part of the New World with more individual rights for more people.

CHAPTER SIX

VALUES: THE LONG STRUGGLE FOR INDIVIDUAL RIGHTS

When economists lately began jettisoning the Blank Slate, turning from the recent short run to the long run, they went very long run indeed. Some have assessed centuries of economic data, finding, for example, that the emergence of individualist values that began at least as far back as the twelfth century has a direct bearing on prosperity today. We will start there and then bring the story of freedom in the Old World forward through the centuries.

THE EMPEROR VERSUS THE FREE CITIES

Holy Roman Emperor Frederick Barbarossa had been trying hard to assert his divine right of kingship in northern Italy since 1154. From his home in Germany he had come to Italy "not to receive as a suppliant the transient favors of an unruly people," he helpfully clarified, "but as a prince resolved to claim, if necessary by force of arms, the inheritance of his forbears."[3]

Arrayed against him was something new in European history—independent cities that recognized freedom for their citizens. Frederick's early attempts to conquer northern Italy showed the free cities what was at stake. When Frederick had laid siege to the tiny city of Crema in July 1159, he tied some Cremaschi prisoners to the siege machines to discourage return fire. Those were the lucky ones—Frederick had other prisoners chopped into pieces. After Crema capitulated in January 1160, he leveled the town.[4]

Two years later, Frederick laid siege to Milan. During the siege, he sent six prisoners of war into Milan to send a message. Five had been blinded; the sixth, left with eyesight to guide the others, had had his nose cut off.[5] Nonetheless, the Milanese resisted until famine compelled unconditional surrender on March 1, 1162. Barbarossa destroyed everything left standing—houses, churches, the old Roman walls, the cathedral and its campanile—brick by brick, dispersing the starving inhabitants to four different unfortified refugee camps. Frederick declared that Milan had ceased to exist. He stationed German troops around the Northern Italian countryside,[6] where they seized as much as two-thirds of the locals' food and raped local women with impunity.[7]

Yet the free cities kept bouncing back. As Frederick invaded northern Italy again in 1176, the free cities—including the rebuilt Milan and Crema—formed the Lombard League to repel the invader. Short on volunteers for his army, Frederick hired mercenary riff-raff with a reputation for brutality even by his own standards.[8]

Near the town of Legnano on May 29, 1176, the two armies stumbled into each other. Frederick's German knights at first routed the Lombard cavalry and infantry. Nine hundred Lombard foot soldiers (later known as the Company of Death) made a last stand, perhaps remembering how Frederick had treated prisoners in previous battles.

The battle that would help determine the future of individual rights turned on a random event—a lance hit Frederick himself, knocking him off his horse. The German troops thought Frederick was dead and retreated in panic. The free cities had won the battle. Frederick had actually survived. He stayed in hiding to evade capture and found his way back to his troops a few days later, but by then it was too late.[9] Neither Frederick nor his successors as Holy Roman Emperor would ever again attack the free cities of the Italian North. Over the succeeding centuries, individual freedom would take shape in these free cities in northern Italy and spread to other parts of Europe.

FROM TYRANNY TO RIGHTS IN EUROPE

It was going to be a long journey to get to individual rights. The starting point in Europe was not hopeful. As one classic study of the individual in the Middle Ages in Europe puts it: "the individual was no more than a recipient of orders, of commands, of the law, and as a layman, in particular, he was merely a passive spectator who was to obey."[10]

Medieval culture placed no value on the individual; it recognized no right for the individual to choose his (much less her) own path. The individual was just an anonymous part of whatever class he was born into. He could not move out of his class, which imposed on him rigid norms of behavior.

The person to be obeyed was the king, who ruled by divine right. Subjects could petition the king, but "a right to demand action or a duty on the part of the king to carry out the petitions of the people could by no means be constructed or was even asserted." The king had a duty to govern his people well, but "if he did not fulfill this duty of his, no power existed on earth to make him do it." On the other hand, those individuals who dared disobey the king's orders were guilty of high treason, which carried the death penalty.[11] The ruler was the de facto owner of all goods and property in his kingdom. The ruler had to cite some *justa causa* for expropriation of property, but the only one deciding whether the *causa* was *justa* was that same ruler.

THE EMERGENCE OF THE FREE CITIES

There is an old German saying—*Stadtluft macht frei* ("city air makes you free")—expressing a customary law of the Middle Ages, whereby a serf who fled to a city and resided there for a year and a day was liberated from further service to his feudal lord. Northern Italian cities started taking more steps toward freedom after the defeat of Frederick Barbarossa in 1176, taking advantage of the Holy Roman Empire's inability to exert control. A form of power emerged that was not yet democratic but that nonetheless was far from the divine right of hereditary monarchs.

In Genoa in the thirteenth and fourteenth centuries, for example, the *compagna* emerged as an alliance among the most prominent families of seafaring merchants to protect trade and enforce contracts. The ruling power in the city was the *consulate*, a rotating board of citizens in power for one year at a time, including heads of the main families. (The word *citizen* in fact appears in vernacular languages around this time meaning "denizen of a city.") Genoa evolved further into a formal assembly of elected members that allowed an even broader range of citizens to participate in government. The assembly's statutes applied equally to all citizens. By the twelfth century, the word *republic* (meaning "public thing") was often used to refer to these citizen-run city-states.[12]

Not all Italian cities were free. Inhabitants of cities that were still in the territory of an absolute ruler lacked the rights of free-city citizens. The Normans had invaded Italy south of Rome and established a monarchy over southern Italy between 1061 and 1091. Before the emergence of free cities, the Normans' Kingdom of Sicily was one of the richest parts of Europe.[13] Its capital Palermo was the largest city in Europe in 1200.

But the future belonged to the free cities. Population growth of free cities throughout Western Europe systematically outpaced that of cities under absolute rule. Freedom in a particular region led to the emergence of more new cities, as individuals accustomed to freedom in their original cities came together to form new cities. The statistical results indicate that, on average, a region developed two new cities (of population greater than 30,000) for every century that it had been free of absolute rule—and the already existing cities in free regions grew much more in population than those in unfree regions.[14]

We see this nowhere more clearly than in Italy itself. While the Italian North had escaped the Holy Roman Empire after 1176, the Italian South would remain under autocratic rule for another seven centuries. Barbarossa's son and successor as Holy Roman Emperor, Henry VI, would conquer the Kingdom of Sicily, succeeding in the South after his father had failed in the North. Henry VI entered Palermo, Sicily, in victory on November 20, 1194, celebrating with a final round of torture for those who had resisted.[15] The South would remain under one absolute monarch or another until Italian unification in 1870.

By 1330, Genoa had grown to twice the size of Palermo, even though the latter benefited from the royal patronage lavished on the capital. Elsewhere in the South, noncapital cities lost even more ground. Salerno had been the fourth largest city in Europe in 1050, and the sixteenth largest in 1200, tied with Genoa. After that, it never appeared again among the thirty largest cities in Europe, while Genoa remained. Today Genoa has four times the population of Salerno and is a lot richer.

The poverty of the Italian South compared to the North is well known. While there are certainly many variables at play, several convincing studies suggest a link to this differential history of absolute rule versus free cities. One study finds that even within the Italian North, those cities that were free at the time of Barbarossa's defeat in 1176—and kept their freedom because of that defeat—are richer today than those cities that were not free.[16] Why would the effects of 1176 last so long? And why do the free cities of 1176 have more organ donors today?

It's Not Personal, It's Business

To get more insight into both the nature of individualist values and why they persist, it helps to compare the Genoese to another twelfth-century group, the Maghribis. The Maghribis had collectivist values that stressed group interests over those of the individual. These values could serve a protective purpose in a lawless world, but collectivist values could not serve for long-run success.

Both groups would have great success in Mediterranean trade. The phrase *genuensis ergo Mercator* ("Genoese, therefore merchant") reflects just how famous the merchants of Genoa became. Since the trade was by sea, they also became pretty good sailors, as reflected in the career of a later Genoese named Cristoforo Colombo.

The Maghribis were Jews who had fled political upheaval in Baghdad and migrated to Tunisia early in the tenth century. Tunisia was part of a region then as now known as the Maghrib, covering northwest Africa. Tunisia was then the capital of the Fatimid Caliphate, but in 969 the Fatimids moved their capital to Cairo. The Jews who had migrated from Baghdad to the Maghrib now re-emigrated to Cairo, where they became known as Maghribis. They were a minority within the larger Jewish minority of Cairo. In the eleventh century, the Maghribis would take over trade throughout the Mediterranean.

The Stanford economic historian Avner Greif first brought the story of the Maghribis to economists' attention in a classic article in 1993, then elaborated their story much more in a 2006 book.[17] Greif documented something surprising. Maghribi merchants used long-distance agents for trade all over the Mediterranean. They advanced large sums of money to the agents to make purchases in distant ports. While they had no formal contracts, or means of enforcing such contracts, few of the agents ever absconded with the money.

Greif noted that in a system of collectivist values, the group could achieve contract enforcement amongst its members without formal laws. The minority Maghribis socialized mainly with each other. They could share information about each other's business, such as whether an agent had ever cheated them. They agreed that they would never hire an agent who had cheated any one of them. When, for example, in 1055, a Maghribi trader caught a Jerusalem-based agent named Abun ben Zedaka embezzling his money, the news spread quickly, and Maghribi traders as far away as Sicily canceled their agency relationships with the cheater.[18]

A Maghribi agent pondering cheating would have to weigh the short-term benefit of taking the money and running against the long-term cost of destroying the rest of his career with his fellow Maghribis. Since the Maghribis had one of the most profitable things going on in the eleventh century—Mediterranean-dominating trade—the agents almost never followed the path of Abun ben Zedaka. These arrangements persisted across generations, as Maghribis married only other Maghribis and sons took over their fathers' businesses (and inherited their blacklists of cheaters). The system motivated each Maghribi to invest further in relationships with other Maghribis to maintain fresh information on cheaters, thus reinforcing the segregation between Maghribis and the rest of society. The group exerted pressure on the individual Maghribis to conform to these norms.

The Genoese, by contrast, did not organize trade by social groups such as ethnic minorities or families. And so they could not count on social ostracism as a means of contract enforcement. Instead, Genoa developed a legal system and permanent courts to enforce contracts.

Each of the two systems had its advantages and costs. The Maghribi system required no investment in formal institutions such as society-wide legal codes and courts. The limitation of the system was that it restricted trades only to those involving Maghribis. The Genoese had to pay the costs of formal enforcement, but, once paid, they could engage in any trade with anyone. The Genoese could handle a large-scale expansion of trade; the small number of Maghribis could not.

The consequences show up in the subsequent histories of the two groups. If you are wondering why you have heard of the Genoese and not of the Maghribis, it is because the success of the latter was short-lived. The Maghribis had lost their hold on the Mediterranean trade by the end of the twelfth century, and they then disappeared back into the Jewish community. The thirteenth century in the Mediterranean belonged to Genoa; in 1314 Genoese trade value was forty-six times larger than it had been in 1160. The population of the city had more than tripled from the year 1200 to 1300, making Genoa the fourth-largest city in Europe.[19]

COLLECTIVIST VALUES

Behind the subtlety of contract-enforcement differences between Genoese and Maghribis is a not-so-subtle difference between individualist and collectivist values. The collectivist Maghribis succeeded by enforcing moral behavior within the group. This worked wonders for protecting group members from being victims of immoral behavior but it did nothing for non-Maghribis.

Under these values, a group member should not cheat fellow group members, but there were no restrictions on cheating outsiders. Everyone behaved according to the same principle, so only insiders could be trusted, not outsiders. In such circumstances, tolerance for different races, religions, or lifestyles was likely low, and outsiders were seldom entitled to the same treatment as the insiders of a given race or religion. In fact, it was acceptable and even expected to cheat or rob them. Obviously, the precept that "all men are created equal" was not widely shared.

The group rules with collectivist values. Membership in the group was involuntary; it was determined by birth. The group expected the individual to interact principally with other group members (including marriage within the group), to act in the interest of the group, and to behave in accordance with the dictates of the group, such as choice of occupation. Every Maghribi pressured every other Maghribi to conform. Group elders could pass binding judgments when there were disputes. The Maghribis' dominance of Mediterranean trade worked well because the group induced individual Maghribis to be Mediterranean traders and to interact with other Maghribis. The punishment for disobeying the group was ostracism. And ostracism by the group was a social death sentence, since the individual could not join other groups—who had their own strictures against outsiders.

It was different for the individualist Genoese, who created formal institutions that gave equal rights under their laws to all citizens. Citizenship was based not on family or ethnicity but just on residence in Genoa. There were also groups in Genoa but membership was more voluntary, and entry and exit were possible. Moral obligations were not as intense as those within the group in collectivist societies, yet moral norms did not distinguish so much between insiders and outsiders. The seed of the later Enlightenment breakthrough on individual rights was in such values.

There was no doubt which set of values autocrats preferred. Collectivist values made supreme the interests of the kingdom over which the autocrat ruled, and autocracy meant that the autocrat was the one who determined what was in the interests of the kingdom. The Maghribis were one among many groups subject to the autocratic Fatimid Caliphate in North Africa. They could prosper under the Caliph's protection—so long as they obeyed the Caliph. In the hierarchical obedience of collectivist autocracy, families had to obey fathers, fathers had to obey the leaders of their own ethnic groups, while the ethnic groups had to obey the autocrat.

As the Italian economist and culture researcher Guido Tabellini puts it: "Lack of trust and lack of respect for others are typical of hierarchical societies, where the individual is regarded as responding to instinct rather than reason, and where instinct often leads to a myopic or harmful course of action. In such societies, individualism is mistrusted and to be suppressed, since nothing good comes out of it: good behavior is deemed to result from coercion. Hence, the role of the state is to force citizens to behave well."[20]

The ultimate inside/outside distinction in autocratic societies was between those who were loyal subjects to the local tyrant and those who tried to assert their own rights. The autocrat might accomplish some good things for the former but had nothing but prison, torture, and execution for the latter. A despotic ruler could play on lack of trust and lack of respect for others by getting the insiders who supported him to spy on and betray the outsiders who might threaten his rule. An insider group loyal to the regime—usually benefiting from its patronage—would see nothing immoral in the repression of the rights of outsiders, whom they do not respect enough to see as deserving such rights. Conversely, trust and respect between groups would facilitate mutual recognition of rights that would facilitate the emergence of freedom, in which there would be checks on the power of government to abuse individuals of whatever group.

The emergence from autocracy toward freedom had happened in a few northern Italian cities. But freedom only had a future if it continued to spread.

FREEDOM MOVES TO THE ATLANTIC

The most famous son of Genoa, Christopher Columbus, would inadvertently make possible the spread of freedom. The boom in European trade after the discovery of the Americas gave freedom new strongholds 800 miles north of Genoa.

Economists Daron Acemoglu and Simon Johnson of MIT and political scientist James Robinson of Harvard have been recent pioneers in reintroducing historical research into economics, with the aim of explaining economic development. They follow earlier giants such as the economic historian of institutions and Nobel Laureate Douglass North. In a prominent 2005 article,[21] they tackled the question of why the frontiers of freedom had shifted from northern Italy to Western Europe in the seventeenth and eighteenth centuries. Looking at data on institutions, economic development, and access to the Atlantic, they discovered that the Atlantic trade was a key factor. The boom in trade with the American colonies caused changing values toward greater individual freedom in those nations with the best access to the Atlantic, especially in the United Kingdom and the Netherlands. The authors started with a purely geographic measure of how much each European country had access to the Atlantic—the amount of Atlantic coastline that each country had relative to its country area. But this identifies a much larger swath of Western Europe than the British and the Dutch. What else could be going on?

The other key insight is that the effect of the Atlantic trade on further institutional change depends on what values and institutions were already there. The key measure of both institutional change and previous institutions is whether the ruler has absolute power or is constrained by constitutional checks and balances. Unconstrained power is associated with collectivist values in which the group is always supreme. Individualist values, in which the individual has some minimum rights, goes with limits on what the ruler can do to individuals.

An important aside before proceeding: note that we have not yet reached the point in history that stresses one of the most famous checks on executive power, majority-vote elections. Such elections are effective checks in that they allow the population to kick out of office any ruler that they feel has abused them. We will reach that stage in the story below. One point to note for now is that the mechanical definition of political freedom as majority-vote elections is a much more recent phenomenon. It is problematic as a sufficient condition for political freedom. Although elections will certainly be important in the story of freedom, the importance of checks on state power continues to be relevant on its own even with elected governments.

Back to the story in the seventeenth and eighteenth centuries, there are now two dimensions—Atlantic access and freedom—that splits the European countries into four groups. Spain and Portugal had Atlantic trade access but they had absolutist institutions and values. Northern Italian cities had relatively free institutions and values but they did not have Atlantic access. Eastern Europe and Russia had neither Atlantic access nor free values. The winners were the United Kingdom and the Netherlands, which had Atlantic access and already had relatively free institutions and values by sometime in the 1600s.

The Dutch had finally triumphed in 1648 in their long rebellion against their former tyrants, the Spanish. The rebellion against the Spanish king had started with a declaration called the Act of Abjuration on July 26,

1581, that helped inspire the text of the American Declaration of Independence almost two centuries later. The Dutch declared that "God did not create the people slaves to their prince, to obey his commands, whether right or wrong, but rather the prince for the sake of the subjects." If this prince "does not behave thus," then "he is no longer a prince, but a tyrant" and the people may "disallow his authority." The Dutch rebels declared "this is what the law of nature dictates for the defense of liberty, which we ought to transmit to posterity, even at the hazard of our lives."[22]

Meanwhile, English liberty had advanced with the triumph of Parliament against the King in the English Civil War (1642–1651). It advanced again with the triumph of the Glorious Revolution in 1688 and the ensuing English Bill of Rights, which further limited the power of the crown and expanded the freedoms of speech and petition.[23]

First the Dutch and then the British economy boomed in the seventeenth and eighteenth centuries. Ports such as London, Amsterdam, and Glasgow flourished relative to other European cities between 1650 and 1800. (Glasgow would later produce Adam Smith, who would add a few more comments on the benefits of trade.) By 1800 the homes of the Atlantic traders became the most urbanized regions in the world by a large margin, compared to Eastern Europe and Asia, though they had begun with the same urbanization rate as Asia in 1600.

What is the theory of change? These authors suggest that commercial interests outside of the royal circle were able to demand checks on the power of the rulers. These restraints on power protected their property and profits from confiscation and ended royal blockages of freedom of entry into the trade. These changes were resisted by the existing economic elite that benefited from royal power, of course. However, profits convey political power. The profits from the Atlantic trade were enough for the new traders to carry the day over the old interests. Then, as we shall see below, free institutions create free values, and vice versa, for a virtuous feedback loop.

THE EFFECT OF AUTOCRACY ON VALUES

Autocracies perpetuate collectivist values; free cities and states perpetuate individualist values.

As many a rebel then and now has discovered at great personal cost, it is not that easy to be an individualist going your own way in an autocracy that can punish rebels with impunity. Those who care about you—above all, your own family—will beg you to conform to the collectivist laws and norms of the group to avoid a life of prison and torture, for you or themselves.

The family is a major vehicle by which values persist from one generation to the next. Parents learn in their own experience the costs and consequences of conformist versus individualist values. They then decide which values to pass on to their children. In an individualist society, where the children's individual initiative as an economic entrepreneur or political reformer will be rewarded, parents pass on individualist values. In a society where individual initiative, such as challenging the right of the autocrat to restrict political or economic activities, might result in social ostracism and a prison term, parents are not so enthusiastic about teaching individualist values. Autocracy induces parents to highlight obedience as the supreme virtue for their children. As academic culture researcher Guido Tabellini puts it, in autocratic societies "the role of parental education is to control the negative instincts of children, often through recourse to violence."[24]

So autocracy breeds collectivist values and collectivist values breed autocracy. Understanding this vicious circle helps us understand that the members of a society with collectivist values do not necessarily prefer these values. Individuals may prefer to assert their own rights but might have no hope of success when collectivist norms hold for everyone else.

This analysis predicts that collectivist values today will be associated with a history of autocracy. The same culture researcher, Guido Tabellini, has tested this prediction on a dataset of sixty-nine Western European regions.[25] Western Europe, like Italy, contains regions with very different histories of autocracy despite sharing many other long-run attributes (Christianity, geography, etc.). So this set of regions is a good laboratory to observe whether past autocracy promotes future collectivist values. And as it turns out, those regions with a history of autocracy have significantly lower values of trust and respect for others—a dimension of collectivist values that we began to explore above. As noted, when the group's interests are supreme, there is an insider/outsider distinction in which members behave well with regard to their own group but are free to cheat and abuse those outside the group. If everyone behaves this way, the average level of trust and respect will be low. And as we saw above, values of mistrust and lack of respect for others in turn facilitates autocratic rule. The insiders who support the regime and receive its patronage see nothing strange in the regime's brutal repression of outsiders whom the insiders do not respect anyway.

Further, the regions with collectivist values and autocratic history are still poorer today than those with individualist values and a more democratic history. The most notable examples are Portugal and Spain (except for Catalonia), and of course southern Italy once again. The most positive examples of individualist values, democratic history, and prosperity are the United Kingdom, the Netherlands, and northern Italy. (The cultural and income differences within Italy may also help explain why many of the values researchers are Italian.)

Another Tabellini study of the values of third-generation US immigrants offers further confirmation of the persistent role of autocratic history.[26] Those immigrants today whose country of origin was autocratic more than a century ago (taking 1850, 1875, and 1900 as base dates of comparison) have lower levels of trust and respect for others than immigrants from historically democratic countries. Even though the immigrants are in a new, democratic environment, the lessons of historical experience for different groups are slow to disappear.

And finally we get to the organ donors. Analyzing data only from within Italy, another set of Italian economists found that the twelfth-century history discussed above still matters for values today. Cities that were free in the twelfth century are more likely to have organ-donor associations today.[27]

Why focus on organ donations? Donating organs is a proxy for insider versus outsider values, because it reflects altruistic behavior toward perfect strangers somewhere else in Italy. The differential autocratic history of the South explains the big differences between northern and southern Italy in organ donations. But even more interesting, whether towns in northern Italy were or were not free cities at the time of the battle of Legnano in 1176 helps predict whether they have an organ-donor association today.

THE CONSOLIDATION OF DEMOCRACY

Once we realize that autocracy versus democracy affects values, and that values in turn determine whether a society will have autocracy or democracy, then the stage is set for a virtuous feedback loop between democracy and individualist values. One value that of course directly determines the prospects for democracy is whether people value democracy itself. Valuing democracy is associated with individualist values, which would prefer that the ruler obey the people rather than that the people obey the ruler.

Our story now finally arrives in the nineteenth and twentieth centuries, when another huge step forward for political freedom appears: majority-vote elections conducted with a broadly defined electorate. One study found that the longer a country today had been democratic in this sense over the previous two centuries, the stronger was the value placed on democracy.[28] This study suggested a concept of *democratic capital,* defined as the length of democratic experience, while weighting more recent experience more heavily.

Since national borders have shifted around a lot over that time, the country may not be such a clear-cut unit to study values and democratic experience (and values do not necessarily divide neatly at national borders anyway). So this study also added a measure of neighboring-country democratic capital as affecting the value that the citizens of a given country place on democracy.

This result suggests a virtuous circle between democracy and values that make it more likely democracy will persist the longer it has already persisted. A military coup is not a surprising event in a young democracy. It is unthinkable in a long-standing democracy like the United Kingdom. This study confirmed with the data that the likelihood of backsliding into autocracy falls continuously as democratic experience accumulates.

The study also suggested that the variable most relevant for testing the age-old question of how democracy affects development is not the current, possibly transient level of democracy, but long-run democratic capital. The investors and innovators that drive development respond to long-run, not short-run, conditions. If there is a high risk of an expropriating despot in your future, you hold back on investment and effort devoted to innovation. If your society has a lot of democratic capital that makes such a despot unlikely, you invest and innovate and your society prospers.

Of course, democratic majorities can also expropriate capital and inhibit investment, or even abuse minorities, a possible outcome we could call *majority tyranny*. This is another way in which democratic capital clarifies the debate. As noted earlier, political freedom is not only about majority-vote elections but also about checks on the power of government to abuse individuals. As democratic experience accumulates, it fosters individual norms as well as the valuing of democracy. Because of this growth of individualism, mature democracies tend to develop more protections for individuals against the threat of majority tyranny in democracy.

This study on democratic capital suggests two ways in which current discussions on democracy and development are wrong-headed. First, there is too much emphasis on majority voting as the mechanical definition of democracy; democracy is really more about unalienable rights and the consent of the governed than about mechanical procedures. Majority voting may be necessary for democracy, but it is certainly not sufficient.

Second, expectations for a new democracy after many years of autocratic rule are usually set too high. The problems of new democracies (such as those in the Arab world since the Arab Spring) are not the fault of the new democracy but of the long years of autocracy that preceded them.

The discussion so far has been limited to Europe and the Mediterranean basin. It is time to consider what is going on on the other side of the Eurasian continent.

ASIAN VALUES

Harry Lee was born in 1923 in Singapore. Although of Chinese origin, he was quite assimilated to British culture. English had been the family's first language for three generations, and Lee only started learning Chinese at age thirty-two for professional reasons. Lee studied at the elite

British-style prep school in Singapore, the Raffles Institution, and was later active in the Old Rafflesians' alumni association. He studied law at Cambridge, graduating with double first-class honors. In the 1960s, the British foreign secretary George Brown would say to him, "Harry, you're the best bloody Englishman east of Suez."[29]

Despite (or because of) his British roots, Lee later turned against Western values in favor of what he felt were Asian ones. He noted "Asia has never valued the individual over society." Instead, "in Asia," he said, the "individual is an ant." The individual does not exist as a separate entity, he only "exists in the context of his family." Society needs "discipline more than democracy." The latter produces "disorderly conditions."[30]

Lee's collectivist views would never have gotten much notice except for his political activities under the Chinese version of his name, Lee Kuan Yew. As Singapore's first prime minister for nearly thirty years, Lee was the long-time autocrat presiding over Singapore's economic miracle, Lee's argument that "Asian values" produced economic development therefore had a tremendous influence on the authoritarian consensus that still reigns supreme in development.

Suppose that Lee's generalizations about Asian values are mostly correct. We have described above how these values reflect a long history of autocracy. And the values are not necessarily "values"—what individuals left to themselves value—since a collectivist society traps its members in collectivist values. Furthermore, Lee follows familiar Blank Slate thinking when he considers the only relevant record on Asian values to be the rapid growth since 1960 under some East Asian autocrats like himself. If we do not start with a Blank Slate in 1960, but rather in 1820 or even 1500, then the long-run story of Asian values is not one of success but of failure. East Asia in 1500 was roughly similar to Western Europe in per capita GDP. In 1820, East Asia's average income relative to Europe was slipping but was still as much as half of Western Europe's, and not too different from poorer European countries like Greece or Finland. By 1960, East Asia was down to only one-seventh of Western Europe's average income. The difference between individualist and collectivist values is one of those great divides that help us understand how Europe pulled ahead and the rest of the Old World fell behind.

THE GREAT DIVERGENCE

Lee Kuan Yew was right about Asian values being collectivist and autocratic. Then Europe left Asia behind despite the latter's history of technological achievement. Of course, we should not dismiss the more recent rapid growth as evidence either. Interpreting that evidence is more complicated than it seems, and it will take an entire Chapter Thirteen on "Benevolent Autocrats" to sort it out.

Two different culture researchers cited earlier, Avner Greif and Guido Tabellini, joined forces on an article on the cultural and economic divergence between China and Europe.[31] It is partly a story of two different religions. Confucianism was based on moral obligations within the extended family. Christianity prohibited many practices that would have strengthened kinship groups—polygamy, concubines, cousin marriage, and forcing women into marriages without their consent. This is not to say that one religion is "better." We should think of the religious differences more as a historical accident, since the propagators of religious rules did not choose them because some "were better for development." In the long run, Chinese society remained based on kinship clans, while free cities transformed Europe.

Chinese clans enforced contracts (and to some extent still do) much like the Maghribis did. Cheating a fellow clan member could cost the loss of future business and social ostracism. No such penalties applied to cheating members of other clans, so Chinese values had the classic insider/outsider distinction on moral behavior. Trading was done by clan and regional merchant groups that were able to conduct long-distance trade with agents from the clan who did not dare cheat the clan.

Just as with the Maghribis, the clan's ability to enforce contracts is a success on one level in making trade possible when no formal institutions are available. But on another level, the reliance on enforcement inside the clan retarded the development of formal laws and institutions that would have made available a much greater scope of trade—such as between clans. As Greif and Tabellini say, "a legal system would have undermined the clans, an outcome opposed by the elders who controlled the clans and the state that used them."[32] China did not institute a commercial legal code until the empire was collapsing in the late nineteenth century.

Cities in China were held back by the lack of cooperation between clans. Clans were responsible for tax collection and educating their members for civil-service exams. Immigrants to the cities remained loyal to their rural-based clans; they did not transfer loyalty to the city. As one scholar says of China in the seventeenth century: "the majority of a city's population consisted of so-called sojourners, people who had come from elsewhere and were considered (and thought of themselves as) only temporary residents." As a result, "suspicions were always rife that sojourners could not be trusted."[33] There was no such thing as city self-government in China as there was in the free cities in Europe. The percent of the population living in cities in China remained at only about 3 to 4 percent long after Europe had passed 10 percent early in the Industrial Revolution.

Chinese family-firms remain an important form of enterprise in China today. As another scholar wrote about modern China: "you trust your family absolutely, your friends and acquaintances to the degree that mutual dependence has been established. With everybody else you make no assumptions about their good will."[34]

We have some data on cultural values today from the World Values Survey.[35] We can see the insider/outsider distinction on trust, using China and Great Britain from the 2005 Survey for comparison (Figure 6.1). If behaving amorally outside the family is acceptable, as in China, the expectation is that everyone will act accordingly, and anyone outside the family is then not to be trusted, not even "somewhat." More generalized moral behavior in Europe, using Great Britain as an example, supports more willingness to trust other religious groups and other nationalities, including strangers.

As we cannot stress often enough, trust and respect for others affects political freedom as well as the potential for trade and contract enforcement. Trusting and respecting other groups leads to widespread support of rights for all groups, which translates into support for checks on the power of the ruler to abuse individuals from any group.

Individualism is so fundamental in free societies that we don't often consciously reflect on it. For the rest of the world, it is difficult to boil down individualistic values to a single survey question that will translate

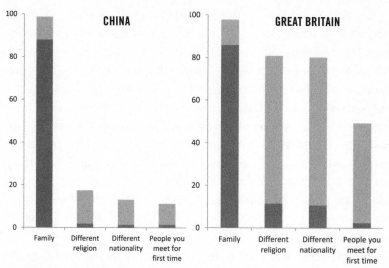

FIGURE 6.1   Percent saying they trust different groups "completely" (black) or "somewhat" (gray) in China and Great Britain.
(Prepared using 2005 data from World Values Survey.)[36]

across cultures. It is so difficult that most global surveys do not even try. We are stuck with some very indirect measures of individualism.

Berkeley researchers Yuriy Gorodnichenko and Gerard Roland have used a survey measure of individualist values that a Dutch researcher named Geert Hofstede originally applied to IBM employees around the world and that has since been validated in broader samples. As they describe it:

the individualism score measures that individuals are supposed to take care of themselves as opposed to being strongly integrated and loyal to a cohesive group. Individuals in countries with a high level of the index value personal freedom and status, while individuals in countries with a low level of the index value harmony and conformity.[The measure reflects] positively on valuing individual freedom, opportunity, achievement, advancement, recognition and negatively on valuing harmony, cooperation, relations with superiors.[37]

We also have available the democratic-capital measure previously discussed, so we can now verify across countries that democratic capital is strongly associated with individualism.

Countries in the bottom third across the world's countries on both individualism and democratic capital include China, Indonesia, Malaysia, Singapore, and Vietnam. The Arab countries today are low on individualism scores but not as low as East Asia. Only regional estimates are available for East Africa and West Africa, but they are both very low on both individualism and democratic capital. Countries in the top third on both individualism and democratic capital include Belgium, Canada, Denmark, France, Germany, Ireland, Italy, Netherlands, Norway, Sweden, Switzerland, United Kingdom, and the United States. Latin America is in between on both individualism and democratic capital.

We have seen here a broad outline of how Europe diverged from the Arab World and East Asia on both freedom and development. Later (in Chapters Seven and Eight) we will also see how Africa, Latin America, and North America wound up in their respective positions on scales of freedom and development.

How Individual Rights Solve Problems

Individual rights are an end in themselves for those with individualist values. Yet of course we are also interested in the practical consequences of individual rights. Can they solve problems as well as an autocrat advised by technocrats?

The technocratic approach pictures a government getting feedback from its appointed representatives. These will communicate to the central authorities what the problems are and how best to solve them, and then the government will solve them. There is both a knowledge problem and an incentive problem with this solution.

Knowledge, of course, is a complex thing, as we learned when we discussed Hayek's ideas about knowledge in Chapter Two. Knowledge is often localized, making it accessible only to neighborhood insiders. Knowledge also is often tacit, in that an individual has difficulty explaining how she or he is able to do something learned by practice. The ease of getting accurate knowledge even on things that seem objectively measurable has been much exaggerated, as we saw with the case of child mortality in Ethiopia in the introduction to Part Three.

There is also an incentive problem: even if the autocratic government has accurate centralized information, is it motivated to solve the problem? It is hard to say what motivates an autocratic government that can act with relative impunity.

A system based on individual rights offers some solution to the knowledge and incentive problems. The individual best informed about how something will affect the individual is usually the individual. Under individual rights that include free speech, a free press, and consent of the governed in the government, individuals will protest any harm the government does to them. They will vote the rascals out of office.

Once again, it is important to go to neither extreme—neither dismissing elections nor making them the only thing that matters. Voting is often overrated because it is not a sufficient condition for individual rights, but it does create the currency of public support or opposition that tends to make politicians listen to complaints. The best way to ensure that the government does no harm is to give individuals the right to protest and to punish those government officials who do harm to them. On the positive side, they will vote to reward officials who do good things for them, like offering public-health services that reduce child mortality.

WHAT DO POOR PEOPLE REALLY WANT?

This chapter has discussed how the group can coerce the individual into autocratic values in an autocratic setting. The evidence confirms that autocratic values are associated with a long history of autocracy.

Values may then be a misnomer, especially under an autocracy, because the ideals expressed by citizens in an authoritarian regime may reflect social norms enforced by the social group or by the state, rather than what individuals really value. Not many defenders of authoritarianism will argue that people coerced into autocratic values by a long history of autocracy yearn for yet more coercion.

But nor should it be open season for those who value individual rights to project those values on everyone else. There is no easy way to observe directly how much different groups of poor people do value individual rights. As noted above, most systematic international surveys do not try. One method that does not meet hard-evidence standards but that is at least suggestive is to carry out a large number of interviews with individuals and groups in different settings and then summarize oft-heard themes. Deepa Narayan, Lant Pritchett, and Soumya Kapoor did this based on 2,000 group discussions and 9,000 household interviews in fifteen countries in Asia, Latin America, and Africa.[38]

Their work provides some themes. Some interviewees spoke of how much they valued what is usually called economic freedom, the checks on government from interfering with the economic activities of individuals. Others spoke of their desire for what would be called political freedom, the restraints on government from suppressing political activities (which themselves act as restraints on government abuses of individuals). But most of the people surveyed do not make distinctions between political and economic freedom. The general picture is that poor people (like rich people) do not like being told what to do; they like to make their own choices. Poor people (like rich people) do not like being told to shut up; they like to speak up to protest any government abuses of them.

The study collected a trove of evocative quotes. On economic freedom, a group of Indonesian men spoke of "freedom of selling, freedom of getting a loan from banks, and freedom to be fishermen and teachers." Similar definitions of freedom are that it means no "interference in whom one transacts with and where" (Tanzania), and "to transact in the market without bureaucratic harassment" (Malawi).[39]

On political freedom, an Afghan farmer said freedom means "one can freely give their opinions." A Filipino group included "the right to vote" but also "the right to protest the laws or policies." A group of men in Morocco said "the judge must not receive telephone calls that dictate to him" and "the oppressor must be judged, and the innocent must be acquitted. There must be liberty of speech." A group of young men in Andhra Pradesh, India, defined democracy as when "people of different castes and religions are treated equally."[40] A group in Cambodia says "freedom means we dare to talk. We have rights to express our opinion on what is right and what is wrong."[41]

Other sentiments do not distinguish between political and economic freedom. Another Filipino woman, Cory, aged forty-two, says freedom is "to live the kind of life you want." A group discussion in Morocco concurs it is the "the choice to decide what we need." To an Indian man in West Bengal, it is "to protest against injustice," to another it is "dignity and respect." To a group of Tanzanian woman, "to be free is to move, to travel, without restrictions."

A Filipino woman named Vanyen describes the absence of freedom as "being controlled from doing what you want because somebody had already set a plan." A man in Tanzania gets more specific: "A local guard came in my home and commanded me to go and transport bricks on my head in order to build a school. Am I not a slave in my own community and country?"[42]

As already mentioned, this survey does not meet the standards of hard evidence (which does not exist on the autocracy-versus-freedom issue either way). The survey does provide a rare opportunity for poor people to speak for themselves. The authors of the survey found a lot of poor people who contradicted the common assumption that poor people don't care about their rights and care only about their material needs.

EVIDENCE AND DEBATE

The patterns discussed here do not *prove* that autocracy and collectivist values cause poverty—correlation is not causation. It could be that people who get rich for some other reason desire more individualism and democracy and are able to get it. Some studies cited here use some formal statistical methods to argue that a history of autocracy *causes* collectivist values, and both autocracy and collectivist values in turn *cause* poverty, but most economists find the methods used not very convincing.

Some who favor technocratic approaches disqualify any discussion of rights because the evidence for positive consequences of rights is not rigorous enough. Some of the individual pieces of the technocratic approach do claim rigorous evidence for "what works," such as evidence that, say, deworming drugs cause a drop in worm infection among children and an increase in the children's school attendance.

Yet refusing to discuss the bigger picture on individual rights just hands the victory by default to the technocratic approach that overlooks or endorses autocrats. All of us make choices for or against the rights view, and the absence of meeting an absolute standard of "rigorous" evidence will not stop those choices.

Those who argued for autocracy in development did not see autocracy as desirable in itself. They argued pragmatically that autocrats would deliver more development than free individuals. Since they argue for giving up something that they agree is valuable—individual freedom—for a material payoff, the burden of proof is on the autocratic pragmatists to demonstrate evidence for such a payoff.

Even if there is no evidence sufficiently rigorous to meet an *absolute* standard of proof for either the technocratic/autocratic or the individualist positions on development, let's at least consider the *relative* weight of the evidence on each side to see if it supports the view that autocrats deliver more development. In light of what we discussed in this chapter, once we looked beneath the Blank Slate, it's hard to argue that the relative weight of evidence is stronger for autocracy than for freedom. We have seen the story of historical success in development is a story of ever-growing freedom and individualist values. At the center of the story are checks on the power of the government to abuse individual rights, precisely the factor ignored in technocratic development discussions today that wind up legitimizing autocrats.

In light of what we discussed in this chapter, it is hard to justify the dismissal of history at the beginning of official development in 1949. It is hard to justify the practices of economists like Gunnar Myrdal that start from scratch on the Blank Slate of an artificially created Third World. It is hard to justify the disqualification of the First World—the countries that actually did develop—as guides to development in the Third World.

The legacy persists to the present, a legacy of failure to challenge the technocratic illusion that would capture Bill Gates and Tony Blair. We will have more to say about autocracy and public health in the next two chapters.

Escape Whenever You Can

The findings on autocracy having a lasting effect suggest one simple lesson: get out of the vicious circle of autocracy and bad values as soon as you can! The sooner you begin the virtuous circle of democracy and good values, and the sooner you get through the rocky transition, the better.

Meles Zenawi, Ethiopia's autocratic ruler, was not explicitly mentioned in the stories of Gates and Blair that began this chapter. Yet Meles was Ethiopia's dictator from 1991 until August 20, 2012, when he died of natural causes. It turns out that the Ethiopia that entranced Gates and Blair in the new millennium had just lost an important opportunity during Meles's regime. In 2005, democracy had come close to winning, but the development-aid-supported autocracy of Meles Zenawi had violently repressed the movement. Gates was not directly involved, but Tony Blair was not so innocent. We turn to that story in the next chapter by way of introducing the deeper roots of autocracy in Africa, in which we will also examine the divergent outcomes across the Atlantic in North and South America.

CHAPTER SEVEN

INSTITUTIONS:
WE OPPRESS THEM IF WE CAN

According to the technocratic view, bad government is itself a problem amenable to technical solutions. According to Tony Blair's African Governance Initiative, for example, governments are "unable to effectively design and implement programmes" because "they lack capacity to use outside assistance wisely and be partners in development." The problem is that "the capacity to implement—to translate vision into results on the ground—is weak."[1]

The AGI's response is designed accordingly: its goal is "strengthening the government's capacity to deliver programmes." The AGI web site explains "To do this we focus on three fundamental delivery processes, the three P's of: Prioritisation, Planning, and Performance management."[2] The "we" apparently refers to experts deployed by the AGI. If experts can fix the problem of bad government, that implies the cause of bad government is at least partly a shortage of such expertise.

Another view of bad government—also known as oppressive institutions—is that wherever people lack rights, and when oppression pays off for the rulers, the rulers will oppress their subjects. Unchecked power is abusive power. However, when the majority of the people are in a position to assert their rights, the government will not oppress them. According to this alternative view, bad government suffers from a shortage of rights, not a shortage of experts. We start first with more information on the current Ethiopia story and then review the long run of historical evidence, again contradicting the Blank Slate.

MORE INSIGHT FROM ETHIOPIA

Another look at the recent experience in Ethiopia praised by Tony Blair sheds more light on this debate.

We saw in the previous chapter how Tony Blair joined Bill Gates in praising Ethiopia's government for its progress on health in 2013. Blair already had a history with Ethiopia's autocratic ruler Meles Zenawi, in power since 1991. In 2005, while he was prime minister of the United Kingdom, Blair appointed Meles Zenawi to his Commission for Africa that was to explain how to use foreign aid to Africa that was surging at the time. This allowed Meles to coauthor a report praising himself with sentences such as how "more and better aid can support positive changes" as demonstrated by "recent advances" in a small number of successes that included "Ethiopia."[3] The Commission Report devoted a special annex to the success of aid in Ethiopia: "progress has been encouraging," "social progress in Ethiopia has been good," and "authorities have worked hard in producing a robust poverty reduction strategy." The donors could do even more "to support the government programmatically in implement-ing its poverty reduction strategy," and "it would be realistic to double aid to Ethiopia over the next five years."[4] The idea of a benevolent auto-crat implementing expert advice to achieve great results in Ethiopia was already in place in 2005, to be echoed in 2013 by Gates and Blair. But Meles was about to demonstrate the weak spot of the benevolent autocrat idea—a ruler with no checks on his powers is likely to abuse individual rights. That issue will be the main point of this chapter.

In 2005, Meles agreed to hold general elections in Ethiopia, hoping to burnish his international stature. Meles may have believed his popularity was sufficient for him to win a free election. Instead, discontent with Me-les was so great that the election gave the opposition surprising victories. Ethiopian economist Berhanu Nega was elected mayor of Addis Ababa for the opposition, and the opposition may have won overall. In response, Meles manipulated the vote count (according to many international and impartial observers) to produce a victory for his own party. When student demonstrators took to the streets to protest, Meles's security forces opened fire, resulting in more than 100 deaths. Meles put Berhanu Nega in jail.

The major aid donors to Ethiopia were then and still are the British Department for International Development (DFID), the US Agency for International Development (USAID), and the World Bank. Tony Blair and George W. Bush may really have believed they were supporting an autocrat promoting development. But, like historic examples of backing autocrats for foreign-policy reasons, it was also politically convenient for the United States and the United Kingdom to support Meles Zenawi as a reliable ally in the War on Terror; Ethiopia was a Christian nation in a sea of Islam.

The aid donors had to respond to the public embarrassment of supporting a ruler who shot down demonstrators and jailed the opposition. The donors made some cosmetic changes—they would direct the aid to local governments rather than to the discredited national government. However, this tactic overlooked the reality obvious to everyone—that the national government controlled the local governments. Tony Blair himself oversaw this policy as he was prime minister until June 2007. Aid was eventually redirected back to unrestricted transfers to the budget of the national government.

Despite the British and American foreign-aid support for his benevolent autocracy, Meles kept offering new object lessons in how autocrats abuse rights, even using the aid funds to do so. On October 19, 2010, Human Rights Watch (HRW) had released a report titled *Development Without Freedom*.[5] An HRW investigation had found that Meles Zenawi was using donor funds to blackmail starving peasants into supporting the regime and punishing opposition supporters by withholding donor-financed food relief.

The report included anonymous quotes from donor officials working in Ethiopia: ""Every tool at their disposal—fertilizer, loans, safety net [welfare payments that include food relief]—is being used to crush the opposition. We know this." "It is clear that our money is being moved into political brainwashing." A World Bank staff member in Addis Ababa wondered "Which state are we building and how? It could be that we are building the capacity of the state to control and repress."[6] A 2009 secret US cable uncovered by Wikileaks also said that the official donors to Meles were "keenly aware that foreign assistance . . . is vulnerable to politicization."[7]

Publicly, however, a spokesman for the group of leading official donors said that, in their own research, they had not found "any evidence of systematic or widespread distortion."[8] The embarrassment of the HRW report in October 2010 induced these aid agencies to promise a field study to investigate the charges. But the same donors then informed HRW in April 2011 that they had canceled the field study, though they did not feel obligated to offer any explanation why.[9] Perhaps they felt the public pressure was off, as there was little public outcry in the US and UK development communities in response. Yet it was a challenge for the donors to keep relying on the public's forgetfulness as Meles kept coming up with new abuses. In September 2012, a courageous Ethiopian farmer, known in court documents as Mr. O (his real identity is a secret for his protection), started legal action against British aid for its support of the Ethiopian government's "villagization" program, which had begun in 2010 in the remote region of Gambella close to Sudan. This program intends to relocate 1.5 million families from their own lands to new "model villages" created by the government that are supposed to be closer to roads and so to access to government services. The government is selling lands in the same region to foreign investors. The government claims the migration is voluntary, and that the villagization program is not related to land sales to investors.

The *Guardian* newspaper and Human Rights Watch have found evidence to the contrary from interviewing villagers in Gambella. Villagers as well as former local government officials report the government took the villagers' lands without their consent and leased those same lands to foreign investors, an echo of the Uganda story that began this book.

Mr. O says that soldiers evicted him at gunpoint from his own farm in the Gambella region, where he also witnessed the soldiers' assault against villagers who resisted. A blind villager named Peter, interviewed by the *Guardian*, says he asked for consideration due to his disability. Instead, soldiers beat him and raped his wife. Mr. O said that the village to which he had been moved was far from improved access to such essential services as land, water, and food. Like many other intended beneficiaries of villagization, Mr. O and Peter wound up fleeing to a refugee camp in Kenya.[10]

This is the political backdrop to the statements by Gates and Blair in 2013 about the positive achievements of Ethiopia's regime, amidst a continuing flood of aid for Ethiopia's government from the United Kingdom that began under Blair's leadership and continues under his successors.

Not even shooting and jailing the opposition, manipulating aid to starve the opposition, seizing the lands of villagers and relocating them against their will, and perpetrating violence against villagers who protested has been enough to shake the technocratic faith that autocrats can be trusted to be benevolent implementers of technical solutions.

THE COST OF OPPRESSION

Oppression has broad consequences that hold back development. It promotes a lack of trust that inhibits trade and facilitates more oppression. It entrenches a hereditary political and economic elite that blocks the creative destruction necessary for development. Oppressive rulers underinvest in public goods for the majority. This last point will bear on the question raised by the contemporary Ethiopia story on whether autocrats are usually good for reducing child mortality.

Of course, the abuses of the Meles regime constitute a very small body of evidence, just as its good performance on child mortality over a few years did in the previous chapter. I need to follow my own admonition to broaden the evidence to include the long record of history. This chapter again discards the Blank Slate to review recent economists' historical studies on these alternative views, going back to the slave trade and European settlement of the New World. It introduces a new factor into the long-run story of oppression: geography. We will see when and where geography made oppression likely to happen. By comparing places with different histories of oppression due to geographic accidents, we get new evidence on the long-run consequences of oppression. This comparative analysis takes us to stories in Colombia and Benin in this chapter, and to New York City and the United States in the next chapter. We begin on the coast of Benin in the 1600s.

THE AJA

The Aja people of West Africa are a good case study of the geography of oppression, because few peoples have ever had a location so unlucky as the Aja.

Located in what is today's Benin, Togo, and Nigeria, the Aja lived in the part of Africa closest to the bulge of Brazil that reaches eastward deep into the Atlantic. The width of the Atlantic was smallest between Brazil and that part of West Africa, only about 1800 miles. The northeast of Brazil near the bulge was a prime slave market beginning in the 1580s. The later slave markets in the Dutch, British, and French Guianas (today's Suriname, Guyana, and French Guiana, respectively) are just above the Brazilian bulge.

Not far north of Suriname, Guyana, and French Guiana begins the chain of Caribbean islands known as the Lesser Antilles, including Barbados, Martinique, and Guadeloupe, also major slave markets. As a certain Italian sailor discovered by accident after 1492, the currents and prevailing winds make the Lesser Antilles the western terminus of one of the fastest routes across the Atlantic. Columbus's second, third, and fourth voyages all first went south along the African coast, then turned west to arrive in the New World at the Lesser Antilles. Even the winds were against the Aja.

What turned all of these parts of the New World into slave markets in the 1600s and 1700s was a crop native to India: sugar cane. The European demand for sugar was exploding at the same time in the seventeenth and eighteenth centuries as a sweetener for two other recently discovered consumer products: tea and coffee. Sugar cane would become the dominant crop of northeast Brazil, the Guianas, and the Caribbean, which all had near-perfect ecological conditions for it.

Sugar cane and slavery went together. Sugar plantations, run by the French, Dutch, British, and Portuguese, had to be large to cover the cost of the cane-processing mills. The plantations required just one (European) manager but a lot of workers. The regions' indigenous people were dying off from European diseases and so were unavailable to handle the brutal labor of harvesting sugar cane. European migrants to the New World did not want to work on sugar plantations when they had better options of owning their own family farms on the unoccupied land elsewhere in the Americas. The Portuguese, Dutch, British, and French plantation owners' solution to their labor problem, then, was to buy slaves from West Africa, among them the Aja. The multinational group of European traders who supplied the slaves were also Portuguese, Dutch, British, and French. The places in the New World that were based on European oppression of slaves would have very different long-run outcomes than those based on European family farms, as we will explore more below and in the next chapter.

The Aja lived close to the coast and close to African kingdoms that captured slaves and sold them to Europeans, specifically the kingdoms of Dahomey and Oyo. While we usually might think of the slave trade as the product of evil Europeans, it was also the product of evil Africans. The profits of the sugar boom brought out the worst in everyone, splitting West Africans into victims and victimizers. The kingdoms of Dahomey and Oyo grew rich on their sales of slaves, which enabled them to buy ever more guns, which enabled them to seize more slaves.

The unlucky Aja entered slavery in two main ways: the African kingdoms would either take them prisoner during wars or kidnap them while working in the fields. Sometimes even the Aja victims' own relatives would sell them into slavery to pay a debt, to settle a score, or simply to buy enough food to survive. The stretch of the West African coast around where the Aja lived would appear on European maps of Africa for several centuries as "the Slave Coast." The Aja alone, although not a very large group, accounted for one out of every twelve slaves that crossed the Atlantic. By 1800, the Aja population still in Africa was half what it had been in the 1680s.[11] Their experience was going to be emblematic of the disastrous long-run consequences of the slave trade in Africa.

SLAVES OR CONSEQUENCES

Leonard Wantchekon is a Princeton political scientist from Benin, the country where the Aja live today. Wantchekon left Benin to get graduate training in economics but returns to Benin frequently now for his research. He has established a sterling reputation as a researcher on African politics and economics. But his experience with oppression in Benin is also deeply personal, as we will see.

In December 2011, Wantchekon published a study with Harvard economist Nathan Nunn on the consequences of the slave trade in Africa.[12] A survey called the Afrobarometer questions households throughout Africa about their lives and values. One of the questions asks how much respondents trust other people, both inside and outside their own ethnic group. That question would reveal a great deal about the consequences of the slave trade for the kind of values that we have already seen prevent prosperity through trade and instead facilitate autocracy and oppression.

Although the victimization of the Aja was mostly over by 1800, the Aja turn out to have long memories. They scored exceptionally low values of trust today toward other ethnic groups and even toward their fellow Aja. It was as if the Aja could still remember how their fellow Africans and even their fellow Aja had betrayed them centuries earlier, slipping over the backyard fence one morning and kidnapping a beloved son who was never to be seen again.

Nunn and Wantchekon statistically confirmed across a large group of households comprising many different ethnic groups that members of those groups that had had the most slaves captured had lower levels of trust than did members of those groups that escaped the slavers. As the previous chapter discussed, trust is very important for both long-run prosperity and freedom. Asia had the kind of collectivist values in which people trusted only their own kin group, which limited the scope for trade so necessary for development. In contrast, the more widespread trust of European individualistic values allowed widespread trade. Yet Asia could at least benefit from effective contract enforcement and trade based on clans and family firms. This part of Africa did not even have that much of a development foundation to build on, since the slave trade had destroyed people's trust even in their own kin groups. As I once heard Wantchekon say in a talk: "if you don't even trust your own family, it's over."

We also saw in the previous chapter how lack of trust and respect for others weakens support for individual rights and opens the door to the unchecked power of autocrats to abuse individuals. Insiders who support and receive patronage from an autocratic regime see nothing strange in the rights violations of outsiders they do not respect anyway. And we also saw already what we see more evidence for here: a history of autocracy and violence breeds more lack of trust.

The slave trade's disastrous effects help explain a result that Nathan Nunn had already found in his doctoral dissertation—that among today's

African nations, those where Europeans had seized the most slaves were poorer than nations that had largely escaped slavery. Benin today is one of the poorest African nations.[13]

EVIDENCE WITH A CAUSE

But once again correlation is not causation. It is plausible that the correlation could also run in reverse: poverty caused enslavement. Poorer people are less able to defend themselves because they cannot afford as many weapons as richer people. Also pre-existing lack of trust could have caused more enslavement. People who were already less trusting and less trustworthy are more likely to help the slavers by betraying their neighbors.

Nunn and Wantchekon's research used the unlucky location of the Aja to address these concerns. Compare the Aja to another, similar group that differed from the Aja chiefly in escaping the slavers because they were farther inland, and farther from Brazil as well. That comparison is in effect an experiment of history in which only geography (that is, the good and bad geographic luck of the peoples being compared) is allowed to vary. If significant differences in poverty/trust outcomes are noted, they are then most likely due to the variation of geography, thus helping eliminate the possible reverse link between poverty/trust and slavery. That is, if the geographically lucky, less-enslaved people are systematically more trusting than the geographically unlucky, more-enslaved people (as it turns out they are in this study), then we can more confidently assert that slavery caused lack of trust, rather than the other way round.

For example, the Soninke people of interior West Africa (along the borders where today's Senegal, Mali, and Mauritania meet) are far away from the coast, and they thus avoided widespread slavery. The Soninke today exhibit much higher levels of trust than the Aja. The Soninke also appear to have long benefited from their high (slavery-free) trust levels— they are one of the great merchant peoples of West Africa, mostly dominating the diamond trade, for example.

I stumbled across the Soninke on one of my first World Bank trips as a young economist in 1985, to The Gambia, a tiny strip of a country, lining both banks of the Gambia River, and entirely surrounded by Senegal except for its short Atlantic coast at the mouth of the river. In The Gambia, the Soninke are known as Serahule, and even an ethnically clueless economist like me quickly discovered that they dominated most of the business in the Gambia. Invoking the usual stereotype, they were called "the Jews of the Gambia." I interviewed an illiterate businessman who was one of the richest men in the country, owning about ten houses (he had lost count) in the capital of Banjul. Again, trust and merchants go together within ethnic groups. There are many merchant tribes scattered across Africa that have internally solved the trust problem.

History ran the same experiment on entire countries that were farther away from slave destinations compared to those that were close. Landlocked Botswana in southern Africa was much farther away than Benin and it is more than three times richer than Benin. Today's Democratic Republic of the Congo was much closer to slave markets across the Atlantic in Brazil, and today is in bad shape. Again it turns out that these comparisons between the lucky and unlucky in slave world geography hold systematically, suggesting that slavery did play a significant role in causing poverty.

Back on the Slave Coast of West Africa, the big winners were powerful slave-trading states that could import more guns from the slave trade and then become even more powerful. The West African slave states such as Dahomey (whose capital was Abomey), and Oyo imported about 180,000 guns a year by 1730, which rose to around 300,000 to 400,000 by the early 1800s. Such force made these states more absolutist, with fewer checks and balances that had traditionally existed, such as councils of elders. These states would make war just to capture slaves.[14] Not even the termination of the international slave trade ended predation by these states. The king of Dahomey shifted from slave exports to exporting palm oil through the old slave trade ports of Whydah and Porto Novo. He found the workers for his palm-oil plantations among domestic slaves.

Lord Hailey and other European creators of the development idea in Africa assumed a Blank Slate and then went on to promote the colonial state as a benevolent autocrat (see Chapter Four). But they were obscuring how the history of their own countries' slave trading had directly violated rights and indirectly strengthened slave kingdoms in Africa, and destroyed trust within the victimized groups, all of which contributed to African underdevelopment.

Two countries that have already appeared in our narrative were also prominent victims of the slave trade. The coastal Akan and Ewe peoples in Ghana suffered from the same locational disadvantages as the Aja in Benin. (The Ewe are also linguistically related to the Aja.) They also became principal targets of slave raiders and traders. The Ashanti Empire in the interior of Ghana in the 1700s and 1800s had conquered and extracted tribute from the coastal Akan peoples and the Ewe and had exported Akan and Ewe slaves to the Europeans. Ghana had Africa's single highest rate of slave exports per square kilometer of land area.

Mistrust and lack of respect between ethnic groups facilitated continued autocracy, even if the same ethnic group did not stay in power. After independence, Ghanaian autocrats tended to assemble anti-Ashanti coalitions from the coastal Akan people (to which Kwame Nkrumah belonged) and the Ewe and to repress the Ashanti-based opposition. Even oppressive economic policies like punitive taxation of cocoa producers had an ethnic angle, because most cocoa producers were Ashanti. This history is part of the story behind Kwame Nkrumah's disastrous dictatorship in Ghana, which beviled the development economist Arthur Lewis, as described in Chapter Four. If development economists had understood the history, perhaps they would not have been so eager to give large developmental powers to postcolonial states in Africa.

Another lesser-known victim of the slave trade is another country we have just been discussing: Ethiopia. Although safe from the Atlantic slave traders, Ethiopia was in the most unlucky place for another group of slave traders: the Arabs. The Arab slave raiders could transport Ethiopian slaves across the Sahara and across the Red Sea. Ethiopia was the fourth largest source of slaves for all slave trades from 1400 to 1900.[15] Ethiopia's indigenous governments since then have consisted of a long series of tyrants that included Haile Selassie and Meles Zenawi. If Gates and Blair had understood the deep roots of Ethiopian government oppression, perhaps they would not have been so quick to embrace Meles as a benevolent autocrat.

Consequences at the
Other End of the Slave Trade

Researchers have also followed the trail of slavery across the Atlantic to show the long life of slavery's devastation at the other end. It turns out that children are dying today from preventable childhood diseases in Colombia because of the legacy of slavery. This begins to provide evidence on the question of how an oppressive history (often reflected in an oppressive present) affects health; it is the beginning of a larger and longer-run body of evidence on autocracy and health that extends beyond the data on, say, child mortality during just the past few years under some modern-day dictator. Oppressive conditions themselves are bad for the health of the oppressed, but autocratic rulers also seldom care enough to take positive action to promote public health among the majority.

Further, we have already seen how a history of autocracy and oppression breeds values like lack of trust and respect for others, fostering an insider/outsider distinction in which the insiders place little value on the rights or well-being of the outsiders. A minority elite of Europeans and their descendants in Colombia would control the government and place little value on the rights or well-being (including the health) of the indigenous people, mestizos, and blacks that made up the majority in Colombia.

One of the authors of the study showing this is a Colombian economist named Camilo García-Jimeno, whose education was financed by a Lauchlin Currie Fellowship from the Colombian central bank Banco de la República that had once hosted Currie. In contrast to Currie and most subsequent generations of development economists, García-Jimeno did not treat Colombian history as a blank slate where development began in 1949.[16] He looked back to 1778, when 26 percent of the population of what is now Colombia were of European descent. The whites' population share was low in part because of a large indigenous population but also because of all the African slaves the whites had brought in by then.

The reason for slavery this time was not sugar cane, but gold. The colonial settlers had discovered gold in the Chocó region of Colombia (south of Cartagena) as early as 1544, but it took another century and a half to figure out how to get the gold. The work of placer mining devoured labor as much as sugar-cane harvesting did, requiring gangs of workers to construct sluices or redirect rivers to expose the riverbed, then pan for the gold. As with sugar cane, the local people were too weakened by European diseases to have the necessary stamina for a life of nonstop oppression. As with sugar cane, mine owners could not attract European immigrants to do the brutal work, because Europeans had the better option of owning some of the abundant land elsewhere in the Americas.

The Colombian oppressors were inspired by their Brazilian cousins to find the answer in slavery. Many Brazilian slaveowners exited from the now declining sugar industry in the early 1700s, taking their slaves to a gold rush in the interior province of Minas Gerais. Colombian whites saw the solution to their Chocó mining labor problem and started importing African slaves through the port of Cartagena in the 1720s. The gold rush was intense but short, mostly over by 1800.

Two centuries later, García-Jimeno and his coauthors demonstrated that the legacy of slavery still shows up in Colombia. They compared municipalities with mines to those that were right next door but that did not have mines. The municipalities where the mines had been, compared to their nonmine neighbors, had more poverty, fewer children in school, and worse vaccination coverage. The gold mines' locations were determined by geological factors unrelated to anything else that would have affected development, so the legacy of mining and slavery appears to be the only explanation for the worse poverty, education, and vaccination rates evident even today in the mining towns compared to their non-mining neighboring towns.[17] Vaccination rates are 15 percentage points lower in the locales that used to have gold mining and slavery than those that did not. Even within Colombia, some places have a more intense history of oppression than others, with consequently worse damage to the health of the oppressed.

THE BIG PICTURE

García-Jimeno's coauthors were Daron Acemoglu of MIT and James Robinson of Harvard, who led the initial breakthrough in which development finally took history seriously around the new millennium. Acemoglu and Robinson expounded on the big picture in their book *Why Nations Fail* (in turn based on earlier academic papers with Simon Johnson of MIT).[18] They followed pioneers who were not development economists at all, but economic historians, the widely venerated pair of Stanley Engerman and the late Kenneth Sokoloff, who in 1997 published a study of how history led to South America's underdevelopment relative to North America.[19]

These authors suggest the problem with South America is that it is government by the elite, for the elite, and of the elite. The elite is more interested in exploiting the rest of the population than in long-term development. It also follows that the elite pampers and perpetuates itself rather than making investments in the masses, such as public health.

A minority of oppressors can get rich seizing most of the pie from the nonwhite majority. Public health and political and economic rights are then privileges for the minority. On the other hand, a majority-led country can get rich only by growing the pie, not by fighting over it with each other. So a ruling majority will put in place much wider political and economic rights and public services that support sustained economic growth for all.

Elites (who are commonly of European descent in the Americas) want to limit political freedom so as not to threaten their rule. They also want to have economic rights for themselves but not for the nonwhite majority that they want to exploit. Economic rights for the majority would prevent the elite from expropriating the lands of the majority. Economic rights for the majority would also create potential new entrepreneurs who could drive some elite-owned firms out of business. So elites typically do not put in place a general system of property rights, contract enforcement, and protection against government expropriation—such rights will therefore not be available to the majority.

This is not to say that an elite-dominated system completely eliminated the possibility for development. Colombia's European economic elite, protected by its European political elite, achieved a certain amount of development doing business with each other and with foreign partners. However, Colombia was to have a century of average growth that still leaves it today at one-fourth of US income.

The difference between minority European societies in South America and majority European societies in North America is in turn mainly determined by the differences in geography. We have already seen the beginnings of this story, as sugar-cane and gold economies led to the oppression of majority populations of blacks and indigenous people by minority European elites. Sugar cane existed in South America and the Caribbean, but not in North America. (We will discuss the slave cotton economy in the US South in the next chapter.)

The other geographic accident that mattered was that pre-Columbian population density was much higher in Mexico and Andean South America than in North America, and it remained so even after the disastrous death rates from European diseases. A large indigenous population made exploitation by a minority a better strategy for Europeans than settlement by a European majority. It would have taken enormous military force in South America to drive off enough of the indigenous population and make enough room for majority European settlement, with not that much immediate gain. A smaller amount of force suffices to just tax the natives for the benefit of a minority group of settlers.

Colombia's European-descended (white) population was 26 percent of the whole in the late 1700s, when the European-descended population of the United States was 81 percent of the whole. Minority Europeans, such as Brazilian and Caribbean sugar planters, could partially develop their societies. But their hold on power was not optimal for long-run development. For example, there were not enough successes in new sectors of the economy to offset the long decline of the sugar industry after its heyday in the seventeenth and eighteenth centuries. The elite had too severely restricted the pool of entrepreneurs who could launch new industries.

Moreover, without economic rights, the majority populations in South America had no incentive to make the investments and innovations necessary for long-run development. An average Colombian outside the European elite that controlled the government would have found little incentive to invest in a new industrial venture that the elite government might confiscate anyway. And so European-minority societies wound up less rich and more unequal compared to the European-majority societies.

The Colombians were not intrinsically less virtuous than Americans, they just had more people to oppress and a smaller group of oppressors with whom to share the spoils. Oppression is a crime of opportunity. If you can do it, and you can get away with it, you will do it. This was true of Colombians who oppressed a majority. It was true of Africans who profited from the slave trade in Africa. It was true of the American South that oppressed a slave minority. This is a bit different from the technocratic assumption that state actors follow the benevolent actions recommended by technocrats.

COLOMBIAN UNDERDEVELOPMENT

Colombia was also a public-health disaster. The European elite lived in the temperate altiplano in mountain cities like the capital Bogotá, where health was better because of the absence of malaria. The elite felt little incentive to invest in combating the health problems of the former slaves or indigenous/mestizo people who lived in the lowlands near the Caribbean coast or in the river valleys where malaria was endemic. As late as 1933, a statistical manual on the rural province of Nariño would describe how more than half the deaths were due to causes like "epidemic and infectious diseases" and diarrheal diseases (described as "diseases of the digestive tract"). Less than 3 percent of the deaths were due to "old age."[20]

Public-health campaigns that target the majority of the population are a necessary ingredient for progress on health. A majority with political rights will demand such public-health services for the majority. A government controlled by a minority elite will not feel such pressure for improving the health of the majority. If the minority elite continues to perpetuate itself as an elite, things do not improve.

Colombia offers a particularly clear example of a self-perpetuating elite in its presidential line, which looks more like a hereditary position than an elective one. Joaquín Mosquera was president in 1830, followed by his relative General José María Obando, while less than 5 percent of the adult male population voted in the 1830s. Tomás Cipriano de Mosquera, another relative of the first Mosquera, became president in 1845, succeeding his own son-in-law. Mosquera's relative Obando became president for the second time in 1853. Cipriano de Mosquera was also president a second time. The Conservative Party later offered the electorate two choices: Cipriano de Mosquera's son-in-law or his nephew. Meanwhile, the archbishop of Bogotá was at one point during this period Manuel José Mosquera, a relative of both Joaquín Mosquera and Tomás Cipriano de Mosquera.

An entrenched political elite also favors an entrenched economic elite, as the former will support privileges and restriction of entry by newcomers. The economic elite will repay the favor with cash donations to help the political elite retain its grip on power.

When controlling the government is a way for the elite to enrich itself, rival elite factions will fight each other for that control. Colombia has been famous since its independence for its nearly constant civil wars between Conservatives and Liberals, two rival European-led parties. This history carried all the way up to La Violencia that broke out while the Currie World Bank mission was commissioned in 1948.

A former senator and supreme court justice, José María Samper, wrote a "Critical History of Colombian Constitutional Law" in 1887. He deplored, seventy-six years after independence, "our great backwardness in agriculture, industry, trade, and the education of the popular masses." Samper deplored the "comedia democrática" in which the elite (the "caciques") manipulated the vote for their own ends. He warned of further "conflicts and disasters" unless there was change.[21]

A little over a century later, José María Samper's direct descendant Ernesto Samper became president of a Colombia that was still having "conflicts and disasters," amidst a scandal in which Samper's campaign allegedly received donations from the Cali drug cartel. Ernesto Samper's Colombia today is still having trouble with the "education of the popular masses," where Colombia's children scored worse on international test scores than India's, despite India's much lower average income.[22]

In short, Colombia was a place where a European elite established rule based on oppression of the majority. The long-run consequences were values that failed to respect other groups outside the insider elite, underinvestment in the health and education of the majority, and a hereditary political elite that helped entrench an economic elite, and vice versa.

Colombia has had some long-run growth, but it began only around 1900, roughly a century later than that in North America. Since then Colombian growth has generally failed to overcome its late start, and Colombian average income certainly has not caught up to North America's.

The growth data on Colombia are notable in another way. Let's recall Lauchlin Currie's 1949 World Bank mission, intended to ignite Colombian development, ostensibly for the first time. In fact, the mission tried to initiate "a determined effort" that was "all that is needed to usher in a period of rapid and widespread development." Despite the hoopla from 1949 to 1951 on the World Bank's first attempt in Colombia to spur development by an authoritarian government, the episode left no obvious mark on Colombia's long-term performance. Colombia's growth from 1900 to 1950 was a little less than 2 percent per capita per year; its growth from 1950 to 2012 was a little less than 2 percent per capita per year.

BENIN

Benin was in an even less favorable position for development than Colombia. It suffered the legacy of mistrust even within kin groups, which, as we have seen, is most toxic for trade, investment, and development. As we saw in the past chapter, an authoritarian history begets more authoritarian history. From the time of the slave trade, we see an unbroken series of predatory kingdoms in Benin, preying upon their own populations.

Benin became independent from France on August 1, 1960. Strife among the Aja and their former enslavers has been unsurprisingly endemic ever since. Initially, four different leaders, from four different ethnic groups, competed for power. For example, one of the leaders was Justin Ahomadegbé-Tomêtin, a descendant of the rulers of the old slave kingdom of Dahomey, from its former capital city of Abomey. Another of the leaders was Sourou Apithy from the old slave-exporting port of Porto Novo. The result of conflict between regional/ethnic leaders has been a constant cycle of coups and attempts at one party-states.

On October 26, 1972, Mathieu Kerekou carried off a military coup and instigated a draconian Marxist state, renamed the People's Republic of Benin. His brutal regime lasted for the next eighteen years, jailing anyone who protested. One of those arrested in July 1985 was a student leader named Leonard Wantchekon. Wantchekon managed to escape in December 1986 and emigrated to Canada and later the United States.

Leonard Wantchekon's warning about the development consequences of mistrust in Benin came to pass. Benin started off among the poorest countries in the world in 1950, when data on relative incomes first becomes available, and the annual rise in living standards since then has been glacial: about 0.4 percent per year from 1950 to 2012, at a time when the world average income per person rose at about 2 percent per year. Virtually every year, the people of Benin fall further behind relative to the world economy.

THE SLIPPERY SLOPE ON THE LEFT

This history of the slave trade in Benin and oppressive minority European rule in Colombia highlights the damaging consequences of wrongs done by authoritarian actors.

It is easy to see how embracing this history could leave one vulnerable to being dismissed as a left-wing extremist who blames everything bad in the world on white oppressors, racists, slave traders, and colonialists. But we should not give in to this temptation. Acknowledging the role of European oppression in the failure of some countries does not require ignoring the domestic roots of autocracy. And, of course, Europeans did not invent the phenomenon of the strong oppressing the weak. The lesson of this history is simply that neither Europeans nor non-Europeans can be trusted with unconstrained power against the rights of individuals.

CHAPTER EIGHT

THE MAJORITY DREAM

As a relief to the grim stories of oppression, there is a very positive side when a majority of the population does manage to assert its rights. These rights set in motion a remarkable ability to generate prosperity and to solve the problems of poverty, including the tragedy of high child mortality. The experience of the North American colonies—the United States and Canada—offers a contrast to the Caribbean and South American experiences in the previous chapter.

WHEN NEW YORK WAS LESS PROMISING THAN SURINAME

One might wonder now why North American colonies, which did not look that different from the South American ones, did not also evolve institutions that perpetrated slavery and oppression by European elites. At first, they did go in that direction, not only in the slave South, but even in a northern colony like New York.

Slavery first appeared in New Amsterdam under the Dutch, who brought 467 slaves from Africa between 1626 and 1664. The Dutch gave "half-free" slaves some land north of the city to farm in 1641 to 1647, in what is now SoHo and Greenwich Village. The gift was not quite as magnanimous as it appears, as the Dutch were at war with the Indians at the time and the blacks formed a buffer. "Half-free" meant that the slaves themselves were now free, but their children would return to slavery.[1] The Dutch gave a half-free slave named Gratia d'Angola a 10-acre farm in the 1640s, centered around what is today one block of Greene Street between Prince Street and Houston Street, in the SoHo neighborhood of Manhattan.[2]

My NYU colleagues Laura Freschi, Steven Pennings, and I have re-searched the history of this Greene Street block between Houston and Prince from the 1600s up to the present using archival records and maps.[3] Aiming to consider a view of development based on individual rights, we wanted to examine the story of the individuals who would come and go on this block during the 400 years of American economic development. This chapter covers the Greene Street block up to 1850; future chapters will pick up on its later history.

The block that began under slavery progressed next to recognize the privileges of a small elite in New York. The owner of the Greene Street block after the slave Gratia d'Angola would eventually be Nicholas Ba-yard. Bayard (1644–1707) belonged to a family that was the New York equivalent of the Colombian Mosqueras, the elite family that had rotated power amongst their members in the nineteenth century in Colombia. Bayard's mother was sister of New Amsterdam's most powerful gover-nor, Peter Stuyvesant, while his father's sister was the wife of Stuyvesant. Bayard trained as Uncle Stuyvesant's private secretary, and then after the British takeover served as both mayor and alderman of New York.

Bayard was able to take advantage of the mistreatment of slaves and freed blacks, along with his political connections, to amass huge amounts of land. The new British regime oppressed slaves even more than had the Dutch. Masters were permitted to punish slaves in any way short of dis-memberment or death. Slaves could not testify against whites. The law promised a horrible death to any slave conspiring with others to revolt. The law did not permit enslaved blacks and free blacks to associate, and it forbade slaves to sell or trade. No former slaves made free after 1712 could own land or houses or pass property to heirs. The 1712 law also said that no slave could be freed without posting a £200 bond [$5800 in today's money], just in case they became a public charge. Life got so miserable in New York for free blacks that they fled to New Jersey.[4]

Bayard apparently benefited from blacks selling their farms north of the city at distress prices. He assembled a large farm around 1700, stretching all the way from the northern edge of what is now Chinatown to cover much of what is now SoHo and the southern part of Green-wich Village. Gratia d'Angola and his descendants were the losers on

Greene Street, while Bayard was the winner who would wind up with the Greene Street block.

At this point around the eighteenth century, there does not seem to be much difference between North and South America, which is a useful corrective to the view that we in the North just had saintly founding fathers compared to those evil oppressors in the South. If there was any difference between North American and South American colonies in the seventeenth and eighteenth centuries, it was that the former were much less promising. After retaking New Amsterdam from the British in a 1667 war, the Dutch traded it back to the British for the sugar plantations of Dutch Guiana (today's Suriname).

ANOTHER GREAT DIVERGENCE

So why did New York and Colombia have such different fates in the long run?

This leads now to the big question of why there was majority European settlement in North America and minority European settlement in South America. Research finds that geography influences the outcome. The temperate zones in North America were more attractive to European migrants than the South American tropics. European agricultural technology transferred more easily to temperate climes, and death rates of settlers were lower in temperate zones than in the tropics.

Slavery, as we began to see above, was chiefly a matter of crops and minerals. Gold and sugarcane did not motivate European immigrants to come as workers but did motivate Europeans to import captive Africans to work the mines and plantations. The British colonies of North America had few minerals, and the predominant crops were wheat and corn. There is no payoff to large landholdings in wheat and corn—they are ideal crops for family farms, because they are just as profitable for smallholdings as they are for large ones. And the vast lands available in North America for such family farms attracted vast numbers of family farmers from distressed regions like the Palatinate region of southwest Germany (destroyed by the Thirty Years' War and famine in the 1600s) and Ireland (chronically in conflict with the British).

The present author is a mongrel mix of rogue Germans (Biebels, Fettermans, Herbeins, Muellers, Tanners, Zirkles, and Oesterles—later Anglicized to Easterly) and rogue Protestant Irish (Atkinsons, Doynes, Dolans, Espys, Longmuirs, McKays, Montgomerys, and McMechens) that all had roughly the same history. They arrived in the early 1700s, they farmed the empty lands of Appalachia, they married each other, they each had twelve children, the children married each other, and they had more children.

The American South was an intermediate example between South America and the Caribbean on one hand and Canada and the northern British colonies of North America on the other hand. There, slave crops like tobacco and cotton perpetuated slavery, but corn and wheat land (and the absence of large indigenous populations) still attracted large-scale European settlement.

Statistical research confirms the broad outlines of this story. The appearance of what Acemoglu and Robinson would call "inclusive institutions" versus "extractive institutions" is indeed correlated with the geography described here.[5]

THE ELITE FAILS TO STAY ELITE IN NEW YORK

Nicholas Bayard and his descendants would be a prime example of how a hereditary elite—either political or economic—was not viable in a society of majority European settlers with both political and economic rights. Things had begun well for a possible Bayard dynasty. Nicholas Bayard had already figured out by 1700 that he could use his farm and its proximity to the port of New York to export food to sugar plantations in the Caribbean that did not want to use scarce sugar land for that purpose.[6] The farm economy of New York City did not need to rely on slave labor. Europeans were glad to do farm work to learn the skills necessary to move on later to start their own family farms.

Bayard's farm would eventually pass to his grandson, Nicholas Bayard II (1698–1765). Nicholas II figured out that other profitable activities in New York included dominating the sugar trade. Slaves were necessary to the production of sugar in the Caribbean but not to the trade in sugar from New York. New Yorkers took the sugar from the Caribbean in return for food from New York. Bayard II then reshipped the sugar to England in return for manufactured goods for New Yorkers. Bayard II participated in the trade as well as the farming, owning two "sugar houses" in the city, one of them on Wall Street near the future Stock Exchange.

The white population of New York City surged in the 1700s, while the black population stagnated. The nearly free land and trade opportunities beckoned the whites to keep coming. The absence of a profitable slave economy in New York—which elsewhere as we have seen required commodities like sugar and gold, and later tobacco and cotton—gave little incentive for anyone to keep importing slaves. By 1784, blacks made up less than a tenth of the New York population.[7] New Yorkers abolished slavery gradually in the late 1700s and early 1800s, with final emancipation in 1827. There was growing religious sentiment against slavery in both England and America, but it is hard to know why this would have affected the Northerners in the United States differently than the Southerners. It is likely that the New Yorkers did not end slavery because they were more virtuous than Southerners, but simply because their geography did not make slavery pay off.

The original Nicholas Bayard surely would have liked to perpetuate a hereditary elite. But the continuing influx of free white immigrants and the free-for-all from economic and political freedom made it impossible. His descendants did not retain the political power that their well-connected ancestor had used for his original landholdings; they could not use such power to restrict entry by new competitors as their Latin American and Caribbean elite counterparts often did. Which industries and trades were profitable kept shifting. The Bayard family business model of trade with the sugar plantations in the Caribbean fell victim to the decline of the Caribbean sugar economy.

Nicholas Bayard III (1736–1802), the great-grandson of the first Nicholas, went bankrupt in 1789 and was forced to sell the Bayard farm to pay his creditors. The old Bayard sugar house disappeared on Wall Street, while down the street at the same time the ancestor of some of the next members of the economic elite was helping to found the New York Stock Exchange. We will meet him below.

Meanwhile, a shipping merchant and real-estate auctioneer, Anthony Bleecker (1741–1816—after whom today's famous Bleecker Street, one block north of our Greene Street block, is named)—bought most of the Greene Street block formerly owned by Nicholas Bayard and Gratia d'Angola.[8]

How Rights Solved Problems in New York

Rights for the majority created a problem-solving system in the United States that was not available in South America. We have seen that the European elite in Colombia tended to act in its own interest instead of the interests of the majority on public goods and services like health. Democratic elections in the United States gave the majority a mechanism for getting the public goods and services they wanted. Elections meant that the social payoff to a public good was related to the private payoff of a political entrepreneur who could deliver the goods. Such an entrepreneur tends to win the next election and so gets rewarded with a longer term in office. This mechanism operates at both the national and local levels.

Political entrepreneurship played a key role in the story of the Erie Canal. The idea of a canal across the Appalachians had been around since the eighteenth century, to address an increasingly severe problem. The growing population of the Midwest was producing huge surpluses in commodities like corn and pork that they could not consume themselves, yet transporting them across the mountains to the big population centers in the East was very costly. Thomas Jefferson, who had a romantic image of the self-sufficient farmer and had always scorned the merchant classes who conducted interregional trade, was not sympathetic. While president in January 1809, he described the proposed Erie Canal as "a little short of madness."[9] Admittedly, the project of digging a manmade river through the mountains was costly and required some vision to appreciate its long-run benefits. So when a New York delegation approached Jefferson for funding about it in 1809, the last year of his second term, he suggested they come back in a hundred years.

But the benefits to the majority of a transportation link to the Midwest were too great to be denied. A pluralistic political system in which many power centers compete to gain the "consent of the governed" has the ability to work around politicians who get it wrong. DeWitt Clinton was such a competitor to Jefferson—both occupying a different level of government (New York state governor) and a different party (Clinton would run for president for the opposition Federalist party in 1812 and almost win). Clinton realized the canal's importance to making New York City the nation's pre-eminent port. As New York State governor, he asked his own state legislature for funding. He finally got the money and construction began in 1817.

Somehow the chaotic and decentralized political system had gotten the right answer. At the time, grain and pork traveling from, say, Ohio to New York City had to travel from Ohio farms to the nearest road or navigable river down to the Ohio River, then down the Mississippi to New Orleans, then by sea to Eastern seaports. The Erie Canal would cut in half the transport cost of farm products from Ohio to New York City, in the process creating an economic transport corridor that lasts until the present.[10] The canal went through the lowest gap in the whole Appalachian Mountains near any major port. The major east–west route of the railways would later follow the same route, as does Interstate 90 today.

On November 4, 1825, Dewitt Clinton stood in a boat off the coast of Sandy Hook, on the Atlantic edge of New York harbor, and poured a keg of water from Lake Erie that had arrived on the first boat to traverse the completed canal into the Atlantic Ocean.[11] The canal had solved a problem for both New York and Midwesterners. Midwesterners got much better prices for their farm products, and they now had cheaper access not only to New York City markets but to all other markets reachable by ship from New York. New York thrived as a port and trading center; the city's population exploded.

GREENE STREET AND A GROWING CITY

The canal's economic benefits would produce a surge in New York City's rising population, and so accelerate the city's northward expansion. The Greene Street block would benefit from New York's growth as a prime residential neighborhood for the middle and upper classes. Anthony Bleecker and other landowners on the Block had carved it up into residential lots. By 1830, only five years after the Canal's opening, the Greene Street block contained twenty-six houses, a shop, and a Dutch Reformed

Church. We have our first data on the block's real-estate value in 1830, a little less than $5 million in today's dollars. There is only one house from this period still standing on the block today. (Figure 8.1)

The real-estate value on this block would increase by a multiple of fifty-six over the next 180 years. This block's most valuable asset was its total freedom to keep reinventing itself, close to other New York City blocks with the same freedom. This would lead the block through many surprising changes that are detailed here and in subsequent chapters.[12]

THE ECONOMIC DEVELOPMENT OF A FAMILY

In contrast to minority rule that oppresses the majority and protects the economic interests of an entrenched elite, majority rule creates incentives and allows opportunity for the majority to get rich. Let's see how this worked out with a tale of an individual, a family, and a neighborhood in New York.

Included in the northward movement of the city was a man named Benjamin Mendes Seixas; born in 1811, he would live until 1871. He had left home at a young age to begin making a living as an importer of cigars. He also would profit as a buyer and seller of real estate in what is today SoHo all around the Greene Street block.

For Benjamin Seixas, both cigar importing and real-estate investment reflected new opportunities that were created by a democratic government's investment in the Erie Canal. The Erie Canal meant that a cigar importer like Benjamin now had access to the vast markets of the American interior. Cigars were not the niche item they are today: mid-nineteenth-century Americans consumed 300 million cigars a year.

Benjamin also benefited from good transportation links to the rest of the world indirectly created by the Erie Canal. Oceanic shipping was developing as a hub-and-spoke system.[13] It was cheaper to run large ships from a hub on one side of the Atlantic to another hub on the opposite side, and then offload the goods onto smaller ships to take them to other ports on each side. With the boost that New York had already gotten from the Erie Canal, it became the hub on the American side. The average size of ships entering New York harbor more than doubled from 1834 to 1860.[14]

FIGURE 8.1   The only remaining building on the Greene Street block from the 1820s–1850s residential era. (Author's photo, 2013.)

Other spokes from the New York hub reached out to the Caribbean and even as far as China. This made it cheaper for Benjamin Seixas to import his cigars. Cigar importing was not the only business that benefited from transportation links. The same links helped Benjamin's brother Jacob to make a living as an importer of dry goods (such as fabrics and clothing).

Booming trade requires a finance industry. Importers need loans to buy their goods, which they then repay after they sell the goods. No finance, no trade. When trade booms, finance booms. Benjamin's uncle and cousins would get rich from finance.

The Seixas family and many other New Yorkers prospering in the city's thriving economic sectors needed good places to live. This was the role of the Greene Street block, well located not far from downtown business and yet not so close as to suffer from the filth and congestion of the dense population downtown. As the income of potential residents on Greene Street grew, it drove up prices: real estate on the Greene Street block doubled in value from 1830 to 1850. Like other early purchasers of real estate in the greater Greene Street neighborhood (what is called SoHo today), Benjamin could buy low and then sell high.

In 1829, Benjamin was living at 24 Vandam Street, five blocks to the west of Greene Street. By 1842, Benjamin had moved to the Greene Street block, eventually settling at 133 Greene Street, where today stands a Christian Dior luxury menswear store. At the time of the 1850 Census, Benjamin was thirty-nine years of age, living at 133 Greene with his wife Mary, six children aged six to nineteen, a housekeeper, a male clerk, and three young Irish maids. His cigar import business was located downtown at 3 Maiden Lane, on the corner with Broadway, about a half hour walk or quick carriage ride away from 133 Greene Street.

Benjamin's real-estate assets are listed in the 1850 Census as the equivalent of what would be about $1 million in today's dollars. That does not sound very rich by today's New York standards, but average incomes in New York and the United States in 1850 were something like one-seventeenth of what they are today; compared to the average income in 1850, Benjamin's wealth would be comparable to about $17 million today. At the same time, American development had already proceeded to the extent that 1850 incomes in Benjamin's time were twice what they had been in 1720 at the time the Greene Street block was part of the Bayard farm.[15] In short, Benjamin's American Dream had succeeded.

There is more to the success story than just Benjamin as an individual, it is also the success story of a family, and the success story of a now-forgotten minority-within-a-minority ethnic group. Individual freedom does not automatically mean asocial individuals who do not care about any group larger than themselves; it means freedom for the individual to choose the groups that he or she values and works with in economic as well as social activities. Many success stories involve individuals working with their extended families and self-defined ethnic group together to achieve success.

How does this differ from the collectivist values of the Maghribi families and Chinese clans, discussed in Chapter Six, as compared to the individualist values of the Genoese and the English and Dutch? The big difference is that dealing with (or even belonging to) your own ethnic group is voluntary in individualist societies, as opposed to mandatory in collectivist societies. There is also more mutual tolerance between groups in individualist societies compared to collectivist ones, as we saw in Chapter Six. Members of ethnic groups in individualist societies can then get the best of both worlds. They benefit from high trust and social networks within the ethnic group to find and make some beneficial deals. But impersonal contract enforcement in individualist societies means they also have the opportunity to make interethnic deals that offer a much wider range of opportunities.

New York's relative freedoms were to make possible success for a group excluded almost everywhere else. Benjamin's success story was a Jewish success story, not exactly unknown in New York, but calling Benjamin "Jewish" does not begin to describe his ethnic group (or match mindless stereotypes).

THE REFUGEES

Benjamin's group was a now-forgotten and tiny group of Sephardic Jews who made their way out of Portugal in the early 1700s to London and Amsterdam, and then to New World locations, including New York City. This group in New York was never larger than about 3,000 individuals before the middle of the nineteenth century, after which they were swamped by Ashkenazim immigrating from Central Europe and their original identity was largely forgotten.[16] But this small group had achieved major success by that time.

Benjamin's great-grandfather, Isaac Seixas, was born in Lisbon, Portugal. Jews were fleeing Portugal because of horrific persecution. Jews who wanted to remain in Portugal after it joined Spain in banning Judaism in 1497 had been forced to convert to Christianity. Some of them really did convert, while others continued practicing Judaism in secret. The Inquisition did not bother to distinguish the two. With varying intensity, the Inquisition stalked all former Jews for evidence of secret religious practice. The intensity increased in the first two decades of the eighteenth century in Portugal, when the Inquisition punished 2,126 for practicing Judaism, of whom 37 were burned alive at the stake.[17] The Inquisition had first stretched suspected "Judaizers" on racks until they confessed. The Inquisitors insisted the Judaizers implicate their wives, parents, and children; many were tortured more than once.

Other Portuguese Jews, some of them still bearing rope burns from the inquisitor's rack, were already in New York by the time Isaac Seixas arrived in 1738. They already had their own synagogue, Shearith Israel, in downtown New York on what is today South William Street. (The exact location is known but there is no historical marker, probably because it is today a six-story parking garage.)

Isaac's son, Benjamin Mendes Seixas (after whom his grandson on Greene Street would be named), was born in 1748. He was a merchant of middling success, as would appear from his advertisement in the *New York Gazette: and Weekly Mercury*, April 15–May 6, 1771:

> Benjamin Seixas, Saddler, At his shop in Broad Street, nearly opposite to his Excellency General Gage, makes and mends all sorts of saddles, chairs, chaises, and harnesses; likewise has for sale the following articles which he will sell cheap for cash, either wholesale or retail: bits and stirrups of all kinds. Curry Combs and brushes. . . . Green livery lace Blue, green, and scarlet fringe Horse nets and chair fringe Horsewhips, cowskins &c With a variety of other articles too tedious to specify. N.B. An allowance will be made to those who buy to sell again.[18]

Benjamin was also politically active, becoming less enamored of the British General Thomas Gage after the Revolutionary War began. Benjamin backed the Revolution, in contrast to the Loyalist sympathies of most New York merchants, perhaps because of New York City's history of equality for Jews. New York in 1777 became the first state in the Western world to give total citizenship to Jews.[19] Benjamin contributed also to the future of New York as one of the founders of the New York Stock Exchange—it is he (with his descendants) who was mentioned earlier in the chapter as replacing Nicholas Bayard III in New York's economic elite.[20] Benjamin had helped launch New York's finance industry that would thrive on the back of its booming trade; his own children and grandchildren would prosper from finance.

The first Benjamin Mendes Seixas had sixteen children who survived to adulthood. With his children mainly marrying into other Sephardic families, they were going to make possible some large family enterprises. (Repeating the same family names over and over, they were also going to make it incredibly confusing for modern researchers—and readers—to keep track of who is who.) His first surviving child, Moses Benjamin Seixas (1780–1839), pursued a modest occupation at the lottery office at 47 Cedar Street but had also begun the family practice of entering the real-estate boom on the ground floor in what is now SoHo, buying a property at 133 Thompson (near the corner with Prince Street) in 1828 for $1200. Many members of the Seixas family would benefit from the doubling of real-estate prices in the neighborhood of Greene Street from 1830 to 1850.

We know from Moses B. Seixas's survivors after his death in 1839 (including his first son, our man Benjamin Mendes Seixas, on Greene Street in the 1840s and 1850s), that the family was doing well. Many of Benjamin's family lived in SoHo near Greene Street. Benjamin's mother—Moses's widow Judith—lived in 1850 at 67 West Houston Street, one block north and west from her son Benjamin, with those of her numerous other offspring still at home. As of the 1860 census, Judith had real-estate assets of more than $400,000 in today's dollars.

Benjamin's younger brother, Jacob Levy Seixas, as we noted already, became a wholesale importer of dry goods. He lived at 21 Wooster Street, the next street over from Greene Street, which is where their father Moses B. Seixas had died in 1839. Later in life, as of the 1870 census, Jacob Levy Seixas had accumulated combined real estate and personal assets of over $900,000 in today's dollars.

Numerous other uncles, aunts, and cousins of Benjamin were moving into the neighborhood that is now called SoHo from the 1830s through the 1840s. Reflecting this movement, the Shearith Israel synagogue itself had moved into the neighborhood, near the corner of Crosby and Spring, in 1834. Part of the value of a booming neighborhood's real estate is the value of being next to other rich and successful people with whom to do business, which in this case included a lot of members of the greater Seixas family.

Our Benjamin Mendes Seixas at 133 Greene Street was not the richest grandchild of his grandfather of the same name. Our Benjamin's uncle, Seixas Nathan, a Wall Street broker, lived down the street from him at 116 Greene.[21] Seixas Nathan had married his first cousin Sara Seixas. Sara was the daughter of the first Benjamin Mendes Seixas, while Seixas Nathan was the son of a sister to that first Benjamin Seixas who had helped found Wall Street. Seixas Nathan followed in that business tradition as a Wall Street broker. The sons of Seixas Nathan and Sara Seixas, Benjamin Seixas Nathan and Mendes Nathan, would continue the family business as stockbrokers.

It was Benjamin Seixas Nathan, first cousin to our Benjamin Mendes Seixas on Greene Street, who would make a fortune as a Wall Street operator. Benjamin Nathan as of the 1840s lived a few blocks away from his cousin at the corner of Bleecker and Thompson, in a large house that is now a Greenwich Village bar called the Back Fence.

We know a little bit more about Benjamin Nathan than other Seixas descendants, because he managed to later get himself sensationally murdered in 1870. The *New York Times* and other papers had lots of coverage of the murder and the victim. Nobody ever figured out who murdered Benjamin Nathan in his bed in the middle of the night, but the coverage did reveal a lot about his wealth. "In his home he was lavish to excess, surrounding himself with every comfort and luxury money could procure," although it also noted Nathan's generosity to charities (he was one of the founding donors of what is now Mount Sinai Hospital).[22] Nathan also had a country estate in New Jersey. The *Times* gave his fortune as what in today's dollars would be almost $9 million, which was again even larger relative to the far lower average incomes in those days. The finance industry had become a remarkable income generator for New York and for the Seixas family.

Let's return to our Benjamin Mendes Seixas of Greene Street. Just before his death in 1871, he had passed the cigar-import business at 3 Maiden Lane to his son Myer. The time of the Portuguese Jews as a distinct ethnic success story was about over. The Sephardim were assimilating into the larger society, marrying into families of Ashkenazim or even Christians (our Benjamin himself had married a Christian named Mary

Ann Jessup). But the Seixas family had demonstrated for a century the potential for prosperity of a city and a country that did not restrict economic rights to an elite.

Benjamin Seixas' Greene Street block would also be an example of the freedom to change at every level necessary for prosperity. We note here its 1850s shift into a new but not very attractive industry. Benjamin Seixas had moved out of the block abruptly in 1852, and other relatives quickly followed, moving out of the surrounding neighborhood for locations farther uptown. It is unlikely that Benjamin lost money on his sudden exit from the neighborhood, for the new owners were willing to pay good money for a town house with many small bedrooms. The block had suddenly turned over to its next surprising incarnation: New York's greatest concentration of whorehouses. To understand why and how that happened will take some more explanation in Chapter Ten. We will see further surprising changes on the block that feature industries more likely to pass moral scrutiny.

DEVELOPMENT AND UNDERDEVELOPMENT IN NEW YORK

Although a free society is a great problem-solving system, as the Erie Canal example suggested, there was one problem that 1850 New York had still not solved: health. This was in part because it had not been solved anywhere yet. We first see how bad the problem was and then finally see whether a free society could cope with reducing it.

Benjamin Seixas on Greene Street, and the greater Seixas family, had benefited from the success of free entry into the economic elite that helps explain New York's and America's successful development. But he and his family would also suffer from the failure of New York's and America's development on health as of 1850. Benjamin and his wife Mary had the tragedy of seeing three of their ten children die as infants (and a fourth would die later at age eighteen). First, their daughter Sara died at three months of age in 1842. In 1849, at eight months of age, their son Daniel died of convulsions (possibly reflecting acute dehydration from a diarrheal disease like cholera). In 1852, their son Washington died at eight months.[23]

Benjamin's relatives, even his wealthy stockbroker cousins Mendes Nathan and Benjamin Nathan, did not escape health tragedies. Benjamin Nathan's daughter Luisa died of scarlet fever at age five on Bleecker Street in 1852. The next year his son Lucien died at the age of seven months.[24]

Mendes Nathan, down Greene Street from Benjamin Seixas at 22 Greene, saw his daughter Constance die from dysentery at the age of nineteen months in 1849. Another daughter died of marasmus (malnutrition) at twenty-six days in 1850, and his daughter Anne died at thirteen months of whooping cough in 1853. Later his son George would die at the age of eight in 1863.[25]

A related health tragedy had showed up earlier in the death of the mother of Mendes and Benjamin Nathan, Sara Seixas Nathan, in 1834 from "childbed fever." A way to try to make up for child deaths was by having more children, but multiple childbirths also subjected the mothers to another gruesome lottery from high maternal-mortality rates.

We know of these deaths because the synagogue Shearith Israel kept comprehensive records of deaths of its members. My coauthors and I have reviewed the records from 1828 to 1855, which covered 443 deaths. Today, we think of the typical dying person as elderly. Today deaths of children under five years of age account for less than 1 percent of all deaths. New York's child mortality crisis in 1850 shows up in the synagogue records when we see that a third of deaths were of children less than five.

The nineteenth-century mortality crisis also made New York of that era abnormally dangerous for older children and young adults as well. Benjamin Seixas's brother Myer died of typhus fever at age twenty-two in 1842, at their mother Judith's home on 67 West Houston. Two years earlier, Benjamin's cousin, Benjamin Isaac Seixas, had also died of typhus three blocks to the east on Crosby Street.

There were too many ways to die in mid-nineteenth-century New York. On April 30, 1852, a stagecoach ran over and killed ten-year-old Moses Seixas, son of Benjamin's brother Jacob Levy Seixas on Wooster Street. Only two weeks later, Benjamin's cousin Zipporah Seixas died of consumption (tuberculosis).

Today, deaths of older children and young adults (say, ages five to twenty-four) account for less than 2 percent of all deaths. In the Shearith

FIGURE 8.2   Child mortality on the Save the Children website.
(Savethechildren.org, 2013.)

Israel records, these ages account for 13 percent of all deaths. Combining the under-five deaths with these, half of all deaths in the Shearith Israel records occurred to people under twenty-five, while today those ages account for less than 3 percent of all deaths. We have other mortality records from 1850s New York that indicate the Shearith Israel patterns were not abnormal.

AFRICA ON GREENE STREET

The website for the charity Save the Children features the arresting statistic that every 3 seconds in the world today a child dies, many from easily preventable causes (Figure 8.2).

It helps us appreciate the success of the fight against child mortality in the United States to know that our own ancestors would have been even more eligible for Save the Children campaigns. The US infant-mortality

rate in 1850 for whites was 217 infant deaths for every 1,000 live births.[26]
(Infant mortality is defined as children's deaths that occur before their
first birthday. Child mortality means children die before their fifth birthday.) This is almost double the worst infant-mortality rates in the world
today, which are in Sierra Leone, Democratic Republic of the Congo, and
Somalia. It is almost double the infant mortality rate in Ethiopia in 1990,
the horrific rate of infant mortality, and also child mortality, that inspired
Bill Gates to overlook Meles's dictatorship. But solving this tragedy in the
United States would not require autocrats.

DEMOCRACY AND CHILD MORTALITY

The solving of child mortality in New York (and in the United States) was
going to be a democratic success story. It took a democracy that allowed
many different groups the freedom to agitate for many different reforms,
because the health crisis had many complex causes.

The first challenge to improving health in 1850 was a lack of knowledge on what caused disease and death. We now know a big part of the
problem was the cycling of the disease agents through human waste into
drinking water. Princeton Professor Angus Deaton shows in his 2013
book, *The Great Escape*, that understanding (which led to correcting) this
problem had the largest single effect on child mortality in rich countries
over this period. We will see in a future chapter how free societies are
the best option for scientific discoveries and technological breakthroughs.
Here we just note in passing that the germ theory of disease needed to arrive in New York. It did so later in the nineteenth century, mainly through
research from England. The physician John Snow's famous identification
of a particular water pump in London as the source of the contaminated
water that spread cholera in 1854 London was a key turning point.[27] Virtually all the scientific discoveries that also enable progress today on child
mortality in poor countries were made in free societies.

The next problem after understanding the science was indeed the lack
of proper water and sanitation in New York. It took a while for the germ
theory to get translated into government action on these services. It would
require monitoring of different water sources, improved engineering on
sewage disposal, and tracking water quality at the other end in neighbor-

hoods.[28] Even the primitive knowledge of the 1850s had already suspected that it was a problem to drink water contaminated by human and animal wastes. Correcting this would require a multipronged attack of government and private actions that lasted for decades.

The third problem was getting the population itself to embrace more sanitary habits. Washing one's hands after going to the bathroom is something we do without thinking today, but it took a lot of effort to get to that point. The population as well as the experts had to embrace the germ theory of disease.

The fourth problem was simply that New York and the United States were still poor by today's standards. Per capita income in the United States in 1850 was one-seventeenth of that today—about the same as Ghana today. Even a rich person like Benjamin Seixas in 1850 would be poor in many dimensions by today's standards. For example, Benjamin Seixas' house in 1850 was small even by the standards of today's cramped New York apartments. To accommodate the thirteen members of the Seixas household in 1850, the house at 131 Greene had only two stories, each measuring 25 by 40 feet. If congestion was this bad for the upper class, imagine how it was in the tenements of the poor. Congestion makes contagion more likely and makes it more difficult to maintain sanitary conditions. As income rises, people can afford to spend more on larger living quarters.

Many other factors that affect health are driven by the material prosperity of the citizens. Most obvious is the total amount available to spend on health problems, both by private citizens and public agencies. Education is also correlated with income and we have just seen that private understanding of how disease spreads was critical to get people to change habits. As New York's environment was favorable for the overall rise in prosperity, this would be part of the solution to the health tragedy of mid-nineteenth-century New York. But general development alone was not enough; health also requires public action to be democratically demanded by the populace.

The founding of the New York City Board of Health in 1805 was a first indication of a majority willing to invest in its own future, but there was a long way to go. In 1842, the government finished the Croton Aqueduct to bring drinking water to the city. Between 1849 and 1865, the new Croton Aqueduct department also laid down a network of sewer pipes.[29] (Prior to that effort, the word *sewer* just referred to an open ditch down the middle of residential streets.) [30] An 1851 map showed the sewer line had reached the Greene Street block, although that was as far north as it went on Greene. Coverage for the city was still minimal. In 1856, New York had about 10,000 "water closets" featuring piped-in water and piped-out sewage for a population of 630,000.[31]

Political reform movements demanded more. Epidemics of cholera (1849, 1854, 1866) and typhus (1851, 1864) helped them make their case.[32] As we have seen with the death of Benjamin Seixas's brother Myer from typhus, contagious diseases were a problem for all classes of society. With contagion, the health of the neighborhood of the rich was also affected by conditions in the neighborhood of the poor.

Two more powerful organizations than the old City Board of Health— the Metropolitan Sanitary District, and a new Board of Health—began operation in 1866, featuring far more intensive inspections of water, milk, and food supplies. The board started enforcing the first sanitary codes in the 1870s and 1880s. Advances in scientific knowledge in the 1890s made possible the founding of a laboratory to test for bacteria, which in turn made it easier to find trouble spots in the public water supply and eliminate the contaminants. Chlorination of water supply arrived in 1911, and pasteurization of milk in 1912.

In 1908, Sara Josephine Baker (1873–1945), a New York pediatrician, started the "first municipal unit in the world devoted to the health protection of mothers and children," a children's hygiene unit at the Board of Health.[33] Public-health nurses taught the importance of hygiene to the mothers—it does not help to have clean water if the water is recontaminated at home. Health education is vital but tedious (again: wash hands after visiting the bathroom!) Baker would be the US representative to the Health Committee of the League of Nations in the 1920s, crossing paths with League of Nations' development efforts that would show up in China (as discussed in Chapter Three).

The simple prediction is that societies with majority rule do better than those with minority rule on giving the majority public services it wants, such as public health. Infant mortality fell drastically in the United States from 1850 to 1920. It reached rates in 1920 that our comparator society of minority rule from the previous chapter, Colombia, would not reach for

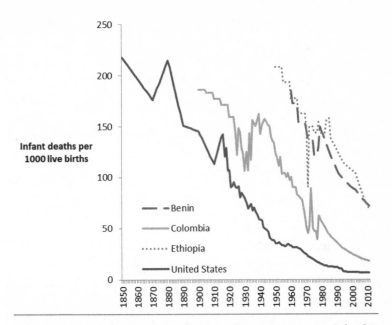

FIGURE 8.3   Long-run trend in infant mortality rates in Benin, Colombia, Ethiopia, and United States.

(Chart constructed by author, using modern data from World Bank World Development Indicators, spliced with historical data from M. Rodwan Abouharb and Anessa L. Kimball, "A New Dataset on Infant Mortality Rates, 1816–2002," Journal of Peace Research 44, no. 6 [2007], 743-754.)

another four decades. The victims of oppression and autocracy in Africa—Benin and Ethiopia—would not reach that rate until 2011 (Figure 8.3). The further success of public health, medical science, and development in the United States would reduce the mortality rate to 6 infant deaths per 1,000 live births today, a long way from the 200 deaths per 1,000 of the nineteenth century.

In short, the child-mortality crisis in Ethiopia that Gates treated as a de novo problem was one the United States had already confronted and solved. Looking beneath the Blank Slate, we see a society with political freedom solving this problem. And part of the progress Ethiopia was later to make on this issue involved the spread to the rest of the world of science, medicines, and water and sanitation methods invented in the United States, the United Kingdom, and other democracies.

FIGURE 8.4   Per capita gross domestic product in the United States, Colombia, and Benin (constant U.S. dollars).

(Graph constructed by author using modern data on economic growth from World Bank World Development Indicators, merged with historical data from Angus Maddison, "Historical Statistics of the World Economy: 1–2008 AD.")

US DEVELOPMENT IN RELATIVE TERMS

Figure 8.4 shows the consequences for the long-run paths of the different degrees of oppression and individual rights featured in this and in the previous chapter. Each series begins when we first have data for that country. As shown, the US economy explodes, Benin at independence starts off extremely poor and stays that way, and Colombia is in between. As noted earlier, Colombia today is at one-fourth of US per capita income. Looking horizontally, Colombia today is about a century behind the United States in attaining a given living standard. Colombia has had steady economic growth but has failed to close the gap with the United States over the long run. Benin's income today is where US income was two centuries ago.

These patterns are confirmed by statistical associations across all countries between institutions that protect rights and long-run prosperity. There is again a problem of causality, which cannot be decisively resolved, on which causes which: does protection of individual rights cause long-run prosperity, or does prosperity bring about protection of individual rights?

Again, our starting point is that freedom is also an end in itself, while autocracy is not. This puts the burden of proof on the autocrat, if he wants to claim that he delivers development in return for surrendering valuable freedoms. Since we have to choose on the basis of relative evidence rather than absolute rigor, the evidence is relatively more unfavorable toward autocracy than freedom.

Discarding the Blank Slate in this part of the book, we saw free Europe outperforming unfree Europe and unfree China. In this chapter, we saw an example of a society in New York and in the United States with individual rights in the long run outperforming two other societies from the previous chapter—Benin and Colombia—with oppression and suppression of rights.

There was no justification to discard this long-run picture in order to enable the consensus for authoritarian development to emerge in the twentieth century. There is no justification today for Gates and Blair to celebrate five years of alleged autocratic success in one country on one shaky dimension—Ethiopia on child mortality—while ignoring centuries of experience from around the world. The Blank Slate has given cover to autocrats for far too long in development; there is no reason for it to continue.

PART FOUR

Nations Versus Individuals

On March 7, 2012, the *New York Times Magazine* published an article by Scottish journalist Matt McAllester entitled "America is Stealing the World's Doctors."[1] The article lamented the move of doctors from poor countries to rich countries, with particular emphasis on those moving from African nations to America. The article focused on a Zambian doctor named Kunj Desai, who had left his native country behind to work at University Hospital in Newark, New Jersey. Dr. Desai felt guilty about leaving his homeland for a more lucrative position in America.

McAllester quoted approvingly an article from the British medical journal the *Lancet,* arguing that recruitment of health workers from Africa should be seen as a crime.[2] The *Lancet* article called doctor "theft" a "very important violation" of human rights. It suggested that those who steal doctors from African nations should be charged at the International Criminal Court, the body that prosecutes war crimes.

The ethos at work here, at face value entirely progressive, is in fact disrespectful of Africans' rights. The African doctors in question are persons. A person can be "stolen" from an African nation only if that person is the property of that nation. Such a crime violates rights only if rights are recognized for nations and not for nationals.

A double standard exists for individuals from rich or poor countries and it reveals our lack of respect for the rights for the latter. Skilled professionals in rich countries migrate without permission. If journalist Matt McAllester

[handwritten margin notes: "borderless world?"; "Role of migration as primary actor rather than corporation in or a ..."; "what about the corporation in or a ..."]

chose to move from a small Scottish newspaper to the *New York Times,* nobody would object, much less claim that he had been "stolen." Presumably, Mr. McAllester would also be content, since his relocation was voluntary.

This anecdote offers a revealing window into the development debate about the prerogatives of nations versus the rights of individuals. The former has triumphed over the latter; development seems to be almost exclusively about the fate of nations rather than about the fate of nationals. We seem to care more about Zambia than about Zambians.

We examine the moral and pragmatic debate on nations versus individuals from two angles in this part. In Chapter Nine we consider migration across national borders from the point of view of both the nation and individuals. In Chapter Ten we then explore the implications of the usual approach in which development analysis primarily takes place at the national level. Of course, nations matter, but do they matter as much as we think? Making the nation the unit of analysis in big-picture development discussions is almost unquestioned and its costs ignored.

This part does not criticize all nationalist ideas and nationalists. Nationalism is in part a voluntary movement and has had some positive achievements. The critique here is of excessive nationalism, what we could call the "nationalist obsession." The nationalist obsession has been very convenient for national governments auditioning for the job of chief developer of their nations; it is part of the core ideology supporting many authoritarian states. More subtly, it is convenient for the development experts whose only plausible counterparts are national government representatives. We should not automatically dismiss the nationalist emphasis on those grounds, nor should we accept a restriction of analysis to the national level only because of political expediency.

CHAPTER NINE

HOMES OR PRISONS?
NATIONS AND MIGRATIONS

As the example of the Zambian doctor showed, the treatment of migration in the development community is unintentionally revealing about just how much stronger are the prerogatives of nation-states than the rights of individuals. There is an ironic echo in this chapter of the 1920s development discussion in China covered in Chapter Three, in which early development ideas gave technocratic cover to US immigration restrictions against the Chinese.

THE MORALITY OF NATIONALISM

Love of country is often a noble thing. New nations emerged in the twentieth century as peoples of one nationality or ethnic group or religious affiliation strove to liberate themselves from rule by other nationalities in multinational empires (like the Austro-Hungarian or Ottoman Empires) or colonial empires. The breakup of such multiethnic empires resolved some tensions by giving each ethnic group its own nation. People found it easier to cooperate on providing public services—agreeing on which language to use in public schools, for example—when they were working with their own co-ethnics rather than straddling ethnic divides.

But the very idea of "love of country" implies choice. Individuals decide where to place their love of country within an array of other allegiances, such as to family, region, or ethnic group based on race, religion, or language. It turned out there were too many such groups to give each group its own nation, so the alternative choices of allegiance did not disappear as much as nationalist ideology expected.

→ root of many of middle eastern

Nationalism becomes authoritarian when such choices are denied to individuals, as some examples can illustrate. When the new nations emerged in the twentieth century in the aftermath of wars and decolonization, some new nationalist leaders defined the identity of a nation as the same as that of a majority ethnic group. National authorities sometimes wanted to suppress minority ethnic-group identification, such as banning the use of the minority's language (e.g., Turkish leaders banning Kurdish). They persecuted minority groups whose beliefs contradicted those of the majority culture (for example, identifying Pakistani nationalism with Sunni Islam, and consequently suppressing the religious and other rights of minority Shiites and Christians). The national authorities violently suppressed anything that looked like separatist movements of a region or ethnic group (for example, Ethiopia's army repressing Somali minorities in southern Ethiopia in the region bordering Somalia).

Authoritarian nationalism contributed to two world wars, which left it discredited in the rich countries. Yet authoritarian nationalism got a new lease on life from development in the poor countries. The rich countries' emphasis on the nation as the sole object of development efforts, born out of their own foreign policy needs as discussed in Part Two, coincided with national authorities' efforts to make national identity trump all other identities. Development lent unintended support for suppressing minority rights in the name of putting the nation's collective well-being above all else.

Authoritarian nationalism in poor countries has left behind a string of war crimes and rights violations, with ethnic minorities such as Tutsis, Bosnian Muslims, Kurds, Tibetans, and Darfuris falling victim to a nationalist majority. The Minorities at Risk project at the University of Maryland has identified no fewer than 283 minority groups that it has classified as At Risk at some point since 1950, almost all of them outside rich countries.[3]

MIGRATION AS PROTECTING INDIVIDUAL RIGHTS

For the last several centuries, an antidote to authoritarian nationalism and ethnic persecution has been migration. Members of an ethnic group op-

struggles

pressed by an autocrat can leave for somewhere else with less oppression. We have already seen one example of this on the Greene Street block in New York with the Seixas family. An early form of authoritarian nationalism in eighteenth-century Portugal, as enforced by the Inquisition, was to equate being Portuguese with being Catholic. The Seixas family and other Portuguese Jews could assert their individual rights by leaving Portugal for New York. Migration is a kind of safety valve, or escape hatch, allowing people to leave an intolerably oppressive situation.

We see the safety valve again on Greene Street when a new wave of Jews arrived as workers on the block in the 1880s; they were fleeing pogroms under the Russian Czar. The Czar identified being Russian with being Orthodox Christian. It was the escape of these Jews that inspired Emma Lazarus in 1883 to write what would later be inscribed on the Statue of Liberty: "Give me . . . your huddled masses yearning to breathe free. . . . I lift my lamp beside the golden door!" Emma Lazarus is another Seixas descendant; she was the granddaughter of Seixas Nathan and Sara Seixas whom we mentioned in Chapter Eight as living down Greene Street from their nephew Benjamin Seixas in the 1840s.[4] The greatest tragedy in the history of migration was that the United States had closed Emma Lazarus's golden door by the time German Jews in the 1930s and 1940s were trying to flee history's worst example of authoritarian nationalism.

Immigration restrictions in the United States of the 1920s included the Oriental Exclusion Act that caused the racial tension with the Chinese described in Chapter Three. Then and now, development unintentionally provided a technocratic rationale for restrictions on immigration to the United States, even when these restrictions were really motivated by racial antipathy rather than dispassionate developmental considerations. The restrictions also benefited autocrats in the would-be immigrants' home countries, allowing them to exploit their subjects without the risk of their escaping by migrating.

Yes, migrants did take away from their home nations the skills and labor that could have contributed to national development at home. There is an understandable concern for those left behind at home. Yet development made no place in its calculations for the well-being of would-be migrants themselves. It made no place for the rights of would-be migrants,

which is potentially everyone, to make their own choices for themselves
and their families.

Development's hostility to the individual rights of migrants could also
merge with humanitarian concern for the well-being of those left behind.
The genius of technocratic development continues to be its ability to serve
groups with nearly opposite values. To those in rich nations with antipa-
thies to other ethnic groups, it justifies immigration restrictions; to those
humanitarians in rich nations concerned about those same ethnic groups,
it offers development in the groups' countries of origin.

so ironic!

Ethnic groups are the most emotive example of migrants having a
welcome escape hatch from oppression, in this case ethnic oppression.
Yet there is no reason to limit the discussion to ethnic oppression. Individuals suffering deprivation of their political and economic rights also
may want to flee their oppressors for somewhere else where they will have
such rights. We are familiar with this idea when famous dissidents from
a repressive regime get political asylum in a free country. Yet why should
we limit the escape hatch only to the most famous? Again, development
based on the economic performance of pieces of territory has little room
for individuals who seek to find a place for their own rights.

Migrants also move for economic reasons, to go from a place where
they have less potential income to one where they have more. It is not
easy to distinguish such cases from those based on seeking greater rights.
Denial of rights and lack of economic potential go together and reinforce
each other. Even if we could identify migrants who move only for economic reasons, it is not clear they deserve any special hostility for that
motivation.

Again, a double standard reveals what little regard we have for the
rights of poor people. Many of us in rich countries migrate for economic
reasons all the time, whether it is from one place to another within our
countries, or even from one industry to another. We cherish the principle
that each of us has the right to realize our maximum potential by changing places. Why do we have a special hostility toward persons from a poor
country crossing a national boundary on their way to realizing their own
potential?

The point of this discussion is not to demand completely open migration everywhere. National immigration policies must consider many complexities that are beyond the scope of this book. The point is that development—based only on maximizing the economic potential of one piece of territory—had a hostility toward the rights of individuals that is revealed whenever those individuals want to migrate. This hostility blinds us to the possibility that migration itself could be a powerful vehicle for both global and individual development.

MIGRATION AS POVERTY REDUCTION

What would you think of a single antipoverty program within one poor country that was responsible for 82 percent of all the escapes from poverty that had ever happened in that country? The development community's actual reaction seemed to be: that's terrible!

The country was Haiti, and the program was called—migration to the United States. Michael Clemens and Lant Pritchett, on whose work I base much of this chapter, did the calculation. They looked at Haitians who had incomes above $10 a day, which is safely above the usual international poverty lines of $1 a day or $2 a day (although still only one-third of the US poverty line). They included the Haitian diaspora as well as Haitians in Haiti. Some 82 percent of the Haitian nonpoor lived in the United States; only 18 percent of the nonpoor Haitians still lived in Haiti.[5]

Of course, there is every reason to care about Haitians who remain in Haiti, but development seems to go to the other extreme of not caring about any Haitians who choose to leave Haiti. The development mind-set is apparently that eliminating poverty only counts if you stay at home. Only achievement on or of the territory called "Haiti" counts, not achievements by or for individual Haitians. This view of development exists independently of anti-immigration feelings in the United States, but it is certainly a welcome gift to those with such feelings.

The nationalist obsession also blinds us to positive effects of migration on *global* development. When a Haitian moves from a place where she earns little to a place where she earns much more, she has increased global GDP. Why should we care only about national development and not about global development?

The Missing UN Summit

It does not take much to hold a UN summit on a global issue. The typical UN summit will declare something to be a problem and suggest international action to solve it. There have been UN summits on women, population, the environment, children, aging, the Millennium Development Goals of poverty reduction, and many other topics that fit this pattern.[6]

The shared responsibility for the international action to address a summit issue will mean that no one national government will be held responsible. The only consequence of inadequate progress on the solutions suggested by a UN summit is usually—another UN summit. This author confesses to having mocked UN summits many times as all talk and no action.

One sign of the political sensitivity of migration as a topic is that it fails to cross even the extremely low bar required for convening a UN summit conference. Despite frequent proposals to do so, there has never been a UN "Summit on Migration." A UN General Assembly resolution had proposed a migration summit as long ago as 1993, before most of the summits on the other topics listed above even happened. But the politics are too difficult. For the rich nations, like the United States, it seems to threaten uncomfortable discussions of what the American Civil Liberties Union describes as "laws that deny immigrants' access to the courts, impose indefinite and mandatory detention, and discriminate on the basis of nationality."[7] There is a faint echo of the attempt to avoid discussion of the Oriental Exclusion Act from nine decades ago that we reviewed at the beginnings of authoritarian development in Chapter Three.

After thirteen years of effort and negotiation, there was an agreement in 2006 to hold a "high-level dialogue" on migration. A high-level dialogue is an even emptier version of a UN summit process that is already almost entirely empty. This twice-empty outcome was apparently an effort to avoid attracting any international attention whatsoever. They succeeded, as this author can testify personally. Despite professional dedication to watching UN efforts on development, despite even an interest in migration, I had never heard of the High-Level Dialogue on Migration of 2006. It took an inquiry to Michael Clemens, the migration specialist, to uncover this nonevent.

The suppression of The-Topic-That-Must-Not-Be-Named was achieved by a 2006 compromise that reflected mainly the interests of the rich nations where migrants most want to go—that is, the United States, Australia, Canada, and the European Union. These nations maybe did not want to draw attention to the miserable way they treat would-be migrants who do make it to their territory, or how they deny refuge to some horribly abused people from other places. The migrant-receiving nations of course do have a legitimate case to determine their own immigration policies, but they do not have a right to censor international discussion of migration and development.

REMITTANCES

In fairness to the World Bank and other parts of the development community, this community contains sensible, caring people who recognize many of the points made in this chapter. The World Bank's page on migration allows that "the overall economic gains from international migration for sending countries, receiving countries, and the migrants themselves are substantial." Yet at the same time, the World Bank emphasizes discussion overwhelmingly only on one narrow dimension of migration, remittances. Before getting to the recognition of "overall gains" just mentioned, the World Bank page begins: "Remittances, the money sent home by migrants, are three times the size of official development assistance and they provide an important lifeline for millions of poor households. Remittances to developing countries are estimated to reach $372 billion in 2011."[8]

The World Bank's topic page on migration is actually called "Migration and Remittances." (In what may be either a random glitch or a Freudian slip, this page has a link to another page called "Migration and Poverty Reduction," but that page is blank.[9]) The World Bank's April 2013 "Migration and Development Brief" of eleven pages mentions the word *remittance* 150 times. The word *rights* is never mentioned.[10]

Remittances are indeed part of the benefits of migration. If you have already migrated, then it is safe to encourage you to send back home as much income as possible. Let us celebrate progress in the development

ones who have the power are the same ones that migrant's are fully @ mercy of

community when it happens: only in the last decade was there even discussion of remittances as a positive force in development.

At the same time, though, there has been little or no discussion of migration at the Bank or anywhere else in the development community as a way for individuals to protect their own rights and escape oppression.

Brain Drain

Which brings us back to the brain drain with which we began this part on nationalism. The idea of a disastrous brain drain has lost some credibility as evidence has accumulated on how much of their foreign incomes brain drainers have remitted back to their home countries.

Economists have also pointed out that the opportunity to migrate is part of the reason individuals invested in skills in the home country at all. The payoff to sacrificing a lot to acquire skills is higher if the worker can work abroad as well as at home. If the payoff falls because the worker cannot work abroad, that worker is less likely to invest in skills. Preventing a brain drain by restricting out-migration means that fewer people will invest in becoming "brains" to begin with. The lower creation of new brains will eventually offset the number of existing brains that were retained by preventing a brain drain. Moreover, if a nation is good at producing some type of skilled workers both for home and for export, like Filipino nurses, that should be something to be celebrated, not something to be choked off.

That it took decades after the beginning of "official development" to figure out such common-sense points shows how bad the nationalist obsession in development has been. Now the discussion on the net effect of brain drain is finally allowed in aid agencies.

Yet still verboten is consideration of the principal beneficiary of brain drain: the out-migrating brain drainers themselves. The brain drainer carries the stigma of being a development traitor, whose gains from migration are somehow illicit. Yet the Invisible-Hand principle works well with migration. The wage paid to the brain drainer reflects the value of their contribution to world output. When drainers leave low-wage jobs for high-wage jobs, they increase their productivity. They benefit not only themselves but world development as a whole. Only a nationalist obsession would ignore such gains in global development.

One of the arguments against brain drainers is that their home nation spent money on educating them, which should force them either to not leave at all or to repay the money. This argument gives suspiciously special treatment to migration. If educated nationals stay at home and fail to add to national production for some other reason—because they joined a monastery, or chose to stay at home with the kids rather than work— there is usually not a call for them to pay punitive damages.

The Lost Republic of West Virginia

Another way to see the double standard we have on coercive nationalism is to examine poorer provinces within nations. Although the logic on the damage of brain drain is the same whether it be a poor nation or a poor region within a nation, the latter does not receive much notice.

West Virginia is the second poorest US state. On a moonless night in late September 1957, two West Virginia brain drainers smuggled themselves and their two children—the youngest just two weeks old—across the Ohio River, en route to jobs in northwest Ohio. These brain drainers were both graduates of West Virginia University, where the man also had gotten a PhD. He was going to use education as his path for upward mobility, to escape the poverty to which he had almost been consigned at age two by the death of his father. But this path required a good job, and the good jobs were in Ohio, not in West Virginia.

The two-week-old along for the ride was this author. From 1950 to 2000, 800,000 other West Virginians—including all of my aunts, uncles, and cousins—left a state that had only 2 million people at the beginning. Nobody has ever reproached my parents for being traitors to West Virginia, nor has anyone asked them to repay West Virginia for their schooling costs.

Ghost Countries

The hostility toward migration as poverty relief in development continues even when migration *does* benefit those left behind. A big reason for

West Virginia's out-migration was the long-term decline of its coal industry. Among other things, the replacement of trains by automobiles shifted
energy demand from coal to petroleum—West Virginia was a victim of
creative destruction. Employment in West Virginia coal declined even
faster than production did, as mines were mechanized. Other industries
suffered badly in West Virginia as its leading industry tanked.

Let's leave behind now the focus only on movement of brains and consider population migration of both skilled and unskilled workers. The huge
out-migration in West Virginia suggests that both skilled and unskilled
workers were leaving; let's now lump them together using economists' jar-
gon as "labor." And let's compare West Virginia with Zambia, which also
had a huge negative shock with the decline of its copper industry. Zambia
was the focus of the "stealing doctors" article with which this chapter began. Kunj Desai, the Zambian doctor who migrated to the United States,
was the exception for Zambians, most of whom could not move due to immigration restrictions elsewhere. Let's broaden our lenses from just brain
drains to the effect of an emigration prohibition on all Zambians.

And while we are at it, let's do a supply-and-demand analysis for labor (again no longer distinguishing skilled and unskilled labor), an analysis suggested by Lant Pritchett in a paper titled "Boom Towns and Ghost
Countries." In both West Virginia and Zambia, outside economic forces
(collapse of coal and copper demand, respectively) caused a collapse in
the demand for local labor. If migration cannot happen, the supply of local labor does not change, so the collapse of the demand for labor at home
means a wage collapse. This was roughly what happened in Zambia, which
had a long decline in per capita income from the 1970s through the 1990s.

However, if people can leave on a large scale in response to the collapse of labor demand, there is a different outcome. Labor supply at home
decreases when people leave, as happened in West Virginia. Wages for
those left behind don't need to collapse if the local labor supply is falling
just as fast as labor demand is falling. Per capita income in West Virginia
actually rose at the same rate as the US average throughout the Great Out-
Migration from West Virginia. West Virginia did not get poor because of
out-migration; it was already poor before the out-migration began, and
the out-migration kept it from getting poorer.

Zambia, in contrast, did get poorer because people could *not* migrate when there was a huge negative shock like the collapse of the copper industry. Pritchett contrasted the phenomenon of "ghost towns"—where people leave when the mine shuts down—to what he suggested we should call "ghost countries"—countries that get a lot poorer when the mine shuts down because people *cannot* leave. Such a nation becomes a prison for poor people.[11]

MOURIDES

Another way in which migration can have a positive effect on those left behind is when it gives them new access to international networks of trade and finance. There is a surprisingly omnipresent yet unknown group in Western cities that illustrates this. To illustrate the omnipresence of this group, go up to any African-looking street retailer in New York, Paris, Madrid, or Milan, and ask them if they are from Senegal. They will almost certainly say yes. Ask them if they are Mouride. Again, they will say yes.

The Mourides are a religious brotherhood that also became an international network of merchants. The Mourides give each other credits to finance purchases of goods and to start new ventures. They make international remittances to family members back in Senegal and provide loans to each other.[12]

During French colonial rule in Senegal in the late nineteenth century, a Muslim critic of the French and Senegalese elite, Ahmadou Bamba Mbacké (1853–1927), founded the Mouride brotherhood in 1883. Bamba advocated hard work, an ascetic lifestyle, and group solidarity as a way to divine redemption. Before his death, Bamba founded the holy city of Touba for the Mourides, where he is now buried.[13] Today, Touba is Senegal's second-largest city, four hours by car to the east of Dakar.

The work ethic of the Mourides coincided with the takeoff of peanut production during the French colonial era, and the Mourides wound up dominating peanuts before and after independence. However, drought and low peanut prices in the late 1970s and early 1980s drove many Mourides to seek other opportunities, most notably via emigration to France, the United States, Spain, Italy, and elsewhere.[14]

The Mourides have kept emigrating despite explicit and implicit barriers to migration. They often arrive without any knowledge of the foreign language or society's rules but receive the support needed to get on their feet in *dahiras*, groups of men (and lately women) who organize housing, financial and spiritual support, and business training or advice for new arrivals.

It was this network of mutual support and trust that made possible the economic network of the Mourides. The network remains based in Senegal. Stalls with corrugated iron roofs packed together in the Sandaga market in Dakar constitute the Wall Street of the Mourides. When a Mouride merchant leaves Senegal to buy electronics or cosmetics in New York, handbags and shoes in Italy, or clothes in France, he deposits cash in the Sandaga market branch of the KARA International Money Exchange. KARA works like Western Union, but instantaneously, with far less expense. Upon the merchant's arrival in New York, he can pick up the amount he has left in Sandaga at the KARA branch on Broadway.[15]

In New York he can receive further credit from one of the emigrants who live around 116th Street and Malcolm X Boulevard in "Little Senegal," the Mouride community in Harlem. He completes all these transactions with neither a written contract nor a notary certification nor any collateral. During his stay in New York, his family back in Senegal might need food or money. The merchant simply calls another Mouride merchant in Sandaga who can dispense cash to the family the same day in a small Sandaga shop.

The Mourides have built a system that allows instantaneous and nearly costless financial transactions. While the aid establishment is supporting microcredit projects around the world with mixed results, almost everyone has overlooked the Mourides, who can pride themselves on decades of successful microfinance.

Their dense network also serves for exchange of market information: one Mouride merchant got a tip through the network to buy plastic storks in New York City's Chinatown to sell to German tourists in the French city of Strasbourg, knowing that Strasbourg's merchants would not be able to match the price.[16]

The Mouride network has made possible prosperity for many of its members, both back in Senegal and abroad. The five Fall brothers from Kaolack, Senegal, grew up in *dahiras* and then started out as cloth traders. The first brother to emigrate, Cheikh Mbacke Fall, arrived in New York in 1973 to purchase some CDs for a businessman from Cameroon. Over the next eight years he developed hairpieces for the African market with a Korean business partner.[17]

Upon returning to Senegal, Cheikh single-handedly created a market for hairpieces in Senegal, and he and his Korean partner opened the first factory for hair products there. His brothers left Kaolack to support Cheikh's business. One of them, Abdouh Lahat, supported Cheikh in importing beauty and electronic products from New York, perfumes and TVs from Saudi Arabia, and radios from Hong Kong. In the 1990s, the Falls moved into the Senegalese market for cosmetic products from the United Kingdom and the United States, and for shoes from Taiwan.

Utilizing the international Mouride network, the Fall brothers ensured payments for both the Mouride participants in their businesses and their non-Mouride business partners. The business of the Fall brothers had started out in the remote village of Kaolack and within one generation employed Mourides all over the globe.

CONCLUSIONS

Migration is the canary in the coal mine on development's attitude toward individual rights versus the prerogatives of nation-states. The hostility toward a skilled professional migrating from Zambia to a rich country reveals a concern for the territorial collective called "Zambia" that shows at the same time a lack of concern for Zambians as individuals with rights.

The bias toward development as a self-contained thing on national territory also shows the inability to think about the role of nonnational or transnational forces or groups, such as the Mourides, in economic development. The next chapter considers more evidence that national forces alone are not as important as usually believed.

- In a way corroborates Friedman's rather globalized perspective

CHAPTER TEN

HOW MUCH DO NATIONS MATTER?

(handwritten in left margin: national growth v. global growth)

(handwritten asterisk in left margin)

If there is one number to which the rights of millions will be happily sacrificed, it is the national GDP growth rate. National leaders believe national growth takes place as the result of national actions. These leaders take great pride in rapid national growth, as do their expert advisers who think their advice is paying off. The unofficial line for a "growth miracle" seems to be annual growth of income per capita of 6 percent. Grow 6 percent, and all will be forgiven.

The national state justifies itself partly as the custodian of economic management charged with promoting growth. The development agencies and experts justify themselves as advisors to these states on how to raise growth. Their claims to be able to raise growth are part of the justification for nation-states and their technocratic advisors to have more power. But if their claims are hollow, they provide little justification for the Tyranny of Experts. So this chapter examines how much evidence there is for these claims.

The broader lesson is that the excessive emphasis on development of nations over development of individuals was yet another tragic, misguided choice on the road to forgetting the rights of the poor. Nations do matter for growth and development outcomes, but not as much as usually believed. When they do matter, it is sometimes for the wrong reasons. By overemphasizing the national unit as the place where development happens, the experts wound up interfering with the rights of peoples from different nations to do mutually advantageous deals with each other.

Development's search for the answer to "what is the right national action to raise growth?" was misplaced. The answer is not the right *national* action; the answer is a system of political and economic rights in which many political and economic actors will find the right actions—both within and across national borders—to promote their own development.

We have already reviewed the long-run historical narrative in which systems based on rights solve public problems and let individuals solve their own private problems, where systems that oppress and repress individuals fail to do so. In this chapter, we see how development's extreme focus on the national unit to the exclusion of individual rights yielded little payoff and sometimes yielded a negative payoff.

DO NATIONAL POLICIES AFFECT GROWTH?

My own research career really began in 1991 when Ross Levine (now at the University of California at Berkeley) and I got a grant from our employer at the time, the World Bank, for a research project entitled "How Do National Policies Affect Long-Run Growth?"[1] The *how* in the title of the project took for granted that national policies do affect growth. This captured perfectly the nation-centric mentality of the World Bank at that time (including this author's mentality at that time) and since.

National policies can of course matter in some extreme situations, as Robert Mugabe demonstrated with a heroic combination of hyperinflation and land expropriation to achieve negative growth in Zimbabwe. But over less-extreme ranges, one of our World Bank project's findings was that there was little evidence that national policies had major effects on national growth, despite some illusions to the contrary that we review in this chapter.

This finding is not only unwelcome at the World Bank and other development agencies, it is unwelcome to autocrats and their expert advisors who want to justify their hold on power by their wisdom at promoting national growth. It will be unpopular with both left-wing and right-wing policy experts, who each claim that their policies will have sizeable national-growth payoffs.

GOOD POLICY OR GOOD LUCK?

Ironically, one of the most successful papers from the World Bank project on "How Do National Policies Do Affect Long-Run Growth?" established just how little national policies actually *do* affect growth. This author and some interesting coauthors wrote the paper: Larry Summers (later treasury secretary and Harvard president), Michael Kremer (later Harvard professor and development superstar), and Lant Pritchett (also later Harvard professor and development superstar).

The paper studied how polices like inflation, government deficits, trade, price controls, and interest-rate controls affect long-run growth. The finding of the paper was simple—national growth success is usually temporary and quickly reversed. This finding has been replicated many times since as new data have come along.[2]

In other words, the fastest-growing countries in one period are not the same countries as those of the next period, or of the previous period. Togo was one of the fastest-growing countries in the 1960s, a success that it has not come remotely close to repeating since. Similar examples for each decade include Paraguay (1970s), Oman (1980s), the Dominican Republic (1990s), and Chad (2000s). If you haven't heard a lot of discussion about the great Togo (or Paraguay or Oman or Dominican Republic or Chad) success story, it is because they each had only a fleeting moment of success, offset by longer periods of mediocrity or outright disaster.

What is going on? Policy differences between countries persist a long time, but growth differences between countries do not. So it is hard to give much importance to national policies (or any other national characteristic that is long lasting—and most national characteristics *are* long lasting). What actually produces a lot of growth variations are temporary factors: booms and busts in commodity prices, the boom-and-bust cycles of international lending, natural disasters and recovery, or (embarrassingly) measurement error in growth rates. Other things that affect growth are so evanescent that researchers cannot even pin them down. Often, we growth researchers simply have to admit that we often do not know what explains sudden changes in growth.

To say it another way, there is a strong tendency for both extreme success and extreme failure to revert toward average. If success and failure reflect mostly temporary factors, these temporary factors are not likely to be repeated next period. Any time a country's growth is above the global average, it is very likely that the growth will fall back down toward the global average in the next period. It will not fall all of the way back, but it will fall most of the way. Between successive decades, for example, about 70 percent of the above-average growth in a country disappears in the next period. Some new countries will suddenly appear as top growers, only to fall back next time themselves, and so on. The best forecast for a rapidly growing country is that its growth will slow down. (The same is true in reverse: below-average growth performance will move back up toward the world average as the temporary bad factors are not repeated.)

Even the Gang of Four, the East Asian growth superstars that have been in the top world rankings of growth the longest, have since fallen back toward the average. The growth of Singapore and Hong Kong was still perfectly respectable from 2000 to 2010, but they were surpassed in that decade by Sierra Leone and Rwanda.

A 2005 study showed the phenomenon of fleeting growth success in a different way. It studied episodes of growth acceleration, in which growth increased by at least two percentage points from one seven-year period to the next. These episodes were surprisingly common: the study documented eighty-three accelerations altogether. Yet it was less common that rapid growth was sustained—almost half of the episodes followed the acceleration period with growth below the global average.[3]

Perhaps most disconcerting was that this 2005 study, like the 1993 study, could shed little light on why growth accelerated. A few of the growth accelerations occurred with well-known episodes of changed policies, such as China's 1978 shift to market-oriented policies. But these examples of well-explained changes in growth were the exception.

The study authors could not be more clear. Growth accelerations *do not* happen when economists expect they will: "most instances of economic reform do not produce growth accelerations." And growth accelerations *do* happen when economists have no reason to expect them: "most growth accelerations are not preceded or accompanied by major changes in economic policies, institutional arrangements, political circumstances, or external conditions."

The 2005 study was not an isolated finding. Harvard economist Dani Rodrik wrote a comprehensive survey on policies and growth in 2007 in the premier *Journal of Economic Literature*. His conclusion was that "the experience of the last two decades has frustrated the expectations . . . [that] we had a good fix on the policies that promote growth."⁴ His conclusion reflected a consensus; other academic economists have been saying the same thing in recent years.

Noise Versus Signal

The pattern that most growth booms are temporary is so important that it deserves yet another angle of vision. Consider Rwanda's high growth rate, a 6 percent increase in per capita income in 2011. This is numerical territory for a growth miracle, which results in observers giving a lot of credit to the national state presiding over the miracle growth. When we get excited about a growth miracle like this, it is because we expect it to last a long time. One year of high growth would not be much of an accomplishment if it only lasted that one year. The difference between 6 percent growth and the global average of 2 percent growth for one year is a 4 percent difference in income, which is good but hardly merits miracle designation.

But if the 6 percent growth of income per capita were really permanent, the consequences indeed would be miraculous. Over fifty years, a sustained average of 6 percent growth produces an eighteen-fold increase in income per capita. Average global growth of 2 percent per capita increases income over the same period at less than three-fold. A three-fold increase in income is great, but it is a lot less than the eighteen-fold increased produced by the 6 percent growth-miracle cases. The power of compound growth has attracted a lot of effort to reach the lasting miracle growth of 6 percent.

Almost all these hopes have been disappointed in the long run. We now have annual data on growth of income per capita for 101 countries over fifty years, and data for shorter periods for another 103 countries. We can use these data to estimate the range of permanent growth rates of countries. Annual growth rates will reflect both permanent differences between countries and the temporary year-to-year variation around the permanent growth rate for each country.

A good guide to how seriously to treat a one-year high-growth rate as permanent is the relative importance of the temporary year-to-year variation in growth versus the permanent growth differences between countries.

If permanent growth differences are large relative to the temporary variations, then we will get excited about the onset of rapid growth. In contrast, if temporary variations swamp permanent differences, rapid growth in the short run will be both very common and very temporary and is hardly grounds for excitement.

The vote of the evidence is a landslide for temporary factors over permanent national differences. Of the total variation of annual growth rates, around 95 percent is temporary; only about 5 percent of the variation of annual growth reflects permanent differences between nations. To put it another way, the year-to-year variability of growth within each country is about 20 times larger than the permanent growth differences between countries. Those nation-states getting credit for growth success in the short run account for surprisingly little of the development action in the long run.

The long-run growth differences do allow for a few really exceptional countries. The most famous are the aforementioned Gang of Four— Singapore, Hong Kong, South Korea, and Taiwan—who maintained a 6 percent per capita growth rate for several decades. China has joined the 6 percent club more recently with its remarkable growth surge. Yet even for these superstars, their long-run growth is very likely less than 6 percent. The greatest successes go to those who are not just good, and not just lucky, but both lucky and good. Even several decades of 6 percent growth included some temporary factors that will not last. The overall data say it is very unlikely that the top-five growth performers out of about 200 countries in the world would have long-run growth more than about 4 percent per capita. We have seen the Gang of Four already slow down. Here is a free prediction that China will slow down, too; it may have already started.

So maintaining 6 percent growth for several decades really is a miracle. Yet virtually all countries have had at least *one* year of 6 percent growth (only 4 out of 101 nations with the most complete data failed to attain 6 percent growth in at least one year). The dominance of the temporary growth fluctuations over permanent differences between nations explains why there are so few of the lasting miracles and yet why almost everyone has had temporary miracles.

The statistical pattern of all countries speaks loudly that most miracle growth rates are one-hit wonders. The evidence is saying that annual growth is mostly noise rather than signal. This is not a welcome finding in development agencies that claim to know how national actions can raise long-run growth within a reasonable horizon for policy makers.

The root cause of these findings is simply that annual growth rates are extraordinarily volatile. The average change in GDP per capita growth rates (in either direction) from one year to the next is over 4 percentage points, usually reflecting the appearance and disappearance of temporary factors like a commodity-price boom. For example, suppose that a temporary oil-price increase boosts growth in an oil exporter. Oil-price increases will first move the oil exporter's growth up above the world average, but a subsequent fall of oil prices will plunge the oil exporter's growth back to average. The oil exporter may have only one good year, or it could have several in a row, but the high-growth boom will end pretty quickly most of the time if most of the action is temporary, like temporary oil-price booms.

If a country maintains a fast growth rate above the average for a longer period, that is evidence that this country does have some more permanent difference from the average—but not as permanent or as different as many might think. Averaging over a long period filters out some of the noise, but the noise is so large that it takes a lot of averaging over a lot of years to minimize the noise and find the signal.

A ten-year horizon is way beyond the horizon of most national policymakers establishing policy today. Sadly, ten years is still not enough averaging to get rid of most of the noise. With ten-year averages of growth rates, we now consider the variation from one decade to the next within each country around its permanent growth rate. We now have reduced the role of temporary noise to 80 percent of the total variation of ten-year-average growth rates, and increased the role of long-run national differences to about 20 percent. That is a pretty disappointing permanent signal after waiting ten years to collect enough data on the nation's permanent growth potential.

We could save a role for national determinants of growth over the medium run, like economic policies, if these policies changed a lot and if growth responded to these changes. The two studies above—confirmed by many other studies as Dani Rodrik emphasized in his survey—found that both conditions fail to be met. Policies do not change that much, and, when they do, growth does not respond much, if at all.

If the claim that national policies can raise growth within a medium-term horizon has little support, that, too, is bad news for the national state–technocrat complex. The sacrifice of individual rights on the altar of maximizing national growth shows little or no evidence of paying off for individuals.

MEASUREMENT ERROR

What is going on with the huge majority of growth variation that is not explained by permanent national determinants? One among many factors that helps explain the volatility of annual growth rates is a particular embarrassment: growth is subject to large measurement errors.

That both the levels and the growth of Gross Domestic Product (GDP) are subject to large errors in measurement has been known for many years, but again has received suspiciously little attention from those prone to worship national growth rates—that is, national policy makers and the experts and aid agencies set up to advise them.

Detectives on the trail of measurement error can point to a couple of damning pieces of evidence. First a review of the output of national statistics offices shows some gaps. When we measure growth in GDP to assess real progress in living standards, we are interested in growth in GDP corrected for inflation. A 2012 study pointed out that the United Nations maintained a complete dataset on inflation-corrected GDP for forty-seven countries in sub-Saharan Africa from 1999 to 2004. Yet as of mid-2006, the UN Statistical Office had actually received data from national statistical agencies for *less than half* of these observations. Fifteen African countries had *never* given the UN *any* data on inflation-corrected GDP.[5] The data for economic growth in those fifteen countries do not even exist. To come up with numbers anyway, the United Nations was doing something between making educated guesses on the numbers and simply making them up.

The second clue for measurement-error detectives is that different sources come up with different numbers for the same GDP growth rate by year and country. This is the same embarrassing problem pointed out with child-mortality statistics in Ethiopia just as Bill Gates was celebrating precise measurement to guide health policy. National policy makers using growth to guide policy also have bad numbers for this guidance.

The standard source for growth data is the World Bank's World Development Indicators (WDI). An alternative source for growth data is an impressive estimation exercise at the University of Pennsylvania done by the Center for International Comparisons of Production, Income, and Prices. The latter produces data known as the Penn World Tables (PWT).[6] Both of these sources are doing their best to measure economic growth, they both have superb reputations, and both are widely used by academic researchers (including this author).

Yet they have a surprising tendency to disagree on what growth is for a given country and year. On average, the difference for all countries between their estimates (in either direction) for any given year in any given country is 2.2 percentage points of growth. For sub-Saharan Africa, where we already had the first clue that measurement error might be severe due to missing and possibly made-up data, the difference between the PWT and WDI estimates (in either direction) for growth rates is 3.4 percentage points.

Take war-torn Democratic Republic of the Congo where the national government does not have full control of the national territory and statistical efforts may not be a top priority. There are some unsurprisingly big differences between PWT and WDI in Congo. In 2003, for example, the WDI saw an economic expansion of 3 percent per capita, while PWT saw a *contraction* of 10 percent per capita—a steep recession. Even though there was confusion about what growth actually was, the World Bank could still claim to discern the national state's effect: "From 2003 to 2005, the transitional government . . . laid the foundations for strong growth."[7]

The World Bank was reckless to be drawing conclusions in the midst of chaos in the Congo. But do not think that big disagreements on growth happen only in war-torn disasters. Disagreement on growth also happens in the much-celebrated growth stars. In Singapore in 2003, PWT saw a slight contraction of 0.1 percent, while WDI saw miracle growth of 6.2 percent. In China for three consecutive years in 1987 through 1989, WDI had China's growth between 3 and 6 percentage points higher per year than did PWT.

Moreover, these sources tend to disagree with their own past selves. When WDI and PWT issue additional years of data, they also revise the old numbers. WDI does not make available the older versions of its data (which is bad), but PWT does (which is admirable). The average change in growth, in either direction, for any given country and year of overlapping data between the most recent revision (round 7) of PWT ("PWT7") and its predecessor version (round 6; "PWT6") is 2.4 percentage points of growth (3.8 percentage points for sub-Saharan Africa).

Even if we think the revisions move in the direction of the truth, we are always dealing with some data that will be revised in the future, including especially the most recent data. This suggests again that all of us should not be taking annual growth rates so seriously. It is unlikely we know with any confidence what they really are.

I torture the reader with this excess of boring detail only because the boredom hides a problem that is not boring. We pass out congratulations or blame to national policy makers because we assume national growth performance is measured with precision—a precision that does not exist and that is sometimes even based on numbers that do not exist.

As with other types of temporary noise, there is a partial remedy available: averaging over longer periods. Since measurement errors go in both directions, they tend to cancel out with averaging. The average difference between WDI and PWT is reduced to 0.7 percentage points for ten-year averages, and the difference between the two PWT versions is reduced to 0.9 percent (the corresponding numbers for Africa are 1.0 and 1.5 percentage points). This is still not trivial, and it still leaves some large decade-growth errors around the average. I mentioned earlier in this chapter that Sierra Leone had surpassed the Gang of Four on miracle growth between 2000 and 2010. I myself fell for the same illusion of precision. A later check showed that only PWT shows Sierra Leone's growth at a miraculous 6.7 percent per year in the millennial decade, while WDI shows a pedestrian 2.6 percent per year for that period.

Yet all this at least leaves us some hope for finding a signal and tells us what to do to find it: look at the long run, and make the run as long as possible. This is yet another reason to disavow the Blank Slate and let the long run of history speak.

REGIONAL GROWTH VERSUS NATIONAL GROWTH

Economists have now spent two decades trying to explain growth differences between countries. They have tried a multitude of national policies and other characteristics, few or none of which hold up as robust predictors of growth differences. One major exception is a robust finding on one national characteristic, but this finding has always been an embarrassment. The national characteristic that does robustly matter is what *region* your nation belongs to. Whether your nation is in sub-Saharan Africa is a good predictor for (bad) growth. Latin American location predicts below-average growth and East Asian location predicts above-average growth. The regional effects hold up for the different datasets on growth (WDI and both versions of PWT), although their magnitude varies somewhat. Roughly speaking, Latin American countries on average grow about 1 percentage point less than East Asian ones, while African countries grow about 2 percentage points less than East Asian ones.

It does not seem to be an accident that the worst growth disasters—such as Zambia, Zimbabwe, Central African Republic, Madagascar, Niger, Liberia, and Democratic Republic of the Congo—are almost all in sub-Saharan Africa. It does not seem to be an accident that those growth stars, the Gang of Four and China (and Japan in earlier decades) are all in East Asia. The idea of a regional growth effect has been especially unwelcome to development experts and aid officials who want to give advice on growth. They can advise the national policy makers, but they cannot give advice to the nonexistent regional policy makers.

Another sign that regional growth is an important part of the action is that regions move together from one decade to the next. For example, Latin American nations in the 1980s collectively had a famous "lost decade." A regional credit bubble had burst: global banks had given the region a supply of easy credit at low interest rates in the 1970s, then interest rates went up and credit was cut off in the 1980s.

A sensible principle for attribution for national growth performance is that a nation does not get special recognition if its performance is just at the average. It would be foolish for a nation to claim credit for growth that is the same as the average for its region. If a nation is above (or below) these averages, then we can talk about special recognition for the nation's growth performance.

This principle further reduces the share of growth variation explained by permanent national differences. Some of the variation in decade growth rates explained by national differences was really explained by regional differences. Recalculating, we now get only a little more than a tenth of the variation in decade growth rates explained by national differences. Regional growth differences explain roughly as much of growth as national growth differences do.

The data are trying to tell us that growth success and failure is more of a regional thing than we think, and less of a national thing—and we, the nation-obsessed, are not listening. What if we listened to the data and took our gaze away from the nation, and considered some nonnational factors, something a little more regional? Who knows what new perspectives we might get, what other stories might deserve consideration?

BACK TO FUJIAN PROVINCE

The last time we saw the port of Quanzhou, in Fujian Province, China, in this narrative, it was to watch the backs of the defeated Nationalists departing for Taiwan after the failure of Chinese development before 1949. Fujian Province has a history and a role in today's development that may help us explain why East Asia has done well as a region. As a bonus, the story also involves migration.

Let's look at one remarkable Fujianese individual to get started. Eka Tjipta Widjaja was born in Quanzhou in 1923. He left Quanzhou and a war-torn Fujian Province in 1932 with his family at the age of nine. His grandson later recalled that they left in boats because "they didn't want to be farmers. They wanted to achieve something in their lives." They were "depending on the wind" to determine where they wound up. That place turned out to be South Sulawesi, Indonesia. Starting from nothing, Widjaja had a retail store that prospered only by his maintaining longer hours than his competitors. He moved to Jakarta and started larger businesses, first a candy manufacturer, then a maker of coconut oil products.[8] In 1962, Eka Tjipta Widjaja founded the business that would make his fortune, Sinar Mas, which grew to be a giant pulp and paper conglomerate. As of 2009, his son Teguh Widjaja was chairman of Sinar Mas Group-APP (the paper division), which alone employed 150,000 people and was valued at more than $20 billion.

Meanwhile, another of Widjaja's sons, Oei Hong-Leong, moved to Singapore, where he became known as the "The Man with the Midas Touch" through his ability to restructure third-tier companies and increase their value.[9] His net worth as of 2013, at age 65, was $745 million.[10]

Next in the family story is Eka Tjipta Widjaja's grandson, Eric Oei Kang, who was born in 1970. He moved to Hong Kong after getting an economics degree from the University of California at Santa Barbara and an MBA at Claremont Graduate University. Today, Eric Oei Kang heads up Creator Holdings, a giant construction company in Hong Kong.

This one family from Fujian contributes to success in three different East Asian tigers: Indonesia, Singapore, and Hong Kong. Meanwhile, the success of this Fujianese family has bounced back to Fujian (and thereby China) itself. The Singapore-based son, Oei Hong-Leong, played an important role in China's economic miracle in the 1990s by buying up a lot of state companies, including forty-one factories in his father's original hometown, the port of Quanzhou, Fujian, from whence his father had left Fujian for Indonesia and from whence Chiang Kai-shek's Nationalists had fled China for Taiwan.[11]

The important role of the overseas Chinese in East Asian success, in facilitating both trade and capital flows within the region, is not exactly a secret. But the term *overseas Chinese,* referring to the Chinese minorities spread throughout East Asia, is an overly broad generalization. A disproportionate share of the migrants came from just one Chinese province: Fujian. The reasons lie deep in history, in yet another defeat for the Blank Slate view of development.

Fujian province is on the coast of China across from Taiwan. The province is mountainous and infertile for agriculture, so the Fujianese, in the words of scholar Edgar Wickberg, "made fields of the sea."[12] Already by the time that Marco Polo arrived in Fujian at the end of the thirteenth century, he found a thriving port he called by its Arabic name Zaytun, crowded with ships and traders. Polo noted there were "rich assortments of jewels and pearls."[13] Zaytun is where we get the word *satin*, one of the port's luxury exports.[14] Marco Polo's Zaytun is known today as— Quanzhou, which by now might qualify as the most important city in world economic history that you have never heard of.

From the thirteenth through the nineteenth centuries, Fujianese traders migrated to Taiwan, Japan, the Philippines, Okinawa, Vietnam, Cambodia, Sumatra, Java, Malaya, Singapore, and the kingdom of Ayut-thaya in what is today Thailand. Already by the seventeenth century they had muscled into the role of key middlemen in East–West trade (in addition to intra-East trade) by playing off the Dutch and the Spanish against each other, trading silk, porcelain, furniture, sugar, and metal wares.[15]

Yet more Fujianese migration happened between the 1860s and 1930s, as European colonial plantations (such as rubber in British Malaya and Dutch Indonesia) were looking for a reliable labor force. The network of Fujianese merchants already in place was happy to help out, recruiting coolie labor back in Fujian, who then moved permanently to Malaya, Sin-gapore, and Indonesia. The coolie laborers' descendants were then avail-able also to join the next generation of merchants in the thriving regional Fujianese trading network.[16]

The advice of the development experts as "official development" began after 1949 was to emphasize national industrialization over international trade. Africa's and Latin America's leaders listened more than did East Asia's to the advice to develop at home rather than through foreign trade. This advice was poorly timed in retrospect: the greatest foreign-trade boom in world history was about to begin. The Fujianese network was one factor in East Asia becoming the biggest and most lasting beneficiary of that boom. East Asia's share of global exports went from 12 percent in 1960 to 31 percent by 2011. The same number in Latin America over the

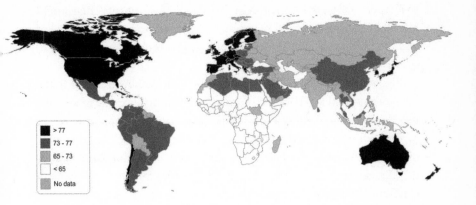

FIGURE 10.1   Differences in life expectancy in 2011 were more regional than national. (Prepared using World Bank Development Indicators data and StatPlanet mapping software.)

What would the giants be w/o globalization—> as this inherently connected to growth

same period declined from 7 percent to 6 percent, while Africa's share of global exports declined from 5 percent to 2 percent.

The overseas Chinese (whom we have seen are disproportionately Fujianese) are sometimes called the "Jews of Asia." The economist Thomas Sowell said it might be more appropriate to call the Jews the "Chinese of Europe."[17] Let us recall again the beginnings of the nationalist idea of development in the interaction of Chinese and American scholars in the 1920s that was a convenient distraction from the racist American restrictions on Chinese immigration. It is ironic that the Chinese migrants— many of them Fujianese—that the United States barred would turn out to be amongst the most productive migrants in history.

TREATING THE NATION-OBSESSED

The obsession with nations extends to measures of development success other than growth rates, though with even less justification. The World Bank conducted a report on global inequality in 2006. One of the main questions asked by the report was "how much does one's country of birth determine one's opportunities in life?" The answer: "We show that the inequalities between countries are staggering." The solution to this problem?

The report will look for "action by [national] governments" that would produce "changes" that will reduce such inequities between nations.[18] But was the problem of global inequity primarily a problem of inequity between *nations*?

The World Bank's President at the time, Paul Wolfowitz, wrote in the introduction to this report of a specific cross-country example of inequality: "we live in a world of extraordinary inequalities in opportunity . . . across countries. Even the basic opportunity for life itself is disparately distributed: whereas less than half of one percent of children born in Sweden die before their first birthday, this is the case for close to 15% of all children born in Mozambique."[19]

The body of the report gave more examples of the inequalities between countries:

> In 2000 the life expectancy of a child born in Sierra Leone (37 years) or Botswana (39 years) was less than half that for a child born in the United States (77 years).[20]

> Opportunities for the consumption of private goods differ vastly between rich and poor countries. Mean annual consumption expenditures range from . . . $279 in Nigeria to . . . $17,232 in Luxembourg. . . . The average citizen in Luxembourg enjoys monetary resources 62 times higher than the average Nigerian. While the average Nigerian may find it difficult to afford adequately nutritious meals every day, the average citizen of Luxembourg need not worry too much about buying the latest generation cell phone on the market.[21]

Does that income even reach the people though?

There are two commonly used measures of overall development success: the growth of income per capita and the level already attained of income per capita. This chapter has already discussed the small share of national differences in growth, but what about levels of development as measured by income per capita? Is it time to salute the remarkable performance of the Luxembourg development experts?

One answer to that question is evident in the map of life expectancy shown in Figure 10.1. Income, infant mortality, and life expectancy are characteristics much more of regions than they are of nations. Luxembourg benefits from being in Europe while Nigeria is disadvantaged by its position in sub-Saharan Africa. This is not surprising given some of what we learned by moving away from the Blank Slate. Factors like cultural values and technology do not show sharp divides at national boundaries. They are products of entire civilizations, not the arbitrary boundaries of today's nations.

The World Bank shows the nationalist obsession in development that could misinterpret such elementary and well-known facts so drastically. This is not stupidity. It is again the political mind-set that shapes development ideas to meet the needs of both the national leaders (usually autocrats) in the poor countries and the aid organizations in the rich countries who deal with those national leaders.

The great social thinker Robert Nisbet had pointed out the absurdity of thinking of development as primarily national back in 1969, using a rich country's history as an example:

"It is not possible to deal with any of the major changes of England save in terms of incessant historical interaction of the English—traders, artisans, scholars, artists, as well as statesmen—with people and ideas and forces of one kind or other which cannot conceivably be localized in England."[22] The danger of overemphasizing the nation is that these interactions between people across borders will be cut off.

THE ALEPPO DISEASE

Suppose we do see a clear example of national borders that do matter. Sometimes that turns out to be a bad thing.

With the end of colonialism, artificial borders hardened into national boundaries around the world. Often they became a sudden new barrier to the flow of goods, services, and people, halting a flow that had benefited people on both sides of the previously nonexistent boundary. This happened in Latin America in the nineteenth century, with a century of little regional progress to follow. The full effect of national borders in Africa only happened in the 1960s with decolonization. New borders had a profound effect earlier in the Middle East with the dismantling of the Ottoman Empire after World War I.

To see the effects of the new national borders in the Middle East, take the example of Aleppo, in what is today Syria. As Aleppo native Nassim Taleb notes, Aleppo may hold the record for the longest record of prosperity in history. It was connected to Quanzhou (Zaytun) because it was a major stop on the Silk (Satin) Road; it also specialized in wheat trading throughout the Mediterranean during the Roman Empire.[23]

When the Ottoman Empire came along in 1516, it eliminated political boundaries from Iran to Algeria and from the Arabian Peninsula to Eastern Europe. Aleppo's traders took advantage of their location at the spot where East meets West. European goods arrived in Aleppo from one direction from London, Marseilles, Amsterdam, and Venice. From the other direction, goods originating in Iran, India, Iraq, Anatolia, and Arabia came in by caravan. Aleppo would thrive on this trade for the next four centuries.[24]

The traders were a diverse group, including Venetians, English, French, Dutch, Arabic-speaking Muslims, Christian Syrians, Turkish-speaking Ottomans, Indians, Bukharans (from modern day Uzbekistan), Armenians, Sephardic Jews expelled from Portugal, Italy, and Spain, and Arabic Jews from all over the Levant.[25]

They traded goods like raw silk, wool, cotton, finished fabrics, camels and camel hair, gallnuts, pistachio nuts, and drugs and gums. They got these goods from northern Syria and the Syrian desert, southeastern Anatolia, Mosul, Iran, Diyarbakr, Arabia, and Basra. From Europe, the goods included woolens, raw metals, and other goods as diverse as firearms, clocks, paper, housewares, and chemical products, not to mention products of the European colonies such as dyes, spices, sugar, and coffee. From Aleppo, most of these goods were destined for re-export to cities in the interior, in Syria, Anatolia, Iraq, and Iran.[26]

The twentieth century was a series of nationalist disasters for Aleppo. After World War I, Aleppo got its first blow from the carving up of the Levant into the French colonies (called League of Nations "mandates") of Syria (containing Aleppo) and Lebanon; the British colonies (mandates) of Palestine, Jordan, and Iraq; and independent Turkey. Independence hardened these borders even further before, during, and after World War II. It became so costly and time-consuming to bring goods across the new borders that Aleppo was cut off both from its natural trading hinterlands in surrounding nations and from its European trading partners. It was a blow from which Aleppo would never recover.

The traders left Aleppo to become a prosperous diaspora in Beirut, Europe, and North America. Nassim Taleb quoted his grandfather asking a friend why he had moved from Aleppo to Beirut at a time when the latter had a horrific civil war. He answered "we people of Aleppo prefer war to prison." All of Aleppo had become a prison.[27]

INTERNATIONAL TRADE

My colleague in the New York University Economics Department, Yaw Nyarko, is from Ghana. Nyarko recently said at a conference that you could hardly have found a worse thing to do to Africa than to slice it up into lots of tiny countries. Ironically for the nationalist obsession in development, one of the regional factors that held back African development was that Africa had too many nations.

To see the possible problems at work in Africa, consider this absurd example. Suppose my apartment building suddenly became "independent" from the United States. I could not keep my job at NYU, a few blocks away in what is now a foreign country, unless the US government authorized the immigration and employment of a foreign national. To judge by the experiences of my foreign friends with the Immigration and Naturalization Service, my paperwork would get lost several times, the rules would be incomprehensible, and I would strain to find the right kind of visa that permits my work. I don't know that I would even qualify for the category that the INS calls "alien of extraordinary ability." Some anti-immigrant forces would criticize NYU for outsourcing to a foreign nation.

Even if I managed to pass the trial by fire of the INS, to perform my job I need a few other things to move across borders. I need to import the iPad I am using right now, which comes from the Apple Store located two blocks away in US territory. Then I will need to export my books into the US market. If the Tenants' Committee of my building had heard about the ideas of nationalist development for Apartmentistan, they might have decided to ban some import categories (like luxury iPads) and heavily tax some exports (like books). Between the INS and the Tenants' Committee, I am at high risk of becoming an Aleppo.

As absurd as this example is, it reflects reality for anyone close to a new national boundary, such as those drawn by colonization and decolonization in Africa. It was an unhappy accident that development thinking stressed development at the unit of the nation and was scornful of trade at the moment of independence of many new nation-states. Development thinking did not go to the extreme of total national self-sufficiency, known as autarchy, nor am I arguing for religious worship of free trade. The point is that development has seldom appreciated the dangers that nationalism can pose for the gains from trade.

How does this point square with the evidence given above that nation-states do not matter as much as we thought for income and growth? Should not trade policy differences show up as differences between nations in either growth or levels of income per capita? The development community's debate for and against free trade has focused almost exclusively on looking for such differences between nations, which shows again the nationalist obsession. In fact, we should look as much or more at regions as at nations for evidence on trade. Whether trade self-destructs or thrives depends not on one nation alone but on a nation and all of its would-be trading partners. Even if a country frees up its own exports and imports, its trading partners must also free up their corresponding imports and exports.

The relevant group could be the whole world, or it could be a region. At the world level, falling transport costs and trade barriers have driven globalization since World War II. This has generated a historic boom in global trade that gets some of the credit for global economic development. Chapter Three noted how the New Zealand economist John Bell Condliffe, who advocated free development in pre-1949 China, also pointed out the opportunities for global development from increased trade. His reward was to be ignored and forgotten, but he has turned out to be right.

On the negative side is the "Aleppo disease" in development: putting barriers between regions that previously thrived on interaction with each other. This may have been a common factor that slowed the efforts of poor regions around the world to catch up with richer ones. The severity of Aleppo disease may have also differed by region, as I speculated above, which could help explain why part of national success and failure was at the regional level. Africa has been a notable development failure. Africa also, as Yaw Nyarko complained, was remarkable for its proliferation of borders of many very small states, and also had the newest states.

PAPIER MÂCHÉ NATIONS

A bridge made out of papier mâché may look exactly like a real bridge, but the difference will become clear if you drive a truck across it. Lant Pritchett has used this metaphor to describe many of the organizations set up by newly independent states after colonialism ended.[28] Each country had all the trappings of a nation—a president, a department of education, and borders—but the "nation" had little ability to do any of the things that nations are supposed to do. It often turned out to be better at the destructive things that nation-states do rather than the constructive things.

Decolonization happened fast and initial conditions were terrible in many new nations in Africa. At the independence of the Belgian Congo on June 30, 1960, only sixteen Congolese had college degrees.[29] Roads were nearly nonexistent and radios scarce, so few of the Congolese learned of their new identity as Congolese. Only a colorful tyrant named Mobutu distracted attention from the papier mâché reality of the Congolese state. Today, a half century later, the Democratic Republic of the Congo is still far more of a "nation" to its many would-be saviors than it is to its own people. This is an extreme case; other states became more functional, and most states have become more functional over time.

Even with the weakest states, some parts of the government apparatus are more functional than others. The parts that might be expected to be most functional would be those that collected their own revenue to sustain themselves, that could get by with staff with minimal qualifications, and whose existence is compatible with political interests. The part of government that fits these requirements almost perfectly is the border police. The salaries of immigration and customs agents can always be paid

arguing for a borderless, but regionally focused world

by the taxes they collect, or more unofficially by the bribes they impose on hapless border-crossers. The jobs of these agents are perfect for political patronage. The income from customs can finance political parties. So the most damaging part of the new nation-states—costly border crossings for people and goods—was also likely to be the most functional part. Nationhood was not as positive as was hoped with papier mâché benefits and concrete costs.

Conclusions

In the debate on the prerogatives of nations versus the rights of individuals, the case for the former depended on development that happened mainly at the national level. Yet nations do not matter for development as much as the development community says they do. When they do matter, it is sometimes in a bad way, as we have just seen with Aleppo disease and trade-destroying borders. The worship of national growth success has often led to giving the national state more powers to pursue this success. The extreme emphasis on national growth performance is misguided, for it shows little evidence of paying off—or even of any way to know whether the national strategy really is paying off or not, according to questionably measured growth rates. The casualties as usual are the individual rights suppressed in the name of the nation's collective pursuit of success.

PART FIVE

Conscious Design Versus
Spontaneous Solutions

Dr. Jim Yong Kim was born in Seoul, South Korea, in 1959 but moved with his family to the United States in 1964. After a career as a physician working in global public health and development, Dr. Kim became president of the World Bank on July 1, 2012. He was the first president of the Bank who had actually worked in development beforehand.

In his first major speech as World Bank president on October 11, 2012, given at its annual meeting in Tokyo, Dr. Kim called for the World Bank to become a "Solutions Bank." The Bank should offer "evidence-based, non-ideological solutions to development challenges." The Bank should reach agreement with other development agencies, with foundations, with academics, and with the private sector "to advance shared goals" for solutions. He called for a new "science of delivery" to implement the evidence-based solutions. This new science would include "the design, execution and demonstration of results."[1]

Dr. Kim could hardly have been more explicit in aligning himself with the consensus view, now decades-old, that conscious design offers the best hope for ending poverty. Part Five of this book considers the case for the neglected alternative of the debate: spontaneous solutions from individuals as market traders, entrepreneurs, and technological innovators. Chapter Eleven covers markets and Chapter Twelve looks at technologies. The last chapter in this section (Chapter Thirteen) picks up the story with Dr. Kim again as he praises the purported successful designs of local autocrats on a visit to China. We will take seriously the claim that autocrats successfully design development, and we review the evidence of both sides of a debate on benevolent autocrats that goes back all the way to Adam Smith.

CHAPTER ELEVEN

MARKETS: THE ASSOCIATION OF PROBLEM-SOLVERS

Chung Ju Yung was from an earlier generation of Koreans than Dr. Jim Yong Kim. He was born in 1915 in the village of Asan, in the Tongchan district on the east coast of the Korean peninsula. Chung as a young man had a problem that really needed one of Dr. Kim's solutions.

Chung's family's farm did not produce enough food to feed him, his parents, and his siblings. In his own words: "The soil was not very fertile and did not produce enough harvest for a big family. . . . In those days you left home before dawn. You worked 15 to 16 hours a day. Even if you worked so hard, you had not enough to eat. . . . We would eat oatmeal late in the morning, skip lunch, eat bean porridge at night and go to bed."[2]

A "Solutions Bank" as visualized by Dr. Kim would have summoned an agricultural development expert. Such an expert could have studied the agricultural problems of Asan and recommended evidence-based, non-ideological solutions to these problems, such as more fertilizer, more irrigation, better seeds, or new crops. That is not what happened.

Chung Ju Yung understood something that Dr. Kim apparently does not, and that most development thinkers never have. Chung knew that the worst way to solve your own problem is to try to solve your own problem. A better way is to join an "association of problem-solvers" in which you dedicate yourself to solving other people's problems, and in which you trust other people to solve your own problems. This association has no president, it holds no meetings, it has no membership fees, and no membership restrictions. But it does solve many problems.

There was an alternative to the direct solution of bad agriculture for

→ Fundamental idea of trade

Chung in the village of Asan. Chung could conclude he was just never going to be good at solving his own hunger problem, given the infertile soils, and look for someone else who was better at producing food for him. Meanwhile he could direct his own energies to solve other people's problems in some other area at which he was better than at growing food in infertile soil. He could exchange his problem-solving talents on behalf of those others, in "some other area," for the problem-solving talents of others in producing food for him.

The "some other area" for Chung was initially modest: he turned out to be good at fixing cars. He opened an auto-repair shop in Seoul, one hundred twenty miles to the southwest, and auto repair was in high demand during and after World War II, first for the Japanese and then for the Americans. He earned enough to send money for food back to his family. We will see later that Chung's contribution to solving Korea's transportation problems would be much bigger than a repair shop.

The "association" of people exchanging their problem-solving abilities with each other also turns out to be much bigger than this modest example shows. Adam Smith developed it more than two centuries ago, it is taught in every introductory course in economics, and it is widely accepted in rich countries. Yet this idea still gets little recognition for solving the problems of poor countries. The mention of Adam Smith invariably triggers ideological wars that reflect not only some genuine issues for debate, but an even larger set of misunderstandings.

THE PROBLEM-SOLVERS ASSOCIATION

A successful problem-solving association has to have two features that this book has mentioned before. First, it must have adequate knowledge for others to solve your problem. Second, the problem-solvers must have adequate incentives to solve your problem.

Chung's example illustrates why knowledge is so important. An agricultural expert in Asan may indeed have had some knowledge that the villagers lacked on, say, fertilizer. However, the expert might find it difficult to find out from local men in the village how unsuccessful a long experience of trial and error with fertilizer had already been. It might be thought he could simply ask, but the history of development is full of failed communications between experts and locals.

Anthropologist James Ferguson once documented a World Bank project meant to promote agricultural development in a region of Lesotho in southern Africa. The World Bank experts never realized what Ferguson had discovered in his field work: the local men had no interest in farming. The men had long ago figured out how poor their local soils were, and had chosen a far more profitable opportunity as migrant workers in South African mines.[3]

Part of the communication problem is that even the successful use of fertilizer involves a lot of adaptation to very specific microlocations in each plot. Success is hostage to constantly changing prices of fertilizer and crops, not to mention the weather. It would be hard for the outside expert to access all this complex history of trial and error, successful and unsuccessful. Moreover, it is hard for the expert to observe each farmer's ability; maybe Chung Ju Yung's problem was not infertile soil but that he just was really bad at farming.

Another way to state the knowledge problem is that success is often a surprise. It is often hard to predict *what* will be the solution. It is even harder to predict *who* will have the solution, and *when* and *where*. And it is even harder when the success of who, what, when, and where keeps changing. This is just restating Hayek's insight about the knowledge problem with conscious design, as discussed in Chapter Two.

All this means that solving the knowledge problem is hard work. A lot of work requires a lot of rewards, so a successful problem-solving system must hand out such rewards to the problem-solvers.

THE MAN FROM GLASGOW

Adam Smith spent his formative years in Glasgow, Scotland. He was the first to explain clearly the problem-solving system that was then evolving in the West and that would later spread around the world.

Glasgow's appearance here may not have been entirely accidental. In the eighteenth century, Glasgow was the kind of rapidly growing free city that we discussed in Chapter Six as so outperforming cities under authoritarian rulers. Within the British Isles, the Treaty of Union in 1707 between Britain and Scotland had also opened up to Glasgow a large free-trade area (including Northern Ireland) that the local merchants quickly exploited.[4] It was also trading with the Caribbean, the North American colonies, and the Continent, surpassing other British cities in particular in the tobacco trade. Its manufacturing and trade boomed hand in hand: it imported raw sugar and tobacco leaf and exported refined sugar and refined tobacco.

So maybe we have nicotine addiction to thank for the brilliance of Adam Smith, the man from Glasgow. Adam Smith was born on June 5, 1723, in the east coast town of Kirkcaldy, into a middle-class family, a sickly child coming along six months after his father died. Smith was going to live a boring life, much of it in the company of his mother. Perhaps he came closest to excitement during a trip to Paris in 1766 after he had already become famous for his first book, *The Theory of Moral Sentiments*. There was a rumor (reported many years after the event) that one Parisian lady had pursued him, overlooking his bad French and bad teeth, and attracted to his intellect. According to the rumor, Smith did not reciprocate the affection in Paris because he was himself in (unrequited) love at the time with an unnamed English lady. That's about as exciting as it gets for Adam Smith gossip. As one of Smith's biographers put it, "It is to be feared that the biographer can do little more with the topic of Smith's sex life than contribute a footnote to the history of sublimation."[5]

Smith's life was instead bound up with the exciting life of the mind at the University of Glasgow, both as a student and as a professor. The university (which in the next chapter will also produce a second Glasgow hero, James Watt) was unusual at the time for its skepticism and challenge to authority. As one of its principal reformers said of professors at *other* universities:

"The weightier Matters of true Learning . . . such as . . . the improvement of Reason, the love of Justice, the value of Liberty . . . are either quite omitted, or slightly passed over: Indeed they forget not to recommend frequently to [their students] what they call the Queen of all Vertues [sic], viz. Submission to Superiors, and an entire blind Obedience to Authority."[6]

Before jumping to Smith's most famous contributions, let's correct some misunderstandings that often prevent appreciating his achievements.

THE MISUNDERSTOOD MR. SMITH →very much also Korten's idea

Smith's faith in the individual as a problem-solver was so revolutionary, then and now, that it creates lots of misunderstandings. Anyone who says "Adam Smith" is assumed to favor pure laissez-faire. This slippery slope came about because Smith's ideas became ideological shorthand for stock positions on both the left and the right in Western countries, obscuring the more important parts of his ideas that are now accepted by all sides in the West.

The most insightful quotes and the most misunderstood quotes are the same quotes:

> By directing that industry in such a manner as its produce may be of the greatest value, [the individual] intends only his own gain, and he is in this, as in many other cases, led by an *invisible hand* to promote an end which was no part of his intention. Nor is it always the worse for the society that it was no part of it. By pursuing his own interest, he frequently promotes that of the society more effectually than when he really intends to promote it.[7]

> It is not from the benevolence of the butcher, the brewer, or the baker that we expect our dinner, but from their regard to their own interest. We address ourselves, not to their humanity, but to their self-love, and never talk to them of our own necessities, but of their advantages.[8]

The Invisible Hand is the critical concept. Adam Smith saw the market in privately supplied goods as "invisibly" providing this "hand" to guide the solving of many of our problems. The suppliers who provide any goods that are profitable in the marketplace do so only to get the profit, but they wind up unintentionally meeting many of our most pressing needs. Our demand to get our most urgent needs met is what makes the

244   The Tyranny of Experts

goods profitable. Smith's Invisible Hand was one of the first introductions of the revolutionary concept of "spontaneous order," which we discussed in Chapter Two as today including biological evolution, the Internet, language, and social norms.

The misunderstanding is that Smith believed "greed is good," which triggers revulsion against his Invisible Hand on the left. Some on the right have the misunderstanding that Smith gives a blanket endorsement to all profits by the existing businessmen. Actually, Smith held many negative views about both the rich and businessmen. In his first classic, *The Theory of Moral Sentiments*, published in 1759, Smith spoke of the rich as a "few lordly masters," consumed by "vain and insatiable desires," not to mention their "natural selfishness and rapacity."[9]

As for businessmen, Smith in *The Wealth of Nations* spoke of "the mean rapacity, the monopolizing spirit, of merchants and manufacturers," which sounds like something he had personally observed in Glasgow. His whole work he described as a "very violent attack" targeting "the wretched spirit of monopoly." Another famous statement of Smith's further develops this:

"People of the same trade seldom meet together, even for merriment and diversion, but the conversation ends in a conspiracy against the public, or in some contrivance to raise prices."[10] Greedy merchants were, for Smith, far from concerned about promoting general well-being. To the contrary, "their interest is . . . directly opposite to that of the great body of the people."[11]

Smith's idea of a free market in this context (still a relevant context today) was not to enrich the existing merchants but to make them *less* rich through the loss of their monopoly rights and privileges. For the same reason, Smith's agenda would not make a "few lordly masters" richer. His free-trade agenda would actually lead to cheap food imports for the poor that would undercut these large landowners.

The Invisible Hand was not the force only of firms' self-interest but also that of consumers' self-interest: "it always is, and must be, the interest of the great body of the people, to buy whatever they want of those who sell it cheapest."[12] It was in this cause that he promoted the abolition of special privileges and monopolies over domestic or foreign markets. It was in this cause that he promoted free trade, both domestic and foreign. Smith did not anticipate that many would later see his ideas as mainly benefiting the rich.

And Smith also understood the problem of greedy merchants who would cheat the public if they could, and he already understood the importance of trust that we discussed in Chapter Six to make markets work. Self-interest was not greed, it was not pursuing monopolies; it was honorable dealing and freedom of entry to whomever could deliver the goods.

Finally, Smith understood that not all problems could be solved by the Invisible Hand of the market. Only the government can solve some problems, and government may need to intervene in some malfunctioning markets, such as public goods that do not deliver enough of a private return. Smith said the government should supply, for example, public schools, roads, bridges, and canals.[13] Let's declare a temporary truce in the market-versus-government wars, so that an appreciation of the Invisible Hand does not automatically imply some extreme view that government has no role in anything. All free societies today, from social-democratic Scandinavia to industrial-policy Japan to the more free-market United States, have relied heavily on the Invisible Hand.

SMITH'S PROBLEM-SOLVING SYSTEM

We can now get to the guts of Smith's vision of a successful problem-solving system. Smith articulated three important ideas that made the Invisible Hand so effective: the division of labor, gains from specialization, and gains from trade. These three ideas are connected so that each makes the other possible.

Again, it does not make these ideas any less powerful that they are elementary concepts taught in introductory economics classes. We are interested in ideas with either moral or pragmatic payoffs, regardless of their originality or prestige. Nobel laureate Robert Solow might have been right when he once said that most or all of what you need to give practical policy advice comes from Econ 101. And actually it will turn out that, despite the recent inclusion of some of Smith's ideas in new academic theories of growth, these ideas are still neglected in debates among nonacademics in the development community.

The Division of Labor. The division of labor is about how much a worker performs *all* the necessary tasks to produce something versus how much the work is divided up into more specialized tasks among workers. To take the modern automobile as an example, you could either have each worker build an automobile from scratch, or you could have an assembly line that divides up the overall task of building an auto into a myriad tiny tasks, each to be done by one in a long succession of workers.

Gains from Specialization. Division of labor then makes possible two particular gains from specialization. First, all of us are much better at some things than others, and specialization allows us to do what we do best. Suppose Roger Federer was too busy assembling his own iPad to play tennis, Beyoncé was too busy playing tennis for her own family to sing and dance, while Steve Jobs was too busy singing and dancing for his friends to make iPads. I think we are all grateful these three could instead specialize in their best area, what is usually called their "comparative advantage."

Second, workers get even better at their best area with experience. As workers perform smaller tasks more often, they get more proficient at doing it through repeated practice. Nearly two centuries after Smith, Nobel Prize winner Kenneth Arrow would call this "learning by doing." The modern theory of economic growth rediscovered learning by doing as a major force beginning in the 1990s. Popular writers like Malcolm Gladwell and Matthew Syed have argued that the kind of success that Federer/Beyoncé/Jobs attained takes "10,000 hours of practice."[14]

I can attest to learning by doing from my own thimble-full of experience in the motor-vehicle field. In the 1970s, the world's top three motor-vehicle firms were General Motors, Ford, and Chrysler, all in Detroit. They bought auto parts from many specialized companies in the northwest Ohio area where I grew up and went to college, including a truck-radiator firm called Modine Manufacturing in Pemberville, Ohio, eighty miles from Detroit. During summer vacation from college in 1977, I worked at the Modine plant. Thanks to division of labor, my job on the assembly line was a specialized one: tightening the bolts on the radiators right before they went to the shipping department. I used an electric screwdriver with an attachment that just fit the nut on the bolt—apply the screwdriver to the bolt, pull the trigger, and tighten the bolt, over and over again for about two dozen bolts on each radiator on one side (a coworker did the same thing simultaneously on the other side), over and over again for countless radiators that kept coming through during an eight-hour shift.

At first, the veterans on the assembly line mocked the college kid who was so slow at tightening bolts. But as practice time accumulated, I found my inner bolt-tightener. By the end of the summer, the veterans begged the college kid to slow down so that the management did not increase the speed of the assembly line in the bolt-tightening department.

Gains from Trade. Gains from trade are simply the payoff to the division of labor and gains from specialization. As each of us specializes, I trade my specialized output for yours. The buyer of a truck with a radiator was buying my bolt-tightening skills. The trucker sells his transportation services to wheat producers, enabling them to move their wheat (perhaps in the form of processed flour—another specialized production task) to my local bakery, where I buy fresh-made bread. Each of us wants to buy as cheaply as possible, which means we buy from the most efficient supplier—who got to be most efficient through gains from specialization. The many specialists in an economy engage in many-sided trades while being (or striving to be) the most efficient anywhere at what they do.

If you could not trade, you would have to make everything for yourself. There would be no division of labor, no specialization, no learning by doing. Trade opens up a large market that makes radical division of labor and specialization possible. The gains from trade for you do *not* imply losses for anyone else, the gains from trade are mutual: everyone wins, even if not necessarily by the same amount.

Writer Thomas Thwaites dramatized these gains from specialization and trade when he decided to make an electric toaster entirely on his own and write a book about it. Thwaites could have bought an electric toaster in the supermarket for $6.10. Instead, it took him nine months,

1,900 miles of traveling, and $1,837.36 spent on raw materials to produce an electric toaster by himself, which he had to concede produced mildly warm bread rather than toast.[15]

Trade does not automatically mean international trade. Chung Ju Yung's initial breakthrough was simply in domestic trade of auto-repair services for food for his family. It makes little difference whether he bought this food within Korea or from foreign suppliers. Despite all the passion exhibited about foreign imports versus domestic production, the "gains from trade" argument makes no logical distinction between your fellow nationals solving your problems and foreigners doing so. Why should it matter which side of the border your problem-solvers are on?

To put it another way, trade is the final piece of the problem-solving system. Each of us has some problems we need solved and we look around for who is best at solving each of our problems. Each of us also decides which of the problems of others we are best at solving. Individual freedom of choice is what decides who is best at solving problems. The chosen problem-solver is often the one who can solve their problem the best at the lowest cost—a lot of customers will choose that one to solve their problems. The customers do not choose the one who does not solve the problem, or solves it badly, or who solves it at a higher cost. If I had really failed to solve the problem of tight bolts on radiators—if the radiators with loose bolts leaked and exploded—the truckers would not have bought them, thus indirectly firing me as their problem-solver on truck-radiator bolts. Freedom to choose is a powerful engine in rewarding the world's best problem-solvers in each area, while getting rid of the inept problem-solvers.

Similarly, individuals freely choose which problems of others they are going to solve. Tightening bolts was the best option that long-ago summer for someone with few skills and little experience. I was lucky to find people who wanted tight radiator bolts, as that job was a better solution for me than my previous options of people who wanted their papers delivered, their windows cleaned, or their lawns mowed.

Adam Smith's radical Enlightenment vision of individual freedom was going to create many different possibilities for individuals to find themselves as the chosen problem-solver. It was also going to let the individual go on a search to find her own chosen problem-solver for each of her problems.

Knowledge

So how does the Invisible Hand solve the knowledge and incentive problems of a successful problem-solving system? How can you process the vast knowledge necessary to find the world's best problem-solver for each of your problems? When you want to solve your automobile problems, you do not need to place an ad in the *Economist* magazine for a worldwide audience—"wanted: skilled problem-solver in the personal transport sector." Of course, there is a range of quality of cars, with the higher quality more expensive, but we can address this by treating each quality level of cars (for example, luxury versus economy) as a separate good with its own market-determined price. To find your automotive problem-solver, you just need to look on the Internet for the lowest-price car of your own desirable quality for sale in your area. All the work has already been done for you by lots of others looking for cars and lots of firms looking to supply cars. This vast search and matching process is summarized in only one piece of information: the price of cars.

At the end of the day only the most efficient problem-solvers are left standing at the prevailing price in the market for cars. This winnowing happens thanks to the individual choices of everyone else in the world in thousands of different locales, which together make up the global market for cars, to buy the cheapest cars for a given quality level—and not to buy the most expensive cars. Soon enough, the worst problem-solvers are out of business and competition forces those who are left to offer the best deal available.

There is some monopoly power of some car producers in some markets that mess up this admittedly idealized picture. But even then, as Adam Smith understood, monopoly is usually self-correcting. Monopoly means high profits, which sends out a signal heard around the world by other suppliers that here are some easy profits to be made by coming in and underselling the monopolist.

Equally, the potential personal-transport problem-solvers do not need exhaustive knowledge of everyone in the world who wants that problem solved and how much they are willing to pay. Everything they need to know is contained in that same small piece of data: the price of cars. If they can do as well or better than that market price, each would-be car-solver is in, otherwise they are out. This price filters back into other prices that coordinate all the specialized suppliers to the final-goods suppliers. The price of trucks is a huge determinant of the price of truck radiators, which is a huge determinant of the going wage for truck-radiator-bolt-tighteners. Knowing the wage available to me at Modine Manufacturing, compared to opportunities in the window-cleaning, paper-delivery, and lawn-mowing industries, was all I needed to know to find my summer's destiny in solving the radiator-bolt problem.

The same applies in deciding in which sector you are going to solve problems. Chung Ju Yung needed to know only two things to move into auto repair: the low income of farmers in Asan and the higher income of auto-repair shop owners in Seoul.

Solving the Incentive Problem

The Invisible Hand solution to the incentive problem is a self-reinforcing system of rewards. Modine rewards me for good bolt-tightening, the trucker rewards Modine for good truck radiators, the farmer and the baker reward the trucker for prompt and reliable delivery of wheat from one to the other, and I reward the baker for the warm, aromatic loaves just out of the oven. Chung got rewarded for auto repair, for solving others' problems, and then he paid others for solving the problem of making food available to his family.

Yet we take for granted this ability to get perfect strangers to solve our problems for us, without realizing how strange it really is. Suppose I walked out of a building into a pouring rain and realized I had no umbrella, I then asked a stranger to give me his umbrella, which he quickly agreed to give me. Could this really happen? Surely the stranger would likely not agree: he is more likely to be surprised and offended at my bizarre behavior. Yet this did happen to me in downtown New York, and a stranger did give me his umbrella. The only additional details necessary to make it comprehensible is that I gave the stranger $5, and he was a street merchant. The market enlists a vast array of strangers in solving our individual problems.

THE KEY

The key principles of the most successful problem-solving system in human history are surprisingly simple. The first requirement is that each individual's private payoff to his problem-solving must be the same as the benefit of his problem-solving to others—the social payoff. The price of bread is what each loaf of bread is worth to the consumers (the *social payoff*), as they revealed by purchasing loaves voluntarily at that price. The price of bread is also the income of the baker per unit of bread supplies (his *private payoff*), which he can use in turn to purchase goods that he values from others. So the baker is getting rewarded per loaf of bread for solving others' bread problems just the amount that the solution is worth to them.

Contrast this with a nonmarket system. Suppose for example that the consumers are able to get bread only from the Bread Production Administration, whose bureaucrats get a fixed salary regardless of consumer satisfaction. These bureaucrats get no private payoff from supplying another loaf of bread anyway, so they are unlikely to adjust their bread problem-solving strategy even if the consumers think the bread tastes like roofing shingles (low social payoff per loaf to consumers). Conversely, if the bureaucrats stumble upon a recipe for high quality bread that consumers love (high social payoff) but it then quickly runs out, the bureaucrats still have no private payoff—and hence no incentive to increase production of the bread that does solve problems. The nonmarket system has no self-correcting reaction to unsolved bread problems.

The market, by contrast, rewards the profit-seeking baker according to just how much the consumers feel the bread is worth at solving their nutritional gluten problem. So the market will self-correct. Suppose there is a high social payoff to making bread for consumers—as measured by what consumers are willing to pay—but nobody is producing any bread to take up consumers on what they are offering. Some supplier in search of profits will start solving the missing bread problem, rewarded by the private payoffs of the revenue per loaf that is aligned with the social payoff to consumers.

The second requirement is individual rights. Everybody must have the right to choose which problems they will solve. You then have a whole society full of problem-solvers seeking the most fanatically efficient solutions possible for each other. This system has nobody in charge, yet finds the best solutions for your problems *and* helps you find your own best role as a problem-solver for others. This is the Invisible Hand.

Again, the wonder of Adam Smith's breakthrough is often lost under a thick layer of ideological abuse of the Invisible Hand by both its proponents and opponents. The Invisible Hand is not utopia; it is not perfect; it is always a work in progress. There are genuine concerns about income distribution, in which the rich get their needs met so much more than the poor. There are still so many things wrong with the private suppliers of our needs that we could also describe the Invisible Hand in reverse: it is the process of driving out of business the incompetent in favor of the mediocre, the mediocre in favor of the good, and the good in favor of the excellent.

PROBLEMS AND SOLUTIONS WITH
MARKETS AND GOVERNMENTS

There are lots of products and activities where private returns are very different from social returns. Adam Smith identified some of them. When producers get together in a monopoly cartel to restrict supply and fix prices above the competitive market level, they create excess profits for themselves at the expense of consumers. Their extra private payoff does *not* correspond to a social payoff; it is just redistribution from consumers to producers. The producers are self-restricting their problem-solving for consumers and getting rewarded for doing so. If you think of an industry where there is lots of monopoly power you might notice how they often are lacking in great customer service. Allow this knowledge about the semimonopolistic airline industry to comfort you the next time your luggage gets rerouted to Idaho.

Economists since Smith have identified lots of other examples of what they call "market failures." These include unintentional spillovers of solving one problem that creates new problems (like improved manufacturing processes that nonetheless then contaminate public water supplies). It also includes public goods where individuals cannot be excluded from the general benefits (like a clean public water supply), from which it is usually not possible to make a private profit. Some of these problems require government intervention.

But the Invisible Hand does not thereby become irrelevant. It is critical to keep avoiding the perception of a slippery slope toward one extreme (problems can be solved perfectly by the market) or the other (problems can be solved perfectly by the government). Sometimes the market failures are contrasted with the ideal case where government policy finds the perfect tax or subsidy to align private and social payoffs. A tax on pollutants to the water supply equal to the damage they cause everyone else, for example, makes the polluter privately bear the social cost. On the other side, there is the abundant record of do-nothing legislators and thieving officials who highlight government failures. The promarket side might go too far by contrasting government failures with market successes, a comparison which is not relevant when there are public goods the market does not handle.

On the ideal government solution, the question remains whether the government actors have the right incentives to find this solution. The incentive problem exists as much for public actors as it does for private actors (a realization that economists achieved only belatedly, around about the 1980s, when they invented a new field called "political economy").

Here's one missing insight that we discussed already in Chapter Seven: the Invisible Hand principle would also make the supply of public goods work much better. Democratic accountability is one of the ways in which we seek to make individual government actors have their private payoffs align with social payoffs. If politicians or officials fail to deliver the public goods, then their private careers will fall victim to the wrath of the voters. The politician feels the heat either directly at an election, or more indirectly (and more commonly) by means of public complaint expressed via a free press or phone calls and e-mails from constituents. These systems are always flawed and cumbersome, but the promarket side should not be comparing these "government failures" to some nonexistent utopia any more than the progovernment side did with "market failures" (such as goods that pollute the environment).

*This discourse does looks at government + markets as mutually exclusive

ANOTHER CRUCIAL MOMENT
IN THE ARGUMENT OF THIS BOOK

The debate about market versus government is thus once again the *wrong* debate. One side pretends market failures do not exist, and the other pretends government failures do not exist. The debate should be as much as making each type of actor—government or private—have their private and social returns aligned better, as much as it is about finding the right mix of government and market to solve problems.

The *right* debate is once again about individual rights versus state power. A unified vision on individual rights—both political rights and economic rights—is about holding both private and public suppliers accountable for their actions.

We have now reached another crucial moment in the argument of this book. The technocratic approach—solutions by experts—arguably gives us the worst of all worlds. Having experts in charge of solving society's problems turns things over to agents who face neither a market test nor a democratic test. If they get the knowledge (including localized feedback) wrong, they suffer neither economic nor political penalties. If their solutions should happen to work, they get neither economic nor political rewards. So there is nothing to spur them on to scaling up successes any more than there is anything to motivate them to kill off failures.

The Invisible Hand spurs development through the virtuous circle of specialization, learning by doing, and gains from trade. The Invisible Hand guides nonexperts to something they are good at doing. They start selling it, and they get even better at it thanks to learning by doing. Trade allows them to keep increasing the scale of the virtuous circle, selling more and more, learning to do it better and better, till they take the world market by storm.

DEVELOPMENT GOALS AND BAD PRINCIPLES

Let's see how often these basic principles of economics are neglected in development today, starting with the idea beloved by Bill Gates, Jim Yong Kim, and the United Nations Millennium Development Goals: setting goals and then finding evidence-based ways to reach them.

This is not the way the "association of problem-solvers" solves problems. The decentralized system finds the cheapest solutions to problems, through market and democratic feedback from individuals. Which problems get solved—which goals get met—are among the many choices that emerge from this decentralized system. The problems that get solved are those where individuals perceive the highest benefits relative to the costs. In my household, the Millennium Development Goal on ratio of educational television to junk entertainment watched is not met. However, our Millennium Development Goal of a nonzero supply of toilet paper is always met.

The UN goal setting, of which Bill Gates and World Bank President Jim Yong Kim are admirers, ignores these common-sense principles. If goals are set in advance, then development programs will wind up pursuing some goals too little ("good" goals with high benefits relative to low costs) and other goals too much ("poor" goals with low benefits and high costs). Major gains in well-being would be possible by moving funds from problems with low benefit-cost ratios to high benefit-cost ratios, but these gains will never happen when the goals are set inflexibly from the beginning.

For example, World Bank goal-driven efforts at solving agricultural problems, like those in Chung's childhood in Korea in the introduction to Part Five, have for decades now shown little payoff to a lot of investment. Gains from maintenance of roads are enormous relative to costs, but road maintenance is chronically underfunded by the goal-driven World Bank. The combination of market and democratic feedback with individual rights is more successful at abandoning marginal lands in agriculture, paving the roads, and selling the motor vehicles that together make it possible to ship food from the areas with good land to those with bad.

THE REPUBLIC OF GREENE STREET

We are biased by our focus on nations to treat international trade as something special compared to domestic specialization and exchange, but in most respects it is not. It is just as important to have domestic trade work well as it is for foreign trade to work well. One way to see this is to just imagine redrawing the borders of a nation to make it smaller, thereby shifting some existing trades from domestic trade to international trade. Nothing changes except the labels. Part of the dynamism of the Invisible Hand is each of these micronations is working well in finding its own comparative advantage, gains from specialization, and gains from trade.

Let's go back to the Greene Street block between Houston and Prince Streets in New York City's SoHo neighborhood, last discussed in Chapter Eight above.[16] Like nations and individuals, the Republic of Greene Street gained from specialization to solve others' problems while generating income for the problem-solvers. Its chosen specialization kept changing as the world around it kept changing, including technological change.

When we last checked in on Greene Street in 1850, the block was solving the needs of New Yorkers such as the Seixas family for residences. The large Benjamin and Mary Seixas family was living at 133 Greene Street. But as I hinted in Chapter Eight, Greene Street was about to discover a new profitable activity. That activity was the second-largest business in New York: prostitution (the first largest business was textiles). What gave this exact block a comparative advantage in prostitution was a large cluster of potential customers staying two blocks away in hotels on Broadway. By 1852, New York's first multimillion-dollar hotel, the St. Nicholas, opened at Spring Street and Broadway. Broadway already had the huge Metropolitan Hotel at the corner with Prince Street.

As for the supply side, prostitution was an ugly solution to an ugly situation for women in the patriarchal society of the 1850s. Alternative female-employment opportunities outside the home were not abundant. If fathers and husbands should die or abandon their families, the best bet for women to survive was sometimes prostitution. The sex trade paid women far more than domestic service, the main competing alternative.[17]

In the 1850s, the Greene Street block rapidly turned over from residences to brothels. The Benjamin Seixas family at 133 Greene Street did not want to live next to brothels, but they were free to go somewhere else. They moved to the West Village. The old Portuguese Jewish synagogue, Shearith Israel, moved in 1859 from its location near the Greene Street block to Fifth Avenue and Nineteenth Street. The previous synagogue location now featured a minstrel hall.[18]

By 1870, there were thirteen brothels on the Greene Street block. The old residences were themselves part of the comparative advantage of the block for prostitution. The home of the thirteen-member Benjamin Seixas family at 133 Greene Street had lots of separate rooms, which made their former abode an advantageous location for a whorehouse. The madam was Laura Barmore, forty-eight years old, an Irish immigrant. The prostitutes were seven women in their twenties: two from New York and one each from New Jersey, Connecticut, Pennsylvania, Georgia, and Ireland.[19]

According to *The Gentleman's* Directory, an 1870 guide to brothels that also provided commentary—sort of a Zagat's for whorehouses—our Greene Street block had the largest number of brothels of any block in all of New York City. *The Gentleman's Directory* describes the block as "a complete sink of iniquity." The "filth and turmoil" evoked "Sodom and Gomorrah."[20]

Yet *The Gentleman's Directory* was conflicted. It also expressed appreciation for "decent bagnios" ("brothels") that are "conducted in good style," where the lady boarders' "loveliness and amiability" make the brothel a "very pleasant place of resort." It gave two brothels on our Greene Street block the "decent bagnio" rating. Laura Barmore's brothel at 133 Greene was not one of them.

But the association of problem-solvers was not done on Greene Street. What happened next would surprise Laura Barmore and her customers and give women better alternatives to make a living. The surprise was a long time in building. The first piece of an alternative comparative advantage for the block was that it was only seven-tenths of a mile to the Hudson River docks that in turn led upstream to the Erie Canal and the markets of the American interior. At the same time, downstream, the Hudson River gave access to the world. We noted already how New York had become a hub for long-distance oceanic shipping thanks to the boost it got as a port from the Erie Canal.

Residents did not want to live next to brothels, but manufacturers did not object so strongly. As the brothel era took over, various manufacturers, including a carriage factory, an ironworks, and an elevator manufacturer, also moved in. For a time the block was specialized by the hour: manufacturing by day, prostitution by night. But there was far more scope to expand manufacturing than there was to expand its night-time complement.

By the middle of the nineteenth century, railroads were taking the same route as the Erie Canal with even faster and cheaper transport of manufactured goods to the interior in one direction, and raw materials in the other. The Hudson River Railroad opened a terminal at St. John's Park (what is now the exit from the Holland Tunnel) in 1868, six-tenths of a mile from Greene Street.

The final piece in the new comparative advantage of Greene Street was another kind of response to the Invisible Hand: Russian Jews and Italians chose high wages in New York over low wages back in Russia and Italy. As we have seen in the migration discussion in Chapter Nine, the Russian Jews were also fleeing pogroms under the Czar. Yet more transportation advances, such as larger and faster steamships on transatlantic routes, made the escape from oppression, violence, and poverty easier and cheaper. Immigration surged in New York after 1880.

The post-1880 takeoff on Greene Street also owed a lot to an earlier wave of Jewish immigrants from Germany in the 1840s and 1850s. These immigrants at first settled on the Lower East Side and had started as tailors or sellers of used clothing.[21] The next generation produced more entrepreneurs, who pioneered a new industry below Fourteenth Street: garment manufacturing. It would now explode on Greene Street.

The influx of Russian Jews after 1880 settled mainly on the Lower East Side (which the earlier German Jews had since left) and a large share worked in the garment industry. One of the few occupations open to Jews to survive in the Russian Pale of Settlement (a zone of Russia to which the czars confined the Jews) had been the "needle trades," including tailors and milliners. As a historian of Jews in America has put it, they also welcomed working for firms that were "almost entirely Jewish-owned. There were no language difficulties, no anomie here among unfriendly Gentiles."[22]

The Italian immigrants were also a good fit for garment work. Many Italian women brought with them a tradition of sewing and embroidery they had done at home back in Italy. Italian immigrants to New York settled in four separate "Little Italies" south of Fourteenth Street, one of which was just to the west of the Greene Street block. For example, Donato Longano, a tailor, and his wife Rosa emigrated from Italy to the United States in 1880 and landed on Sullivan Street, four blocks west of

Greene Street. They and their five children were part of the nearby labor pool for work in Greene Street garment businesses.

Two German Jewish brothers, Henry and Isaac Meinhard, were able in 1882 to see a block of whorehouses as a place where they could combine access to cheap transport with cheap labor. The turnover of the economic elite continued even inside the Jewish community, as German Jews like the Meinhards replaced the Portuguese Sephardim like the Seixas family as the leading entrepreneurs.

The Meinhard Brothers bought up the house at 133 Greene that had been the Benjamin Seixas family residence in 1850 and then Laura Barmore's brothel in 1870. They also purchased two other brothels next door, and in 1882 tore all three down and built two six-story cast-iron buildings to use as combination factories and warehouses. These buildings still stand today (Figure 11.1).

Once everything came together, the Greene Street block changed fast. All but two of the small brick houses were razed and replaced by the same kind of cast-iron buildings as the Meinhard Brothers'. The ground floors displayed men's and women's wear, while upper floors were used for back offices, storage, and manufacturing. Real-estate prices on the Greene Street block nearly tripled from 1880 to 1890; the boom lasted through 1910.[23]

In 1901, a directory lists the wholesalers and manufacturers on the Greene Street block as selling cotton, fur and fur trimmings, cloaks and suits, textiles, buttons, ladies' hats, and shawls.[24] An 1896 Factory Inspectors Report listed 22 garment businesses on the Greene Street Block, employing 399 men and 758 women.[25]

A description in 1910 captures Greene Street and surrounding blocks:

> Approach from Broadway and you pass crowded workrooms where men's clothing is made by the wholesale, hats turned out by the gross, and flowers and feathers pasted, branched, and packed for shipment to the farthest corners of the country. You pick your way through the narrow, crowded streets of Mercer, Greene, or West Broadway, where heavily loaded trucks are delivering huge rolls of cloth or carrying away the finished products in the form of underwear, neckwear, shirtwaists, or mattresses and burial supplies.[26]

FIGURE 11.1
The factory/
warehouse that
Henry and Isaac
Meinhard built
in 1882 to replace
three brothels.
(Author's photo, 2013.)

FUR CUTTINGS.
HIRSCH & CO.,
Furs, Skins, Hatters' Raw Stock and Fur Cuttings,
139 GREENE STREET, NEW YORK.

Headquarters for "Manufacturers and Fur Dressers" to obtain Highest Prices for all kinds of Fur Cuttings, Skunk Tails, etc. Send for Price List when you are ready to sell.

CONSIGNMENTS SOLICITED.   PROMPT RETURNS MADE.

FIGURE 11.2   Advertisement in the *Fur Trade Review* (1901) for a furrier on Greene Street.

The Invisible Hand had brought together on 486 feet of pavement along Greene Street in the 1880s a first immigrant wave of German Jewish entrepreneurs and a later immigrant wave of Italian Catholic and Russian Jewish workers, railroad and shipping operators, as well as customers and suppliers, in markets in the American Midwest, American South, Europe, South America, and Asia. They all came together on a block previously full of whorehouses to create a textile boom at the epicenter of American industrialization. As the entrepreneurs, workers, and shippers specialized in the problem of clothing everyone else, they solved their own problems with the income they generated for themselves. New work opportunities for women and Jews would contribute to the erosion of discrimination against them, pointing them toward more nearly equal rights.

Yet the block would not stay at the epicenter, it was about to go into a decline that would last for decades. Chapter Twelve will pick up the story of the Greene Street block's decline and fall after 1910.

SPECIALIZATION AND SUCCESS

We now have lots of contemporary data available to explore the role of specialization and trade in the success of many individuals escaping poverty. Unfortunately, data are widely available only on trades that do cross borders. Despite the importance of domestic specialization and trade, we will have to turn now to international data to illustrate the amazing potential of specialization and trade.

Let's take the world motor-vehicle market as an illustration. Only four countries produced half of all road-vehicle exports in the world in 2011. The first three are familiar motoring countries: Germany, Japan, and the United States. The fourth is what until recently would have been a big surprise: South Korea.

The success of a "country" at specialization is really the success of a firm; the success of a firm is really the success of an individual. Korea's success at exporting automobiles is traceable to an individual and a firm that we have already met: Chung Ju Yung and his auto-repair shop.

As we pick up Chung's story again at the end of World War II, his Motor Service is rehabilitating old vehicles discarded by the American occupation forces that arrived in September 1945. He even retrofits old Japanese cars to run on charcoal because of gasoline shortages. Chung renamed his Motor Service in 1946, using the Korean word for "modern": Hyundai.

Hyundai today is the world's fourth-largest auto company, with operations in every part of the world. The quality-award-winning Hyundai Sonata sedan thriving in the American market today is a long way from the vehicles Chung and his team rigged up from whatever junk was available in Seoul in 1946.

Let's see the consequences of what Chung wrought for South Korea's specialization today. First, check statistics on specialization by a product like "road vehicles." South Korea has road vehicles as one of its top exports, accounting for an eighth of all export revenues. But road vehicles are still too broad a category to understand specialization. The United Nations has a set of nested categories at finer and finer levels of specialization: there are 97 two-digit categories of exports ("road vehicles" is category 87), which can be further broken down into 1,222 four-digit categories, which in turn can be broken down into 5,053 six-digit categories.

Two-thirds of South Korea's road-vehicle exports come from just one four-digit category, 8703: "Motor cars and other motor vehicles principally designed for the transport of persons . . . including station wagons and racing cars" (other alternatives are trucks, tractors, and auto parts). We are getting more specialized now, but still not specialized enough. Moving to the six-digit level of breakdown yields specialization by type and size of both the passenger car itself and its engine. Category 870223, passenger vehicles "with spark-ignition internal combustion reciprocating piston engine, of a cylinder capacity >1500cc but not >3000cc" accounts for two-thirds of South Korea's exports of passenger vehicles. To recap, South Korea specializes in road vehicles, within which it specializes in passenger cars, within which it specializes in small but not too-small cars with internal combustion engines.

We are still not done specializing. Retail networks are necessary to sell the cars in each destination country, and an exporter is going to be better at retailing in some markets than others. So exporters specialize not only by product but also by destination. South Korea's top auto export destination is the US market, which is four times larger than its second-largest destination, China.

We can now see that trade opens up a remarkably wide world of possible specialization opportunities by good and by market, but specialization also means focusing on remarkably few such opportunities. At the six-digit product-definition level, there are those 5,053 products. But the top twenty of these products accounted for 42 percent of Korea's export revenue. There are 243 possible destinations (countries or territories), making 1,227,879 possible product-destination combinations. South Korea had 121,854 nonzero product-destination combinations out of the possible 1,227,879, or about 10 percent.

Then given what we said above about these nonzero product-destination combinations, South Korea specialized yet again. The top-twenty product-destination combinations (about 0.02 percent of the number of nonzero entries) produced a fifth of all Korean export revenues.

Looking at the same data worldwide uncovers many surprisingly bizarre combinations of hyperspecialized product, origin, and destination: Egyptians export ceramic toilets to Italy, Filipinos send electronic integrated circuits to the United States, and Nigerians export floating docks to Norway. Entrepreneurs from Lesotho export cotton trousers to American men, while Fijians send cotton suits to American women. Each one of these examples is notable for being both a large share of the origin country's export revenues *and* a large share of the destination market's import of that product.[27]

Changing Specializations

To make the knowledge problem even worse, the hyperspecializations keep changing as circumstances change in the source country, the destination country, the exports from third parties, the industry, the technology, and any number of other factors. Of the top-twenty product-destination combinations in South Korea in the year 2000, only two were still in the top-twenty in 2011 (one of which was small passenger cars with internal combustion for the US market). This is a typical pattern.

We also see this turbulence from the product point of view. Italy, Sweden, and Britain had been top-ten motor-vehicle exporters in 1980 but were no longer in the top ten in 2010. They were replaced by South Korea, Mexico, and China. Among automobile firms, Chrysler, Fiat, and British Leyland were in the top ten in motor-vehicle production in 1970 but were gone by 2010. Leyland disappeared altogether, while Chrysler went through near-bankruptcy and bailout under Jimmy Carter. One of the firms that remained near the top in 2010, General Motors, was not actually General Motors (which went bankrupt in 2009), but a bailed-out company of the same name.

Specialization in trade is like trying to crack a fiendish security system in which the right combination to open the lock changes every two minutes. Somehow the safe gets opened anyway with the help of that wily safecracker, the Invisible Hand, which constantly updates successful combinations by sending out price signals as to what are the most profitable specializations.

There are three things to note about the remarkable volatility and unpredictability of success in markets. First, it is not markets that are volatile, it is life. Markets adjust rapidly to changing circumstances and, compared to not adjusting, this is a virtue rather than a vice.

Second, this volatility should alleviate some of the anxiety about corporate power. "Powerful corporations" are only temporarily powerful, because they are at the mercy of market forces that make them vulnerable to loss of market share and even bankruptcy. Moreover, any given corporate chieftain is even less secure, since he or she will be out with the first sign of trouble even if the corporation hangs on.

Third, the volatility does have upsides and downsides. On the upside, it is constantly creating a lot of new opportunities. If you work hard and keep trying, your ship will come in sooner or later. On the downside, success does not last forever. It is very painful for the employees of an enterprise when circumstances change and the enterprise is no longer viable. But even then, remember that new enterprises are creating new jobs to replace the old ones.

The Invisible Hand works by constant searching for the right domestic and international trade opportunity, for the right person in the right firm in the right country to make the right product for the right market at the right time. Every one of these dimensions often produces a surprise. The biggest surprise in the world automobile market of the last six decades was the emergence of the world's fourth-largest auto company: Chung Ju Yung's Hyundai in South Korea.

A KOREAN ADAPTING TO CHANGE

Chung Ju Yung brought to Hyundai a lot of practice adapting to change. When he was born in 1915, Korea had only recently abolished a rigid class system (including slaves and "out-castes") in which the peasant Chung would have had little future. Korea had been the "hermit kingdom" sealed off to all Western contacts (not to mention trade) until the 1880s. This isolation was barely ended before the country's independence was over. After the Russo-Japanese War of 1904 to 1905 and even more after World War I, the Western powers initially endorsed the brutal Japanese rule over Korea, which would last until the end of World War II.

Koreans were on the long list of peoples whose hopes Woodrow Wilson had raised and then betrayed with his promises of self-determination after World War I. When it became clear that these promises were for Europeans only, and as the Japanese were only too happy to have their 1910 annexation of Korea endorsed in the Versailles Treaty, Koreans took matters into their own hands. Public demonstrations against Japanese rule on March 1, 1919, brought 2 million Koreans into the streets. The crowds cheered for a declaration of independence authored by the poet Ch'oe Namson: "We hereby declare Korea as an independent state and its people as free. This we declare to all the nations of the world in order to make clear the rightness of human equality. . . . The age of might has passed away, and the age of morality has come. . . . By protecting our individual right to freedom our joy shall be full."[28]

The Japanese colonial rulers were less enthusiastic, killing 7,500 demonstrators while torturing and jailing 46,000 more. In Cheamni village, near Suwon, the Japanese herded all the villagers into the local church, then burned it down with the villagers inside. The barbarities never stopped coming for the rest of Japanese rule until 1945, including even forcing Koreans to speak Japanese and use Japanese names. It is no wonder that Chung's business only began to take off after the Japanese defeat and he started doing business with the American occupation forces.[29]

First, a rigid aristocratic class system and then a psychotic occupation by a foreign power gave Koreans little incentive to invest in their own future development. Second, starting from that abysmally low point, Chung's and the South Koreans' story is of a positive *change* in economic and political freedom while still deficient in the *level* of individual freedom for most of the story.

Chung's success story shows how complicated it is to assess the roles of the government and the Invisible Hand, because the Invisible Hand helps to adjust to the ever-changing government. Chung was a master at cultivating a long line of autocrats that began with US army generals, independent Korea's first dictator Syngman Rhee, then dictator Park Chung Hee, and then yet another dictator, Chun Do Wan.

Chung was adept at seizing opportunities created by government contracts in the Korean War and the Vietnam War, and possibly opportunities created by Park's industrial policies. The industrial policies are the most controversial part of the story. I will not try to resolve it here; Chapter Thirteen will discuss the evidence for the "developmental leaders" that Korea may have had, also known as "benevolent autocrats."

Because it is cited so often, I have held back until now on one of the most famous comparisons of nations with and without the Invisible Hand: the comparison between South and North Korea, south and north of the thirty-eighth parallel north. National borders may not usually matter as much as we think they do, but they do when one side of the border has insane totalitarian rulers. One of the most evocative comparisons is to look at the nighttime satellite photos of the Korean peninsula. The South is ablaze with light. The lights abruptly switch off at the thirty-eighth parallel, leaving all of North Korea without any visible light (Figure 11.3). Chung's home village of Asan, in the Tongchan district, was left behind in the darkness after the partition. It still today has not solved its famine problems.

GAINS FROM SPECIALIZATION

What do we learn from patterns of specialization? Let's develop further where the specialization gains come from. First, specialization allows producers to use a lot of what they have a lot of, while economizing on the

FIGURE 11.3   North and South Korea by night. Almost the lone bright spot in North Korea, the capital city of Pyongyang would be lost amid the myriad blazing lights of South Korea. (Data courtesy of Mark Imhoff of NASA.)

things that are scarce. At the crudest level, they specialize based on their relative amounts (beginning "endowments") of the three basic inputs into production: unskilled labor, skilled labor, and physical capital (machinery and equipment). Their endowments form the basis of their comparative advantage: they are best at making things that use a lot of what they already have and they economize on what they do not have.

One of the big changes in global auto production is the migration of production from high-wage (i.e., labor scarce) to low-wage (i.e., labor abundant) production. Ford first arrived in Korea in the 1960s looking for local counterparts to produce cars with cheap Korean labor. Indeed Korean auto production has remained more labor intensive than its international competitors because of its reliance on cheap labor. In 1990, a Korean vehicle took thirty-three days of labor time to assemble, while a US vehicle took twenty-six, and a Japanese vehicle took seventeen.

Yet the cheap-labor story is far too broad a brush to explain the specialization patterns. Why did a Hyundai emerge in Korea and not in dozens of other cheap-labor places? Why did Korea wind up producing small gasoline-powered passenger cars and not diesel cars? Part of the answer is that comparative advantage is a lot more subtle than just cheap labor, it is having the right skills, geography, raw materials, culture, and other things that give a comparative advantage at something. The researcher is often at a loss to explain exactly what these are.

But there is one group that knows a lot more about what the idiosyncratic endowments are: the exporters and workers themselves. For example, I can tell you that I at least briefly survived in the competitive market for bolt-tighteners in Pemberville, Ohio, in 1977 because I happen to have a peculiar kind of manual dexterity for repeated operations that was a good fit for bolt-tightening. My immediate supervisor could also confirm this after a little trial and error—that is, after a failed stint in the shipping-crate-building department that involved a misunderstanding between me and a nail gun. The point is that knowledge of what local workers are best at is, not surprisingly, very localized knowledge, not available to anyone else. The advantage of the Invisible Hand is that it utilizes such localized knowledge of the agents themselves to find what they are best at because they are the ones who decide what to do under the Invisible Hand.

Suppose that I am going a bit overboard on the localized knowledge thing, and that it is possible for a sufficient number of top-down experts to eventually figure out what an economy is best at doing. That's OK, but do not forget the core principle of trade and specialization that producers economize on scarce resources and do not want to specialize in things that require a lot of what they do not have. Expert-run management of the export business itself requires a scarce and expensive factor: experts. One of the advantages of the Invisible Hand is that it economizes on the use of scarce experts and utilizes only the localized knowledge of the abundant supplies of nonexperts. (This doesn't automatically dismiss the top-down experts, but it raises the bar for them to prove their worth.)

The other explanation already offered by Adam Smith for the gains from specialization, if not hyperspecialization, is learning by doing. The narrower a laborer's specialty, the better the laborer gets at doing it. Another one of the big drivers of specialization is that workers already have some previous learning by doing that is relevant to some narrow sector. Then once they choose that sector they accumulate even more learning by doing. This argues strongly for specializing even more in that sector, until the other sectors drop away and they are hyperspecialized. This can also help solve the mystery of specializing by destination. Retailers' learning to please the whims of their customers is a destination-specific form of learning by doing.

We still see the signs of learning by doing in the top automakers today: Germany, Japan, and the United States, the top three, together account for 42 percent of global auto-exports today. Germany and the United States have been among the automobile pioneers for a century. Japan's success story is only somewhat more recent at this point, having surpassed the United States as long ago as 1980. Learning by doing is also all over the story of Chung's success with Hyundai.

CHUNG LEARNS TO MAKE CARS

This is not to say it is a simple story. The Chung Ju Yung story keeps getting stranger. There was no straight line leading from Hyundai Motor Service in 1946 to today's global car giant. Chung actually sold Hyundai Motors in the recession following the Korean War in the early 1950s.

Nevertheless, when Ford arrived in the 1960s looking for a Korean manufacturer to make cheap cars, Chung impressed them with the grease-monkey savvy left over from his days in auto repair. "The other two company presidents did not know anything about cars," said Chung. "However, there was nothing I did not know about a car. That was why my company got the contract." On February 23, 1968, Ford and Chung signed "a standard overseas-assembler franchise agreement."[30]

A small amount of learning by doing had given Chung and Hyundai the edge, then they were going to do a lot more learning. Initially, Hyundai was just going to assemble cars from complete kits of parts, little more than what a father does assembling a toy on Christmas morning. Ford did not take it too seriously when Chung refused to allow Ford any "management participation." They were a global behemoth humoring an unknown company from a country that had barely seen a car until World War II.

Likewise, they indulged Chung when he wanted to move from assembling kits to actually doing Korean models collaboratively with Ford engineers. Hyundai started making diesel trucks with 80 percent of the parts from Ford of Europe, even the engines and transmissions. Korean engineers also started tinkering with the car designs with Ford engineers looking over their shoulders. "They taught us everything—how to read a drawing, what is a manufacturing standard, how to do quality control," said Lee Soo Il, a Korean engineer who joined Hyundai in 1969.[31] Ford had once again underestimated the company that would later surpass them.

By the early 1970s, Ford belatedly woke up to the reality that Chung's goal was to produce Hyundai's own car under its own name. The Ford–Hyundai partnership fell apart. Chung now turned to Mitsubishi in Japan for his technological needs, borrowing an Italian designer and a British engineer along the way. Against all odds, Hyundai's first car, the Pony, came off the assembly line in December 1975. It was an immediate success in South Korea. Although there were only 100,000 cars in South Korea in 1975, that number would increase a hundred-fold over the next twenty-five years as the South Korean economic miracle continued. Chung had found the right car for the fastest-growing market in the world.

Yet the Korean market was still not enough for Chung: he wanted a global market. By luck or by design, Chung had produced a cheap small car right at the moment when the OPEC oil crisis and the environmental movement had shifted demand away from gas-guzzlers. Using markets in Africa, Latin America, and Canada as laboratories for further learning by doing, it would take Hyundai another decade to crack the US market with the Excel. The Excel won awards as best new car in the United States in 1985.

Chung and Hyundai had made incredible progress, but not nearly enough. Hyundai in 1989 to 1993 still had an average of 200 defects for every 100 of its new cars during the first ninety days, compared to 130 for GM and Ford, and fewer than 100 for Toyota and Honda. As Hyundai produced the first generation of the Sonata in 1987, it could not even get into the US market because it failed to meet emissions standards (Hyundai remained grateful for the always-forgiving Canadian market).

The third-generation Sonata still sold fewer than 25,000 units a year to Americans from 1993 to 1999. The sales breakthroughs finally arrived with the fourth generation, then the fifth generation started winning awards, and today the seventh generation sells nine times more cars than the third generation did. We can now see South Korea's remarkable payoff to its vehicle specialization included specializing and learning by doing, not only by specific product niche and by market, but even by model of car.[32]

How to Scale Up Success

To understand the South Korean specialization success, you need to know it was not just great, it was insanely great. The top three exports from South Korea (defining products very narrowly at the six-digit level), including the small gasoline-powered passenger cars, generate $94 billion in export revenue by themselves. These three exports alone generated revenue of $1,888 for each and every South Korean. In contrast, while Lesotho benefited from specializing in cotton men's trousers, as mentioned above, it stopped a good way short of this scale of success. The top three six-digit specialties in Lesotho generated only $87 for each and every person in Lesotho.

The Invisible Hand helps with scaling up success as well as with finding success in the first place. Once workers get into a virtuous circle of learning by doing and increasing production on your chosen specialty, they still need the Invisible Hand to keep scaling up. They need it to efficiently get them the scale of the inputs, both domestic and imported, that go into producing the increasing scale of specialized output at which they are becoming so good. To free up those inputs, the Invisible Hand has to shut down many other specialties at which they are not so good.

One way this happens is probably the most hated and misunderstood part of the Invisible Hand. There is one type of trade in the market that has always seemed sinister: trading money today for money tomorrow. A rapidly growing industry or firm will produce higher output tomorrow than it did today. Having only today's revenue at hand, though, it does not have enough money to pay for today's inputs for tomorrow's outputs. That is when the guys who trade money tomorrow for money today come in. They advance the growing firm money today to pay for their inputs today, and in exchange the firm gives them some money tomorrow from their future output revenues. Let's dub this a "bank loan." Alternatively, the finance guys could give the firm money as a partial ownership claim today, and the firm would then pay them part of its profits tomorrow, corresponding to their ownership claim. Let's dub this a "stock market."

We have already met the finance guys in 1850s New York who thrived from advancing funds to New York's booming domestic and international trade. The success of our man Benjamin Mendes Seixas, the cigar importer on Greene Street, depended in part on the finance industry in which his cousin Benjamin Seixas Nathan became a great success. Now we see that finance is necessary for entrepreneurship as well as for trade.

The finance guys give funding to the industries they expect to keep growing and they therefore expect to be able to pay them back. And the finance guys have to cut off industries that are contracting, because they won't be able to pay them back. So finance plays a big role in cutting off the failures and scaling up the successes. The combination of the goods market and the financial market is a double death threat to any specialized activity that is not thriving, while giving abundant life to any specialized activity that is succeeding.

Part of South Korea's scale of specialized success is due to a banking sector that is twice as large relative to the scale of the economy as Lesotho's. Another part is due to a thriving stock market in South Korea, where the value of stocks traded is 182 percent of GDP. As for the Lesotho stock market, don't ask.

I have deliberately simplified the explanation of finance to just show how basic and essential it really is, and because there is much dislike and mistrust of finance.

University of California at Berkeley economist Ross Levine has provided a whole career's worth of evidence for the central role of finance in development. Let me borrow his summary from a recent paper:

Finance is powerful. It mobilizes savings, allocates those savings, [and] monitors the use of funds provided to firms and individuals. . . . How well financial institutions and markets perform these functions exert a powerful influence on economic prosperity.

When financial systems perform these functions well, they tend to promote growth and expand economic opportunities. For example, when banks screen borrowers effectively and identify firms with the most promising prospects, this is a first step in boosting productivity growth. When financial markets and institutions mobilize savings from disparate households to invest in these promising projects, this represents a second crucial step in fostering growth.[33]

There may indeed be more scope in finance than in goods markets for activities that generate private returns that are not social returns, such as deception, embezzlement, and outright Ponzi schemes. As explained by the great book satirically titled *This Time Is Different,* by Carmen Reinhart and Kenneth Rogoff, cheating in finance did not start with the horrific financial crisis of 2007 to 2008; it has been happening for centuries.[34] Yet somehow, despite the cheating, finance keeps providing the essential services without which large-scale success would not be possible.

ADAM SMITH AND DEVELOPMENT

In 1986, just as Hyundai was cracking the US market, the *Journal of Political Economy*, one of the most prestigious journals in economics, published an article titled "Increasing Returns and Long-Run Growth." The key insight was that investment in a sector not only boosted production in that sector, it also facilitated learning by doing in that sector that was the key to future success. The article began a revolution in academic thinking on economic growth and development in which learning by doing was a key driver.

Another round of insight came a few years later in a 1993 article in another distinguished journal, *Econometrica*. The article, titled "Making a Miracle," specifically aimed at explaining what had happened in South

Korea. At the heart of the story was learning by doing when workers specialize in doing the same thing over and over again. Growth and development theory based on these insights has flourished for the two decades since. The insights of Adam Smith are back at the center of development after an unforgivable absence of decades.

We will see in the next chapter that new theories of growth and development stimulated by these two articles would also extend the Invisible Hand into another type of problem-solving: inventing new technologies.

CHAPTER TWELVE

TECHNOLOGY: HOW TO SUCCEED
WITHOUT KNOWING HOW

The United Nations' Broadband Commission for Digital Development, cochaired by the Rwandan dictator Paul Kagame, may be a hint that someone in the development community believes technology is driven by top-down design.

The Broadband Commission for Digital Development produced in September 2012 its third annual report, *The State of Broadband 2012: Achieving Digital Inclusion for All.* They explain their design for bringing broadband Internet to everyone:

> The Report recognizes a clear need for policy leadership to establish a strong vision among stakeholders and prioritize the deployment of broadband at the national level. A growing number of countries now have a national broadband plan, policy or strategy in place, with some 119 countries having a policy in place by mid-2012.

> Governments play a critical role in convening the private sector, public institutions, civil society and individual citizens to outline a vision for a connected nation.

> Policy leadership provides the structure to identify constraints, opportunity gaps and actions around the supply and demand of broadband deployment and adoption.

Advocacy Target 3: by 2015, 40% of households in developing countries should have Internet access.[1]

President Kagame himself opined:

> The transformational impact of broadband on people's lives and global economies is no longer questionable; the remaining challenge is to extend these obvious benefits to the majority of global citizens and allow them to unleash their creative potential to fully integrate in the information driven global economy. This will require new frameworks for global cooperation in areas of investment, research and technology. The Broadband Commission for Digital Development will work to realize this potential.[2]

Some dissidents questioned what President Kagame had implicitly commanded them *not* to question: the "obvious benefits" of the "transformational impact of broadband."

University of California at Berkeley researcher Kentaro Toyama cites surveys that show when a village gets hooked up to the Internet on a PC, "the dominant use is by young men," who are "playing games, watching movies, or consuming adult content."[3] On the other side of the ledger, India's IT industry has captured 35 percent of the world market for business-process outsourcing while India ranks 114th in the world in average Internet connection speed.[4]

Wiring the world to end poverty overlooks how many less-faddish technologies are still lacking among the poor. The development audience gets excited about farmers in a remote but wired village finding out prices in real time for their crops. It fails to ask whether those farmers have motor vehicles to transport the crops to the market to get that price.

The point is the same as that made repeatedly throughout this book. The top-down leaders and experts in technology do not have enough knowledge or incentives to get it right for the reality of what is happening at the bottom. They promised to end poverty with broadband and they gave us young men watching porn.

THE MISSING CAUSE OF DEVELOPMENT: TECHNOLOGY

If we do not understand technology's role in development better, it is partly the fault of the whole field of economics. Adam Smith's Invisible hand in 1776 applied to goods that were already in existence, and this remained the dominant framework in economics for the next two centuries. For most of the history of economics, the field spent most of its energies on explaining a static economy in which existing goods could be allocated with ever-increasing efficiency. The field never had quite enough to say about the most important two things going on over those two centuries: the invention of new goods and perpetual economic growth.

Nobel laureate Robert Solow at last placed innovation at the center of growth in a 1957 article. He showed that traditional factors like investment in plant and equipment could not account for most of American economic growth. There was something else, and the obvious candidate for "something else" was invention.[5] After Solow, most economists accepted that economic growth happened through technological innovation.

Yet still unexplained was why and how innovation happened, a state of affairs that continued for the next three decades. Many tried to explain innovation, many came up with promising insights, but they failed to generate an overall convincing theory of innovation. Finally, in 1983, a young student of Nobel Laureate Robert Lucas at the University of Chicago, a student named Paul Romer, handed in a PhD dissertation that offered a simple but paradigm-shifting theory of innovation. It was this dissertation that resulted in the 1986 "Increasing Returns and Long-Run Growth" article mentioned at the end of the last chapter.[6] The theory would be refined much more by Romer himself, by Lucas (who wrote the "Making a Miracle" article about learning by doing also mentioned in the last chapter),[7] and by a whole new generation of economists ever since that created what came to be called "the new growth theory." These economists would have to explain both how technologies got invented (innovation) and how they spread (imitation). The theory and evidence they produced will allow us here to address again the big question of development as the result of conscious direction versus spontaneous solutions.

THE PEOPLE MODEL

One simple innovation model suggested by the new growth theorists was the ultimate in spontaneous solutions emerging from the bottom.[8] Innovation just means coming up with new ideas. In this simple model, the number of new ideas is proportional to the number of people. Think of each person as a problem-solver, constantly trying to find a better way to do his or her own work. They could be testing out things by trial and error, or a new idea could just strike them. The more problem-solvers there are, the more solutions they generate on new and better ways to get the work done.

So suppose a number of people are involved in farming and trading. One problem is how to move farm produce from the producers to the consumers. One person thinks of a wooden box to carry the wheat, as opposed to just carrying wheat stalks in his arms. Another person suggests putting wheels on the box to make it easier to move, which prompts another person to suggest clearing some cart paths on which to move the wheeled box. Yet another person suggests hooking up the wheeled box to a horse. We have just invented the horse-drawn cart, one of the most important innovations in human history.

The increased stock of ideas makes larger production possible. The horse-drawn cart frees up a large labor force that was previously devoted to carrying grain by hand. Now this labor can work in the fields instead. So now more wheat can be grown. Increased production of wheat means larger populations can now be fed.

Ideas are powerful multipliers of production because of one peculiar property they have. If I am using a horse-drawn cart to move my wheat, no one else can be using the same cart at the same time. If I am eating the bread, no one else can eat the same bread. Most goods are "rival" in that use of them by one person precludes the use of them by a rival person.

But ideas are "nonrival." If I am using the *idea* of a box, wheels, and a horse, that does not preclude anyone else from using the same idea for their purposes. If I am using the formula $1+1=2$ to count the wheat, that doesn't preclude anyone else from using the same formula at the same time to count their wheat. If I construct a physical wheeled cart, I am the only user, and only my production increases. But if I come up with the

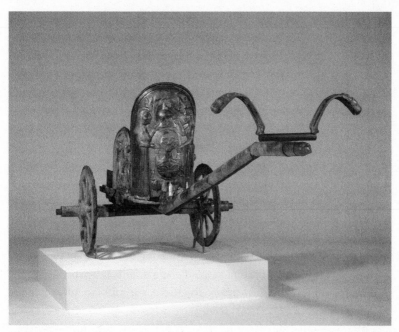

FIGURE 12.1 Bronze Etruscan chariot from the sixth century BC. The pairing of draft animal and wheeled vehicle was a momentous innovation that spread rapidly across Eurasia.

(©Metropolitan Museum of Art Image source: Art Resource, NY.)

idea of a wheeled cart, everyone with whom I am in contact can become users, and everyone's production increases.

We are now in a virtuous circle. A large population produces a lot of new ideas, so we have greater production, which feeds an even larger population. The larger population now produces an even greater number of new ideas, so now we have an even higher growth of production and population. The growth of population, technology, and production all keep accelerating over time.

TESTING THE PEOPLE MODEL

The only evidence we can find for this bottom-up story of innovation is— all of human history. The story first predicts that the higher the initial population, the higher population growth will be. At the time of Christ, world population was about a quarter of a billion. Global population growth for the next fifteen centuries was about 4.5 percent per century. By AD 1500, global population had risen to 438 million, and population growth over the following century was 27 percent. Global population first surpassed a billion early in the 1800s. Over the century from 1820 to 1920, there was population growth of 79 percent. By 1920, global population was 1.86 billion, from which population growth of 281 percent has followed since. Global population growth has indeed been higher, the higher the initial global population is.

The story next predicts that the higher the initial population, the more innovation there will be. The world as a whole confirms this prediction, as the rate of technological progress kept accelerating as the world population rose. The most surprising explanation for the industrial revolution was that it was not a revolution at all; it was a gradually accelerating process over centuries that just finally reached a critical mass of people for producing ideas.

Of course, growth of population cannot keep accelerating forever: there is a biological maximum on human reproduction. At some point, there will be a momentous shift. Instead of using the increased production only to sustain a larger population, a good part of the increased production will go to increasing the standard of living of the whole population. The historical data suggest this shift happened around 1820, just as the Industrial Revolution was spreading from Britain to North America and Western Europe. World income per capita growth now started accelerating as the population kept rising.

We can also test the story by comparing different parts of the world with each other. The prediction of this simple story is that the more-populous parts of the world will at any moment have better technology than less-populous parts. The more-populous parts will also have more technological innovation than less-populous parts.

How to divide up the world to test this prediction? The key principle was already given above: my nonrival ideas spread to everyone with whom I am in contact, so the right unit is those who are in contact with each other. The correct unit is *not* the nation-state, which did not even exist at this time. The correct unit for most of human history is more likely to be something like regions or even continents. Most of the Eurasian continent developed enough trade and transportation links amongst its different parts to be considered a single population. The Silk Road connected East Asia to the Mediterranean and Europe by land, through Central Asian steppes. There was oceanic travel all around the edges of Eurasia, including all around the coasts of Europe, along the coasts adjoining the Indian Ocean, and amongst the archipelagoes of Southeast Asia and East Asia.

In contrast, a number of other human groups were relatively isolated from everyone else. Sub-Saharan Africa was mostly isolated by the Sahara. Even more isolated were what are now Australia, New Zealand, and North and South America. Eurasia had over 200 million people at the time of Christ, while sub-Saharan Africa had only 8 million. Even more miniscule was North America with less than 800,000 at the time of Christ, and Australia had less than 400,000. (It goes without saying that these numbers, which come from the late economic historian Angus Maddison, are speculative.[9])

And indeed, as predicted, the great technological divide in human history is between Eurasia and everyone else. The year 3000 BC is roughly the common date of archaeological findings confirming wheeled vehicles scattered across Eurasia. For example, there was a wooden wheel with a hole for an axle in Ljubljansko, Slovenia;[10] a pictograph of a four-wheeled wagon in Uruk, Mesopotamia; and a ceramic model of a four-wheeled wagon in eastern Hungary.[11] A bit later (1200 BC), the chariot shows up in a site in Anyang, China, with wheel construction oddly similar to a spoked wheel dated to the second millennium BC in Lschashen, Armenia.[12] A site on the Taedong River basin in Korea dated to about 100 BC shows horse trappings and carriage fittings.

The archaeological evidence keeps accumulating to confirm that virtually all of Eurasia had wheeled vehicles pulled by draft animals in the first centuries after Christ. The rest of the world did not even have the wheel. It would not appear in sub-Saharan Africa, Australia, New Zealand, or North and South America until after Columbus.

This Is Crazy, but Is It Crazy Enough?

The discussion of population and development here is different from the conventional mind-set that always prefixes *over-* to the word *population*. I once gave a population and development lecture at Hebrew University in Jerusalem, setting out a narrative like the one above. A generous donor concerned about the problem of overpopulation had financed the lecture series.

It is the only time I have ever lectured where I then heard the chairman of the session apologize to the audience for the lecture they had just heard. To think of (over)population as a good thing was just too crazy for a respectable audience. (The donor also was present and was very gracious.)

In fairness to the session chairman, the conventional view of overpopulation does have its own sensible theory. For most of human history, land was a very important input into production. As population rises, there is less land per person, which would imply less production per person. Unlike nonrival ideas, land is a rival good: if some recently born people take more of the land, there is less for those previously born.

So increasing population has negative rival effects (decreasing land per person) and positive nonrival effects (increasing ideas). Which tendency wins will be settled by the data. The great long-run view of all of human history suggests the nonrival effects of population win.

One can imagine many other regions or eras in which the negative, rival effect will win. Doomsday thinkers are so worried about the rival effects that they forecast famine, war, and reality television whenever population grows. Sub-Saharan Africa has since had a population explosion that did not yield the predicted technology explosion, but neither did it yield the doomsday predictions. We will see below that the strength of the idea–population link depends on some other factors we have not covered yet.

Technological Virtuous Circles

The virtuous circle of technological innovation is even stronger than the population–technology story alone would predict because technology also feeds on itself. The more technology one already has, the faster is the rate of technological innovation. This is another piece of theory and evidence in favor of innovation as a bottom-up process.

There are many reasons why more innovation usually happens the more technology one already has. I will just give one reason: many new inventions are just combinations of previous inventions. (The writer Matt Ridley in his book *The Rational Optimist: How Prosperity Evolves* described it as "ideas having sex."[13]) We have already seen this with the horse-drawn cart, which was a combination of three previous inventions: a wooden carrying box, the wheel, and the domestication of horses as draft animals. This principal of new inventions combining previous inventions would continue throughout the history of transportation.

The same miraculous year, 1776, that brought us Adam Smith and Thomas Jefferson also brought us James Watt. Watt (1736–1819) is the other hero from the University of Glasgow promised in the last chapter. There were many connections: Watt was Adam Smith's friend and Glasgow neighbor. Another of Watt's intellectual friends was William Small (1734–1775), a Scottish philosopher and mathematician who was Thomas Jefferson's favorite professor at the College of William and Mary.[14]

In 1776, Watt installed the world's first steam engines, one in a coal mine and one in an ironworks. Watt was himself combining several previous discoveries. The first was the discovery in the seventeenth century that steam was evaporated water, creating high pressure that could be used to push a piston. Watt relied upon inventions from military industry (especially the cannon) to do the precision tooling of the piston and cylinder necessary to create a fuel efficient engine.

Watt's breakthrough would have its biggest impact far from the coal mines. It would eventually make it possible to replace the horse in the horse-drawn cart with a steam engine.

This possibility was only realized after other innovations that drew upon other previous technologies. One intermediate step was a horse-drawn iron railway using cast-iron rails (a metallurgical invention of its own) in 1805. Then by September 27, 1825, a British engineer named George Stephenson (1781–1848) had managed to put everything together in Stockton, England, for a steam locomotive to haul eighty tons of coal and flour and a car full of passengers nine miles in two hours. In other words, the huge innovation of the railroad was simply a combination of previous inventions of horse-drawn wheeled vehicles, the steam engine, and iron rails.

One amusing illustration of the partnership of past and present in technology is that the railroad gauge (the distance between the wheels, or the width of the railroad track) that George Stephenson used in the world's first train in 1825 was 4 feet 8.5 inches (1.4 meters). This became the most common railroad gauge worldwide. The distance between the wheels inferred from wheel-rut spacing found on Cretan roads built in 2000 BC had also been 1.4 meters.[15] There are no very compelling reasons in chariots, carriages, or railroads to prefer 1.4 meters to something smaller or larger. Each generation of innovator had no reason to change the width of the carriage from the previous generation, regardless of whether it was pulled by a draft animal or a steam locomotive, and so an arbitrary wheel gauge persisted from 2000 BC to AD 1827. Today, the 1.4-meter gauge is still the standard on rail lines in Europe, North America, Australia, Japan, and China.[16]

The key prediction is that innovation is usually faster the more technology one already has. We can explain again the same technological great divide between Eurasia (including China) and the rest of the world that we have already explained once with population. Eurasia had more advanced technology than the rest early on, which correctly predicts that Eurasia would be where most of the action was on innovation for the last millennium.

We can refine this test further. On both sides of the great divide, there was still a lot of variation. Some parts of technologically advanced Eurasia were more technologically backward than others. Some parts of the technologically backward Rest were more technologically advanced than others. Is there an association between where a patch of ground was technologically in AD 1500 and where it is today?

To capture these different little patches of ground, some coauthors and I used the territories of today's nation-states and collected data on their technology in 1500 and their technology today. This method does not imply that nation-states were what mattered. How could they, when they did not even exist in 1500? The territory of today's states just happens to be the only way to track different patches of the earth's surface through time, because we have the national data today, and we can approximately reconstruct the technology available on the same pieces of territory back in 1500. And we took into account the nonnational reality of the story by using a statistical technique that allows for adjoining nations today to be treated as parts of the same territory for the purposes of the persistence of technology from 1500 to today.

To get the AD 1500 historical data, we asked a series of simple questions about whether a technology existed at all in each territory. For example, in transportation technology: did they have the wheel? Did they have horse-powered vehicles, or the magnetic compass, or ocean-going ships? In other areas, we asked about technologies such as iron, steel, moveable block printing, paper, books, and the plough.

We confirmed that technology in 1500 predicts technology (and thus per capita income) today. In fact, 78 percent of the income difference today between Europe and sub-Saharan Africa can be explained by technology that was already in place by 1500.[17]

Moreover, the historical roots of technology are even deeper. We have some very crude data on technology in 1000 BC and in AD 1. There is a strong correlation between technology in 1000 BC and that in AD 1, and between technology in AD 1 and technology in AD 1500. We can also jump right to a strong correlation between 1000 BC and technology in AD 1500.

So we find that a very simple theory of bottom-up innovation can explain many of the big facts about technology around the world today. But there is one fact conspicuously left unexplained.

East Versus West in Eurasia

No simple story ever fits the data perfectly. The AD 1500 data show what is already well known, that China was among the most advanced in 1500, yet it is still relatively poor in income and technology today. Why did China not benefit from 1500 to the present from the same process of bottom-up innovation? Will that point to some other factor we have left out?

China was famous for its precocious technological innovations (such as gunpowder and the compass), which is consistent with the population and technology story. But the population story is of no help in explaining why the Western edge of Eurasia would pull ahead beginning in the late eighteenth century and leave the Eastern edge far behind. Why did the West invent the steam engine and railroad, and not the East? We need something else.

That something else is already on the table: the Western idea of the individual that emerged from the Enlightenment. That miraculous year 1776 is again the key symbol: Jefferson declares all men equal, Adam Smith declares all men free to choose, and James Watt installs his first steam engine. There are two key mechanisms by which the new Western idea of the individual helped innovation: the challenge to authority and the private return to innovation.

QUESTION AUTHORITY

The challenge to authority is also a challenge to the idea of conscious direction of technical innovation, or of development in general. The philosopher Immanuel Kant summarized the whole Enlightenment as *sapere aude*, which can be variously translated from the Latin as "dare to know" or as the bumper sticker "question authority."[18] The old hierarchical view of human society, the demand that the individual conform to the group, was not fertile for innovation.

The economic historian Joel Mokyr in his superb book *The Enlightened Economy* attributes the British industrial revolution to these new Enlightenment ideas about the individual's right to dissent: "intellectual innovation could only occur in the kind of tolerant societies in which sometimes outrageous ideas proposed by highly eccentric men would not entail a violent response against 'heresy' and 'apostasy.'"[19] Mokyr points out that the word *innovation* was previously a "term of abuse." Innovators showed an insulting disrespect for venerated ideas, institutions, thinkers, and rulers. After the Enlightenment, innovation became "a word of praise."[20]

With this new perspective, technological and scientific knowledge became "contestable," meaning that "there were no sacred cows and that nothing would be accepted on authority alone, and that, moreover, doubts and criticism of conventional wisdom would not be penalized."[21] (I can't wait until the Enlightenment arrives in the development community.)

One mechanical illustration of the benefits of "question authority" is to think of innovation as resulting from a lot of experiments by many individuals in which the odds against an experiment's yielding a useful innovation are high (a good description of the real world of innovation). You can still beat a thousand-to-one odds if you have a thousand individuals running different experiments and only one has to succeed.

The key words here are *different experiments*. A conformist society does not permit "different experiments." The hierarchical authorities and group pressure forces individuals to conform, or, in other words, they will all be prone to run the *same* experiments. The chances of finding a one-in-a-thousand technological breakthrough are dismal if a thousand different people are all running the same experiment.

Having Paul Kagame force everyone to run the same experiment on broadband, which will be called "best practice" by the expert advisors to Kagame and the Broadband Commission, is not promising. That is *not* the way technological progress happened in history, nor the way it still happens today. We can now start to see why the individualist West pulled ahead of the conformist East after the eighteenth-century Enlightenment.

THE PRIVATE RETURN TO INNOVATION

The other Enlightenment idea that boosted Western innovation was that the inventor could keep the rewards of his own invention. This created much more powerful incentives to make innovations in the West compared to the East, with the predictable result that the former had a lot more innovation than the latter.

Having the inventors realize private returns was a bit more complicated than it was for sellers under Adam Smith's Invisible Hand. The miracle of the Invisible Hand of the baker is that his private return to bread was the same as the social return to bread, but the private and social returns to ideas are not equal. Since ideas are nonrival (i.e., they will be used by everyone else), the social return (return to everyone else) to your coming up with a productive idea is a lot higher than your private return to yourself. This means that incentives for innovation are inadequate. Individuals do too little innovation compared to the ideal world where private returns would be equal to social returns.

There is no perfect solution to this problem, but there are solutions. The classic response is patent protection for inventions, which allows only the inventor to commercially benefit from the invention. The West's respect for the individual and his or her property rights carried it into the realm of ideas, where one can get "intellectual property rights" for his or her idea. This has the strong advantage of raising the returns to invention, to get inventors to do more of what is so beneficial to society.

By the time he installed his first steam engine in 1776, James Watt had been working on his steam engine for twelve years. He kept going with financing from a factory owner with deep pockets. Watt's spending twelve years improving an invention and a factory owner's financing him only happened because Watt had gotten a patent on his steam engine.

Conventional wisdom is that patents are the main or only way the West solved the inadequate incentives for invention problem. But there is also an even more bottom-up solution that was first sketched out by Joseph Schumpeter early in the twentieth century in his famous theory of "creative destruction."

Schumpeter postulated that an innovator has a jump on everyone else on commercializing his or her own idea. The innovator can develop new products that use his ideas, keeping the idea itself secret from other would-be users. What this means is that he has a monopoly on a product, the new product that resulted from his idea, and as with all monopolies he can realize high profits. The monopoly profits are what give the innovator a generous return for the new idea. This is the "creative" part. In contrast to Adam Smith, Schumpeter saw monopoly as socially beneficial, because of its stimulation of innovation.[22]

The high monopoly profits should not freak out Mr. Smith too much. Profits from invention do not last forever. Your rivals see your profits from your nonrival idea and they are plotting your destruction by inventing another idea that will replace yours. This is the "destruction" part of "creative destruction."

AND AT LAST WE HAVE
A THEORETICAL MODEL OF INNOVATION

In academic economics, a theory is never fully accepted until it can be put into a mathematical model. Paul Romer's 1990 article "Endogeneous Technological Change" was the first widely accepted theory to capture Schumpeter's ideas, and Romer has been followed by many other theorists since.[23]

Romer's and others' recent theories of innovation offered several new wrinkles. Romer drew upon another old idea, monopolistic competition, proposed by Edward Chamberlin back in 1933. Monopolistic competition, seemingly an oxymoron, is when monopolists produce consumer goods that are almost-substitutes for each other. Firms can freely enter to make new products when profits to the old ones are still high. The competition of monopolists making similar products keeps the monopolists' profits down.

The new product will soon be followed by other new products that are imperfect substitutes for it, so the innovator is a monopolistic competitor rather than a monopolist. For example, Apple was a monopolist on the iPad for a while, but Samsung, Google, and Amazon Kindle soon came up with imperfect substitutes that took away some of its market. It is this prospect of future competition that supplies the "destruction" of which Schumpeter spoke. The bottom line is that the private return to invention will be generous but not exorbitant compared to the social return. Innovation will happen in a decentralized market system, and growth will happen thanks to innovation.

James Watt was able to anticipate returns from his steam engine, not only because of his patent, but also because of his temporary monopoly on the steam engine. He continued to make better steam engines than anyone else, as he continually tinkered to improve the fuel efficiency of his engines. By the mid-1780s James Watt had perfected an engine that would not be overtaken for another fifty years. His son James Watt Jr. (1769–1848) took over the business for many years after his father had retired.

THE SPREAD OF TECHNOLOGY

The other new wrinkle in Romer's theory is extremely important because it gives us a simple theory of how technology spreads. Romer followed up his 1990 article with another one in 1994 that used the 1990 theory to make one more simple point. As mentioned above, another problem in the theory of technology is understanding how technologies spread from the original area in which they are invented (innovation) to other areas (imitation).

Romer's 1994 theory was that new technology became embodied in new products and moved as those products were exported to other areas. If you want to imitate a new technology invented in some other part of the globe, Romer suggested in 1994, all you need to do is import that new product.[24]

This insight raises the stakes further on letting trade happen. Now trade is not only a matter of benefiting from the gains to specialization, as in the previous chapter. It is also the vehicle by which you can adopt a new technology. If you want to join the automobile technology revolution, start by importing an automobile. Chung Ju Yung in the previous chapter had launched Hyundai Motors based on his experience with repairing imported cars in South Korea.

MOVING PEOPLE

There is one other well-documented way that technology spreads, which is further support for the bottom-up spontaneous order view of technology. For good measure, it also contradicts the nation-centric view of technology and development. To move a technology, all you need to do is move a person.

Again, the long, long view gives the best evidence for this. We have already seen that technology in AD 1500 predicts technology and income today. There was a big set of exceptions: the regions that would later become the United States, Canada, Australia, and New Zealand were all cut off from the rest of humanity and they had very little technology in 1500, or at any earlier date, yet they are technologically advanced today.

The reason the lands of North America and Oceania were an exception is most likely that Europeans settled in these lands in large numbers and brought their technology with them. (Geography does matter at the very least in determining where people go, as we have already discussed with the temperate zones in North America that proved attractive to Europeans.) Latin America is an intermediate example, where there were minority European settlements that today yield middle-income countries, richer than similar countries without European settlements.[25] (This supplements the institutional explanation in Chapter Seven why Colombia was much more successful than Benin, though not as successful as the United States.)

We can do a more systematic test. Is it places or people that matter for today's technology and income? We have already done the place-based measure of technology in AD 1500. For the people-based measure of technological heritage, we measure the technology of the AD 1500 ancestors of today's peoples, regardless of whether today's peoples have changed location since then.

The prediction contest is no contest: the people-based measure of technological heritage from 1500 drastically outperforms the place-based measure in predicting today's technology and income. This result has been replicated many times in the new development research that stresses the importance of historical roots: it is the history of people rather than of places that matter.[26]

THE POWER OF THE PEASANTS

It was not only Europeans who were carrying technology around the globe after the Old and New Worlds made contact. Understanding this is further evidence for the spontaneous people-based view of technological diffusion. It is also yet another contradiction of the Blank Slate view of Africa and Asia as places where nothing had happened until the beginning of "official development" in 1949, where passive peasants had no potential.

We have already mentioned the cocoa production in Ghana's Ashanti region in the discussion of Ghana's first president, Kwame Nkrumah, who after independence in 1957 taxed the cocoa growers nearly to death as part of toxic political conflict between ethnic groups. But where had that cocoa come from?

Ghana became one of the world's largest cocoa producers in the early twentieth century in spite of, not because of, the colonial administration. The British had picked coffee as the promising commodity in the Gold Coast (as Ghana was known before independence).[27] The colonizers also tried introducing cotton. Both failed at the time, and neither has ever taken off since in Ghana.

Cocoa was native to the New World and unknown to the Old, but it quickly spread after the Atlantic trade began. In 1879, a Ghanaian farmer and trader named Tetteh Quarshie visited Fernando Po (an island now called Bioko, off the coast of Cameroon, in what is now the nation of Equatorial Guinea). Farmers on Fernando Po were already growing cocoa. Tetteh Quarshie helped himself to a few plants and carried them back to the Akwapim people of southeastern Ghana.[28] The Akwapim farmers experimented with the new crop in the 1880s, utilizing their previous experience with palm oil farms.[29] They found local conditions were good for cocoa and it sold for more than alternative crops, so its popularity spread.

Even after local farmers had introduced cocoa into the Gold Coast (Ghana), the British almost succeeded in killing it. The colonial government had an incentive to make the Gold Coast pay off for the colonizers. They thought cocoa should be grown on "modern" plantations on a large scale. They could not believe that primitive local farmers had already found the most efficient farm size. After six different attempts at plantations failed, with large losses for the colonial budget, colonial officials finally gave up. What the Akwapim knew, and the British did not, was that small holders could mix cocoa with food crops, making small plots preferable. Modern research has confirmed that mixing cocoa with food crops actually helps the cocoa plants. The food crops offer ground cover and weed control to the cocoa plants. As one modern source puts it, the "continuous care" that smallholders "lavished" on their crop mix of food and cocoa benefited both crops.[30]

By 1891, just thirteen years after Tetteh Quarshie's trip, Ghana began to export cocoa to world markets. Within two decades, the Gold Coast became the world's largest cocoa producer. The linguistic cousins of the Akwapim, the Ashanti people in the middle of the Gold Coast around Kumasi, also adopted cocoa as small holders. The Ashanti would produce most of Ghana's supply of cocoa at independence.

It was this Ashanti production of cocoa that made them a tempting target for Kwame Nkrumah's destructive schemes to redistribute the wealth between ethnic groups, unintentionally endorsed by Sir Arthur Lewis, as discussed in Chapter Four. Ghanaian governments more recently have refrained from punitive taxation of Ashanti cocoa farmers, and these farmers are once again among the world's leading suppliers of cocoa today.

On the other side of the globe, we have seen in Chapter Three how, when historian R. H. Tawney visited Tianjin, China, in 1932, he had described China as a "static civilization . . . little influencing the West and little influenced by it."[31] As a historian, he should have known this was nonsense; China had been trading with the West for centuries.

Chinese peasants were sufficiently nonstatic to introduce a new technology that increased the calories, vitamins, and nutrients produced by a given amount of land, thus sustaining a larger population for a given amount of land. The new technology was called the potato. The Spanish had borrowed the potato from the South American Andes (in what is now Colombia, Ecuador, Peru, and Chile) after the conquest by Francisco Pizarro in 1532, and other Europeans learned about it from the Spanish. Chinese farmers learned about the potato from Dutch traders in the 1600s. The potato made it possible for farmers to plant in mountainous areas previously unsuitable for agriculture. Chinese farmers also substituted the potato for other crops that produced less food value per hectare, like barley, oats, and wheat.

It was partly due to the potato that China's masses became what the comic strip *Doonesbury* once called "friendly but teeming." According to a recent quantification of the potato's impact, it could account for as much as a fourth of the substantial population growth in China and the rest of the Old World between 1700 and 1900.[32] It is off balance that all the talk today about the huge size of China's economy concentrates only on recent leaders like Deng Xiaoping; a lot more credit should go to Mr. Potato Head.

TECHNOLOGY TRANSFER AND CREATIVE DESTRUCTION: THE GREENE STREET BLOCK

The textile boom story on the Greene Street block already featured an important role for technological improvements in transportation. New Yorkers got access to the new technologies by importing products embodying them from Great Britain—such as the railroad and the steamboats—with further refinements by New York innovators.

Other technologies important to the garment boom on Greene Street were also borrowed from Britain and then improved further, such as those for the cast-iron buildings. The British had pioneered cast iron as a strong, cheap, and more fireproof building material in the late eighteenth century. New Yorkers adopted cast iron after about 1850, with further refinements from local pioneers like New York architect James Bogardus (1800–1874).[33]

Another important technology for the new cast-iron buildings on Greene Street was the elevator. Again this was a technology imported from Britain, but its real breakthrough happened because of a New York inventor named Elisha Graves Otis, who made a significant innovation to the original British design. Elevators at the time were subject to fatal plunges if the cables holding them should break. In 1853 Otis invented a safety brake that kicked in if the cable broke.[34] Elevators became a lot more popular once their users no longer had to worry about falling to a horrible death. Embodying the monopolistic return to innovation, the Otis Elevator Company is still today the world's largest manufacturer of elevators.

Once the cheap labor from the immigration boom arrived, the technology of cast-iron buildings with elevators took over Greene Street in the 1880s. The innovators on Greene Street got their reward in the block's textile boom between 1880 and 1910.

But the rewards to Greene Street were bounded by creative destruction. Elevators and other technologies that allowed larger and taller buildings, and new assembly-line technologies in the garment business, meant that the Greene Street buildings were no longer adequate. It was cheaper to build new buildings than retrofit older ones, and so by 1922 garment manufacturing had shifted all the way north to between Twenty-Third and Thirty-Fourth Streets around Seventh Avenue.[35] The new buildings were as tall as twenty-four stories (compared to six stories on Greene Street). Each floor was as large as 30,000 square feet (compared to 4,000 square feet on Greene Street), with the larger floors obviously preferable for assembly-line technology.

Technology gives, and technology takes away. With the loss of the garment business, Greene Street block went into a long industrial decline. Real-estate values on the block by 1920 were a fourth of what they had been during the boom, and they would remain roughly unchanged through 1970.

After 1970, after a near-death experience, the block would enter on a surprising new phase of the creative destruction cycle. We will discuss it in the next chapter.

More on Technological Diffusion

There are two more important facts that govern the spread of technology. It is easier and cheaper to imitate a technology invented elsewhere than it is to invent a technology for the first time. However, it is not so easy and cheap that new technology spreads everywhere instantaneously.

If technology imitation is still somewhat costly, that suggests that the same individualism and incentive forces that form the theory of invention could also make up a theory of imitation. Societies that allow individuals to *sapere aude* (dare to know! question authority!) are going to be more permissive for individuals to adopt foreign technologies that challenge the social status quo. Conformist societies that obey the elders in sticking to the old ways will not be fertile for imitating foreign technology any more than they were for inventing technology.

Incentives will also matter. If the individual gets to keep the rewards for adopting a productive technology from abroad, adoption is more likely to happen. This requires the same kind of respect for individual rights that was necessary both for the invisible hand and for invention.

We have discussed above how innovation is complementary to previous technology. The same is true with imitation: the richer your own technology history, the easier it is to adopt new technologies from abroad.

Catching Up or Falling Behind

Technological imitation explains some patterns in postwar economic growth.[36] Let's divide countries into two groups. Some countries have already adopted most or all of the most advanced technologies in each sector, usually known as the technological frontier. Let's call them the frontier countries. The rest of the world has not adopted most of the advanced technologies. We will just call them the nonfrontier countries. Since technology is a principal determinant of income per capita, these two groups are equivalent to the rich countries and the poor countries.

The countries at the frontier have (mostly) opened themselves to innovations by lowering barriers such as laws that ban new technologies or protect old ones. They have good incentives in general for technology adoption (that is why they are at the frontier). This also implies that a new innovation in one frontier country quickly spreads to the other frontier countries. The frontier keeps gradually moving outward as new technologies are invented like, say, the successive versions of the iPad. Since we identified technological progress as the long-run driver of growth, this suggests that the frontier countries will all grow at roughly the same rate.

Those far from the frontier potentially have much more variable outcomes, based on whether the environment is favorable for imitating frontier technology. At one extreme, some countries continue to suppress individual rights so much that there is little or no incentive for either imitation or innovation. They will have worse growth than the frontier countries.

At the other extreme are countries with a rights regime favorable for technology adoption. They can benefit both from the fact that imitation is cheaper than innovation, and from the large technological leaps toward the frontier that imitation makes possible. Compare the productivity increase from upgrading from one version of an iPad to another to the productivity jump from upgrading from a typewriter to an iPad. Such countries can have very rapid catch-up growth over a long period.

The prediction is simply that poor countries will have much more variable long-run growth than rich countries. Do data confirm this prediction? Let's go back to the exercise of Chapter Ten, in which we used the data on growth for all years and all countries to distinguish between temporary and permanent differences between national growth rates. We found permanent differences were swamped by the temporary differences in growth, but permanent differences between nations did exist.

Now let's divide up countries between rich and poor depending on income per capita at the beginning of the whole period (in either 1960 or 1970). How important are long-run differences between national growth rates in the two groups? The prediction that long-run growth varies more in the poor countries is abundantly confirmed. In fact, in some of the exercises (using the different growth datasets), we find no evidence for any long-run growth differences between rich countries. This matches the prediction that frontier countries tend to grow at the same rate, while nonfrontier countries might have favorable conditions for rapid catch-up growth, or they might not.

What are "favorable conditions" for technological imitation and catch-up? We have described how they are societies that have strong individualism and incentives to adopt technology and a strong technological heritage. The most favorable conditions for rapid growth due to catch-up are to have adequate incentives today for imitation and an advanced technical heritage but a low current income for some other reason. We have already discussed extensively in this book one possible candidate for "some other reason": a history of oppression that suppressed individual rights.

CHANGES IN FREEDOM AND CATCHING UP

A history of lack of freedom in a society means that many technological advances happening elsewhere in the world pass that society by. The positive way to put this is that there will be a lot of pent-up technological catching up that will be unleashed if there is a systemic change from autocratic oppression to recognition of individual rights. Such change is usually gradual (and hard to measure) but there are a few cases that could match the story.

The world's largest imbalance between extensive technological history and low current income in 1950 was China. The systemic changes in China that improved individual incentives after 1978 are a major change toward greater freedom. So China after 1978 had practically ideal conditions for rapid catch-up growth: strong technology history and a positive change in freedom. It is strange that we evaluate rapid Chinese growth (which is the percentage of *change* in technology and income levels) relative to the *level* of freedom today in China. It makes more sense to relate *changes* in income and technology adoption to *changes* in freedom in China.

Since technological history travels with people, the imbalance between this history and initial income in 1950 could also be relevant to places with a Chinese diaspora. Such places include three of the four members of the Gang of Four: Taiwan, Singapore, and Hong Kong. And these places were notable for large increases in, at least, economic freedom. So we now have a story that covers most of the growth superstars.

At the other extreme, low income that matches a feeble technological heritage and past and present poor incentives—unchanged today, with continuing autocracy and oppression—created unfavorable conditions for catching up. Sub-Saharan Africa could appear to fit this story.

So the Blank Slate that labeled both China and Africa as at the same starting place would be off the mark. A possible story for China in the long run is that it just had a bad century and a half: Western semicolonial depredations, internal war and strife between warlords, the Japanese invasion, the Chinese civil war, the brutal crushing of individual incentives by Communism, Mao's Great Famine, and the Cultural Revolution. Such disasters and oppression by foreign and domestic actors drove Chinese income way below its long-run technological potential given by its past history. Once the disasters were over by 1978, and there was a systemic change toward freedom, there was great potential for catch-up.

This section, and this chapter, considers whether the theory of innovation and imitation outlined here matches the big facts about worldwide patterns of growth. The verdict is yes. It is also illustrated by case histories like China (and the Chinese diaspora) and Africa.

One could wish for additional evidence for this theory, such as statistical proof that a specific measure of a "favorable rights regime for imitation" or "increased freedom" *causes* rapid growth. We have seen already in Chapter Ten that research on national-growth differences has been unable to supply robust evidence linking particular measures of national characteristics to growth, even before getting to the issue of which causes which.

But we do not have to declare total ignorance in the absence of rigorous statistical proof. We do not really have the option of believing in nothing. We choose explanations based on the *relative* strength of the evidence for one theory or another. The innovation and imitation theory described in this chapter does well matching many different big facts in the data.

I am still not claiming any decisive evidence that this is the whole story in everyone's favorite case of China. I am offering the story both as a possibility to be weighed next to others and as illustration of how catch-up could work. In Chapter Thirteen we will weigh this evidence against another popular story for both China and for many other cases of rapid growth—that benevolent autocrats get the credit for high growth.

THE KNOWLEDGE PROBLEM IN INNOVATION: THE PRINCIPLE OF SURPRISES

Innovation has the greatest of all knowledge problems. The essential point is as ignored as it is obvious: you cannot plan or predict innovation. If innovation could be predicted in advance, it would not be innovation. If the invention is already known, it does not need to be invented. What this means is that the path of innovation is always a surprise. Who will be the innovator is equally a surprise.

Take Hollywood as an example. Each new movie is an invention, and it is never certain in advance which movie will be a hit with the audience.

As veteran Hollywood screenwriter William Goldman said, *Raiders of the Lost Ark*

> was offered to every single studio in town—and they all turned it down . . . except Paramount. Why did Paramount say yes? Because nobody knows anything. And why did all the other studios say no? Because nobody knows anything. And why did Universal, the mightiest studio of all, pass on *Star Wars*? . . . Because nobody, nobody—not now, not ever—knows the least goddam thing about what is or isn't going to work at the box office.[37]

But there are solutions to this the unknowable knowledge problem. Let's see how. First, the solution will not give a large role to a distinguished panel of experts chaired by Paul Kagame.

Second, the solution is to have many independent individuals trying lots of different things. Hayek has a good statement (already quoted in another context in Chapter Two) about how important it is to have independent individuals because of the unpredictability of innovation: "The growth of reason is based on existence of differences . . . [between] individuals, possessing different knowledge and different views. Its results cannot be predicted. . . . We cannot know which views will assist this growth and which will not."

Let me also repeat a quote from Hayek given earlier in the book: "It is because every individual knows so little and . . . because we rarely know which of us knows best that we trust the independent and competitive efforts of many to induce the emergence of what we shall want when we see it."

Hayek's solution is the "independent efforts of many," where the many "possess different knowledge and different views." Innovation and individualism go together, innovation and conformism do not. You do actually need us annoying dissidents insulting your conformist views.

Third, that word *competitive* summons us back to the Invisible Hand of the previous chapter. Many different innovators compete for the affections of the audience. The market tests which innovations are hits and which are duds. In other words, we consumers choose which new products we want and which we do not. Hayek was right that we consumers often do not know ourselves what we will want in advance, but we shall want it when we see it. We might have thought that we wanted Halle Berry in *Catwoman* in 2004 (later named worst movie of the year), but what we really wanted was Anne Hathaway playing Catwoman in *The Dark Knight Rises* in 2012 (box office champion of the year).

THE SURPRISING AUTOMOBILE

You might have thought the automobile was a can't-miss invention if there ever was one. But it took a while to catch on after it was invented. In 1769 a Frenchman invented the first steam-engine-driven carriage to run on the roads.[38]

But the steam carriage did not survive the competitive efforts of the railroad builders. The problem was that steam engines were too large relative to the power they delivered for an individual vehicle. Transport by steam vehicles cost ten times what horse travel did. The vehicles made a racket, doused the passengers with fumes, and were prone to explode. So steam taxis and steam omnibuses failed the market test.

It would take many generations of innovation before the automobile became feasible, none of which could have been foreseen in advance. The inventors have names still recognizable today. The steam engine would be replaced by the internal-combustion engine, which then had to be made smaller in volume and weight (finally achieved by Daimler and Maybach in 1885). The fuel would be gasoline instead of coal. By 1894, Benz produced the first successful car, selling 1,200 units, mainly to Frenchmen. Another early success was a Daimler racing car with the world's first honeycomb radiator. The car's marketing director named it after his eldest daughter, Mercedes, and the manufacturer later merged with Benz. By 1901, Peugeot (originally a bicycle company) had taken over. Louis Renault took another step forward with the invention of the drive shaft, and the Michelin brothers developed pneumatic tires.

The most famous innovation in manufacturing occurred in December 1913 in Detroit, Michigan: Henry Ford's assembly line for the Model T. Ford was already producing the Model T before the assembly line, but the line's efficiency allowed him to cut the car's price from $825 to $345 (only $8,000 in today's dollars). The global auto market would be dominated by Americans for quite a while. The United States produced 73 percent of the world's cars in 1933, while the former market leaders of Germany and France produced 4 percent and 8 percent, respectively. Japan in 1933 produced 191 cars, compared to 1.6 million in the United States.

The end of US dominance after World War II emerged at first from a surprising source. Adolf Hitler had commissioned a "people's car" ("Volkswagen") from Ferdinand Porsche, but little was produced of Porsche's design before the war. After the war, no Germans were in a great position to make Volkswagens. They offered the design to Britain and to the United States, but there were no takers. The British auto industry association reported the model "does not meet the fundamental technical requirements of a motorcar" and it "is quite unattractive to the average motorcar buyer. It is too ugly and too noisy." By the end of 1959, the Germans had sold 400,000 VW Beetles in the United States.[39]

Hitler's surprising role in the Volkswagen may open some role for planned government innovation. As with the previous chapter, let's have a truce on whether industrial policy could sometimes work in innovation. Even if it did, the rest of such an industrial policy success would depend on the spontaneous forces that develop the innovation further, in interaction with the spontaneous forces of markets.

Another surprising source of competition for the United States was Toyota. The first Toyota attempt at exporting a car to the United States, the Toyopet in 1957, did not turn out well, even after the launch by the reigning Miss Japan, Kyoko Otani. The traffic authorities in Los Angeles declared the Toyopet not roadworthy: the rearview mirrors were too small, the headlights too weak, and the turn signals did not signal.[40] And the Toyopet cost 40 percent more than a VW Beetle. US sales of the Toyopet were not strong. A better-performing innovation was the Toyota Corolla in 1968, which by 1970 was already selling 200,000 units in the United States.

The oil-price shocks in the 1970s shifted the global demand toward small cars. The Toyota Corolla was the perfect oil-shock car, with close to the highest fuel efficiency in the world. Toyota and other small-car Japanese automakers took off. By 1980, Japan was the world's leading car exporter.

The same names from automobile history are still around today among the top world automakers—Daimler, Mercedes, Benz, Peugeot, Renault, Ford, Porsche, Volkswagen, and Toyota—showing how long the private return from innovation for the monopolistic competitors really does last.

The automobile history also shows again the importance of long-run technology history in technological catch-up. Whether your ancestors had advanced transport technology in AD 1500 is an excellent predictor of your automobile production today. The rise of Japan and then South Korea as auto exporters has idiosyncratic explanations but also reflects East Asia's ability to regain the technological prowess it had achieved before modern times. The newest example of that East Asia story is the world's newest occupant of the number-one position in number of units of motor vehicles produced by country: China.

THE CUSTOMERS INSIST ON THEIR OWN EXPERTISE

The Broadband Commission for Digital Development was of course right that new communications technologies are exciting. They offer the large potential gains from leaping to the frontier, as discussed above. Yet the technology is evolving based on what the customers—not expert commissions—want. Mobile phones are already doing much of the work for which the commission thought they needed broadband.

The number of mobile-phone subscribers in Africa has quintupled in the last seven years, to reach nearly 500 million.[41] They have been applied to unexpected uses. Just as cell phones themselves bypassed dysfunctional land lines in Africa, Africans are using their cell phones to bypass inefficient state-regulated traditional banks. The firm MPESA in Kenya originally intended to be a microcredit organization but found that its customers wanted to use the technology they devised for repaying microcredits for something else. MPESA had stumbled by chance into a huge market for financial transfers by cell phone. Three years after its founding in March 2007, MPESA was reaching 40 percent of Kenya's adult population.[42] MPESA now processes more transfers within Kenya than Western Union does internationally.[43]

Outsiders tend to overlook another less sexy but still transformative technology in Africa: motor vehicles. Cell phones and cards for minutes of talk time are sold through millions of tiny kiosks. Where are most of those kiosks located? On the roads. How were most of the physical mobile phones and cards delivered to the kiosks? By motor vehicles.

And it is not only mobile phones. Motor vehicles delivered the oral rehydration kits and vaccines that saved millions of African babies. Motor vehicles transport the teachers and textbooks responsible for the big advances in education. Motor vehicles allow marginal farmlands to be abandoned, transporting their ex-farmers into cities where they are more productive, while transporting food back to the rural neighbors and families they left behind. Motor vehicles make commodities located in the interior into valuable exports.

The 1950 average for sub-Saharan Africa (outside of the white-settler areas of Rhodesia and South Africa) was less than one car for every 1,000 population. By 1980, it was seven cars for every 1,000, and today it is about nineteen cars for every 1,000 population.

Africa is part of a worldwide trend of the spread of automobiles in which the number of cars corresponding to a given level of per capita income keeps shifting up, decade by decade. Or in other words, poorer countries today have access to the same level of car penetration that much richer countries had in earlier decades. South Korea in 1980 had about the same number of cars per capita that Germany had in 1950, while Mali reached this same level by 2010.[44]

And yet there is still so far to go (or to put it positively, so much catch-up potential!) South Korea has a car ownership rate (cars per 1,000 population) thirty-two times higher than Mali; Germany's rate is sixty-three times higher than Mali.

We can predict that Africa's future transport technology is impossible to predict. When the surprises of the static Invisible Hand are combined with the surprises of technology, there are always more surprises.

Paul Kagame's own Rwanda produced a surprise in the last few years due to technology. As a coffee fanatic, I noticed a few years ago that Rwandan coffee suddenly showed up in the favored shops of the Manhattan espresso cult. On further investigation, it turned out that Rwandan coffee growers had learned how to move into the high end of the world coffee market by innovations as simple as washing the beans by hand.

The export was only possible because of motor vehicles that could haul the coffee from locations all over Rwanda to the nearest export port. But finding an export port was itself another problem. Landlocked Rwanda is surrounded by countries with bad roads and dysfunctional ports. So shipping the coffee by motor vehicle to the nearest oceanic port was not the best path to profits. The Rwandan coffee innovators chose to use another engine-powered vehicle that bypassed surrounding countries: an airplane. Air-freight companies charge more per ton than ocean freight. This helps explain why Rwandan coffee exporters chose to shift to the high end of the coffee-quality ladder. High-end coffee has a high value-to-weight ratio (Rwandan coffee goes for as much as $24 per pound), meaning that costly air shipping does not destroy profits. The flexibility of specialization sometimes allows occasional compensation for some areas that are still technologically backward. Other export successes by air freight in Africa are cut flowers (and of course coffee) from Kenya and Ethiopia, and fresh fish shipped frozen from Uganda and Tanzania.[45]

CONCLUSION

Technology is another spontaneous order, like markets, and these two spontaneous orders interact with each other. You choose to solve others' problems in exchange for having them solve yours. Others exchange the discovery of new solutions with those who meet their needs in the meantime with the old solutions. We as individuals solve the complex knowledge problem of millions of product specializations, using our decentralized knowledge. As many independent innovators, we even solve the worst knowledge problem of them all: the knowledge of what does not yet exist. We are a long way from the development model of solving problems with technocratic goals and expert commissions. We are a long way from conscious design and a lot closer to spontaneous solutions.

Yet there is still one big intellectual temptation left to believe in conscious design: the idea that benevolent autocrats deserve the credit for some of development's biggest successes. How much credit, for example, belongs to Paul Kagame for Rwanda's high-end coffee success that has transpired on his watch? We consider that in the next chapter.

CHAPTER THIRTEEN

LEADERS: HOW WE ARE SEDUCED BY BENEVOLENT AUTOCRATS

World Bank president Dr. Jim Yong Kim paid a three-day visit to the People's Republic of China in November 2012. He presumably knew that the Chinese government was a dictatorship, but he apparently thought it was a benevolent one. According to Dr. Kim, China's leaders had already met "the challenge of actually delivering on truly aspirational goals." The Chinese government had been "explicit in writing them down and looking at itself in terms of what more it needs to do, and also looking at its great accomplishments."[1] He announced in China a new World Bank initiative to spread "practical knowledge from China's successes in reducing poverty" to other World Bank members.[2]

The World Bank's report on China's future "China 2030: Building a Modern, Harmonious, and Creative Society" was a joint effort of Bank experts and staff appointed by Chinese leaders. Kim made frequent references to the report during his tour. The report encapsulates the view that great development outcomes are the result of great leaders willing those outcomes: "A successful outcome will require strong leadership and commitment, steady implementation with a determined will." The closing sentence of the report says that outcomes depend "on the wisdom, strength, and determination of the Chinese leadership."[3] The World Bank still seems to prefer the same authoritarian development approach to 2013 China that Western actors held for 1930s China (Chapter Three).

Autocratic Miracles

There is a strong tradition of folklore about benevolent autocrats who deliver development to their people. And indeed the list of autocrats who seem to have worked miracles goes on and on: Deng Xiaoping in China, Lee Kuan Yew in Singapore, Park Chung Hee in South Korea, Chiang Kai-shek in Taiwan, Augusto Pinochet in Chile, Suharto in Indonesia, and Mahathir Mohamad in Malaysia. The evidence that autocrats cause rapid growth seems overwhelming. We now must confront the evidence that there really are benevolent autocrats. Such evidence would favor conscious direction over spontaneous solutions. It could be evidence that the Tyranny of Experts actually does deliver development.

But evidence is not always what it seems. In fact, this chapter offers some strong reasons to believe that these growth episodes happened in spite of autocrats, not because of them.

The idea of benevolent autocrats is nonetheless hard to kill, evidence or no evidence, because of a combination of psychological biases that all of us (including this author) have. It takes some hard work first to understand the evidence properly, and second to try to disable psychological biases. But the payoff is a new respect for the democratic rights of remote and voiceless poor people.

Evidence or Consequences

There are two variants of the benevolent-autocrat idea. The first and stronger variant is simply that autocrats are better than democrats for development (by *development* in this context we usually mean "rapid economic growth"). The second, weaker variant is that the best autocratic leaders are better for growth than the best democratic leaders, while conceding that the worst autocrats are worse for growth than the worst democrats.

Even with the stellar autocratic success list, it does not take long to dispose of the first variant, that autocrats are good for growth. You only have to know one additional thing: autocrats also presided over most of the world's recent growth disasters. The list of the disasters is again long: Robert Mugabe in Zimbabwe, Kim Il-sung and offspring in North Korea,

Mohammar Qaddafi in Libya, Daniel Ortega (the first time around) in Nicaragua, Joseph Mobutu in Zaire, Ferdinand Marcos in the Philippines, Kenneth Kaunda in Zambia, Jean-Bedel Bokassa in the Central African Republic, Julius Nyerere in Tanzania, the military junta in Burma, and many other lesser-known despots.

So the success of *some* autocrats does *not* imply that autocracy delivers rapid growth *on average*. For every Lee Kuan Yew, there is a Robert Mugabe. In the postwar period, the average growth is the same or lower under autocrats compared to democrats. In the longer run, including the historical growth of today's now rich democracies, as we saw in Chapters Six, Seven, and Eight, the growth advantage is with democrats.

We have lost any presumption that autocrats are benevolent in general, but it is still very possible that some autocrats are benevolent. Since autocratic leaders are a lot less constrained than democratic ones, it is plausible that a benevolent autocrat (Lee Kuan Yew) could do more good for growth than a democrat, while a malevolent autocrat (Robert Mugabe) could do a lot more damage to growth. This is a plausible theory that this chapter will take seriously. We will test it most directly against the evidence at the end of the chapter. Before we get there, we have to deal with some issues on how we interpret evidence.

DANGEROUS PROBABILITIES

Unfortunately, before we can get to testing the weaker variant that *some* autocrats are benevolent, we have to deal with some psychological biases in favor of the stronger variant that *most or all* autocrats are benevolent and produce high growth.

Psychologists have documented systematic biases in the way we think about evidence. The leading psychologist on these topics is the Nobel laureate Daniel Kahneman, whose book *Thinking, Fast and Slow* is essential reading. Kahneman discusses how "thinking fast"—acting on gut reactions—can be an amazing problem-solver for most real-life situations, when there is not enough time for formal deductive reasoning ("thinking slow"). However, one area where thinking fast does badly is probability and statistics—in other words, in interpreting evidence.[4] Thinking fast, then, has systematic biases, and most of these biases reinforce strong beliefs in benevolent autocrats.

One major bias involves mixing up probabilities that sound similar but in fact are wildly different. Here is an illustration from a very different area. After almost every tragic mass shooting that happens somewhere in the United States, the shooter is diagnosed as mentally ill, and this brings with it a wave of misguided thinking.

For example, we think that the person already treating this mentally ill person should have seen it coming. Going even further, one recent proposal after the horrific Newtown, Connecticut, school shooting suggests that the mental-health records of individuals be automatically turned over to law-enforcement agencies.

Of course, a diagnosis of mental illness is almost useless to predict who will do a mass shooting. We are prone to confuse two probabilities that sound similar: the probability that a mass shooter will be mentally ill, and the probability that a mentally ill person will be a mass shooter. The first probability may be high. The second probability is miniscule: a few new mass shooters appear every year out of a population of the mentally ill that numbers in the millions.

We have gone through this uncomfortable example because of a similar mistake we make with autocrats and growth. We are similarly prone to confuse two statements: most high growth happens under autocrats, and most autocrats have high growth. The first may be true (for reasons we will explore, such as most high growth happening in poor countries, who also happen to mostly have autocrats), but the second is certainly false, as we have already seen above. It is the second (false) statement that is relevant in considering whether we should be willing to sacrifice political freedom (of ourselves or others) to an autocrat in return for high growth.

The mistake of confusing two opposite probabilities only matters when they are very different. Two types of circumstances tend to make them very different:

1. when the outcome being considering ("high growth," "mass shootings") is rare, and/or

2. when extreme positive outcomes are offset by extreme negative
   outcomes

Either one of these is enough by itself to make the two probabilities
very different and so make the mistake of confusing them very costly.

Only circumstance 1 holds in the cases of mass shootings, which was
enough by itself to cause misguided recriminations. We do not sufficiently
appreciate how rare mass shootings are, to be open to the possibility that
such incidents would also be extremely rare among mentally ill people.

Growth miracles are not quite as rare as mass shootings. But the way
we celebrate growth miracles still makes them rare: our attention to them
increases the greater the growth miracle, but, the greater the growth miracle, the more unlikely it is. The ones most universally celebrated are the
Gang of Four—Singapore, Hong Kong, South Korea, Taiwan—and more
recently, China. These are only five countries out of approximately two
hundred countries. Moreover, even for these five countries, they only had
growth miracles for some periods and not for others.

The cutoff that seems to attract "miracle" designation is growth of income per capita of about 6 percent per year, as we discussed for nations
in Chapter Ten. China did not have miracle status before 1980. For the
Gang of Four, the miracle is already over today by this definition, after
lasting for four decades (1960–2000) in which income increased around
ten-fold.

To sum up, it is because growth miracles are rare that the true statement "most growth miracles are autocrats" is so very different from the
false statement "most autocrats are growth miracles." Our confusion on
this point is so strong that I will pound away at it just a bit more. This
same psychological mistake contributes to stereotyping of certain unpopular minority groups, as in the case of the "violent mentally ill." It could
be true that "most terrorists are Muslim," but it is definitely not true that
"most Muslims are terrorists." Prison statistics could indicate that "most
violent felons are black," but it is definitely not true that "most blacks are
violent felons." Racism has many toxic causes, but one of them is just the
racists' incompetence at probability. The same incompetence makes us
believe autocrats produce high growth.

Circumstance 2 contributes to this probability mistake when extreme positive outcomes are offset by extreme negative outcomes. As we have seen, autocrats are associated with both growth miracles and growth disasters. Some economists like Dani Rodrik at the Institute for Advanced Study interpret the autocrats and growth evidence as showing that autocracy is like a very risky bet: you can win big with Lee Kuan Yew, or you could lose it all with Mobutu.[5]

Unfortunately, we have just seen that our psychological biases confuse statements like "most growth miracles occur under autocrats" with "most autocrats produce growth miracles." This means that we also confuse the strong and weak variants of the benevolent-autocrat hypothesis. We interpret evidence for the weak variant—that *some* autocrats can produce miracles—as evidence for the strong variant—*most or all* autocrats produce growth miracles. The abundant evidence against the strong variant goes to waste when our psychological biases take over.

It makes our biases even worse when we hear a lot more about successes than failures. Research indicates that the *New York Times* was four times more likely to mention successful autocratic countries than failed ones over 1960 to 2008.[6] The same results hold for lots of other publications. I am not alleging a conspiracy. The media just report what their readers want to read about, which is apparently a lot more about success than about failure. Apparently, we want to hear a lot more about Lee Kuan Yew than about André Kolingba, who was the unsuccessful dictator of the Central African Republic from 1981 to 1993.

The Parable of Sam and Joe

The list of psychological biases toward autocrats keeps growing longer. We are too prone to believe in benevolent autocrats because we are too prone to use only the most recent data. This is a variant of the Blank Slate belief that the long run of history is not relevant. But here it is triggered by psychological biases, not by development thinkers.

Let me tell you about two individuals, Sam and Joe. Sam's initial choices made him almost five times richer than Joe. Then for most of their lives, Joe's income stayed at the level of dire poverty while Sam's kept growing steadily. By the time they reached middle age, Sam had become twenty times richer than Joe. From that low point, things finally turned around big time for Joe and he started catching up to Sam. The last four years in particular saw Sam's income stagnate and Joe's keep rising. But today Sam is still 5 times richer than Joe, just like in the beginning.

Whom would you prefer to be, Sam or Joe? If Sam followed one career approach and Joe followed another, would you rather imitate Sam or Joe? I think most of us would prefer to imitate Sam.

Please file away that example for future use and let's go back to development. In the last three decades, China has had a remarkable rate of growth while US growth was mediocre. The financial crisis of 2008 devastated the United States but left China untouched.

Notable development economists Nancy Birdsall and Francis Fukuyama in 2011 noted the effect of the 2008 crisis on ideas favoring autocracy (they make clear they are summarizing others' views, not their own view): "Leaders in both the developing and the developed world have marveled at China's remarkable ability to bounce back after the crisis, a result of a tightly managed, top-down policymaking machine that could avoid the delays of a messy democratic process. In response, political leaders in the developing world now associate efficiency and capability with autocratic political systems."[7]

The *New York Times* columnist Thomas Friedman was similarly enthusiastic: "One-party autocracy certainly has its drawbacks. But when it is led by a reasonably enlightened group of people, as China is today, it can also have great advantages. That one party can just impose the politically difficult but critically important policies needed to move a society forward in the 21st century."[8]

It is probably not a surprise to learn that Sam is the United States and Joe is China from the standpoint of long-run history. Why does the parable version cause us to favor Uncle Sam, while the real-life version causes us to favor Uncle Zhao? This example combines two common errors in processing evidence. First, we use too little data. Second, we draw mistaken conclusions about the future based on these data.

With regard to data, in the China–US comparison, we discount, ignore, or erase the historical record and look only at recent experience: the growth rate in the last three decades, or even the growth rate in the last four years. We ignore the long history of superior US performance compared to China. Again, it is yet another example of the belief in the Blank Slate, which discards history.

And it is surprising how often development discussions are based on so little data, as this book already has complained regarding Bill Gates's discussion of child-mortality reductions in Ethiopia. Ethiopia shows up again here as a recent alleged authoritarian growth miracle, which aid agencies proclaimed after only seven years of high growth. British aid celebrated that "Ethiopia has experienced impressive growth and development in recent years,"[9] while the US Agency for International Development (USAID) also affirmed "tremendous progress."[10] Even though the USAID discussion makes clear that part of the growth was simply better weather compared to a calamitous drought seven years ago, the United States is now sure that "Ethiopia" (meaning its autocratic government) is transforming "its economy and society toward middle income status."[11] World Bank President Jim Kim joined the chorus celebrating Ethiopia's "transformational change," which he attributed to a "stable" government that pursues "prudent economic policies," and takes "a long-term perspective."[12]

THE MYTH OF THE "HOT HAND"

After using too little data to christen a particular leader's "growth miracle," the second psychological mistake is to take temporary success as a long-run trend. We project that today's (temporarily) high growth will continue to be miraculous forever. We give autocrats credit for a future that has not even happened yet and that will likely never happen.

The key insight on this subject came from a paper about basketball.[13] One author of this study was Kahneman's longstanding coauthor of many key insights, psychologist Amos Tversky, who died in 1996. In basketball, a player has a "hot hand" when he or she has made a string of baskets in a row. The obvious recommendation to that player's teammates would seem to be to pass the ball to the player with the hot hand the next time they go down the court. But Tversky compiled actual data on shots, made baskets, and missed baskets and found this recommendation was wrong—the "hot hand" player is no more likely to make the next basket than any other player. How could this be?

Tversky subtitled his paper "on the misperception of random sequences." Making baskets is a combination of skill and luck. Even the best players make baskets only about half the time. So for a skilled player, a shot is like flipping a coin, where your skill has gotten you to an even chance of heads. Just as with flipping a coin, if you keep flipping long enough you will get a string of heads in a row. But the probability of a head on the next coin flip is still fifty-fifty.

So it was with the "hot hand" of the skilled basketball player who sinks half his shots. He will periodically have a string of made baskets, but the probability of making the next shot remains at 50 percent. So while his rate of making baskets temporarily reached 100 percent while he had a "hot hand," we should expect him to regress to his average rate of making baskets 50 percent of the time. This is called "regression to the mean" (*mean* in the sense of "average").

Similarly, a string of very high growth rates requires skill by many participants in the economy—let's call it "good fundamentals." But to attain the very highest growth rates may also require a dose of good luck, such as high prices for your exports and/or drops in the prices of materials you import for production, not to mention long stretches of fortuitous weather. We have even seen in Chapter Ten's discussion of national growth rates how important measurement error is in explaining growth volatility. Some lucky "benevolent autocrats" will get growth measured as higher than it turns out later really to have been. In the future, though the same national skills will still be there, the good luck (or the measurement error) will not continue indefinitely. Your high growth would then regress to your average performance based on the fundamentals.

Economists have abundantly confirmed regression to the mean in economic-growth rates. We have already discussed this evidence in Chapter Ten, showing why national differences in growth rates are usually temporary. The same is true with differences in growth rates between leaders. A streak of high growth will make us think a leader has a "hot hand," but these streaks are usually temporary. But we seem to have psychological blinders on when it comes to regression to the mean. We are prone to ignore it and we expect good performance to continue unchanged. We continue to believe in the "hot hand" in both basketball and growth.

What this means in practice is that we incorrectly expect a string of high growth rates under a given autocrat to continue. We also attribute the high growth rates to the skill of this benevolent autocrat. So we are giving him credit twice for the same string of high growth rates: now and in the incorrectly predicted future. The bottom line is that the argument for benevolent autocrats is a long way from proven by just observing *some* high growth rates while *some* autocrats are in power. We will now see two alternative explanations.

IS THERE MORE TO GROWTH THAN AUTOCRATS?

It is time to add two more facts to the discussion, both of which come from previous chapters:

1. Poor countries are more likely than rich countries to be led by autocrats.
2. The dispersion of growth rates is much greater in poor countries than in rich countries.

We have already discussed fact 1 in Part Three on the Blank Slate versus long-run history as possible evidence that autocracy causes poverty and freedom causes prosperity. Chapter Ten already reported fact 2. In poor countries, there are both growth miracles and growth disasters, and everything in between. Rich countries (notwithstanding recent difficulties) are paragons of long-run stability by comparison. Long-run growth in rich countries fluctuates around a narrow range about 2 percent per person per year, and it has been that way for decades.

Chapter Ten also gave already a plausible explanation of fact 2. Technologically backward countries (also known as poor countries) have the potential for rapid growth due to the "catch-up" advantage that they can cheaply imitate technologies already invented in rich countries, and do not have to go through the longer and more costly process of invention. However, if technologically backward countries fail to imitate and start adopting the advanced technology, they will fall even further behind the rich countries. We noted that both incentives and a long history of technological experience often make the difference between the success or failure of catch-up growth.

With fact 2 giving us greater dispersion of growth rates in poor countries than in rich countries, the highest growth rates in poor countries will be greater than the highest growth in rich countries. Fact 1 says that some autocrats will be on the scene in poor countries while this "highest growth" is happening. However, if the catch-up story is the correct explanation for fact 2, autocrats have little to do with the fast growth happening under fact 2, it was really just about the speed of technological imitation.

LEVELS PRODUCE LEVELS, CHANGES PRODUCE CHANGES

Let's continue the quixotic quest to have logic and evidence rule. There is still another alternative explanation of success under autocrats. Fact 1 tells us that lack of freedom is more common in poor countries. This fact is about the level of political freedom, but we can throw in economic freedom for good measure. All of the previous discussion in this book about freedom was about the level of freedom—that a society of free individuals is more likely to solve political, economic, and technological problems and produce a higher level of development (as crudely measured by, say, per capita income).

Stories about growth miracles and freedom often miss the point about levels versus changes that we discussed in the previous chapter. There we discussed how an increase in freedom could unleash technological catching-up, which the previous low level of freedom had pent up. There is a more general principle. If the level of freedom did explain the level of development, then we would expect the change in freedom to explain the change in development.

Economic growth is about a percentage change in development, not about the level of development. So a leading candidate to explain growth would be the change in freedom. It makes sense to explain the change in development with a change in freedom. Why should the discussion be on whether the *level* of freedom explains the *change* in development?

So another possible explanation for growth miracles is a positive *change* in freedom. To take everyone's favorite example, China has actually had a strong positive change in both political and economic freedom since the death of Mao and the loss of power by his cronies. Mao and cronies created recurrent terror, the Great Famine, and the Cultural Revolution, which destroyed incentives for individuals to invest in their futures. Chinese citizens today enjoy stronger rights than they did in those dark days, most obviously in the rights to avail themselves of the Invisible Hand. Even political and personal rights, while well short of attaining a good level of freedom, do qualify for a positive change in freedom. Yet another contender for explaining the Chinese growth miracle is simply that the economy had a large positive response to a large positive change in freedom.

In short, the benevolent-autocrat story—for both China and other autocratic growth miracles—suffers from a surplus of too many other explanations for the same facts.

AUTOCRATS AND CHANGES IN ECONOMIC FREEDOM

The China example illustrates an odd asymmetry between giving autocrats credit for increases in economic freedom, as opposed to increases in political freedom. Both represent a reduction in the power of the state and increased rights for individuals. In both cases, autocrats are surrendering some of their own power.

When autocrats make moves toward increased political freedom, we often see this as happening under pressure from protest movements (as indeed it often is). Yet when autocrats increase economic freedom, we see this almost exclusively as reflecting deliberately chosen policies by a wise autocrat promoting market-led development. This interpretation could be correct, but we do not even consider the possibility that increases in economic freedom can be granted unwillingly by autocrats under pressure from resistance movements.

Individuals can also protest the absence of economic freedoms just as they do the absence of political freedoms, even though the forms of protest are different. The resistance to state control over individuals' economic choices happens naturally in a decentralized way.

Suppose, for example, that there is a price control over a crop that farmers sell that redistributes the profit from the sale from the farmer to the state. The state buys the crop at the (low) official price and exports it at the (high) world market price. Let's use again our story about how Ghana's autocrats since Nkrumah controlled the price of cocoa for Ashanti growers. Facing low producer prices, farmers are not motivated to plant as much of the crop. Farmers can also make some crop sales away from the eyes of the state officials who enforce the price controls, switching their sales to the black market. Eventually there will be little crop production left to control and the autocrat is forced to abandon the attempt at control. This is a plausible story for cocoa in Ghana. By 1983, cocoa growers had so drastically reduced their plantings, and they were smuggling so much of what was left across the border to Côte d'Ivoire, that the state got almost nothing from its attempt to buy at the controlled price and resell at the market price. Ghana's dictator at the time, Jerry Rawlings, finally gave up and allowed producer prices for cocoa to rise toward the world market price. Since the 1980s, cocoa production in Ghana recovered and Ghana once again became one of the world's leading cocoa producers.[14] Ghana's resurgent cocoa boom owed less to Rawlings's "benevolent" leadership than to the decentralized responses of the cocoa producers in the face of government-imposed restrictions.

China's famous switch from collective farming to family farms after 1978 may also have as much to do with farmer resistance as with the deliberate choices of the Chinese leader at the time, Deng Xiaoping. Farmers had been trying for years to evade their obligations to produce for the collective farm (where they got little private payoff) and to increase their production on their own family plots. Brutal force under Mao at the height of the Cultural Revolution in 1966 to 1967 had enforced collective farming, but the cost was anemic crop production. In Mao's last years (1968–1976), the state gave farmers more machinery, fertilizer, pesticides, and improved seeds, but collective farm incentives were so weak that agricultural output barely kept up with population growth.

With less-ruthless power at the center after the death of Mao in 1976, farmers finally found an opening. They could bribe the local party cadres to overlook switching some of their time from collective farms to their family plots. One farmer couple in a poor village in Heilongjiang Province wrote to their local party cadre: "no one wants us because we are so poor. We have an idea to get rid of poverty—which is to divide the land and allocate it to the household. We will pay 4.5 yuan per mu to the [collective] team, if the team leaves us alone."[15]

These deals happened most where farmers were under severe pressure from drought and famine, such as in Anhui and Sichuan Provinces in the late 1970s. Cadres either sympathized with the farmers' plight or were simply happy to increase their own incomes from farmers' bribes. As family farming paid off for both farmers and local cadres, it spread in a decentralized, chaotic way. It was not until 1982 that a central-party document recognized the reality on the ground and acknowledged family farming "as one of the responsibility systems of the socialist collective economy."[16]

The moral of this section is that autocrats get too much credit for episodes of increased economic freedom. While there surely are cases in which autocrats intentionally liberalize policies to increase economic freedom, there is no reason to *assume* this is the norm without more detailed examination. There are two alternative plausible stories: particular state leaders choose on their own to reduce the economic controls imposed by the state, or resistance from below triggers the reduced economic controls of the state. We have just seen as examples of the latter how the state's repression of individuals making their own economic choices generates a natural decentralized resistance to the state, with consequent bottom-up changes in the state's economic policies.

We keep seeing a tension between, on the one hand, explanations of some positive outcomes that feature benevolent autocrats who make deliberate choices, versus, on the other hand, alternative explanations that do not involve intentional leader choices. We will do a more specific test of benevolent autocrats below. But let's first review some more of the psychological biases that also determine which explanations we prefer.

THE WISH FOR HEROES

This chapter is starting to look like one of those action movies in which the hero slays one monster only to find it replaced by a more formidable one, over and over. An even more potent bias in favor of stories of benevolent autocrats is called the "fundamental attribution error."

Demonstrated in many experiments, this error refers to the tendency of people to attribute an outcome too much to individual personality, intentions, and skill and not enough to external factors. The typical experiment takes some volunteers (known as test subjects) and shows them a situation and asks them to interpret it. An experimenter in the 1960s assigned individuals to write letters about Fidel Castro. The experimenter would instruct each individual to either criticize or praise him according to the experimenter's randomly chosen assignment, regardless of each individual's true feelings about Castro. The assignment to write a pro-Castro letter was random. Furthermore, the experimenter *told* the test subjects that the assignments were randomly assigned. Then the test subjects read the pro-Castro and anti-Castro letters. Finally the experimenter asked the test subjects to interpret the letters.

The result? Even though the test subjects knew the writing assignments for and against Castro had been randomly assigned, they believed that the writers of the pro-Castro letters personally held favorable opinions of Castro. The test subjects ignored the circumstances—that assignments were not handed out according to personal beliefs—and instead went with their gut feelings that if someone wrote a pro-Castro letter, it must be because that person harbored pro-Castro sentiments.

That we attribute even random outcomes to intentions or skill is a striking feature of many experiments. Another early experiment showed actors performing a task in view of test subjects. The test subjects were told that payments would be given randomly to the actors, unrelated to performance, and the experimenter designed it so that the real performance was indeed the same amongst all actors. Test subjects gave a higher performance rating to those actors receiving payments. The test subjects instinctively attribute the higher payments to skill and yet again ignored their knowledge of the circumstances—that the payments were random.

Let's apply this knowledge to the benevolent-autocrat situation. Even in the extreme situation that the autocrat had nothing to do with the high economic growth that happened during his reign, it suggests that we would still be disposed to favor stories that attribute the high growth to his personal skill. We believe that since high growth happened during his rule, he must have intended for it to happen.

Another form of the attribution bias is even more relevant to biasing us toward benevolent-autocrat stories. We attribute too much of a group outcome to the skill and intentions of the leader rather than to characteristics of the whole group. A 2001 experiment demonstrated this by showing test subjects two groups who were trying to solve a task. One of each group was randomly designated the "leader." The experiment was designed so that it was the circumstances of the group rather than leader skill or intentions that determined which group did better (since the "leader" was not even the leader!) Specifically, one of the groups was larger than the other, and this was the true cause of the differential success of the two groups at solving the task. However, the test subjects attributed the better outcome in the larger group to leadership "effectiveness."[17]

So there is a conflict between, on one side, two explanations for growth that do not depend on autocratic leadership as a major factor—that is, relying on technological catch-up for rapid growth, and/or experiencing an increase in political and economic freedom that spurred investment and innovation—and on the other side, our psychological preference for personality-based explanations.

Probably the single leader most likely to be anointed a "benevolent autocrat" is Lee Kuan Yew, the long-serving dictator in Singapore, which was one of the world's fastest growing countries over the last half-century. Did Singapore benefit from Chinese culture's long familiarity with technology to be able to catch up fast to the technological frontier in rich countries? Did Singapore's merchants demand more economic freedom in a trading port, or else they would move to other trading ports? Or did Lee Kuan Yew guide Singapore to greatness with skill and dedication?

It's no contest: personality-based stories usually win. Henry Kissinger wrote a preface to a laudatory book by Western authors about Lee Kuan Yew. The book includes tributes to Lee from just about every political leader in the Western world except the prime minister of Malta. Kissinger wrote: "As to the ancient argument—whether individuals shape events or are their register—there can be no doubt about the answer with regard to Lee Kuan Yew, a man of unmatched intelligence and judgment. . . . The Singapore of today is his testament."[18]

THE LAST TEST ON BENEVOLENT AUTOCRATS

Let's brave all the psychological biases and go back to the evidence. We saw first in this chapter that every high-growth autocrat is offset by a low-growth autocrat. Even if autocrats got the credit for this growth, autocracy would be a gamble, striving for a miracle but risking disaster. Then we saw some alternative explanations for high growth that do not even give the credit to the leaders: technological catch-up and high positive changes in freedom. We did not yet test whether the evidence favored the alternative stories over the "good autocrat, bad autocrat" story. We are now in a position to test the latter. We have to cover some tedious details to do this test, but it seems worth the effort after so much hoopla about benevolent autocrats.

There is one test that considers directly whether some autocratic leaders are extra good for growth and others extra bad. The test is simple: let's look at the timing of growth booms and busts to see if they coincide with times when different autocrats were in power. If most of the big changes in growth happen when the autocrats change, that is evidence for big effects of particular, individual autocrats on growth (either positive or negative). If most of the big changes in growth happen when there has been no change in leadership, however, this suggests that individual autocrats do not matter so much as other conditions for growth.

What do the data say?[19] We first have to confront a problem that has surfaced before: different sources do not agree when growth is high. We have four different datasets on growth: the World Bank World Development Indicators (WDI); the Penn World Tables (PWT, version 7.1 and an earlier version 6.1); and different growth estimates from economic historian Angus Maddison. We are considering the period 1950–2000 except for the WDI which covers 1960–2000. (We stop in 2000 because that is where the database on leaders stops.) Depending on the dataset, we have data for around 600–800 leaders. Let's consider the top-performing leaders as those for whom growth during their term was in the top 5 percent of growth for all leaders. We do this for each of the datasets and list leaders that appeared in the top 5 percent in any one of them.

This gives us a list of around thirty-five would-be benevolent autocrats, including such familiar names as Deng Xiaoping (China), Park Chung Hee (South Korea), and Lee Kuan Yew (Singapore), and a more recent candidate, Paul Kagame (Rwanda). The problem is that, because the datasets do not agree how high (or low) the rates of growth have actually been, they therefore do not agree *when* exemplary rates of growth actually occurred. Consequently, the datasets cannot agree on whose watch it was that exemplary growth happened; that is, they cannot agree on who are the would-be benevolent autocrats. Only around a quarter of the would-be top leaders have had growth during their terms that ranks in the top 5 percent according to *all* four datasets. Some leaders may have had high growth, but the growth data are so error-ridden that we often can't say for sure who they are.

Despite this damning flaw in the evidence for benevolent autocrats, we will give the autocrats a pass on this one. We will ignore measurement error and go back to the exercise of seeing whether growth changes when the leaders change. We will do this for each of the four datasets on growth rates to assess the importance of "good" leaders in each dataset, even if the datasets do not agree who the "good" leaders are.

The next problem is that we have to distinguish leaders' roles from the countries' roles in growth rates. We saw in Chapter Ten on national growth rates that the size of the effect of national characteristics on growth is not as large as usually believed, but it is not zero. There is a case to be made that a leader under whom high growth is achieved should be accorded credit for it only when the growth in his term exceeds the average growth of the country he is leading. To put it another way, if all of the leaders in a given country achieve high growth, that is really evidence that the country itself matters more than do the leaders in influencing growth. For example, the list of high-performing leaders above includes three different leaders from South Korea: the dictators Park Chung Hee and Chun

Do Wan, and Roh Tae Woo who oversaw a transition to democracy. Together these three leaders account for most of South Korea's growth data, so it is more likely that conditions and events in South Korea mattered more than did the policies of any of the individual leaders. (Or, possibly, it was the region of East Asia that mattered rather than South Korean leaders. We saw also in Chapter Ten that some of these country effects are really regional effects. What we are calling country effects now in this chapter would include both regional and country effects.)

Comparing country (including regional) effects to leader effects is important here because the rival stories for high growth under autocrats do involve country (or regional) effects, such as the catching-up of technologically backward countries (or regions) and a positive change in overall freedom in the country (or region). So what does the evidence say?

The data show little evidence that leaders matter for growth rates. The timing of changes in growth simply do not match the timing of leadership changes. Many of our estimates of the effect of leaders on growth using alternative datasets and methods are close to zero, which we find almost too shocking to be believed. This finding does not *prove* that leaders do not matter at all, because noisy data implies some margin of error around any estimate, including around zero. But even allowing for a margin of error, we can be confident that the effects of leaders are small, explaining very little of the action in growth rates.

We have already found some evidence in Chapter Ten that national and regional characteristics do matter some in the long run, even if their role is usually exaggerated in the short term. So the long-run evidence is more consistent with the country- or region-based stories for major growth successes like China and the Gang of Four, who illustrate technological catch-up growth strategies and/or the impact of a positive trend toward greater freedom.

Let's review again why attribution of growth miracles to leaders is still so common. In the above results, we find indications of the very high annual volatility of growth that Chapter Ten also found in studying the evidence for the extent to which national characteristics matter for growth rates. The component of annual growth rates that is *not* explained by either national characteristics or the effect of leaders is remarkably large.

It is this boom-and-bust nature of growth rates that explains why there would be so many spurious attributions of growth to leaders even if leader effects are in fact small or nonexistent. Some leaders just get lucky to have part of a large growth boom happen while they are in office. The results say the timing of the boom often began before they took office and/or ended after they left office, so the boom itself provides no evidence that their leadership matters. But even having part of a boom while these lucky leaders are in office is enough to inflate the average growth during their terms, and so they spuriously get credit for high growth anyway.

The bottom line here is that there is little evidence for good and bad autocrats. The best the evidence allows for here is that leaders matter very little. What we are really seeing with good and bad growth outcomes under leaders is national or regional effects, or boom-and-bust cycles in growth unrelated to leaders. We have seen that the data do not even agree which autocrats are having high growth.

This is not good news for the experts. If leaders do not drive growth, then the experts advising them do not drive growth either. The experts had promised to deliver high growth in return for giving them and their autocratic pupils more power. There is no evidence that they have delivered. The growth–payoff justification for the Tyranny of Experts has turned out to be spurious.

THE AUTOCRATIC STATUS QUO

Alas, the Tyranny of Experts in development continues regardless of evidence. The belief in conscious direction of leaders continues to trump the alternative of spontaneous solutions arising from political and economic rights.

The World Bank's Ethiopia web page in September 2012 noted that it was "Ethiopia's largest provider of official development assistance." The Bank said it was "partnering with GoE [Government of Ethiopia] to look for pragmatic solutions" in support of the latter's "public sector-led growth strategy." The Bank would help "the GoE to improve public service performance management and responsiveness," launching a "Public

Sector Capacity Building Program." The GoE had committed to reforms including "democratic representation" and "human rights and conflict prevention," commitments which the GoE would strictly enforce upon itself.[20]

Meanwhile, less than two months earlier, on July 13, 2012, the GoE sentenced the peaceful Ethiopian blogger and journalist Eskinder Nega to eighteen years in prison. The sentence punished crimes such as factually reporting the Arab Democratic Spring as it happened.

This was a crime of which Robert Zoellick, the World Bank president from 2007 to 2012, was entirely innocent. Zoellick managed to give a whole speech on the Arab Democratic Spring without ever using the word *democratic*.[21] In fact, in systematic monitoring of his speeches during his entire five-year term, he never used the word *democracy* in any of its normal variants. Upon further inquiry, the World Bank Press Office confirmed Zoellick's inability to say the word *democracy*. They attributed it to that "non-political-interference" clause of the World Bank's Articles of Agreement that we discussed in Chapter Five.

As we have seen, that clause has been violated in almost every other way throughout the World Bank's history, such as when the United States supported its allies with World Bank loans during the Cold War, and now during the War on Terror. Under President Zoellick, the Bank even supported foreign military intervention in some poor countries, which would seem like a prima facie violation of a "non-political-interference" clause. The World Bank said in 2011 that military intervention by the United Nations and other "external forces" can "begin to restore confidence . . . in post-conflict settlements." Those forces "can also deploy troops to provide physical security guarantees against a relapse" so as "to confront violence in a timely manner."[22] The only time the noninterference clause is binding, apparently, is preventing the Bank from recognizing any democratic rights of any poor individuals in any of their member countries.

The Ethiopia and Zoellick stories illustrate the authoritarian status quo that still remains in the development community made up of the World Bank, the United Nations, the development efforts of rich nations, and the professional class of development consultants.

How Democracies Resist Technocrats

Why don't those of us in societies based on individual rights fall prey to the same psychological blinders that make us worship leaders when things go well and might make us give those leaders too much power? Even if we did believe in heroic leaders, a society with political and economic rights makes it possible for individuals to resist leaders' ambitions one episode at a time. Whenever the leaders threaten the individuals' rights or well-being with one particular project, democracies allow individuals to mobilize resistance.

A return to the Greene Street block illustrates how democracies resist experts who aspire to technocratic power.[23] The story highlights again that what is most important is having individual rights in place, and demonstrates how an allegedly apolitical "expert solution" is a threat to such rights.

The Greene Street block by the 1930s had fallen far. During the Depression, squatters formed a camp called Packing Box City at the north end of the block.[24] The block's fortunes did not improve with the end of the Depression.A report in 1946 noted that the entire neighborhood around Greene Street had reached "a state of depreciation and obsolescence."[25] Urban planners began to study how to fix the problem.

Urban planning in the United States marked the last manifestation of the most enthusiastic New Dealers' wish to see experts plan the US economy. It also exemplified faith in technocrats who were appointed public officials, like Robert Moses in New York, with few checks on their power. The US Housing Act of 1949 endorsing "slum clearance" would give a technocrat like Moses the power to tear down whole neighborhoods and replace them with public housing.[26] But the technocrat Moses would face some fierce democrats on Greene Street.

The 1946 plan recommended all of what is now SoHo for "clearance and redevelopment." In a phrase that sounds familiar from development, the plan said "the depreciation is so widespread that improvement cannot take place except by concerted action." The planners suggested coercion, using eminent domain "to prevent obstruction through holdouts." [27]

The Greene Street block was singled out because it had the lowest real-estate values of all, only half of what it had been two decades earlier: "None of the present buildings in the block are really worth preserving.

FIGURE 13.1   Packing Box City at Houston and Greene Streets, 1933.
(Percy Loomis Sperr/©Milstein Division, The New York Public Library.)

This is a clear case calling for complete demolition and complete replacement. The situation is most extreme."[28]

Robert Moses was one of the enthusiasts for these plans. He proposed using the 1949 federal funds for "slum clearance" in SoHo. In 1951, Moses proposed demolishing 53 acres in SoHo, to be replaced by both market value and low-income housing, along with a public school and a playground. He would turn Fifth Avenue into a four-lane highway, extended south through Washington Square Park, cutting through SoHo to Broome Street. Another eight-lane east–west superhighway would pave over Broome Street and tear down its borders.[29] Moses said in 1953: "I take this occasion to plead for the courageous, clean-cut, surgical removal of all our old slums." "There can be no real neighborhood reconstruction," he said, "without the unflinching surgery which cuts out the whole cancer and leaves no part of it which can grow again, and spread and perpetuate old miseries."[30] The problem with technocrats is not only that they make the wrong predictions. Their even bigger problem is their confidence in their own predictions.

In a seemingly unrelated event in 1947, the artist Jackson Pollock painted *Cathedral*. It was one of the first works in what would be a successful New

York–based art movement called Abstract Expressionism.[31] For the Greene Street block, what was important about Pollock's painting was not its content but its measurements: six feet by three feet. Large canvasses of this kind were common in the new movement, and both the artists and galleries had trouble displaying them in Manhattan's cramped spaces. To move a piece of Abstract Expressionist art sometimes required dismantling stairwells and doorframes. One neighborhood that did not have this problem with space was the Greene Street block and similar blocks around it. The former factory floors in the cast-iron buildings had spaces that delighted the artists, such as "a room that was 33 feet wide and 110 feet deep with a 16-foot high ceiling."[32]

The Greene Street block would be the epicenter of a revolution in both the neighborhood and the art world, which would see SoHo revived by artists and art gallery owners. Artist Joyce Silver reports that she moved into 127 Greene Street in 1960. She is still there today. She remembers that the neighborhood had "lost industrial companies, and so there were all these empty spaces." The industrial world's loss was the art world's gain, for "artists needed big spaces and these were empty and cheap. When I moved in here," said Silver, "it had been a carpentry shop and there was literally a foot of sawdust over everything."[33]

Meanwhile, Greenwich Village residents were horrified at what the Moses plan would do to their neighborhood. The SoHo artists formed an anti-Moses alliance with the Village residents. A West Village resident named Jane Jacobs engaged Moses on the same debate that failed to happen in development: spontaneous solutions versus conscious direction. In a classic book first published in 1961, Jacobs mocked the urban experts' "pseudoscience of city rebuilding and planning" where "a plethora of subtle and complicated dogma have arisen on a foundation of nonsense." Jacobs praised the local neighborhoods as having organically evolved to meet the needs of residents, as embodiments of social networks that helped prevent crime (her famous "eyes on the street"), and as incubators of innovation.[34] She might have added that they also were a source of democratic resistance to technocratic officials who would eradicate those same neighborhoods if they could. The belief in all-knowing experts fades when they are applying their conscious direction to *you*.

Moses had won almost all of his previous battles in New York, but he lost this one, the last of his career. Greene Street had survived its near-death experience. What happened next vindicated Jane Jacobs's position even more.

The art boom took over. On the Greene Street block alone, at least thirty-five art galleries would appear from the 1970s through the 1990s. In 1980, Leo Castelli, the art dealer representing Robert Rauschenberg, opened a gallery at 142 Greene Street. Castelli's gallery also featured Roy Lichtenstein and Andy Warhol, among many other successful artists.

At 133 Greene Street, the former site of the 1850 Benjamin Seixas family home and Laura Barmore's 1870 brothel was going to see yet another surprising shift. The six-story cast-iron building that the Meinhard Brothers built as a garment factory in 1883 survived. Joyce Silver remembers it from the 1960s as a gigantic cardboard boxes company. In 1971, an artist from Waterbury, Connecticut, named Joseph Catuccio moved into the basement of 133 Greene Street. He started in his new home what he called the Project of Living Artists.[35] Ironically, this particular project was a counterrevolution to the Abstract Expressionism revolution that first made possible the art boom on Greene Street. Catuccio's main effort was to promote drawing of the human form, using live models. According to the project's own self-description, it provided a "warm atmosphere where artists, bankers and petty thieves alike are encouraged to engage their shared interest in studying the human form," helping foster a creative dynamic that is "something intangibly beautiful and ferocious . . . shared between artist and model" and "which has carved out an internationally renowned reputation for the Project as—THE PLACE TO DRAW."[36] Four other more mainstream galleries would occupy other parts of the building at 133 Greene Street over the next few decades.

The artists and galleries helped others perceive the Greene Street block as something more than a block where a 1946 city planner thought "None of the present buildings in the block are really worth preserving," where the only option was "complete demolition and complete replacement." The art galleries first attracted wealthy shoppers and tourists, who in turn attracted high-end retail shops, which also attracted affluent residents. As always with creative destruction, the gentrification of the neighborhood

332

FIGURE 13.2   View of 133–135 Greene Street sometime between 1950 and 1973.
(Collection of the New York Historical Society.)

FIGURE 13.3   View of 133–135 Greene Street today.
(Author photo, 2013.)

FIGURE 13.4   Views of the same portion of the Greene Street block, 1940 (left) and 2013 (right). People in foreground in 2013 are in a line for a new iPhone model at the Apple store down the block.

(1940 image Courtesy NYC Municipal Archives; author photo, 2013.)

represented a loss for some people and some tastes and a gain for others. In June 1997, Joseph Catuccio and the Project of Living Artists moved from 133 Greene Street to Brooklyn. The art boom on Greene Street was nearing the end, and the luxury retail era was beginning. Today, 133 Greene has a Christian Dior menswear store on the ground floor.

The upper floors of 133 Greene Street today are a co-op with seven apartment lofts. The average sales price for each of these lofts over the last few years is $2,729,000. The residents today include the son of a garment manufacturer, architecture professors from Princeton and Columbia, an art-museum curator, the manager of a home-furnishings retailer, and a man specializing in renovation and resale of lofts in SoHo.

The block around 133 Greene Street today has a Ralph Lauren shop, other luxury retailers, and a few remaining art galleries. It has also the supreme embodiment of centuries of development: an Apple Store. After

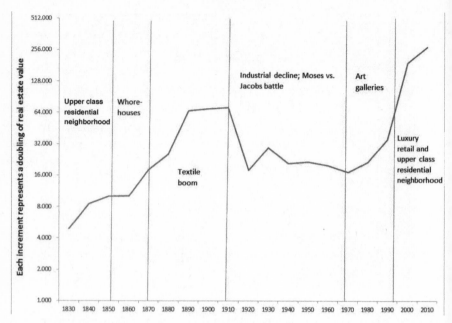

FIGURE 13.5   Market value, Greene Street block, 1830–2010 (in millions of real 2012 dollars). (Figure from Easterly et al., "A Long History of a Short Block.")

the defeat of Robert Moses, real-estate values on the block from 1970 to the present rose sixteen-fold.

Figure 13.5 shows the real-estate value of the Greene Street block in today's dollars from 1830 to 2010, through all phases of its history. The graph uses a special scaling method in which every increment on the scale represents a doubling over the previous value. The block's value kept doubling from 1830 to 1910 through the eras of upper-class residences, whorehouses, and booming textile factories. It went into a long decline from 1910 to 1970. Since then, the upward trend has resumed, with real-estate value doubling with art galleries and luxury retail and residential co-ops. Under the Invisible Hand, the high payoffs were not only to the owners of the galleries, stores, and residences, but to their customers and suppliers in the larger society. The value of the block in the long run was simply the freedom to be whatever its residents and customers wanted it to be.

The moral of the most recent phase of the Greene Street story is not just that Jane Jacobs was proven right after winning her debate with Robert Moses to save SoHo and Greene Street. Not every such debate has a positive outcome. The story just happens to conform to a broader pattern, for which we have seen evidence throughout this book. A system based on individual rights—both economic and political—tends to reward positive actions and stop negative ones. It tends to stop the hubris of conscious direction and leave room for the spontaneous solutions that actually create most of the prosperity we enjoy today.

THE LONG DEBATE

The debate on benevolent autocrats goes back much further than Lee Kuan Yew, or Myrdal versus Hayek, or Moses versus Jacobs. It actually goes all the way back over 250 years to a book on *Despotism in China*, published in 1767 by the French economist François Quesnay. The book did not criticize despotism, it celebrated it. Quesnay was the French counterpart to Adam Smith, and Smith used and cited many of his ideas. Yet there was a fundamental division between them that was a division in the Enlightenment itself: Smith's branch wanted to free people to act in their own interests; Quesnay's branch wanted the educated and talented minority of intellectuals to act on behalf of the majority. Smith's branch of the Enlightenment became the basis not only of the new field of economics but of the liberal society of individual rights and freedoms.

Quesnay's branch of the Enlightenment emphasized that intellectuals knew better than the people themselves what was in their interests. An enlightened vanguard would give people what they would want and should want if only they were able to properly understand their own interests—which they don't. It was one of the very first versions of the Tyranny of Experts.

The Tyranny of Experts lost out in the free societies that emerged in the West, but it remained influential among intellectuals up to the present. In the twentieth century, it was Quesnay's Tyranny of Experts rather than Smith's Invisible Hand that became the mainstream approach in development that we have debated in this book.

The disagreement over the Tyranny of Experts is reflected in Quesnay's book on China. Quesnay's picture of China in 1767 was of a benevolent despot advised by wise scholars. He and others thought of eighteenth-century China as a development success because of its proven ability to sustain a large population. Regardless of whether his picture of China was accurate, Quesnay used it to sketch out his ideal society and government.

Quesnay thought bad government resulted from bad experts: "ignorance is always the principal cause of the most disastrous errors of government, of the ruin of nations, and of the decadence of empires." But Quesnay said that China's tradition of having scholars advise the emperor had saved it from such disasters. These scholar-experts "occupy the foremost rank in the nation," and allow the emperor to lead the people "by the light of reason."[37] The Chinese emperor's job was to select his experts on merit, then simply "follow their advice."[38]

Quesnay considered ideas for putting limits on the emperor's powers but rejected any such limits as a hindrance on the autocrat's ability to form the perfect society. The emperor would let his experts decide, because the experts would be able to "point out with certainty the order of laws most advantageous to the ruler and the nation."[39] Conversely, a society without guidance by experts is doomed: "unenlightened nations can form only transitory, barbarous and ruinous governments," which would be only "uncultivated land, inhabited by ferocious animals."[40]

Quesnay's vision of the benevolent autocrat even included his own version of the Blank Slate: history was useless as a guide to the perfect government. "Let us not seek into the history of nations or into the mistakes of men, for that only presents an abyss of confusion."[41] In contrast, the experts use the "free exercise of reason" in order to "make progress in economic science, which is a great science, for it is the one that underlies the government of nations."[42]

Ironically, after all this, Quesnay's vision of perfect laws was very much laissez-faire, a word originated by his school of like-minded French economists called the Physiocrats. Quesnay's preferred benevolent autocrat was very much like the free-market autocrats we have occasionally mentioned in this book, like Augusto Pinochet of Chile. In his enthusiasm for the

Blank Slate and the instant jump to the perfect government, Quesnay was an eighteenth-century proponent of what today we call shock therapy.

Adam Smith borrowed some free-market ideas from Quesnay but was horrified by just about everything else. Unlike the naïve Quesnay, Smith had no illusions about how political leaders behaved when given unchecked power. He spoke of the "capricious ambition of kings and ministers," and "the violence and injustice of the rulers of mankind." Political freedom cut close to home with Smith, who knew what a narrow escape his own group of Protestants had with the almost-triumph of Catholic rule in Scotland. He spoke of "the pretious (sic) right of private judgement for the sake of which our forefathers kicked out the Pope and the Pretender."[43] (The "Pretender" was James, whose father, James II of England, was deposed in 1688 for his Catholicism. The son, also a Catholic, had unrealized pretensions of regaining his father's throne as James III.)

Smith's leading success story was the American colonies (whose side he took in their dispute with the Crown just as the *Wealth of Nations* was published). Their secret was "plenty of good land, and liberty to manage their own affairs their own way." The word *liberty* appears eighty-five times in the *Wealth of Nations*. As one biographer, Nicholas Phillipson, put it, Smith's life's work was "a call to his contemporaries to take moral, political and intellectual control of their lives."[44]

In a remarkable and little-known paragraph criticizing Quesnay, Smith is starting to see that a free political system could also have an Invisible Hand:

> [Quesnay] seems not to have considered, that in the political body, the natural effort which every man is continually making to better his own condition, is a principle of preservation capable of preventing and correcting, in many respects, the bad effects of a political economy. . . .
> In the political body, however, the wisdom of nature has fortunately made ample provision for remedying many of the bad effects of the folly and injustice of man; it the same manner as it has done in the natural body.[45]

Smith never completed a planned third book on the political order, so it was left to his successors to flesh out the idea of political freedom as a self-correcting system just as much as economic freedom was with the Invisible Hand. But Smith already had in mind a bottom-up system of individual rights in which *both* politics and economics were self-correcting, even with the "folly and injustice of man."

Quesnay was counting on rulers advised by experts to make top-down government so perfect that it did not need to self-correct. Given that folly and injustice are always in excess supply, the future belonged to Smith and not to Quesnay in the West. But Quesnay won in the Rest: development economists in the twenty-first century still imagine benevolent autocrats with wise advisors.

The psychological preference for personality-based stories is one reason why the debate on conscious direction versus spontaneous solutions is usually won by the former, even regardless of evidence. We are all prone to a mental model of the world in which outcomes are the result of intentional action by an identifiable actor. A world in which outcomes are the unintended result of the interaction of many actors with differing intentions just seems too strange to be believed.

The prosperity of our society at home does not necessarily require that anyone have the exactly right mental model of how our society works. We just resist those attempts at conscious direction that threaten our own individual rights. We let spontaneous solutions happen without even needing to understand how they happen.

Yet those thinking about development in another society did require such a mental model. So here the psychological biases trumped the evidence. Conscious direction defeated spontaneous solutions. The Tyranny of Experts defeated the rights of the poor. It did not deserve to win.

CHAPTER FOURTEEN

CONCLUSION

If you are reading this book, you likely care as I do about the material sufferings of the world's poor, including premature mortality, hunger, and poverty. You are confronted as I have been throughout my career with the question, "What must we do to end global poverty?" What do we do with our caring about material deprivation of the world's poor?

There is one thing the history in this book has shown us that we must not do: we must not let caring about material suffering of the poor change the subject from caring about the rights of the poor. It doesn't mean that we care less about the material suffering; it means that we understand that the autocrats have offered a false bargain to meet material needs while we overlook their suppression of rights.

One of many examples this book gave was that of Lord Hailey, who during World War II stressed material development as a way to avoid a discussion of racism in the British Empire. He emphasized material development to avoid a discussion of the political rights of colonial subjects under the absolute power of the empire. He focused on material development to avoid a discussion of equal rights of whites and nonwhites. We discussed how Hailey was able to strike an implicit deal with the Americans: he would not embarrass them about their denial of equal rights to African Americans at home if the Americans would not embarrass the British Empire about its denial of equal rights to Africans. Both would agree to talk only about improved material well-being and not talk about rights.

This strategy had already been part of FDR's New Deal approach toward racial issues, when he needed support from both blacks and Southern segregationists. We talked in Chapter Four about how Eleanor

Roosevelt suggested in 1940 to black leader Ralph Bunche that racism was most "effectively attacked on the economic front." We talked about how New Dealers sought to get blacks to "concentrate on the attainable goal of economic progress and to postpone the challenge to segregation."[1]

That New Deal strategy fell apart only a few years later with the civil rights movement. Martin Luther King Jr. cared deeply about the poverty of American blacks, but he would not let that caring change the subject from equal rights. He understood that unless the principle of equal rights is accepted, you cannot talk only about actions and not about principles. He understood that action cannot happen without principles to guide such action. He understood that as long as there was no agreement about the principle of equal rights for blacks and whites, he could not and would not ever stop talking about equal rights for blacks and whites.

Although King cared deeply about black poverty, he did not feel the appropriate way to frame the issue was, "What must we do to end black poverty?" King's dream was not about an expert plan to reduce poverty among blacks. King's dream was about a nation that lived out the true meaning of its creed—that we hold these truths to be self-evident, that all men are created equal.

King's dream was that blacks would be able to say they were "free at last." He did not first require an expert plan to make blacks "middle class at last."

Colonialism has ended, and racism is not as bad as it was in Hailey's day. But to some extent Hailey's ideas are still succeeding in having material needs change the development subject away from equal rights for the poor and the rich, away from equal rights for those in the West and those in the Rest, away from equal rights for the world's whites and blacks. Far too many rights abuses still happen, even by the development agencies themselves, and are then far too quickly forgotten.

As you wonder what you can do about global poverty, there are many options for your own individual actions. There are many other books about how humanitarian relief of horrific disease and hunger could work best, including a previous book by this author. This book is about a different option for what you can do. This option already exists, but it receives much too little effort and attention. What you can do is advocate that the poor should have the same rights as the rich. You can protest when your own governments trample upon the rights of the Rest, either through their aid agencies or through their many other military and foreign-policy actions.

Not Forgetting Rights in Ethiopia

This assertion of the rights of the poor is needed now more than ever. To give just one example, the world's premier development agency, the World Bank, seems as far from recognizing rights as ever. On July 22, 2013, Human Rights Watch (HRW) issued a fifty-nine-page report, *Abuse-Free Development: How the World Bank Should Safeguard Against Human Rights Violations.* The report documented disturbing indifference to rights in World Bank projects.

HRW condemned the World Bank for financing part of the Ethiopian government's forced-villagization program in the Gambella region. As was discussed in Chapter Seven, the program was also supported by British and American aid. The World Bank board approved a renewal of a project called "Promoting Basic Services" that finances villagization, despite the evidence that the Ethiopian army is taking farmers' land at gunpoint, killing resisters, and involuntarily resettling 1.5 million people. The new "model villages" to which the army moved the villagers lacked those basic services that the World Bank claims to be promoting. Ethiopian government officials designing and implementing the villagization program have part of their salaries paid by the World Bank project. World Bank officials denied any involuntary resettlement and violence even after receiving firsthand testimony to the contrary in a meeting between Bank officials and some of the refugee victims on September 14, 2012. The World Bank board then renewed the Promoting Basic Services project eleven days later.[2] There was far too little protest in the West about this egregious rights violation at the time; there is still far too little now. If you wonder what you can do about global poverty, here is virgin territory for action.

Chapter Seven also mentioned yet another, earlier rights violation in the same country. A 2010 HRW report subtitled *How Aid Underwrites Repression in Ethiopia* documented how Meles Zenawi used donor funds to blackmail starving peasants into supporting his regime, denying donor-financed food relief to opposition supporters. The report included anonymous quotes

from donor officials in Ethiopia such as ""Every tool at their disposal—
fertilizer, loans, safety net [welfare payments that include food relief]—is
being used to crush the opposition. We know this." The embarrassment
of the HRW report in October 2010 forced the aid agencies to promise
an investigation. But the same donors then informed HRW in April 2011
that they had canceled the investigation—they did not feel obligated to say
why. The donors—the UK and US governments and the World Bank—
succeeded at least temporarily in forgetting all about the whole affair.

There is room for all of us to care more about such rights violations.
There is room for us to refuse to forget those Ethiopians who starved
only because they would not endorse their own oppression. We should
not let the Western governments, the Western aid agencies, or the self-
designated "development community" forget.

The jailed Ethiopian dissident Eskinder Nega, mentioned in the previous chapter, published a "Letter from Ethiopia's Gulag" in the *New York
Times* on July 25, 2013. He described being jailed with around 200 other
inmates in a wide hall, sharing only three toilets. He shares a small open
space with about 1,000 other prisoners at Kaliti Prison. His wife had also
been jailed, and his son was born in prison. He sadly remembered the
optimism after the end of the Cold War, when an idea was briefly considered: "no democracy, no aid." That idea has long been forgotten by aid
agencies. World Bank aid, British aid, and US aid not only fund forced
relocation, they help pay the salaries of the brutal jailers of Eskinder Nega.
We can choose not to let our own governments and our own development agencies forget democracy, not to let them forget rights, not to let
them forget Eskinder Nega in jail.

NOT FORGETTING IN UGANDA

This book opened by telling the story of famers in Mubende, Uganda,
whose farms soldiers took at gunpoint under the auspices of a different
World Bank project on February 28, 2010, financing a British company's
forestry project. The story had appeared on the front page of the *New York
Times* on September 21, 2011.

On July 8, 2013, Oxfam, who documented the original abuses, made a low-key announcement that the community had reached an agreement with the British company, the New Forests Company (NFC): "NFC will contribute funds into a community-run cooperative that has been set-up by the Mubende community. NFC will also implement development projects to benefit the affected community. The community remains far from restoring its livelihoods. . . ." A further update in April 2014 by Oxfam noted that the community cooperative had purchased 500 acres for resettlement and fields for the farmers.[3]

The details of the settlement were confidential, so nobody else will ever know just how "far from restoring its livelihoods" the agreement left the Mubende farmers. The World Bank never kept its promise to investigate its own role in supporting the forestry project that became the tragedy of the Mubende farmers. The World Bank is supposed to have safeguards against involuntary resettlement in its own internal policy guidelines. The World Bank's own Office of Compliance Advisor/Ombudsman (CAO) played a role in the mediation but said that the mediation option precluded any CAO assessment of the World Bank's own complicity in the original outrages. It is a bit hard to understand the rules of a World Bank Compliance Office that does not enforce World Bank compliance with its own rules that it should not harm its own project beneficiaries

All parties were sworn to secrecy, with the added incentive to keep quiet that another community victimized by the World Bank–NFC project was still negotiating a similar deal with the NFC. Even this author hesitated to speak out for fear of jeopardizing the other negotiation. The July 8, 2013, agreement on the inadequate deal for Mubende received virtually no notice in the media or development blogs. (This author himself found out about the July 8, 2013 agreement through personal notification by Oxfam; a Google web/news/blog search turned up no news reports and only one inconspicuous blog mention. This author was also unaware of the April 2014 update until making a search for any update on the Oxfam and CAO websites.) The World Bank's confidential mediation process had gotten some compensation for the victims, which is good. But the World Bank's confidential mediation also had made the story disappear.

It is impossible to prove whether this was the intention of the confidential mediation all along, but it was an outcome very much in the interests of the NFC and the World Bank after the embarrassing *New York Times* story. The World Bank was never held accountable for Mubende, which would have been important to change World Bank behavior to prevent future Mubendes. Some four years after the tragic rights violation of the Mubende farmers, the rights violations really have been forgotten.

The book opened by noting how inconceivable the Mubende story would have been if it had happened in Ohio. It is also inconceivable that such a rights violation in Ohio would have led only to confidential settlements for victims, with no accountability for public officials. It is time for a new concern for rights in development, in which a rights violation of Mubende farmers deserves not to be forgotten just as much as a rights violation of Ohio farmers would not have been forgotten.

GROUNDS FOR HOPE

Despite these depressing stories of rights abuses of poor people that are overlooked and forgotten by rich people, the campaign for poor people's rights is far from hopeless. Despite the neglect of freedom in development, poor people around the world are asserting more and more their own freedom.

Despite the trampling of rights by Western governments and development agencies, there are plenty of grounds for hope when we see how much the global change in freedom is positive anyway. Both political and economic freedom are much more widespread today than they were at the beginning of official development, or even than they were two decades ago, as measured by the imperfect measures we have on the different kinds of freedom.

This book does *not* say that nothing good will happen until some utopian ideals on rights are attained. No, this book argues the opposite: an incremental positive change in freedom will yield a positive change in well-being for the world's poor. These incremental changes are already happening.

We discussed Benin's history as both victimizers and victims of the slave trade. We left off the story of Benin in Chapter Seven with a brutal military dictator named Mathieu Kerekou, who had been in power since 1972.

In 1989, a wave of strikes and protests challenged the economic mismanagement and corruption under Mathieu Kerekou. On January 9, 1989, teachers at high schools in Cotonou and the old slave-exporting port of Porto Novo went on strike. Students at the Abomey-Calavi campus of National University went on strike a week later. Strikes spread to civil servants in the government itself. On December 7, 1989, Kerekou announced a National Conference, which turned out to generate more demands for democracy. The end result, after further to and fro, was that on April 4, 1991, Mathieu Kerekou became one of the first African rulers to voluntarily surrender power after defeat in a fair democratic election.

Democracy is making gradual progress in Africa. In 1988, there had been only two African countries classified as politically free by the advocacy organization Freedom House. In 2012, there were eleven. Freedom House divides the rest between "partly free" and the most ruthless dictatorships as "not free." In 1988, there were thirty-one "not free" African dictators; in 2012, the number has been reduced to nineteen.

Those waiting for hours to vote in the hot sun in the new elections in Africa seem to have their own interest in freedom. Again I will quote from the interviews collected by Deepa Narayan and Lant Pritchett. A group of young Tanzanian girls says the opposite of freedom is "being jailed," as well as being "humiliated, beaten, or interrogated at one's home." To a man in Uganda freedom just means "I do whatever I want with my cow."[4]

We discussed Ghana as another locus of the slave trade, with the Ashanti people as enslavers and the coastal Akan people as the enslaved. This divisive legacy may have contributed to the dispiriting story of the independence hero Kwame Nkrumah (himself from the coastal Akan), who in 1957 jailed the Ashanti-based opposition party. Nkrumah's brutal repression dismayed the technocratic economist Sir Arthur Lewis, as we saw in Chapter Four, though he chose to keep silent so as not to harm the cause of African independence.

In Ghana, an election in 2000 led to a peaceful transfer of power from the autocrat Jerry Rawlings (from the Ewe ethnic group) to a democratic

346 The Tyranny of Experts

Ashanti politician named John Kufuor, the political heir to the Ashanti-based opposition to Nkrumah. Kufour was reelected in 2004, but then his party lost to the opposition in 2008 and 2012. Power changed hands peacefully.

We have seen in the previous chapter how economic freedom in Ghana had increased even before the transition to more political freedom. The Rawlings government since 1983 had been forced by the collapse of cocoa production to reduce the destructive controls on Ashanti cocoa growers, allowing the industry to revive. The legacy of the slave trade for political and economic repression of the Ashanti by other ethnic groups in Ghana has faded as economic and political freedom increases.

This book has cautioned a lot against reading too much into volatile and error-ridden national economic-growth rates. Yet we all want to know what little we can learn from growth anyway (which I will keep insisting is not that much). Ghana's per capita growth rate in the new millennium is nearly 4 percent per year. The average growth for all of sub-Saharan Africa (worth only a little bit more than Ghana's by averaging out horrific measurement error over more countries) turned around in the mid-1990s. Since the new millennium began, Africa's growth is the highest in its history.

In Latin America, Albert Hirschman, the development economist who had worked on the World Bank Colombia report, had sounded the alarm in 1979 on how technocratic development "brings with it calamitous side effects in the political realm, from the loss of democratic liberties at the hand of authoritarian, repressive regimes to the wholesale violation of elementary human rights" (as discussed in Chapter Five).[5] Hirschman's alarm was ignored in development, but the progress of liberties in Latin America happened anyway. The military rulers in Argentina, Brazil, Chile, Paraguay, and Uruguay that dismayed Hirschman in 1979 had lost power by the end of the 1980s.

Today, in Latin America and the Caribbean, Freedom House classifies only one country—Cuba—in the most autocratic "not free" category, while it classifies thirteen Latin countries in the most democratic "free" status. To again check whatever we can learn from growth numbers, the chronically underperforming region of Latin America recovered from its "lost decade" in the 1980s, which was discussed in Chapter Ten, and has since returned to a growth of income per person of 2 percent per year, which is the world average.

WHAT ABOUT THOSE EAST ASIAN "BENEVOLENT AUTOCRAT" SUCCESS STORIES?

In 1987, the government of South Korean dictator Chun Do Wan tortured and murdered Park Jong-chul, a student protester from Seoul National University. Massive demonstrations broke out across the nation, with protestors demanding democracy and eventually getting it.[6] South Korea has now been a democracy for a quarter-century. Hyundai, and the economy, continue to thrive. The idea that autocracy was necessary for progress in Korea was contradicted by its own later experience. We have also seen that there is *no* international evidence for the idea that Korea first needed a benevolent autocrat to generate high growth, because we found the international evidence did not support benevolent-autocrat stories. For Korea specifically, we pointed out how it makes more sense to attribute the high growth associated with successive authoritarian, transitional, and democratic leaders to the broader circumstances of the country rather than to the plans of specific leaders. A more plausible country story is that this positive change in freedom, combined with a long experience with technology, made possible rapid technological catch-up growth.

A similar narrative likely applies in another East Asian success, Taiwan. In 1987, Chiang Ching-kuo, the successor to his father Chiang Kai-shek as dictator of Taiwan, ended the martial law that had been in force in Taiwan for thirty-eight years. Democratization continued gradually up through the presidential elections of March 1996.

The March 1996 ballot was the first time in history an ethnic Chinese nation had held free elections for its leader.[7] The ruling party won the first election but peacefully passed power to an opposition winner in 2000. Today, the Kuomintang, the same Nationalist Party for which the long-forgotten H. D. Fong and the Institute of Pacific Relations had formulated authoritarian development in the 1930s, competes in a multiparty democracy. Economic growth continues to be high.

LESSONS OF DEVELOPMENT ON GREENE STREET

A short time ago, I had lunch with Naomi Seixas at a café on the corner of Greene and Houston, on the block whose history is covered throughout this book. Naomi is a young professional who works in New York. She is also a descendant of the Seixas family that lived on or near the Greene Street block from the 1830s through the 1850s. She kindly helped me find additional sources on Seixas family history.

When Benjamin Mendes Seixas lived at 133 Greene Street in 1850, as noted in Chapter Eight, average income in the United States was one-seventeenth of today's incomes. The United States in 1850 was roughly at the average income level of Ghana today.

The death of three of Benjamin's children in infancy reflected a horrific child-mortality rate in New York and the United States that was about double the worst mortality rates today in Africa. In 1850, 22 percent of American children died before their first birthday; today 0.6 percent of children die before their first birthday. The nineteenth-century outcome reflected in part the city's squalid sanitation, in which an open sewer ran down the middle of Greene Street.

Development on Greene Street emerged from spontaneous solutions by individuals. They had given us a textile boom at the epicenter of American industrialization in 1880 to 1910. After a downturn on the block in the twentieth century, whose nadir was the 1933 Packing Box City for the unemployed homeless, they gave us a surprise boom by artist studios, then art galleries, then luxury retail. Today, eight decades later, the Aroma Espresso shop, where Naomi and I had lunch, sits on the site of the 1933 Packing Box City.

The health improvement was made possible both by spontaneous technological solutions—some of them borrowed across borders from other free societies—in new medicines and sanitation, and action by a government that was democratically accountable to its citizens in implementing sanitation.

Today we take for granted our standard of living, our healthy children, our streets without open sewers. Even we in rich countries are prone to forget how much effort our ancestors had to make to achieve the freedom

FIGURE 14.1   Packing Box City at Houston and Greene Streets, 1933.
(Perry Loomis Sperr / © Milstein Division, The New York Public Library.)

FIGURE 14.2   The Aroma Espresso Shop, corner of Greene and Houston, 2013.
(Author photo, 2013.)

that made this possible. The even greater tragedy was that the development debate ignored the historical success of a free society in solving poverty and child mortality.

CAN THE DOUBLE STANDARD END?

One interpretation of trends today is that the Rise of the Rest challenges
the free values of the West. Focusing on the last few decades, the high
growth in autocratic China seems like a particular assault on the Western
model. But this book has offered another interpretation from a longer-run
perspective: free values are gradually spreading from the West to the Rest,
including to China, and the Rise of the Rest reflects precisely that spread
of free values. The idea that individual rights are "Western values" may be
an anachronism that is becoming clearer.

The global double standard of rights for the rich and not for the poor
is very much alive in the technocratic worldview of development. But this,
too, could be a casualty of the Rise of the Rest and the spread of freedom.
The disrespect for poor people shown by agencies such as the World Bank
and the Gates Foundation, with their stereotypes of wise technocrats from
the West and helpless victims from the Rest, may become increasingly
untenable. Development may have to give up its authoritarian mind-set
to survive.

Even from his jail cell in Ethiopia, the courageous dissident Eskinder
Nega expressed hope that "Democracy would no longer be the esoteric
virtue of Westerners but the ubiquitous expression of our common humanity. . . . Tyranny is increasingly unsustainable in this post-cold-war
era. It is doomed to failure."[8]

OUT OF CHINA

The history of authoritarian development began about a century ago in
China with Sun Yat-sen, Chiang Kai-shek, and the economist H. D. Fong,
supported by the Rockefeller Foundation in the 1920s and 1930s, and US
nation-building efforts in the 1940s, as discussed in Chapter Three. It would
be fitting to conclude the story of the battle of ideas in the same place.

Chen Guangcheng is a blind, self-taught lawyer from China's province of Shangdong.⁹ Shangdong is the same province that the Allies ceded to Japan after World War I, provoking outrage from Sun Yat-sen and the Chinese.

In 2006 Chen filed a class-action lawsuit against local officials who had forced women to undergo late-term abortions to comply with China's one-child policy. The national authorities responded by putting Chen in prison for four years, then putting him under house arrest in 2010. On April 22, 2012, Chen escaped from his house-prison. With the help of underground activists, Chen was able to reach the US embassy in Beijing. Under the pressure of worldwide publicity, the Chinese government allowed Chen and his family to leave for the United States.¹⁰

On January 30, 2013, Chen Guangcheng gave a speech at the Washington National Cathedral to an overflowing audience. Chen accused his own government: "Communist party officials are not our rulers, they're our kidnappers." Yet Chen hoped for freedom: "as more and more Chinese people speak out and demand their rights, change in China will become unstoppable." Chen did not believe in benevolent autocrats: "We Chinese must fight for our own rights, we cannot expect an enlightened emperor to bestow our rights upon us."¹¹

Chen understood what many in development still do not. However benevolent an autocrat may appear for the moment, unrestrained power will always turn out to be the enemy of development.

It is time at last for the debate that never happened to happen. It is time at last for the silence on unequal rights for rich and poor to end. It is time at last for all men and women to be equally free.

ACKNOWLEDGMENTS

The writing of this book benefited enormously from generous supporters.

The front line that made this book happen features Lara Heimert, the Publisher at Basic Books, Tim Bartlett, my amazing editor, Andrew Wylie, my agent extraordinaire, and Karl Yambert, the copy editor. They gave critical comments, suggestions, encouragement, and support that were remarkably far-seeing and helpful.

I am deeply grateful to Chris Blattman, Michael Clemens, Elizabeth Dalton, Angus Deaton, Laura Freschi, Steven Pennings, Lant Pritchett, and Dennis Whittle for vital comments on the first draft of the book.

There is an invisible college of my old and new co-authors on work used in this book, or work that formed a background to this book. These mentors and co-authors deserve fulsome thanks for all that I have learned from them. They include Alberto Alesina, the late Michael Bruno, Michael Clemens, Alejandro Corvalan, Diego Comin, Carlos Esteban Posada, Stanley Fischer, Erick Gong, Robert King, Michael Kremer, Ross Levine, Norman Loayza, Peter Montiel, Nathan Nunn, Lant Pritchett, Sergio Rebelo, Ariell Reshef, Shanker Satyanath, Julia Schwenkenberg, Klaus Schmidt-Hebbel, Luis Serven, Joseph Stiglitz, Lawrence Summers, Romain Wacziarg, and Michael Woolcock.

One piece of serendipity that helped the book was that my early work on the book inspired a proposal to the John Templeton Foundation for a research grant to the NYU Development Research Institute (DRI) of which I am co-director. The book then benefited from both the writing of the proposal and then the early research after that grant was approved. I am very grateful to the John Templeton Foundation for this enormous contribution. (Please note, however, that the opinions expressed in this book are those of the author and do not necessarily reflect the views of the John Templeton Foundation.) The staff, post-docs, and student workers of DRI over the last few years helped with general brain-storming, research, and fact-checking that helped the Templeton proposal, the early research, and/or the book, or all of the above. These include Diego Anzoategui, Lauren

Bishop, Tanja Goodwin, Lauren Hanson, Adam Martin, Vivek Nemana, Andrew Peterson, John Schellhase, and Claudia Williamson.

One person at DRI deserves extraordinary recognition for the single largest contribution to the book, one that is so major that it is difficult to adequately describe. Laura Freschi, the Managing Director of DRI, contributed to this book (sometimes also in symbiosis with the Templeton proposal and research) in many intangible and tangible ways, including supervising the student workers, doing her own research and fact-checking, co-authoring the work on the history of Greene Street, and heroic problem-solving whenever there was a crisis close to a deadline.

The support of NYU for the Development Research Institute (DRI) was also critically important to being able to do this book. I want to thank in particular the co-director of DRI, Yaw Nyarko, the Provost of NYU, David McLaughlin, the Economics Department Chairman Alessandro Lizzeri, my Economics faculty colleagues Hunt Allcott, Jess Benhabib, Raquel Fernandez, and Boyan Jovanovic, Professor Kevin Davis from the NYU Law School and Bruce Bueno de Mesquita, Adam Przeworski, and Shanker Satyanath from NYU Politics.

Steven Pennings played a crucial and remarkably helpful role as my Research Assistant on my own work, as co-author on the Greene Street history, and as co-author of work on "benevolent autocrats" and economic growth.

I am grateful to Michele Alacevich for guidance and references on historians' research on the development idea, to Peter Boettke and Bruce Caldwell for questions and discussions about Friedrich Hayek, and to Naomi Seixas for help on Seixas family history.

To my amazing kids Rachel, Caleb, and Grace, you got it exactly right in combining interest and encouragement in my work with the gleeful irreverence that makes it impossible for a father to take himself too seriously. To my wonderful step-kids and step-daughter-in-law, Gennie, Luke and Dana, I am so grateful that you have doubled down on that combination in cahoots with your step-siblings.

Last of all to thank the one who deserves the most gratitude and recognition, my spouse Lizzie, I seek to avoid the awkward spouse-thanking formulas that seem hard for authors to avoid. Lizzie, your contribution to this book, and to my life, is far beyond what words can express.

NOTES

CHAPTER 1: INTRODUCTION

1. Josh Kron, "In Scramble for Land, Group Says, Company Pushed Ugandans Out," *New York Times*, September 21, 2011; Matt Grainger and Kate Geary, "The New Forests Company and Its Uganda Plantations," Oxfam International Case Study, 22 September 2011, http://www.oxfam.org/sites/www.oxfam.org/files/cs-new-forest-company-uganda-plantations-220911-en.pdf. accessed September 6, 2013.

2. World Bank, "Strengthening World Bank Engagement on Governance and Anticorruption," March 21, 2007, p. 33. *http://siteresources.worldbank.org/EXTPUBLICSECTORANDGOVERNANCE/Resources/GACStrategyPaper.pdf,* accessed September 6, 2013.

CHAPTER 2: TWO NOBEL LAUREATES
AND THE DEBATE THEY NEVER HAD

1. Gunnar Myrdal, *Development and Under-Development: A Note on the Mechanism of National and International Inequality* (Cairo: National Bank of Egypt, 1956), p. 65.

2. Gunnar Myrdal, *An International Economy: Problems and Prospects* (New York: Harper, 1956), 145.

3. Gunnar Myrdal, *Asian Drama: An Inquiry into the Poverty of Nations,* 3 vols. (New York: Twentieth Century Fund, 1968), quoted in P. T. Bauer, *Dissent on Development: Studies and Debates in Development Economics* (Cambridge, MA: Harvard University Press, 1976), 187.

4. Ibid., 189.

5. F. A. Hayek, *The Road to Serfdom: Text and Documents; The Definitive Edition,* ed. Bruce Caldwell, Volume 2, *The Collected Works of F. A. Hayek* (Chicago: University of Chicago Press, 2010), Kindle edition, location 1740.

6. Ibid., 4038.

7. F. A. Hayek, *The Constitution of Liberty: The Definitive Edition,* ed. Ronald Hamowy, *The Collected Works of F. A. Hayek,* Volume 17 (Chicago: University of Chicago Press, 2011), Kindle edition, locations 13822, 13901, 13836.

8. Ibid., 13869.

9. Ibid., 13862–863.

10. Hayek, *Road to Serfdom*, 5842.

11. Hayek, *Constitution of Liberty*, 13840–41.

12. Ibid., 13920.

13. Gunnar Myrdal, *Economic Theory and Under-Developed Regions* (London: Duckworth, 1957), 84.

14. Bruce Caldwell, *Hayek's Challenge: An Intellectual Biography of F. A. Hayek* (Chicago: University of Chicago Press, 2008), Kindle edition, location 2744. Another complication about his last name was that *von Hayek* became his legal last name in Britain when he became a citizen because it was the name on his birth certificate.

15. Leif Wenar, ed., *Hayek on Hayek: An Autobiographical Dialogue* (Oxford: Taylor and Francis, 2007), Kindle edition, location 1306.

16. Ibid., 1164–70.

17. Sylvia Nasar, *Grand Pursuit: The Story of Economic Genius* (New York: Simon and Schuster, 2011), p. 375.

18. German History in Documents and Images, Volume 7, *Nazi Germany, 1933–1945*, Decree of the Reich President for the Protection of the People and State ("Reichstag Fire Decree"), February 28, 1933, http://germanhistorydocs.ghi-dc.org/pdf/eng/English%20 3_5.pdf, accessed September 4, 2013.

19. Hayek, *Road to Serfdom*, 5974, 5991.

20. Wenar, *Hayek on Hayek*, 1011–14.

21. F. A. Hayek, *Studies on the Abuse and Decline of Reason*, ed. Bruce Caldwell, Volume 13, *The Collected Works of F. A. Hayek* (Chicago: University of Chicago Press, 2010), Kindle edition, locations 8903–8908.

22. Hayek, *Road to Serfdom*, 3601.

23. Ibid. 1225.

24. Ibid. 1140.

25. Clifford Geertz, "Myrdal's Mythology," *Encounter* 33, Number 1 (July 1969): 29–33; quote is from page 31.

26. Myrdal, *International Economy*, 201.

27. Hayek, *Road to Serfdom*, 1814.

28. Ibid. 1753.

29. Ibid. 1814.

30. Allan Carlson, *The Swedish Experiment in Family Politics: The Myrdals and the Interwar Population Crisis* (New Brunswick, NJ: Transaction Publishers, 1990), 94, 95, 90.

31. Beatrice Cherrier, "Gunnar Myrdal and the Scientific Way to Social Democracy, 1914–1968." *Journal of the History of Economic Thought* 31, Number 1 (March 2009): 33–55.

32. Hayek, *Road to Serfdom*, 1810.

33. Hayek, *Abuse and Decline of Reason*, 1677–85.

34. Myrdal, *International Economy*, 201.

35. Ibid., 201.

36. Ibid., 204.

37. Quoted in Bauer, *Dissent on Development*, 187.

38. Ibid., 187.

39. Hayek, *Road to Serfdom*, 3893.

40. Ibid., 2981.

41. Ibid., 2631.

42. Ibid., 4038.

43. Myrdal, *International Economy*, 154.

44. http://www.cgdev.org/content/calendar/detail/1426888/, accessed August 16, 2013.

45. Hayek did however have one major disagreement with the mainstream economists at that time. The mainstream was happy to assume that everyone involved in the economy had perfect knowledge about what was going on with everyone else. This was (and remains) a very convenient assumption to be able to generate predictive models of the economy. This left open the theoretical possibility that the government could know enough to predict the general equilibrium outcome of any government policy, which left the door open to government planning. Hayek considered this assumption ridiculous.

46. Kenneth Arrow, *Collected Papers of Kenneth J. Arrow*, Volume 2, *General Equilibrium* (Cambridge MA: Harvard University Press 1983), 107–8.

47. Quoted in Daniel Yergin and Joseph Stanislaw, *The Commanding Heights: The Battle Between Government and the Marketplace That Is Remaking the Modern World* (New York: Simon and Schuster, 1998), 150–51.

48. Hayek, *Road to Serfdom*, 1750.

49. Ibid., 1202.

50. Ibid., 1829.

51. F. A. Hayek, ed., *Collectivist Economic Planning: Critical Studies on the Possibilities of Socialism by N.G. Pierson, Ludwig von Mises, Georg Halm, and Enrico Barone* (London: Routledge and Kegan Paul, 2011), Kindle edition, locations 152–57.

52. Hayek, *Constitution of Liberty*, 1980.

53. Hayek, *Road to Serfdom*, 180.

54. Gunnar Myrdal, *Development and Under-Development: A Note on the Mechanism of National and International Inequality* (Cairo: National Bank of Egypt, 1956), 63 and 65.

55. Quoted in Bauer, *Dissent on Development*, 187.

56. Ibid., 206.

57. Ibid., 207.

58. Ibid., 189.

59. Hayek, *Road to Serfdom*, 2216.

60. Hayek, *Constitution of Liberty*, 13831.

61. Hayek, *Road to Serfdom*, Kindle location 4350.

62. Ibid., 4070.

63. Gunnar Myrdal, "The Equality Issue in World Development," 1974 Nobel Prize Lecture in Economic Sciences, March 17, 1975. Available at http://www.nobelprize.org/nobel_prizes/economic-sciences/laureates/1974/myrdal-lecture.html, accessed September 22, 2013.

64. Friedrich August von Hayek, "Banquet Speech," Nobel Banquet, December 10, 1974. Available at http://www.nobelprize.org/nobel_prizes/economic-sciences/laureates/1974/hayek-speech.html, accessed September 22, 2013.

65. Friedrich August von Hayek, "The Pretence of Knowledge," 1974 Nobel Prize Lecture in Economic Sciences, December 11, 1974. Available at http://www.nobelprize.org/nobel_prizes/economic-sciences/laureates/1974/hayek-lecture.html, accessed September 22, 2013.

66. Hayek, *Constitution of Liberty*, 1983.

67. Myrdal, *Economic Theory and Under-Developed Regions*, 84.

68. Quoted in Bauer, *Dissent on Development*, 69.

69. Myrdal, *An International Economy*, 201

70. Hayek, *Road to Serfdom*, 4338.

71. Ibid., 4331.
72. Ibid., 4334.
73. Ibid., 4339.
74. Myrdal, *Development and Under-Development*, 65
75. Ibid., 63, 65.
76. Myrdal, *Economic Theory and Under-Development* 80.

PART TWO: WHY THE DEBATE NEVER HAPPENED—THE REAL HISTORY OF THE DEVELOPMENT IDEA

1. Woodrow Wilson, Addresses of President: Wilson: Addresses Delivered by President Wilson on His Western Tour . . . (Washington, DC: Government Printing Office, 1919), 73.

CHAPTER 3: ONCE UPON A TIME IN CHINA

2. Woodrow Wilson, Addresses of President: Wilson: Addresses Delivered by President Wilson on His Western Tour . . . (Washington, DC: Government Printing Office, 1919), 329.
3. F. D. Lugard, *The Dual Mandate in British Tropical Africa* (Edinburgh and London: William Blackwood and Sons, 1922), 69, 70, and 72. Sir Charles Eliot (1862–1931) was a former British ambassador to the United States and commissioner of British East Africa.
4. Quoted in Suke Wolton, *Lord Hailey, the Colonial Office and the Politics of Race and Empire in the Second World War: The Loss of White Prestige* (Oxford: Palgrave Macmillan, 2000), 40.
5. Quoted in Wolton, *Lord Hailey*, 132–33.
6. Quoted in William E. Leuchtenburg, *Herbert Hoover* (New York: Herbert Holt and Company, 2009), 57.
7. Sun Yat-sen, *The International Development of China* (Shanghai: Commercial Press, 1920).
8. Julie Lee Wei, Ramon H. Myers, and Donald G. Gillin, eds., *Prescriptions for Saving China: Selected Writings of Sun Yat Sen* (Stanford CA: Hoover Institution Press, 1994), Google Play electronic edition, 272–73.
9. Quoted in Paul B. Trescott, *Jingji Xue: The History of the Introduction of Western Economic Ideas into China, 1850–1950* (Hong Kong: The Chinese University of Hong Kong, 2007), 52.
10. Ibid., 47.
11. Ibid., 54.
12. Wei, Myers, and Gillin, eds., *Prescriptions for Saving China*, 313–14.
13. Tomoko Akami, *Internationalizing the Pacific: The United States, Japan and the Institute of Pacific Relations in War and Peace, 1919–45* (London: Routledge, 2013), Kindle edition, location 1397.
14. Ibid., 1423.
15. Ibid., 1360.
16. Ibid., 1444.
17. Ibid., 1244.
18. Ibid., 1374.

19. Ibid., 6778.

20. Ibid., 6729.

21. Quoted in Paul F. Hooper, ed., *Remembering the Institute of Pacific Relations: The Memoirs of William L. Holland* (Tokyo: Ryukei Shysha Publishing, 1995), 452.

22. Following the French defeat of the British navy off Minorca in 1756, the British Admiralty executed its own Admiral John Byng. Voltaire satirically commented that it was good to kill an admiral from time to time "in order to encourage the others."

23. H. D. Fong, *Reminiscences of a Chinese Economist at 70* (Singapore: South Seas Society 1975), 29.

24. Yuan Chen, "Post-War Foreign Policy," in *What the Chinese Think About Postwar Reconstruction: Internal Economic Development, Volume 19, Number 16 (November 1, 1943) of Foreign Policy Reports* (New York: Foreign Policy Association, Inc.), 223–28; quote is on page 226.

25. "Industrialization in the Pacific Countries (Summary of Round Table Discussions)," in J. B. Condliffe, ed., *Problems of the Pacific 1929, Proceedings of the Third Conference of the Institute of Pacific Relations* (New York: Greenwood Press, 1969), 70–71; originally published by the University of Chicago Press, 1930.

26. Hsien-t'ing Fang, *Toward Economic Control in China* (Shanghai: China Institute of Pacific Relations, 1936), 5.

27. Paul Trescott, "H. D. Fong and the Study of Chinese Economic Development." *History of Political Economy* 34, no. 4 (2002): 789–809.

28. http://www.rockefellerfoundation.org/about-us, accessed August 21, 2013.

29. James C. Thompson, *While China Faced West: American Reformers in Nationalist China, 1928–1937* (Cambridge, MA: Harvard University Press, 1969), 139.

30. Quoted in Frank Ninkovich, "The Rockefeller Foundation, China, and Cultural Change" *Journal of American History* 70, no. 4 (March 1984): 799–820.

31. Thompson, *While China Faced West*, 138–39.

32. Socrates Litsios, "Selskar Gunn and China: The Rockefeller Foundation's 'Other' Approach to Public Health" *Bulletin of the History of Medicine* 79, no. 2 (Summer 2005): 295–318.

33. Yung-Chen Chiang, *Social Engineering and the Social Sciences in China, 1919–1949* (Cambridge UK: Cambridge University Press, 2001), 226.

34. R. H. Tawney, *Land and Labor in China* (London: George Allen & Unwin Ltd, 1932), 11, 19, 20.

35. Ta Chen, "Chinese Migrations, with Special Reference to Labor Conditions" *Bulletin of the United States Bureau of Labor Statistics No. 340.* (Washington DC: Government Printing Office, 1923). See also Chen Da, "Emigrant Communities in South China," review by Barbara Celarent, *American Journal of Sociology*, Vol. 117, No. 3 (November 2011): 1022–27.

36. Akami, *Internationalizing the Pacific*, 2728.

37. Condliffe, *Problems of the Pacific 1929*, 95.

38. James T. Shotwell, "Extra-Territoriality in China," in J. B. Condliffe, ed., *Problems of the Pacific 1929, Proceedings of the Third Conference of the Institute of Pacific Relations* (New York: Greenwood Press, 1969), 346–47; originally published by the University of Chicago Press, 1930.

39. Wu Ding-chang, "International Economic Co-Operation in China," in J. B. Condliffe, ed., *Problems of the Pacific 1929, Proceedings of the Third Conference of the Institute of*

Pacific Relations (New York: Greenwood Press, 1969), 374–75; originally published by the University of Chicago Press, 1930.

40. Maxwell S. Stewart, *War-Time China: China's Soldiers, Leaders, Farmers, Progress, Problems, Hopes, I.P.R. Pamphlets No. 10* (New York: American Council Institute of Pacific Relations, 1944).

41. Chiang, *Social Engineering*, 244.

42. H. D. Fong, The Post-War Industrialization of China (Washington DC: National Planning Association, 1942), 78.

43. Article II. Quoted in Trescott, *Jingji Xue*, 286.

44. Creighton Lacy, *Is China a Democracy?* (New York: John Day, 1943), 140.

45. J. B. Condliffe, "Preface," in *World Economic Survey 1931–1932* (Geneva: League of Nations, 1932), 10.

46. Ibid., 10–11.

47. J. B. Condliffe, "The Value of International Trade," *Economica* 5, no. 18 (May, 1938): 123–37; quote is from pages 136–37.

48. J. B. Condliffe, "The Industrial Development of China," speech given at Chinese National Reconstruction Forum at Berkeley on January 24, 1943. Reprinted in Committee on Wartime Planning for Chinese Students in the United States, *National Reconstruction, 1943*, 73–80; quote is from page 79.

49. J. B. Condliffe, *Agenda for a Postwar World* (New York: Norton and Company, 1942), 213.

50. J.B. Condliffe, "The Road to Serfdom," *Think* 10 (December 1944): 34–35.

51. Condliffe, *Agenda for a Postwar World*, 175.

52. J. B. Condliffe, "Point Four: Economic Development," in *Point Four and the World Economy*, Headline Series Number 79 (New York: Foreign Policy Association, 1950), 5–54; quotes from pages 27, 10, and 21.

53. Ibid., 45, 50.

54. Yuan-li Wu, *China's Economic Policy: Planning or Free Enterprise?* (New York: Sino-International Economic Research Center, 1946), 40.

55. Wu, *China's Economic Policy*, 39.

56. Ibid., 48.

57. Ibid., 49.

58. Quoted in Trescott, *Jingji Xue*, 20.

59. United Nations, Department of Economic Affairs, *Economic Survey of Asia and the Far East 1949*, prepared by the Secretariat of the Economic Commission for Asia and the Far East (New York: Lake Success, 1950), 412.

60. Ibid. 380.

61. Myrdal, *International Economy*, 205; footnote is on page 357.

CHAPTER 4: RACE, WAR, AND THE FATE OF AFRICA

1. Minute by A. Dawe, December 13, 1939, quoted in Frank Furedi, *The Silent War: Imperialism and the Changing Perception of Race* (New Brunswick NJ: Rutgers University Press, 1998), Kindle edition, location 2139.

2. This chapter draws heavily on the story and interpretation given by Suke Wolton, *Lord Hailey, the Colonial Office and the Politics of Race and Empire in the Second World War: The Loss of White Prestige (Oxford: Palgrave Macmillan, 2000)* and Mark Mazower,

No Enchanted Palace: The End of Empire and the Ideological Origins of the United Nations (Princeton NJ: Princeton University Press, 2009).

3. Lord Hailey, "Some Problems Dealt with in the 'African Survey,'" *International Affairs* 18, no. 2 (March–April 1939): 194–210.

4. Quoted in Wolton, *Lord Hailey*, p. 55.

5. The Committee on Africa, The War, and Peace Aims, *The Atlantic Charter and Africa from an American Standpoint* (Committee on Africa, The War, and Peace Aims: New York City, 1942), 121–23 for quotes on Africans, viii for "almost all."

6. Quoted in Wolton, *Lord Hailey*, 40.

7. Quoted in Mazower, *No Enchanted Palace*, 49.

8. Quoted in Frank Furedi, *The Silent War*, 1505.

9. Ibid., 716.

10. Ibid., 724–26.

11. Gerald Horne, *Race War! White Supremacy and the Japanese Attack on the British Empire* (New York: NYU Press, 2003), Kindle edition, location 4620.

12. Wolton, *Lord Hailey*, 62, 173

13. Quoted in Wolton, *Lord Hailey*, 77.

14. Furedi, *The Silent War*, 2312–14; statement made March 19, 1944.

15. Robert L. Tignor, *W. Arthur Lewis, and the Birth of Development Economics* (Princeton NJ: Princeton University Press, 2006), 47-53.

16. John W. Cell, *Hailey: A Study in British Imperialism*, 1872–1969 (Cambridge UK: Cambridge University Press, 1992), 215.

17. Quoted in Cell, *Hailey*, 221.

18. J. M. Lee, *Colonial Development and Good Government: A Study of the Ideas Expressed by the British Official Classes in Planning Decolonization, 1939-1964* (Oxford: Clarendon Press, 1967), 9.

19. Cell, *Hailey*, 220–21.

20. Lord Hailey, *An African Survey* (Oxford University Press: London, 1938), xxiv-xxv.

21. Ibid., vi.

22. Ibid., 962.

23. Natasha Gilbert, "African Agriculture: Dirt Poor," *Nature* 483 (29 March 2012): 525–27.

24. Food and Agriculture Organization, "Green Manure/Cover Crops and Crop Rotation in Conservation Agriculture on Small Farms" *Integrated Crop Management* 12 (2010).

25. Hailey, *African Survey*, 1662.

26. The Lord Hailey, "A New Philosophy of Colonial Rule," United Empire XXXII (1941): 163–69; quote is page 165.

27. Ibid., 165.

28. Ibid., 166.

29. Ibid., 166.

30. Quoted in Wolton, *Lord Hailey*, 108–9.

31. Ibid., 107.

32. Ibid., 51.

33. Ibid., 130.

34. O.G.R. Williams, Memorandum on future policy in West Africa, ref: CO 554/132/10, 1943; downloaded PDF file "The National Archives, Learning Curve, Education Service Workshops AS/A2, Decolonisation: Malaya and the Gold Coast 1940–1960, Document 1,"

n.d., from www.learningcurve.gov.uk/workshops/decolonisation.htm, accessed October 10, 2012.

35. Sir George Gater, "Cover Note to Williams, Memorandum on future policy in West Africa," February 9, 1943 (The National Archives, UK).

36. O.F.G. Stanley, "Cover Note to Williams, Memorandum on future policy in West Africa," February 19, 1943 (The National Archives, UK).

37. Quoted in Wolton, *Lord Hailey*, 129.

38. Cell, *Hailey*, 278–79.

39. Furedi, *The Silent War*, 2066–69.

40. Quoted in Horne, *Race War!* 5626.

41. Horne, *Race War!* 4090.

42. Quoted in Wolton, Lord Hailey, 50.

43. Horne, Race War!, 4685.

44. Quoted in Christopher Thorne, *Allies of a Kind: The United States, Britain and the War Against Japan*, 1941–1945 (New York: Oxford University Press, 1978), 8.

45. Horne, *Race War!* 5740.

46. Lippmann and Welles quoted in Wolton, *Lord Hailey*, 47.

47. Gunnar Myrdal, *An American Dilemma: The Negro Problem and Modern Democracy*, with the assistance of Richard Sterner and Arnold Rose (New York: Harper and Brothers, 1944), 488–89.

48. Quoted in Wolton, *Lord Hailey*, 69–70; original quotation is in Myrdal, *American Dilemma*, 486.

49. Ibid., 70.

50. The unattributed quotation is from Wendell Wilkie, quoted in Myrdal, American Dilemma, 488–89. Wilkie had run against Roosevelt in 1940 and at the time of Hailey's writing was a possible third-party candidate in the November 1944 election.

51. Quoted in Wolton, *Lord Hailey*, 132.

52. Furedi, *The Silent War*, 1300.

53. http://www.un.org/en/documents/charter/preamble.shtml, accessed August 22, 2013.

54. Quoted in Mark Mazower, *No Enchanted Palace*, 61.

55. Ibid., 62–63.

56. F. A. Hayek, *The Road to Serfdom: Text and Documents; The Definitive Edition*, ed. Bruce Caldwell, Volume 2, *The Collected Works of F. A. Hayek* (Chicago: University of Chicago Press, 2010), Kindle edition, location 5757.

57. Lord Hailey, *An African Survey* (London: Oxford University Press, 1957): 246–47.

58. United Nations, Department of Economic Affairs, *Economic Development in Selected Countries: Plans, Programmes and Agencies* (New York: Lake Success, 1947), iii, xv.

59. S. Herbert Frankel, "United Nations Primer for Development," *The Quarterly Journal of Economics* 66, no. 3 (August 1952): 301–26; primer quotation and Frankel response on pages 303–4.

60. Ibid., 323.

61. Ibid., 314; Hailey, "New Philosophy," 166.

62. This section draws heavily on the superb book by Tignor, *W. Arthur Lewis*, cited in n.15 above.

63. W. Arthur Lewis, *The Principles of Economic Planning: A Study Prepared for the Fabian Society* (1949; reprinted Oxford: Routledge, 2003), 14.

64. Tignor, *W. Arthur Lewis*, 172.

65. Ibid., 171.

66. Ibid., 210.

CHAPTER 5: ONE DAY IN BOGOTÁ

1. Devesh Kapur, John P. Lewis, and Richard Webb, *The World Bank: Its First Half Century*, Volume 1, *History* (Washington DC: Brookings Institution, 1997), 83.

2. International Bank for Reconstruction and Development (IBRD), *The Basis of a Development Program for Colombia*, Report of the Mission to Colombia, headed by Lauchlin Currie (Washington DC: International Bank for Reconstruction and Development, 1950).

3. Roger J. Sandilands, *The Life and Political Economy of Lauchlin Currie: New Dealer, Presidential Adviser, and Development Economist* (Durham NC: Duke University Press, 1990), 162

4. IBRD, Development Program for Colombia, 2.

5. Ibid., 5.

6. Ibid., 615.

7. Ibid.

8. Ibid.

9. http://en.wikipedia.org/wiki/Second_Bill_of_Rights, accessed August 23, 2013.

10. Sandilands, *Lauchlin Currie*, 168–69.

11. David Bushnell, *The Making of Modern Colombia: A Nation in Spite of Itself* (Berkeley, CA: University of California Press, 1993), 202.

12. Frank Safford and Marco Palacios, *Colombia: Fragmented Land, Divided Society* (New York: Oxford University Press, 2002), 348.

13. Norman A. Bailey, "La Violencia in Colombia," *Journal of Interamerican Studies* 9, no. 4 (October 1967): 561–75; quote is on page 563.

14. Quoted in Michele Alacevich, *The Political Economy of the World Bank: the Early Years* (Stanford CA: Stanford University Press, 2009), 38.

15. Ibid., 46.

16. Ibid., 57.

17. Ibid., 149.

18. Kapur et al., *World Bank*, 101.

19. Sandilands, *Lauchlin Currie*, 120.

20. United Nations, *Economic Development in Selected Countries: Plans, Programmes, and Agencies*, Volume 2 (Lake Success, New York: United Nations Department of Economic Affairs, February 1950), 77.

21. Lloyd C. Gardner, *Economic Aspects of New Deal Diplomacy* (Madison, Wisconsin: The University of Wisconsin Press, 1964), 109; remarks made in 1940.

22. William Adams Brown Jr. and Redvers Opie, *American Foreign Assistance* (Washington DC: The Brookings Institution, 1953), 19.

23. Ibid., 16–18.

24. Gardner, *Economic Aspects of New Deal Diplomacy*, 199; see also http://www.rockarch.org/bio/narchron.pdf.

25. IBRD Articles of Agreement: Article IV, available at http://go.worldbank.org/5VD3CH4OB0, accessed September 22, 2013.

26. Benn Steil, *The Battle of Bretton Woods: John Maynard Keynes, Harry Dexter White, and the Making of a New World Order* (Princeton and Oxford: Princeton University Press, 2013), 125.

27. Part of White's 1942 proposal is reproduced in J. Keith Horsefield, *The International Monetary Fund, 1945-1965, Volume III: Documents* (Washington DC: International Monetary Fund, 1969), 72. These statements were in the IMF part of the proposal and later seem to have drifted into the World Bank part.

28. Another part of White's 1942 proposal is reproduced in Robert W. Oliver, *International Economic Co-Operation and the World Bank* (London and Basingstoke: Macmillan, 1975), 280.

29. Quoted in Fred L. Block, *The Origins of International Economic Disorder: A Study of United States International Monetary Policy from World War II to the Present* (Berkeley, CA: University of California Press, 1977), 46.

30. This note was only recently uncovered by Steil, *The Battle of Bretton Woods*, as described on page 42; quote is from page 137.

31. Quoted in Block, *Origins of International Economic Disorder*, 46.

32. Quotes from Oliver, *International Economic Co-Operation*, 283, 291, 301, 316, 322.

33. Gardner, *Economic Aspects of New Deal Diplomacy*, 267.

34. Colin Clark, *The Conditions of Economic Progress* (London: MacMillan and Co, 1940), 54.

35. Eugene Staley, *World Economic Conditions*, 1938.

36. Gerald M. Meier and Dudley Seers, eds., *Pioneers in Development* (New York: published for the World Bank by Oxford University Press, 1984).

37. P. N. Rosenstein-Rodan, "Problems of Industrialisation of Eastern and South-Eastern Europe," *The Economic Journal* 53, no. 210/211 (June–September, 1943): 202–11.

38. P. N. Rosensenstein-Rodan, "The International Development of Economically Backward Areas," *International Affairs* 20, no. 2, 157–65; list is from page 159.

39. The 1961 essay was reprinted in Albert Hirschman, *A Bias for Hope: Essays on Development and Latin America* (New Haven: Yale University Press, 1971); quote is from page 275.

40. Ibid., 293.

41. Ibid., 292.

42. Ibid., 294.

43. Ibid., 295.

PART THREE: THE BLANK SLATE
VERSUS LEARNING FROM HISTORY

1. Bill Gates, "My Plan to Fix The World's Biggest Problems," Wall Street Journal, January 25, 2013, available at http://online.wsj.com/article/SB10001424127887323539804 578261780648285770.html, accessed August 24, 2013.

2. Craig Baker et al., "The New Prosperity: Strategies for Improving Well-Being in Sub-Saharan Africa," The Boston Consulting Group and Tony Blair Africa Governance Initiative, May 2013, available at http://www.bcgperspectives.com/Images/BCG_The _New_Prosperity_tcm80-133457.pdf, accessed August 24, 2013.

CHAPTER 6:
VALUES: THE LONG STRUGGLE FOR INDIVIDUAL RIGHTS

3. Marcel Pacaut, *Frederick Barbarossa*, trans Arnold J. Pomerand, (New York: Charles Scribner's Sons, 1970), 69.

4. Ibid., 88.

5. Peter Munz, *Frederick Barbarossa: A Study in Medieval Politics* (Eyre and Spottiswoode: London, 1969), 181.

6. Pacaut, *Frederick Barbarossa*, 100.

7. Munz, *Frederick Barbarossa*, 275.

8. Ibid., 299.

9. Munz, *Frederick Barbarossa*, 311.

10. Walter Ullmann, *The Individual and Society in the Middle Ages* (Baltimore, MD: The Johns Hopkins Press, 1966), 17.

11. Ullman, *The Individual and Society*, 23, 25.

12. Luigi Guiso, Paola Sapienza, and Luigi Zingales, "Long Term Persistence," NBER Working Paper 14278, National Bureau of Economic Research, Cambridge, MA, 2008, 8; available at: http://www.nber.org/papers/w14278.pdf, accessed August 24, 2013.

13. Guiso et al., "Long Term Persistence," 10.

14. J. Bradford De Long and Andrei Shleifer, "Princes and Merchants: European City Growth Before the Industrial Revolution," *Journal of Law and Economics* 36, no.2 (October 1993): 671–702.

15. Giorgio Falco, T*he Holy Roman Republic: A Historic Profile of the Middle Ages*, trans K. V. Kent (New York: A. S. Barnes and Company, 1964), 229.

16. Guiso et al., "Long Term Persistence."

17. Avner Greif, *Institutions and the Path to the Modern Economy: Lessons from Medieval Trade* (Cambridge UK: Cambridge University Press, 2006); Avner Greif, "Contract Enforceability and Economic Institutions in Early Trade: The Maghribi Traders' Coalition," *American Economic Review* 83, no. 3 (June 1993): 525–48.

18. Avner Greif, *Institutions and the Path to the Modern Economy: Lessons from Medieval Trade* (Cambridge, UK: Cambridge University Press, 2006), Kindle edition, location 1465.

19. Ibid., 5182.

20. Guido Tabellini, "Culture and Institutions: Economic Development in the Regions of Europe" *Journal of the European Economic Association* 8, no. 4 (June 2010): 677–716; quotation is from page 685.

21. Daron Acemoglu, Simon Johnson, and James Robinson, "The Rise of Europe: Atlantic Trade, Institutional Change and Economic Growth," *American Economic Review* 95, no. 3 (June 2005): 546–79.

22. Oliver J. Thatcher, ed., *The Library of Original Sources: 9th to 16th Century, Editors Edition* (New York: University Research Extension, 1907), 190.

23. "English Bill of Rights 1689," The Avalon Project: Documents in Law, History and Diplomacy, Yale Law School, 2013, available at http://avalon.law.yale.edu/17th_century/england.asp, accessed September 13, 2013.

24. Tabellini, "Culture and Institutions," 685.

25. Ibid.

26. Guido Tabellini, "Institutions and Culture: Presidential Address," *Journal of the European Economic Association* 6, Nos. 2–3 (April 2008): 255–94.

27. Guiso et al., "Long Term Persistence."

28. Torsten Persson and Guido Tabellini, "Democratic Capital: The Nexus of Political and Economic Change," *American Economic Journal: Macroeconomics* 1, no. 2 (July 2009): 88–126.

29. Sunanda K. Datta-Ray, *Looking East to Look West: Lee Kuan Yew's Mission India* (Singapore: Institute of Southeast Asia Studies, 2009), 12.

30. Quoted in Kenneth Christie and Denny Roy, *The Politics of Human Rights in East Asia* (London: Pluto Press, 2001), 9.

31. Avner Greif and Guido Tabellini, "Cultural and Institutional Bifurcation: China and Europe Compared," *American Economic Review* 100, no. 2 (May 2010): 135–40. Available at SSRN: http://ssrn.com/abstract=1532906 or http://dx.doi.org/10.2139/ssrn.1532906, accessed August 24 2013.

32. Ibid., 137–38.

33. John Friedmann, "Reflections on Place and Place-Making in the Cities of China," *International Journal of Urban and Regional Research* 31, no. 2 (2007): 274; quoted in Greif and Tabellini, "Cultural and Institutional Bifurcation."

34. Gordon S. Redding, *The Spirit of Chinese Capitalism*, second edition (Berlin: Gruyter, 1993), 66; quoted in Greif and Tabellini, "Cultural and Institutional Bifurcation."

35. http://www.worldvaluessurvey.org/, accessed September 23, 2013.

36. The author is grateful to Claudia Williamson for sharing culture datasets for academic work in progress with the author.

37. Yuriy Gorodnichenko and Gerard Roland, "Culture, Institutions and the Wealth of Nations," NBER Working Paper 16368, Cambridge, MA, National Bureau of Economic Research, September 2010; quotation is from page 11.

38. Deepa Narayan, Lant Pritchett, and Soumya Kapoor, *Moving Out of Poverty: Success from the Bottom Up* (Washington DC: Palgrave MacMillan and World Bank, 2009), 9–11.

39. Ibid., 76–81.

40. Ibid., 231–32.

41. Ibid., 78.

42. Ibid., 76–81.

CHAPTER 7:
INSTITUTIONS: WE OPPRESS THEM IF WE CAN

1. Tony Blair Africa Governance Initiative, "Our Vision," available at http://www.africagovernance.org/africa/pages/our-vision, accessed September 6, 2013.

2. Tony Blair Africa Governance Initiative, "Our Approach," available at http://www.africagovernance.org/africa/pages/our-approach, accessed September 6, 2013.

3. Commission for Africa, "Our Common Interest: Report of the Commission for Africa," March 2005, 99, available at http://www.commissionforafrica.info/2005-report, accessed September 6, 2013. The Commission for Africa was appointed by Tony Blair in early 2004 and had seventeen members.

4. Ibid., 343–45.

5. Human Rights Watch, *Development Without Freedom: How Aid Underwrites Repression in Ethiopia* (New York: Human Rights Watch, 2010). Available at: http://www.hrw.org/sites/default/files/reports/ethiopia1010webwcover.pdf, accessed August 25, 2013.

6. Ibid., 34, 51, 52.

7. Human Rights Watch, *World Report 2012: Ethiopia*, available at http://www.hrw.org/world-report-2012/ethiopia accessed September 6, 2013.

8. Human Rights Watch, Development Assistance Group (DAG) Ethiopia, DAG Statement, Human Rights Watch (HRW) Report: *Development without Freedom: How Aid Underwrites Repression in Ethiopia*, October 21, 2010, available at http://www.europarl.europa.eu/meetdocs/2009_2014/documents/droi/dv/404_dagstatementv2_/404_dagstatementv2_en.pdf, accessed September 22, 2013. See also http://www.hrw.org/news/2010/12/17/ethiopia-donors-should-investigate-misuse-aid-money, accessed September 6, 2013.

9. Jan Egeland, "Ethiopia: Letter Regarding UK Development Assistance," Human Rights Watch, September 29, 2011, available at http://www.hrw.org/news/2011/09/29/ethiopia-letter-regarding-uk-development-assistance, accessed September 6, 2013.

10. Annie Kelly and Liz Ford, "DfID under fire for poor response to human rights concerns in Ethiopia," The Guardian.com, Friday 21, December 2012, http://www.theguardian.com/global-development/2012/dec/21/dfid-human-rights-ethiopia. Clar Ni Chonghaile, "Ethiopia's resettlement scheme leaves lives shattered and UK facing questions," The Guardian.com, Tuesday, 22 January 2013, http://www.theguardian.com/global-development/2013/jan/22/ethiopia-resettlement-scheme-lives-shattered accessed September 6, 2013. Human Rights Watch, "'Waiting Here for Death': Forced Displacement and 'Villagization' in Ethiopia's Gambella Region," January 2013, http://www.hrw.org/sites/default/files/reports/ethiopia0112webwcover_0.pdf, accessed September 6, 2013.

11. Patrick Manning, *Slavery, Colonialism and Economic Growth in Dahomey, 1640–1960* (Cambridge, UK: Cambridge University Press, 1982), 32.

12. Nathan Nunn and Leonard Wantchekon, "The Slave Trade and the Origins of Mistrust in Africa," *American Economic Review* 101, no. 7 (December 2011): 3221–52.

13. Nathan Nunn, "The Long-Term Effects of Africa's Slave Trades," *Quarterly Journal of Economics* 123, no. 1 (February 2008): 139–76.

14. See also the discussion in Daron Acemoglu and James A. Robinson, "Why is Africa Poor?" *Economic History of Developing Regions* 25, no. 1, 21–50; see for example page 30.

15. Nunn, "Long-Term Effects."

16. Daron Acemoglu, Camilo García-Jimeno, and James A. Robinson, "Finding Eldorado: Slavery and Long-Run Development in Colombia," *Journal of Comparative Economics* 40, no. 4 (June 12, 2012): 534–64, available at: http://www.economics.mit.edu/files/8048, accessed August 25, 2013.

17. Acemoglu et al., "Finding Eldorado."

18. Daron Acemoglu and James A. Robinson, *Why Nations Fail: The Origins of Power, Prosperity, and Poverty* (New York: Crown Publishers, 2012).

19. Stanley L. Engerman and Kenneth L. Sokoloff, "Factor Endowments, Institutions, and Differential Paths of Growth Among New World Economies: A View from Economic Historians in the United States," in *How Latin America Fell Behind*, ed. Stephen Haber (Stanford, CA: Stanford University Press, 1997), 260–304.

20. Michael Clemens, William Easterly, and Carlos Esteban Posada, "Inequality, Institutions and Long-Term Growth in Colombia," New York University, March 2004, photocopy, revised draft of paper presented at Banco de la República seminar, "The Political Economy of Equity and Growth," Bogotá, Colombia, November 19, 2002, page 12.

21. Clemens et al, "Long-Term Growth in Colombia," 28.

22. Eric A. Hanushek and Ludger Woessmann, "Schooling, Educational Achievement, and the Latin American Growth Puzzle," *Journal of Development Economics* 99 (2012): 497–512, available at: http://hanushek.stanford.edu/sites/default/files/publications/Hanushek%2BWoessmann%202012%20JDevEcon%2099%282%29.pdf, accessed August 25, 2013.

CHAPTER 8:
THE MAJORITY DREAM

1. Thelma Wills Foote, *Black and White Manhattan: The History of Racial Formation in Colonial New York City* (New York: Oxford University Press, 2004), 39.

2. "Map of Original Grants and Farms" (Plates 84B-a and 84B-b), in I. N. Phelps Stokes, *The Iconography of Manhattan Island, 1498–1909*, Volume 6 (New York: Robert H. Dodd, 1928).

3. William Easterly, Laura Freschi, and Steven Pennings, "A Long History of a Short Block: Four Centuries of Development Surprises on a Single Stretch of a New York City Street," DRI Working Paper No. 96, Development Research Institute, New York University, New York NY, 2013.

4. Ira Berlin and Leslie Harris, eds., *Slavery in New York* (New York: New Press, 2005). This was the book corresponding to an exhibition at the New York Historical Society, whose page on the laws is "Closing the Vise: New York's Slave Laws," at http://www.slaveryinnewyork.org/gallery_3_2.htm#, accessed September 10, 2013.

5. Daron Acemoglu and James A. Robinson, *Why Nations Fail: The Origins of Power, Prosperity, and Poverty* (New York: Crown Publishers, 2012).

6. Edwin G. Burrows and Mike Wallace, *Gotham: A History of New York City to 1898* (New York: Oxford University Press, 1999), 122–23.

7. Ira Rosenwaike, *Population History of New York City* (Syracuse, NY: Syracuse University Press, 1972), 18.

8. Stokes, *Iconography of Manhattan Island*, 70–78.

9. Quoted in Peter Bernstein, *Wedding of the Waters: The Erie Canal and the Making of a Great Nation* (New York: W. W. Norton & Company, 2005), 23.

10. Easterly et al. with "A Long History of a Short Block."

11. Peter Bernstein, *Wedding of the Waters*, 318–19.

12. Easterly et al., "A long history of a short block."

13. Edward L. Glaeser, "Urban Colossus: Why New York Is America's Largest City," *Federal Reserve Bank of New York Economic Policy Review* 11, no. 2 (2005): 7–24.

14. Robert Albion and Jennie Barnes Pope, *The Rise of New York Port* (New York: Charles Scribner's Sons, 1939), 398.

15. Maddison Project Database, http://www.ggdc.net/maddison/maddison-project/home.htm.

16. Aviva Ben-Ur, *Sephardic Jews in America: A Diasporic History* (New York: NYU Press, 2009), Kindle edition, locations 1886–87.

17. Mark I. Greenberg, "One Religion, Different Worlds: Sephardic and Ashkenazic Jews in Eighteenth-Century Savannah," in *Jewish Roots in Southern Soil: A New History*, eds. Marcie Cohen Ferris and Mark I. Greenberg (Waltham, MA: Brandeis University Press, 2006).

18. "Benjamin Seixas, Saddler," *New-York Gazette: and Weekly Mercury*, April 15–May 6, 1771. From the American Jewish Historical Society Oppenheim Collection, 1650–1850. Series I. Individuals, Benjamin Seixas (b 1747) and wife Zipporah, box 12, folder 18. New York, New York: American Jewish Historical Society, Center for Jewish History.

19. Deborah Dash Moore, ed., *City of Promises: A History of the Jews of New York*. 3 vols. (New York and London: New York University Press, 2012), Kindle edition, location 1726.

20. http://www.jewishencyclopedia.com/articles/13396-seixas.

21. *Doggett's New York City Directory* 1848 and 1851 (New York: John Doggett Jr.).

22. "Horrible Murder," *New York Times*, July 30, 1870, accessed September 6, 2013, http://query.nytimes.com/mem/archive-free/pdf?res=F30E13F63B59107B93C2A A178CD85F448784F9.

23. Malcolm H. Stern, "First American Jewish Families: 600 Families, 1654–1988," The Jacob Rader Center of the American Jewish Archives, Genealogies, Seixas family, http://americanjewisharchives.org/publications/fajf/pdfs/stern_p265.pdf and Shearith Israel Register of Interments, 1828–1855 (original archival research for Easterly et al., A Long history of a Short Block.")

24. Stern, "First American Jewish Families," 226.

25. Ibid., 227.

26. Michael Haines, "Fertility and Mortality in the United States," *EH.net Encyclopedia*, February 4, 2010, accessed September 6, 2013, http://eh.net/encyclopedia/article/haines. demography.

27. The story is told in Angus Deaton, *The Great Escape: Health, Wealth, and the Origins of Inequality* (Princeton, NJ: Princeton University Press, 2013), 95.

28. Ibid., 97.

29. Joanne Abel Goldman, *Building New York's Sewers: Developing Mechanisms of Urban Management* (West Lafayette, IN: Purdue University Press, 1997).

30. John Duffy, *A History of Public Health in New York City 1625–1866* (New York: Russell Sage Foundation, 1968), 183, 274.

31. Martin Melosi, *The Sanitary City: Environmental Services in Urban America from Colonial Times to the Present* (Pittsburgh, PA: University of Pittsburgh Press, 2008), 62.

32. David Rosner, ed., *Hives of Sickness: Public Health and Epidemics in New York City* (New Brunswick, NJ: Rutgers University Press, 1995), 31.

33. Leona Baumgartner, "One Hundred Years of Health: New York City, 1866–1966," *Bulletin of the New York Academy of Medicine* 45, no. 6 (June 1969): 563.

PART FOUR: NATIONS VERSUS INDIVIDUALS

1. Matt McAllester, "America Is Stealing the World's Doctors" *New York Times Magazine* (March 7, 2012). Available at: www.nytimes.com/2012/03/11/magazine/america-is-stealing-foreign-doctors.html?pagewanted=all&_r=0, accessed August 27, 2013. The coverage here was inspired by Michael Clemens, "What Is Not Owned Cannot Be Stolen: Stop Dehumanizing African Health Workers," Center for Global Development blog, Views from the Center, March 12, 2012. http://blogs.cgdev.org/globaldevelopment/2012/03/what-is-not-owned-cannot-be-stolen-stop-dehumanizing-african-health -workers.php, accessed September 9, 2013.

2. Edward J Mills et al., "Should Active Recruitment of Health Workers from Sub-Saharan Africa Be Viewed as a Crime?" *Lancet* 371, no. 9613 (23 February 2008): 685–88, doi:10.1016/S0140-6736(08)60308-6.

CHAPTER 9: HOMES OR PRISONS? NATIONS AND MIGRATIONS

3. The Minorities at Risk Project, Center for International Development and Conflict Management, University of Maryland, http://www.cidcm.umd.edu/mar/about.asp, accessed September 9, 2013.

4. http://americanjewisharchives.org/publications/fajf/pdfs/stern_p150.pdf; http://americanjewisharchives.org/publications/fajf/pdfs/stern_p226.pdf.

5. Michael Clemens and Lant Pritchett, "Income per Natural: Measuring Development for People Rather Than Places," *Population and Development Review* 34, issue 3 (September 2008): 395–434, discussed in Michael Clemens, The Best Way Nobody's Talking About to Help Haitians, Aid Watch blog, January 25, 2010, http://aidwatchers.com/2010/01/the-best-way-nobody%E2%80%99s-talking-about-to-help-haitians/, accessed September 9, 2013.

6. This section draws upon "Dodging International Migration at the United Nations" by Joseph Chamie and Barry Mirkin at the blog PassBlue, January 29, 2013, that covers the United Nations. I am grateful to Michael Clemens for pointing out this article to me.

7. http://www.aclu.org/immigrants-rights, accessed August 27, 2013.

8. http://go.worldbank.org/0IK1E5K7U0.

9. http://go.worldbank.org/HZK5B1Z8E0.

10. World Bank, *Migration and Development Brief* 20, Migration and Remittances Unit, Development Prospects Groups, April 19, 2013.

11. Lant Pritchett, "Boom Towns and Ghost Countries: Geography, Agglomeration, and Population Mobility," *Brookings Trade Forum* 2006 (Washington DC: Brookings Institution Press, 2006): 1–42.

12. Serigne Mansour Tall, "Senegalese Émigrés: New Information and Communication Technologies," *Review of African Political Economy* 31, no. 99 (2004): 31–48.

13. David Robinson, "The Murids: Surveillance and Collaboration," *Journal of African History* 40, no. 2 (1999): 193–213.

14. Cheikh Anta Babou, "Brotherhood Solidarity, Education and Migration: The Role of the Dahiras Among the Murid Muslim Community in New York," *African Affairs* 101, no. 403 (2002): 151–70.

15. Mamadou Diouf, and Steven Rendall, "The Senegalese Murid Trade Diaspora and the Making of a Vernacular Cosmopolitanism," *Public Culture* 12, no. 3 (2000): 679–702. Serigne Mansour Tall, "Senegalese Émigrés: New Information and Communication Technologies," *Review of African Political Economy 31*, no. 99 (2004): 31–48

16. Eric Ross, "Globalising Touba: Expatriate Disciples in the World City Network." *Urban Studies* 48, no. 14 (2011): 2929–52.

17. Victoria Ebin, "À la recherche de nouveaux "poissons": stratégies commerciales mourides par temps de crise," *Politique Africaine* 45 (1992): 86–99.

CHAPTER 10: HOW MUCH DO NATIONS MATTER?

1. William Easterly, Robert King, Ross Levine, and Sergio Rebelo, "How Do National Policies Affect Long-Run Growth?" A Research Agenda," Country Economics Department, the World Bank, Policy, Research, and External Affairs Working Papers, October 1991, WPS 794.

2. William Easterly, Michael Kremer, Lant Pritchett, and Lawrence H. Summers, "Good Planning or Good Luck? Country Growth Performance and Temporary Shocks," *Journal of Monetary Economics* 32, no. 3 (1993): 459–83.

3. Ricardo Hausmann, Lant Pritchett, and Dani Rodrik, "Growth Accelerations" *Journal of Economic Growth* 10, no. 4 (December 2005): 303–29; available at: http://www.nber.org/papers/w10566.pdf, accessed August 27, 2013.

4. Dani Rodrik, "Goodbye Washington Consensus, Hello Washington Confusion?" *Journal of Economic Literature* 44 (December 2006): 969–83.

5. Alwyn Young, "The African Growth Miracle," *Journal of Political Economy* 120, no. 4 (August 2012): 696–739.

6. Alan Heston, Robert Summers, and Bettina Aten, "Penn World Table Version 7.1," Center for International Comparisons of Production, Income and Prices at the University of Pennsylvania, November 2012.

7. World Bank, "Democratic Republic of Congo Overview," available at: http://www.worldbank.org/en/country/drc/overview, accessed August 28, 2013.

8. Russell Flannery, "Youth Movement," Forbes.com, September 8, 2006, http://www.forbes.com/global/2006/0918/058.html.

9. Vivian Wai-yin Kwok, "Asian Tycoon Sues Citi over Losses," Forbes.com, May 19, 2009, http://www.forbes.com/2009/05/19/oei-citi-lawsuit-face-singapore.html.

10. Forbes.com, "Singapore's 50 Richest 2013, Hong Leong Oei," http://www.forbes.com/profile/hong-leong-oei/.

11. Xiaohua Yang, *Globalization of the Automobile Industry* (Westport, CT: Praeger Publishers, 1995), 184.

12. Edgar Wickberg, "Localism and the Organization of Overseas Migration in the Nineteenth Century," in *Cosmopolitan Capitalists: Hong Kong and the Chinese Diaspora at the End of the Twentieth Century*, ed. Gary G. Hamilton (Seattle: University of Washington Press, 1999), 35–55.

13. Charles C. Mann, *1493: Uncovering the New World Columbus Created* (New York: Vintage Books, 2012), 517.

14. Luc-Normand Tellier, *Urban World History: An Economic and Geographical Perspective* (Quebec: Presses de l'Université du Québec, 2009), 221.

15. Gungwu Wang, *The Chinese Overseas: From Earthbound China to the Quest for Autonomy* (Cambridge, MA: Harvard University Press, 2000), 28.

16. Jamie Mackie, "Changing Patterns of Chinese Big Business in Southeast Asia, in *Southeast Asian Capitalists*, ed. Ruth McVey (Ithaca, NY: Cornell Southeast Asia Program Publications, 1997).

17. Thomas Sowell, *Migrations and Cultures: A World View* (New York: Basic Books, 1996), 176.

18. World Bank, *World Development Report 2006: Equity and Development* (Washington DC: World Bank and Oxford University Press), 56.

19. World Bank, *Equity and Development*, xi.

20. Ibid., 55.

21. Ibid., 6.

22. Robert Nisbet, *Social Change and History: Aspects of the Western Theory of Development* (Oxford: Oxford University Press, 1969), 256.

23. Nassim Nicholas Taleb, *Antifragile: Things That Gain from Disorder* (New York: Random House, 2013), 94.

24. Abraham Marcus, *The Middle East on the Eve of Modernity: Aleppo in the Eighteenth Century* (New York: Columbia University Press, 1989), 145–46.

25. Bruce Masters, *The Origins of Western Economic Dominance in the Middle East: Mercantilism and the Islamic Economy in Aleppo, 1600–1750* (New York: NYU Press, 1988).

26. These lists are taken from Marcus, *Middle East on the Eve of Modernity*, 148.

27. Taleb, *Antifragile*, 95.

28. Lant Pritchett, "The Financial Crisis and Organizational Capability for Policy Implementation," in *New Ideas on Development After the Financial Crisis*, eds. Nancy Birdsall and Frank Fukuyama (Baltimore, MD: The Johns Hopkins University Press, 2011), 215–39; reference to papier mâché on page 216.

29. Harry Gilroy, "Lumumba Assails Colonialism as Congo Is Freed," *New York Times*, July 1, 1960; http://partners.nytimes.com/library/world/africa/600701lumumba.html, accessed August 28, 2013.

PART FIVE: CONSCIOUS DESIGN VERSUS SPONTANEOUS SOLUTIONS

1. Remarks as Prepared for Delivery: World Bank Group President Jim Yong Kim at the Annual Meeting Plenary Session, Tokyo, Japan, October 11, 2012; http://www.world bank.org/en/news/speech/2012/10/12/remarks-world-bank-group-president-jim-yong -kim-annual-meeting-plenary-session, accessed September 9, 2013.

CHAPTER 11:
MARKETS: THE ASSOCIATION OF PROBLEM-SOLVERS

2. Donald Kirk, *Korean Dynasty: Hyundai and Chung Ju Yung* (Armonk NY: M. E. Sharpe, 1994), 22.

3. James Ferguson, *The Anti-Politics Machine: Development, Depoliticization, and Bureaucratic Power in Lesotho* (Minneapolis: University of Minnesota Press, 1994).

4. Ian Simpson Ross, *The Life of Adam Smith*, second edition (Oxford: Oxford University Press, 2010), Kindle edition, locations 1231–39.

5. Ross, *Life of Adam Smith*, 6131–39.

6. Nicholas Phillipson, *Adam Smith: An Enlightened Life* (New Haven, CT: Yale University Press, 2010), Kindle edition, location 727.

7. Adam Smith, *Wealth of Nations* (Beijing, China: Dolphin Books, 2008), Kindle edition, locations 6696–98. There is something evocative and/or ironic about a Chinese company producing an electronic edition of Adam Smith sold on Amazon for $1.00. Emphasis added.

8. Ibid., 212–14.

9. Adam Smith, *The Theory of Moral Sentiments* (MacMay, 2008), Kindle edition, location 3585; http://www.amazon.com/dp/B001NPDN46/ref=rdr_kindle_ext_tmb.

10. Smith, *Wealth of Nations*, 1989–90.

11. Ibid., 7327.

12. Ibid., 7324–25.

13. Ibid., 11016.

14. Malcolm Gladwell, *Outliers: The Story of Success* (New York: Little, Brown, and Company, 2008), 39–42; and Matthew Syed, *Bounce: Mozart, Federer, Picasso, Beckham, and the Science of Success* (New York: Harper, 2010), 32.

15. Thomas Thwaites, *The Toaster Project: Or a Heroic Attempt to Build a Simple Electric Appliance from Scratch* (New York: Princeton Architectural Press, 2007), Kindle edition, location 1239.

16. William Easterly, Laura Freschi, and Steven Pennings, "A Long History of a Short Block: Four Centuries of Development Surprises on a Single Stretch of a New York City Street," DRI Working Paper No. 96, Development Research Institute, New York University, New York, NY, 2013.

17. William W. Sanger, *The History of Prostitution: Its Extent, Causes, and Effects Throughout the World* (New York: Harper & Brothers, 1858).

18. Deborah Dash Moore, ed., *City of Promises: A History of the Jews of New York*. 3 vols. (New York and London: NYU Press, 2012), Kindle edition, location 3641.

19. William Easterly, Laura Freschi, and Steven Pennings, "A Long History of a Short Block." The original source was 1870 Census Records.

20. *The Gentleman's Directory*, 1870. Digitized by the *New York Times*, http://documents.nytimes.com/a-vest-pocket-guide-to-brothels-in-19th-century-new-york-for-gentlemen-on-the-go, accessed September 9, 2013.

21. Moore, *City of Promises*, 3130.

22. Howard M. Sachar, *A History of the Jews in America* (New York: Random House, 1993), 145–49.

23. Easterly et al., "A Long History of a Short Block."

24. *The Trow (formerly Wilson's) Copartnership and Corporation Directory of the Boroughs of Manhattan and the Bronx*, City of New York, 1901, accessed on Google Books September 9, 2013, http://books.google.com/books?id=7cYpAAAAYAAJ&printsec=frontcover&dq=The+Trow+(formerly+Wilson's)+co+partnership+and+corporation&hl=en&ei=jU7tTbqCCNDTgAf4oZnYCQ&sa=X&oi=book_result&ct=result&resnum=1&ved=0CC0Q6AEwAA#v=onepage&q&f=false.

25. Documents of the Assembly of the State of New York, Volume 11, 1896, "10th Annual Report of the Factory Inspectors," accessed on Google Books September 9, 2013, http://books.google.com/books?id=n9EaAQAAIAAJ&pg=PA441&dq=%22144+greene+Street%22&hl=en&sa=X&ei=SIXbT5HXH8b66QGxm-SHCw&ved=0CD8Q6AEwAQ#v=onepage&q=%22greene%20Street%22&f=false.

26. Louise C. Odencrantz, *Italian Women in Industry: A Study of Conditions in New York City* (New York: Russell Sage Foundation, 1919), 31–32.

27. This section and the following ones on trade specialization draw on data and findings from William Easterly and Ariell Reshef, "African Export Successes: Surprises, Stylized Facts, and Explanations," NBER Working Paper Number 16957, National Bureau of Economic Research, Cambridge, MA, December 2010; William Easterly, Ariell Reshef, and Julia Schwenkenberg, "The Power of Exports," World Bank Policy Research Working Paper 5081, The World Bank, Washington DC, October 2009; and William Easterly and Ariell Reshef, "Big Hits in Manufacturing Exports and Development," New York University, Department of Economics, photocopy, October 2009, http://williameasterly.files

.wordpress.com/2010/08/4_easterly_reshef_bighitsinmanufacturingexportsanddevelop ment_wp.pdf, accessed September 12, 2013.

28. Djun Kil Kim, *The History of Korea* (Westport, CT: Greenwood Press, 2005), Kindle edition, locations 1797–807.

29. Besides Djun Kil Kim, *History of Korea*, another important source on Korean history for this section was Michael J. Seth, *A History of Korea: From Antiquity to the Present* (Lanham, MD: Rowman & Littlefield, 2011), Kindle edition.

30. Donald Kirk, *Korean Dynasty: Hyundai and Chung Yu Yung* (Armonk, NY: M. E. Sharpe, 1994), 124, 126.

31. Ibid., 127.

32. Another important source consulted on Hyundai was Russell D. Lansbury, Chung-Sok Suh, and Seung-Ho Kwon, *The Global Korean Motor Industry: The Hyundai Motor Company's Global Strategy* (London: Routledge, 2007), Kindle edition.

33. Ross Levine, "In Defense of Wall Street: The Social Productivity of the Financial System," in *The Role of Central Banks in Financial Stability: How Has It Changed?* eds. Douglas Evanoff, Cornelia Holthausen, George Kaufman, and Manfred Kremer (Singapore: World Scientific Publishing Company, 2013), 2011 working paper available at http:// faculty.haas.berkeley.edu/ross_levine/Papers/2011_ChicagoFed_DefenseofWallStreet.pdf, accessed September 12, 2013.

34. Carmen M. Reinhart and Kenneth S. Rogoff, *This Time Is Different: Eight Centuries of Financial Folly* (Princeton, NJ: Princeton University Press, 2009).

CHAPTER 12:
TECHNOLOGY: HOW TO SUCCEED WITHOUT KNOWING HOW

1. Broadband Commission, *The State of Broadband 2012: Achieving Digital Inclusion for All* (Geneva, Switzerland: International Telecommunication Union, 2012), 5, 35, 43. Available at: http://www.broadbandcommission.org/Documents/bb-annualreport2012 .pdf, accessed August 31, 2013.

2. Broadband Commission for Digital Development, "Biography of H. E. Mr. Paul Kagame, President of Rwanda," http://www.broadbandcommission.org/Who/Biographies/1. aspx, accessed September 12, 2013.

3. Kentaro Toyama, "Can Technology End Poverty?" *Boston Review* 36, no. 5 (November–December 2010); http://bostonreview.net/forum/can-technology-end-poverty, accessed September 12, 2013.

4. Charles Kenny, "No Need for Speed," *Foreign Policy*, May 16, 2011; http://www .foreignpolicy.com/articles/2011/05/16/no_need_for_speed.

5. Robert M. Solow, "Technological Change and the Aggregate Production Function," *Review of Economics and Statistics* 39, no. 3 (August 1957): 312–20.

6. Paul M. Romer, "Increasing Returns and Long-Run Growth," *Journal of Political Economy* 94, no. 5 (October 1986), 1002–37.

7. Robert E. Lucas Jr., "Making a Miracle," *Econometrica* 61, no. 2 (March 1993): 251–72. An earlier article that was extremely influential also was Robert E. Lucas Jr., "On the Mechanics of Economic Development" *Journal of Monetary Economics*, 22 (1988): 3–42.

8. In this and following sections, I draw upon the exposition in Charles I. Jones and Paul M. Romer, "The New Kaldor Facts: Ideas, Institutions, Population, and Human Capital." *American Economic Journal: Macroeconomics* 2, no. 1 (2010): 224–45. Avail-

able at: http://www.aeaweb.org/articles.php?doi=10.1257/mac.2.1.224, accessed August 31, 2013.

9. Angus Maddison, Historical Statistics of the World Economy: 1–2008 AD, Maddison Project Database; http://www.ggdc.net/maddison/oriindex.htm, accessed September 9, 2013.

10. Katarina Čufar et al., "Dating of 4th Millennium BC Pile-Dwellings on Liubliansko Barge, Slovenia, *Journal of Archaeological Science* 37 (2010): 2034. doi: 10/1016/j.jas.2010.03.008.

11. David W. Anthony, *The Horse, the Wheel, and Language* (Princeton: Princeton University Press, 2007), 66, 69.

12. Stuart Piggott, "Chariots in the Caucasus and in China." *Antiquity* 48 (1974): 19.

13. Matt Ridley, *The Rational Optimist: How Prosperity Evolves* (New York: HarperCollins, 2010).

14. Joel Mokyr, *The Enlightened Economy: An Economic History of Britain, 1700–1850* (New Haven CT: Yale University Press, 2012), 53; http://www.monticello.org/site/jefferson/william-small, accessed August 31, 2013.

15. M. G. Lay, *Ways of the World* (New Brunswick, NJ: Rutgers University Press, 1992), 34.

16. Douglas J. Puffert, *Tracks Across Continents, Paths Through History* (Chicago: University of Chicago Press, 2009), 13, 4.

17. Diego Comin, William Easterly, and Erick Gong, "Was the Wealth of Nations Determined in 1000 BC?" *American Economic Journal: Macroeconomics* 2 (July 2010): 65–97. Available at: http://williameasterly.files.wordpress.com/2010/08/60_easterly_comin_gong_wealthofnations_prp.pdf, accessed August 31, 2013.

18. Charles W. J. Withers, *Placing the Enlightenment: Thinking Geographically About the Age of Reason* (Chicago, IL: University of Chicago Press, 2007), Kindle edition, locations 92–93; and Mokyr, *Enlightened Economy*, 34 (on "bumper sticker").

19. Mokyr, *Enlightened Economy*, 30.

20. Ibid., 33.

21. Ibid., 42.

22. Joseph Schumpeter, *Capitalism, Socialism, and Democracy* (New York: Harper and Brothers, 1942).

23. Paul M. Romer, "Endogenous Technological Change." *Journal of Political Economy* 98, no. 5, pt. 21 (October 1990): S71–S102.

24. Paul M. Romer, "New Goods, Old Theory, and the Welfare Costs of Trade Restrictions," *Journal of Development Economics* 43 (1994): 5–38.

25. William Easterly and Ross Levine, "The European Origins of Economic Development," NBER Working Paper 18162, National Bureau of Economic Research, Cambridge, MA (June 2012), confirm that colonial European settlement is associated with higher incomes today.

26. Enrico Spolaore and Romain Wacziarg, "How Deep Are the Roots of Economic Development?" *Journal of Economic Literature* 51, no. 2 (2013): 325–69.

27. R. H. Green and S. H. Hymer, "Cocoa in the Gold Coast: A Study in the Relations Between African Farmers and Agricultural Experts," *Journal of Economic History* 26, no. 3 (September 1966): 299–319.

28. J. Edwin and W. A. Masters, "Genetic Improvement and Cocoa Yields in Ghana." *Experimental Agriculture* 41 (2005): 491–50; and David Ould et al., "The Cocoa Industry in West Africa: A History of Exploitation." *Anti-Slavery International*, 2004; http://www

.antislavery.org/includes/documents/cm_docs/2008/c/cocoa_report_2004.pdf, accessed September 9, 2013.

29. Polly Hill, "The Migrant Cocoa Farmers of Southern Ghana," *Africa: Journal of the International African Institute* 31, no. 3 (July 1961): 209–30.

30. Francois Ruf et al., "The 'Spectacular' Efficiency of Cocoa Smallholders in Sulawesi: Why? Until When?" in *Cocoa Cycles: The Economics of Cocoa Supply*, eds. Francois Ruf and P. S. Siswoputranto (Abington, England: Woodhead Publishing Ltd., 1996), 351.

31. R. H. Tawney, *Land and Labor in China* (London: George Allen & Unwin Ltd, 1932), 11, 19, 20.

32. N. Nunn, N. Qian, "The Potato's Contribution to Population and Urbanization: Evidence from a Historical Experiment," *Quarterly Journal of Economics* 126, no. 2 (2011): 593–650.

33. Margot Gayle and Carol Gayle, *Cast-Iron Architecture in America: The Significance of James Bogardus* (New York: W. W. Norton and Company, 1995).

34. *The Encyclopedia of New York City*, second edition, ed. Kenneth Jackson (New Haven: Yale University Press, 1995), s.v. "elevator."

35. B. M. Selekman, Henriette R. Walter, and W. J. Couper, "The Clothing and Textile Industries," in *Regional Survey of New York and Its Environs*, Volume IB: *Food, Clothing and Textile Industries Wholesale Markets and Retail Shopping and Financial Districts*, eds. R. M. Haig and R. C. McCrea (New York: Regional Plan of New York and Its Environs, 1928).

36. This section borrows heavily from the exposition in Jones and Romer, "New Kaldor Facts," 224–45.

37. William Goldman, *Adventures in the Screen Trade: A Personal View of Hollywood and Screenwriting* (New York: Warner Books, paperback edition 1984), 40–41.

38. Erik Eckermann, *World History of the Automobile*, trans. Peter Albrecht (Warrendal, PA: Society of Automotive Engineers, 2001), 16. This is the source for much of this section.

39. Ibid., 168.

40. Wanda James, *Driving from Japan: Japanese Cars in America* (Jefferson, NC: McFarland and Company, 2007), 37–38.

41. Data from World Bank World Development Indicators.

42. Ignacio Mas and Daniel Radcliffe, "Mobile Payments Go Viral: M-PESA in Kenya," in *Yes Africa Can: Success Stories from a Dynamic Continent*, eds. P. Chuhan-Pole and M. Angwafo, World Bank, August 2011; http://web.worldbank.org/WBSITE/EXTERNAL/COUNTRIES/AFRICAEXT/0,,contentMDK:22551641~pagePK:146736~piPK:146830~theSitePK:258644,00.html, accessed September 12, 2013.

43. "Regional Economic Outlook: Sub-Saharan Africa: Sustaining the Expansion," International Monetary Fund, World Economic and Financial Surveys, October 2011, 50; http://www.imf.org/external/pubs/ft/reo/2011/afr/eng/sreo1011.pdf, accessed September 12, 2013.

44. Data are from Diego Comin and Bart Hobijn, "The CHAT Dataset," NBER Working Paper 15319, National Bureau of Economic Research, Cambridge, MA, September 2009 for 1950 and 1980 and from World Bank World Development Indicators for 2008.

45. Easterly and Reshef, "African Export Successes," 2010.

CHAPTER 13:
LEADERS: HOW WE ARE SEDUCED BY BENEVOLENT AUTOCRATS

1. Hu Shuli and Li Zengxin, "In Search of Solutions," *Caixin Online* (December 10, 2012). Available at: http://english.caixin.com/2012-12-10/100470749.html, accessed on August 31, 2013.

2. Ding Qingfen, "China Offers Example in Anti-Poverty Campaign," *China Daily* (December 5, 2012). Available at: http://usa.chinadaily.com.cn/epaper/2012-12/05/content_15988313.htm, accessed on August 31, 2013.

3. World Bank and Development Research Center of the State Council (P. R. China), *China 2030: Building a Modern, Harmonious, and Creative Society* (Washington DC: World Bank, 2013), xxiii, 69. Available at: https://openknowledge.worldbank.org/bitstream/handle/10986/12925/9780821395455.pdf?sequence=5, accessed August 31, 2013.

4. Daniel Kahneman, *Thinking, Fast and Slow* (New York: Farrar, Straus and Giroux, 2011).

5. Dani Rodrik, "Institutions for High-Quality Growth: What They Are and How to Acquire Them," *Studies in Comparative International Development* 35, no. 3 (Fall 2000): 3–31.

6. William Easterly, "Benevolent Autocrats," DRI Working Paper Number 75, Development Research Institute, New York University, New York, NY, 2011.

7. Nancy Birdsall and Francis Fukuyama, "The Post-Washington Consensus: Development After the Crisis," *Foreign Affairs* 90, no. 2 (March/April 2011): 51. Available at: http://iis-db.stanford.edu/pubs/23124/foreignaffairs_postwashingtonconsensus.pdf, accessed August 31, 2013.

8. Thomas L. Friedman, "Our One-Party Democracy," *New York Times* (September 8, 2009). Available at: http://www.nytimes.com/2009/09/09/opinion/09friedman.html?_r=0, accessed August 31, 2013.

9. United Kindgom Department for International Development, Ethiopia Country Page, http://www.dfid.gov.uk/ethiopia, accessed January 14, 2013.

10. US Agency for International Development, Ethiopia (USAID Ethiopia), Country Development Cooperation Strategy 2011–2015: Accelerating the Transformation Toward Prosperity, March 2012, page 3; http://ethiopia.usaid.gov/sites/default/files/images/CDCS-Ethiopia.pdf, accessed September 12, 2013.

11. USAID Ethiopia, Country Development Cooperation Strategy 2011–2015, page 3.

12. World Bank President Jim Kim speech at Brookings Institution, July 19, 2012; http://www.worldbank.org/en/news/2012/07/18/world-bank-group-president-jim-yong-kim-brookings-institution, accessed January 14, 2013.

13. Thomas Gilovich, Robert Vallone, and Amos Tversky, "The Hot Hand in Basketball: On the Misperception of Random Sequences," *Cognitive Psychology* 17 (1985): 295–314. Available at www.psych.cornell.edu/sites/default/files/Gilo.Vallone.Tversky.pdf, accessed August 31, 2013.

14. In 2010 Ghana was the world's second largest producer of cocoa beans (after Côte d'Ivoire). Source: *International Cocoa Organization Quarterly Bulletin of Cocoa Statistics* Vol. XXXIX, No. 2.

15. Quotation is from Kate Xiao Zhou, *How the Farmers Changed China: Power of the People* (Boulder, CO: Westview Press, 1996), 54, which is the principal source for this narrative.

16. As paraphrased by Zhou, *Farmers Changed China*, 57.

17. Roberto Weber, Colin Camerer, Yuval Rottenstreich and Marc Knez, "The Illusion of Leadership: Misattribution of Cause in Coordination Games," *Organization Science* 12, no. 5 (September–October, 2001), 582–98.

18. Graham Allison and Robert D. Blackwill, with Ali Wyne, *Lee Kuan Yew: The Grand Master's Insights on China, the United States, and the World,* Foreword by Henry A. Kissinger, (Boston: MIT Press, 2013), Kindle edition, locations 20–21.

19. What I describe here is the culmination of several years of research as coauthored most recently with World Bank Economist Steven Pennings in a paper: William Easterly and Steven Pennings, "How Much Do Leaders Explain Growth? An Exercise in Growth Accounting," DRI Working Paper No. 95, Development Research Institute, New York University, New York, NY, from October 2014. These results refined those based on an earlier paper I wrote in 2011 and presented at academic seminars (Easterly, "Benevolent Autocrats," 2011). There was an earlier paper Jones, B and B Olken (2005) "Do Leaders Matter? National Leadership and Growth Since World War II" *The Quarterly Journal of Economics* 120 (3): 835-864.that found evidence from a small sample for autocratic leaders having a growth effect. However, Pennings and I found that the Jones and Olken finding did not survive a retesting with the most recent revisions of the growth data they used.

20. "Ethiopia: Country Results Profile," http://web.worldbank.org/WBSITE /EXTERNAL/NEWS/0,,contentMDK:22896813~menuPK:141310~pagePK:34370 ~piPK:34424~theSitePK:4607,00.html, accessed September 23, 2013.

21. Robert B. Zoellick, "The Middle East and North Africa: A New Social Contract for Development," Speech, Peterson Institute, Washington DC, April 6, 2011; http://live .worldbank.org/speech-robert-zoellick-new-social-contract-development. Zoellick used the word *democratizing* but applied it strangely to "development economics," not to the usual meanings of more democratic governments or more democratic rights of citizens in individual countries.

22. World Bank, *World Development Report 2011: Conflict, Security, and Development* (Washington DC: World Bank, 2011), 188 and 192. Available at: http://siteresources.world bank.org/INTWDRS/Resources/WDR2011_Full_Text.pdf, accessed August 31, 2013.

23. This entire section draws heavily upon William Easterly, Laura Freschi, and Steven Pennings, "A Long History of a Short Block: Four Centuries of Development Surprises on a Single Stretch of a New York City Street," DRI Working Paper No. 96, Development Research Institute, New York University, New York, NY, 2013.

24. "Shacktown Pulls Through the Winter," *New York Times,* March 26, 1933, accessed September 10, 2013, http://select.nytimes.com/gst/abstract.html?res=F00C1FFE3 D5E1A7A93C4AB1788D85F478385F9.

25. Arthur C. Holden, "Planning Recommendations for the Washington Square Area" prepared for the Washington Square Association, 1946, 12.

26. Hilary Ballon, "Robert Moses and Urban Renewal," in *Robert Moses and the Modern City: The Transformation of New York,* eds. Hillary Ballon and Kenneth T. Jackson (New York: W. W. Norton & Company, 2007).

27. Holden, "Planning Recommendations," 17, 42.

28. Ibid., 54.

29. "South Village: Slum Clearance Plan Under Title I of the Housing Act of 1949," January 1951 and "Washington Square South: Slum Clearance Plan Under Title I of the Housing Act of 1949," January 1951, Robert Moses Papers, New York Public Library Manuscript and Archives Division, New York.

30. "Talk by Robert Moses at The Baruch Houses Dedication, Wednesday Afternoon, August 19, 1953," Robert Moses Papers, New York Public Library Manuscript and Archives Division, New York.

31. http://www.metmuseum.org/toah/hd/abex/hd_abex.htm, accessed August 31, 2013.

32. Jessamyn Fiore, *112 Greene Street: The Early Years* (1970–1974) (New York: Radius Books/David Zwirner, 2012), 10.

33. Joyce Silver, interview by Laura Freschi, October 19, 2012, New York.

34. Jane Jacobs, *The Death and Life of Great American Cities* (New York: Random House, 2002), 13, 35.

35. Joe Catuccio, interview by Laura Freschi, June 29, 2013, New York.

36. "The Project of Living Artists," http://www.newyorkartworld.com/gallery/project-livingartists.html, accessed August 31, 2013.

37. François Quesnay, *Despotism in China: A Translation of François Quesnay's Le Despotisme de la Chine* (Paris 1767), in Lewis A. Maverick, *China: A Model for Europe* (San Antonio, TX: Paul Anderson Company, 1946), 302.

38. Ibid., 161.

39. Ibid., 272.

40. Ibid., 280.

41. Ibid., 273.

42. Ibid., 277.

43. Ian Simpson Ross, *The Life of Adam Smith* (Oxford: Oxford University Press, Second Edition, 2010), Kindle edition, locations 5372–73.

44. Nicholas Phillipson, *Adam Smith: An Enlightened Life* (New Haven, CT: Yale University Press, 2010), Kindle edition, location 4356.

45. Ibid., 3609.

CHAPTER 14: CONCLUSION

1. Frank Furedi, *The Silent War: Imperialism and the Changing Perception of Race* (Brunswick, NJ: Rutgers University Press, 1998), Kindle edition, location 1300.

2. Human Rights Watch, *Abuse-Free Development: How the World Bank Should Safeguard Against Human Rights Violations* (New York: Human Rights Watch, 2013), available at: http://www.hrw.org/sites/default/files/reports/worldbank0713_ForUpload.pdf, accessed September 1, 2013.

3. "Ugandan Community Reaches Agreement with British Company," Oxfam International, http://www.oxfam.org/fr/grow/node/32124. and https://www.oxfam.org.uk/get-involved/campaign-with-us/latest-campaign-news/2013/07/mubende-agreement, accessed September 1, 2013.

4. Deepa Narayan, Lant Pritchett, and Soumya Kapoor, *Moving Out of Poverty: Success from the Bottom Up* (Washington DC: Palgrave MacMillan and World Bank, 2009), 76–81.

5. Quoted in Michele Alacevich, *The Political Economy of the World Bank: The Early Years* (Stanford, CA: Stanford University Press, 2009), 149.

6. Daniel Tudor, *Korea: The Impossible Country* (New York: Perseus Books Group, 2012), Kindle edition, locations 1530–31.

7. Shelley Rigger, *Why Taiwan Matters: Small Island, Global Powerhouse* (Lanham, MD: Rowman and Littlefield, 2011), Kindle edition, locations 1685–86; and John F. Copper, *Taiwan: Nation-State or Province*, fourth edition (Boulder, CO: Westview Press, 2003).

8. Eskinder Nega, "Letter From Ethiopia's Gulag," *The New York Times*, July 24, 2013, http://www.nytimes.com/2013/07/25/opinion/letter-from-ethiopias-gulag.html. accessed September 11, 2013.

9. Joseph Kahn, "Advocate for China's Weak Crosses the Powerful," *New York Times*, July 20, 2006, http://www.nytimes.com/2006/07/20/world/asia/20blind.html?_r=0, accessed September 1, 2013.

10. "Times Topics: Chen Guangcheng," *New York Times*, http://topics.nytimes.com/top/reference/timestopics/people/c/chen_guangcheng/index.html, accessed September 1, 2013.

11. Video, "In Search of China's Soul: Money, Politics, and the Pressure of Social Change," Washington National Cathedral, available at: http://www.nationalcathedral.org/exec/cathedral/mediaPlayer?MediaID=MED-61PM7-N00006&EventID=CAL-5VSVR-JS0009, accessed September 1, 2013.

INDEX

Ethiopia (*continued*)
  individual rights in, 341–342
  and Nega, Eskinder, 327, 342, 350
  oppression in, 156–159
  "promoting basic services" program
    in, 341
  slave trade/slavery in, 165
  "villagization" program in, 158–159,
    341
  and World Bank, 326–327, 341, 342
  and Zenawi, Meles, 156–158, 159
Experts, 6, 9, 95, 155, 326, 335
  in Africa, 82, 87–88
  and benevolent autocrats, 335–337,
    338
  in China, 47, 55–58, 60, 65, 69, 70, 72,
    74
  in Colombia, 106, 108–109, 110–111,
    113, 114
  in Ethiopia, 156
Extraterritoriality, and China, 47–48,
    52–53, 66, 67–70, 75–76

Fall brothers, 213
Ferguson, James, 241
Finance, 76, 183, 186, 188, 211–213,
    272–273
Financial crisis of 2008, 313
Fong, H. D., 47, 48, 55, 61–63, 63–64, 65,
    75, 78, 79, 347, 350
  *The Post-War Industrialization of
    China* (Fong), 72–73
  "Tianjin Industrialization Project," 60
Ford, Henry, 301–302
Franco, Francisco, 110
Frankel, S. Herbert, 98–100, 101
"Free China" image, 70–71
Free cities, during the Middle Ages,
    129–130, 131–133
Free development, 7. *See also*
  Authoritarian/technocratic
    development versus free
    development debate
Free market, 244
  versus government debate, 11–12
  See also Invisible hand; Market versus
    government debate; Markets

Free trade, and invisible hand concept,
    243–245. *See also* Invisible hand
Freedom, 137–139, 150–151, 297–299, 344
  versus autocracy, 11, 24–25, 152
  See also Economic freedom; Political
    freedom
Freedom House, 344–345, 346
Freschi, Laura, 176
Friedman, Thomas, 313
Fujian Province, China, 79, 226–229. *See
    also* China
Fukuyama, Francis, 313

Gains from specialization, 245, 246–247,
    247–248, 266–269, 271. *See also*
    Specialization
Gains from trade, 245, 247–248. *See also*
    Trade
Gaitán, Jorge, 109
Gang of Four, 220, 298, 311
García-Jimeno, Camilo, 166–167
Gater, Sir George, 91
Gates, Bill, 254, 255
  and Ethiopia, 123–127, 153, 156, 158,
    165, 196, 197, 314
Gates Foundation, 55, 88, 123–127, 350
Geertz, Clifford, 25
General Agreement on Tariffs and Trade,
    76
The Gentleman's Directory, 257
Geography, 291
  and oppression, 159, 169–170
  and slave trade/slavery, 163–165,
    177–178
Ghana
  authoritarian/technocratic
    development in, 101–103
  benevolent autocrat in, and economic
    growth and freedom, 319
  economic growth in, 319, 345–346
  political and economic freedom in, 345
  slave trade/slavery in, 345
  and technology, spread of, 291–293
  See also Africa
Gladwell, Malcolm, 246
Gómez, Laureano, 110–111, 112
The Good Earth (P. S. Buck), 65–66

United States (*continued*)
  per capital income in, 195 (fig.), 196
  racism in, 93–95
US Agency for International Development
  (USAID), 157, 314
USAID. *See* US Agency for International
  Development
"The Use of Knowledge in Society"
  (Hayek), 37, 38

Values, 142, 149–150, 153. *See also*
  Cultural values
Vietnam War, 70–71, 266
"Villagization" program, 158–159, 341

Wantchekon, Leonard, 161–162, 163,
  172–173
War on Terror, 9, 70, 105, 118, 157, 327
Warhol, Andy, 331
Watt, James, 242, 283, 286, 288, 289
WDI. *See* World Development Indicators
The Wealth of Nations (Smith), 244
Well-being, and freedom, 344
Welles, Sumner, 93
West Virginia, 209–210, 211
White, Harry Dexter, 114–115, 116–118
White, Walter, 83
WHO. *See* World Health Organization
Why Nations Fail (Acemoglu and
  Robinson), 167–168
Wickberg, Edgar, 228
Widjaja family, 226–227
Wilbur, Ray, 56
Williams, O. G. R., 85, 90–91
Wilson, Woodrow, 43–44, 48–49, 50, 51,
  52, 56, 265
Winant, John, 85
Wolfowitz, Paul, 230
World Bank, 5, 75, 115, 117–118, 157, 237,
  241, 350
  Articles of Agreement ("nonpolitical-
    interference clause"), 115–118, 327
  "China 2030: Building a Modern,
    Harmonious, and Creative Society,"
    307

in Colombia, 110–111, 112–113,
  113–114, 118, 121, 172, 346
and conscious design versus
  spontaneous solutions debate,
  326–327
and development goals, 255
in Ethiopia, 326–327, 341, 342
and individual rights, 341
"Migration and Remittances," 207
in Mubende, Uganda, 3, 4, 5, 6, 12,
  342–343
and national policies and national
  economic growth, 216–217
and nations, inequities between,
  229–231
and New Forests Company, 343
and "promoting basic services"
  program, in Ethiopia, 341
and Third World, 119
and "villagization" program, in
  Ethiopia, 158–159, 341
World Development Indicators,
  223–224, 225, 323
World Development Indicators (WDI),
  223–224, 225, 323
World Health Organization (WHO), 126
World War I, 56, 79, 83–84. *See also*
  Treaty of Versailles
World War II, 59, 76, 81–82, 116–117,
  240, 339
Wu, Yuan-li, 77–78
Wu Ding-chang, 69–70

Yale Club group, 55–58
Yew, Lee Kuan, 92, 144, 145, 308, 309,
  322–323, 324
YMCA, 56–58

Zambia, 199–200, 210–211, 213
Zedaka, Abun ben, 134
Zenawi, Meles, 153, 156–158, 159, 165
Zoellick, Robert, 327